D1105252

Towards Understanding Relationships

This is a volume in
EUROPEAN MONOGRAPHS IN SOCIAL PSYCHOLOGY

Series Editor: Henri Tajfel

A complete list of titles in this series appears at the end of this volume.

EUROPEAN MONOGRAPHS IN SOCIAL PSYCHOLOGY 18
Series Editor: HENRI TAJFEL

Towards Understanding Relationships

ROBERT A. HINDE

*Medical Research Council Unit on the Development and Integration of
Behaviour, Madingley, Cambridge*

1979

Published in cooperation with
EUROPEAN ASSOCIATION OF EXPERIMENTAL
SOCIAL PSYCHOLOGY
by
ACADEMIC PRESS
A Subsidiary of Harcourt Brace Jovanovich, Publishers
London   New York   Toronto   Sydney   San Francisco

ACADEMIC PRESS INC. (LONDON) LTD.
24/28 Oval Road
London NW1

United States Edition published by
ACADEMIC PRESS INC.
111 Fifth Avenue
New York, New York 10003

British Library Cataloguing in Publication Data

Hinde, Robert Aubrey
    Towards understanding relationships.—(European
    monographs in psychology; 18).
    1. Interpersonal relations
    I. Title II. Series
    301.11'2   HM132   79–40921

ISBN hardback 0–12–349250–5
ISBN paperback 0–12–349252–1

Film set in 11/13 point Baskerville
Printed in Great Britain
by W & J Mackay Limited, Chatham

Preface

The study of relationships between people, for long the preserve of novelists and biographers, now lies within the domain of a variety of disciplines from the social, medical and natural sciences. Diverse theoretical approaches are available. What seems to be lacking, at any rate to an outsider (and I was trained as a biologist), is integration between them. My aim here is to explore how far integration is possible. Can we build a science, in the sense of an integrated body of knowledge, concerned with relationships between individuals?

One theme in this book is that such a science must rest on a firm descriptive base. Relationships must be described and classified before much progress can be made. Of course our descriptions and classifications will be influenced by our preconceptions—even if we could discard our particular scientific spectacles, we can never divest ourselves entirely from those provided by our culture. But only when we have some sort of descriptive base can we specify the realm of applicability of our theories, only then can we see how far they do indeed compete and how far they feed on different facts.

A second theme is that data about interpersonal relationships necessarily involve a number of levels of complexity. Interactions can have properties not present in the actions of isolated individuals, and relationships have properties not present in their constituent interactions. The issue here is not whether social phenomena can be explained in terms of principles derived from a psychology of individual behaviour, but simply that additional descriptive concepts are needed at each level. And since different theoretical approaches relate to different levels of complexity, we must both try to delimit the range of applicability of each approach, and bear in mind how the explanatory concepts used at one level may relate to those at another.

The focus is on dyadic relationships, and this involves limitations of at least three types. First, properties of units larger than the dyad are not discussed. This is of course an arbitrary limit. Yet just as interactions and relationships each have their own emergent properties, so also do groups have properties not present in their component relationships. One has to stop somewhere, and collusion, deviance and other properties specific to groups are not discussed.

The other limitations are more basic, and concern dialectics of at least two types. The first concerns that between "personality" and "relationship". Each of us can perceive threads of continuity reaching back through our lives. We are in some measure the same persons as we were yesterday, last week, last year. The study of those constant threads is the study of "personality". At the same time we are sometimes surprised by how what we do changes depending upon whom we are with. What transpires in each of our relationships depends not only on ourselves, but on the other participant. Colloquially we say that, in each of our relationships, we show different facets of our "personality". But used in that way "personality" implies potentialities for behaving, and, while some of those potentialities are realized in many relationships, others may never be: A might surprise himself and others if he were ever to meet Z. Thus prediction of the nature of a relationship from the known personalities of the participants may be far from straightforward.

Furthermore, the influences are two-way. The personalities of the individuals affect the nature of the relationship, but so also does the relationship affect, to a greater or lesser degree, the participants. We not only contribute to the relationships in which we are involved, we are changed by them.

Because our personalities are determined by the relationships we have experienced, and the nature of relationships is markedly influenced by, but is perhaps not wholly predictable from, the (previously assessed) personalities of the participants, it is important to come to terms with this dialectic between personality and relationships. Hitherto the major effort has gone into the study of personality, so perhaps it will be helpful for a while to focus on relationships. If we can build up an ordered body of knowledge about relationships, then the study of personality and the study of interpersonal relationships, which at present have only an intermittent flirtation, may one day be united. Perhaps developmental psychology will assist the resultant labour.

Second, every dyadic relationship exists in a social setting. The participants have relationships with other individuals which affect their relationship with each other, and their standards, fears and aspirations are markedly affected by the norms of the cultures in which they have lived. Indeed they are likely to bring to their relationships somewhat different premises and expectations in part because of their differing social experiences. In turn, such norms are developed, passed on and refurbished through the agency of the dyadic (and higher order) relationships that constitute the society. A science of interpersonal relationships must thus eventually come to terms not only with the dialectic between personality and relationship but also with that between relationship and society. For this book, however, that would be too ambitious an aim, and the discussion has been focussed, thus:

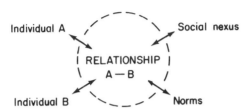

Even within those limits, I would not want to suggest that the progress achieved here is very great. I have proposed categories of dimensions that may be useful for describing relationships and I have indicated the way in which the concepts used by different theoreticians could be related, though not in any definitive way. At most I have attempted to sketch the sort of shape a science of interpersonal relationships might have. I have not attempted, nor would I have been able, to review comprehensively the scientific literature on interpersonal relationships, though I have tried to provide an entry to it. Though I may not have done justice to many of the viewpoints expressed, my main aim has been to relate them. My belief is that, so long as sociologists, anthropologists, psychiatrists, psychologists and biologists attempt to divide the phenomena of human interpersonal relationships into categories suitable to their own specialities, their endeavours are likely to founder. If I may adapt Henri Tajfel's (1972) phrase, all are dealing with biopsychosocial man.

The book is organized into five sections. Part I (Chapters 1–3) is concerned with some general strategic issues—why we need a science of relationships between people and why we have not already got one; with what we mean by relationships and what sort of concepts are necessary for their understanding; and with the principles underlying the search for a descriptive base for such a science. These are matters with which a science of interpersonal relationships must come to terms, but if the reader finds the discussion heavy-going he should skip over them, returning later for what seems pertinent.

Part II (Chapters 4–11) concerns eight categories of dimensions which may be useful for describing relationships, and a discussion of their limitations.

Part III (Chapters 12–20) sketches four sources of principles concerned with the dynamics of relationships—social and other extra-dyadic influences, balance theories, learning and exchange theories, and consideration in terms of positive and negative feedback.

Chapters 21 and 22 are devoted to developmental issues, and the final part (V, Chapter 23) stresses the limitations of the material in the preceding chapters.

In writing this book, I have been greatly helped by critical and constructive comments from a number of friends and colleagues. I would like to mention especially Renford Bambrough, Patrick Bateson, German Berrios, Judy Dunn, Colin Fraser, Nicholas Humphrey, Norman Kreitman, Martin Roth, Joan Stevenson-Hinde and Henri Tajfel. Each of these read the whole or a large part of an earlier draft, and the final form owes much to their help. I am deeply indebted to them for the trouble they took. In addition L. Anne Peplau made valuable comments on Chapter 10, and H. H. Kelley sent me an advance copy of his recent (1979) book, permitting me to insert in the proofs some references to his current views. Finally, I would like to thank Mrs P. Naylor for help with the final preparation of the manuscript.

Whilst preparing this book my own work was supported by the Royal Society, the Medical Research Council and the Grant Foundation.

September, 1979   R. A. HINDE

Contents

III

The Dynamics of Interpersonal Relationships

1

Prolegomena

1

Obstacles to a Science of Interpersonal Relationships

For most of us, relationships with other people are the most important part of our lives. As individuals we know, though not necessarily at a conscious level, a great deal about how those relationships work. We have been learning about relationships between people since we were born. Indeed some would argue that, by virtue of our evolutionary history, we are predisposed to learn about relationships quickly and to use that knowledge with skill (Osgood, 1969; Humphrey, 1976). Although each of us has only a limited range of experience, we can learn about aspects of relationships that we do not experience ourselves from watching and talking with others, and from the distilled wisdom of novelists and biographers. Furthermore, the study of interpersonal relationships comes within the orbit of a number of scientific disciplines. Psychiatrists, concerned primarily with their patients as individuals, must nevertheless see them in terms of their relationships with others (e.g. Sullivan, 1938); those concerned, for instance, with problems of childhood or marriage often treat the relationship rather than the individual. Anthropologists and sociologists are often concerned with the nature of particular types of relationships in the societies with which they deal, and with differences in those relationships within or between societies. Social psychologists, especially in the last fifteen years, have employed experimental and observational approaches to many aspects of interpersonal relationships with considerable effect. Most recently, child developmentalists have seen that children's social and cognitive development depend on the changing patterns of relationships in which they are involved.

And yet, in spite of all these sources of knowledge, it cannot yet be said that we have an integrated science of interpersonal relationships. Although there are some issues about which we know a great deal, that knowledge has been gained in a number of more or less isolated skirmishes, and as yet lacks cohesion.

Perhaps that is the nature of things. Perhaps the subject of interpersonal relationships is such that it is bound to be of peripheral interest to a number of scientific disciplines, but central to none. For reasons that I hope will become plain in the following chapters, I do not believe that to be the case. If we assume that a cohesive body of knowledge about interpersonal relationships is attainable, we must first ask, would it be useful? We get the impression that most of the relationships in which we are involved just happened, and that their natures are a more or less inevitable consequence of the sorts of people we are and the sorts of people with whom we interact. But it is equally clear that what we are is determined at least in part by the relationships we have had. Early family relationships have a special importance here, but relationships all through life continue not only to affect us in the short term but also to influence our subsequent behaviour and relationships. Even apparently trivial everyday relationships have a cumulative effect upon us. Each individual's life is in fact a continuing dialectic between the self he is or believes himself to be and the relationships he forms, with each affecting the other. If we are to understand the complex processes involved, if we are to manage our own relationships successfully, if we are to help and advise others wisely, if we wish to strive to create a society in which positive relationships flourish, we must surely attempt to build up a systematic body of knowledge about relationships. We need a science. We must therefore ask, what is it that has so far hindered its development?

First there are prejudices from outside science. Some argue that full understanding of any relationship is possible only for the participants. Others say that the complexity and diversity of relationships are such that generalizations are unattainable, so that each must be content with such know-how as he can obtain from the array of instances he encounters, with full understanding for ever beyond his grasp. But *full* understanding of all aspects of all human relationships is not what we are after here—we seek only, or at any rate first, for an understanding adequate to achieve our goals. And from that aim we need not be diverted by complexity.

Yet others fear that full understanding of interpersonal relationships would destroy something of value. "Analysis is total, knowledge is boundless. But I can't stand it," says one of Bergman's characters in a perceptive play on marital relationships (Bergman, 1974, p. 192). But if such an argument is to be mounted, it should be directed against all attempts to understand interpersonal behaviour, including those of biographers, novelists and playwrights, and not just against those of scientists. Furthermore, as in all such cases, the question should be phrased, "Will the harm, if any, outdo the good?" But the issue is an old one, and need not be pursued. Analytic understanding does not eliminate the whole; Newton did not destroy the beauty of the rainbow.

Another prejudice involves the supposition that relationships possess subtle properties beyond the reach of the scientist, and must therefore remain the exclusive preserve of novelists, biographers, playwrights and clinicians (in so far as the latter are not scientists). It may well be that the penetrating insights into individual cases that some writers have achieved would not be attainable in any other way. Perhaps instances of the dialectic between personality and relationship are, at least for the moment, best encapsulated in literary form. But when it comes to systematic knowledge, to abstracting generalizations from their wisdom, even the most sensitive literary criticism, in which the material is assessed not only in its own terms but against the yardstick of life (e.g. Black, 1975), produces conclusions no different from those of the scientists and perhaps less securely based.

Of course there may well be properties of relationships that the scientists' instruments cannot detect—they are in no position to argue about that. But they are obliged to *attempt* to fashion tools suitable for all natural phenomena that they encounter. Hopes, fears, ambitions, tenderness, indifference, empathy, sensitivity and many other seemingly intangible entities form the stuff of which relationships are made, but already progress has been made in coming to terms with them. And if for the moment some subtle properties of relationships are beyond scientists' reach, such properties may nevertheless be correlated with properties that are more accessible. For many practical purposes, it is the extent of such correlations that are important. Some of the properties of an affectionate relationship can be specified with reasonable precision (see p. 42), though there may be others that are more intangible. If we could use the properties with which we can now cope to discover, for example, the conditions necessary to promote relationships having those properties, it is at least possible that the same conditions would prove to be propitious also for the more intangible ones.

Yet another obstacle to a science of interpersonal relationships arises from the very fact that each of us knows, or thinks he knows, so much about them already. But even our cherished beliefs may be wrong, or may apply only to a limited range of relationships or in a limited range of contexts. Clearly we must use our intuition, but only with the greatest circumspection. But this very need for care, for validating every finding and testing the limits of every generalization, can lead us into complex endeavours which may at times seem to achieve little beyond proving what is already known. The difficulty here is to maintain a proper balance. On the one hand, the temptation to pursue a line of research just because it yields hard data, even though those data are trivial and unlikely to lead anywhere new, must be resisted. On the other, it is necessary to formulate each piece of knowledge in a manner that enables it to be incorporated alongside others, and thus contribute to the edifice of knowledge. This must be done even with what we think we know, in part because even if we are correct, the generality of what we know for other contexts and other cultures must be tested.

Other prejudices come from within science, for the study of interpersonal relationships does not at first sight provide the sort of material that would allow it to rank highly on the ladder of scientific respectability. Science tends to grow like an *Amoeba*, putting out pseudopodia now here and now there to engulf areas of ignorance, but rejecting indigestible fragments and avoiding areas uncongenial to it. This method of growth leads to the structuring of a value system. Areas of research in which the problems are clear, and where precise techniques are available so that the results can be checked in half a dozen laboratories, become respectable. But it is foolhardy and disreputable to enter areas where the course ahead is murky, where the complexity of the material makes it difficult to follow the same path twice, and where the conceptual jungle chokes the unwary. But, if science is not to be trivial, such anticipations of possible difficulties must be reconciled with the importance of problems. The dilemma between the need for rigour and the need for relevance is not new to psychologists (Bronfenbrenner, 1977), and a growing body of hard-headed scientists have shown that love and hate, and even the trivia of the family breakfast table, are proper grist for their mill.

A more specific problem, and one that provides the central argument to this book, concerns the importance of a firm basis of description and classification. A science, according to the Oxford Dictionary, consists of (or at least, one might interject, depends on) systematic and formulated knowledge. On this view Chemistry became a science when Mendeléef's Periodic Table of elements provided a means for systematizing knowledge. Biology became a science because a theory of evolution provided a basis for the work of taxonomists and systematists. The study of interpersonal relationships lacks such a means for systematizing the knowledge gained. Only when we can describe relationships, categorize their properties, and classify them can we transform our limited knowledge and our experimental findings into generalizations with specified ranges of validity. Here I do not mean to imply that we are totally without such means, but only that the instruments we have are as yet inadequate, and have been insufficiently used.

Hitherto, most research on social interactions and relationships has been paradigmatic, in the sense that it has involved taking one theoretical model or set of postulates, based perhaps on classical or operant conditioning, or on the concepts of norms or of complementary needs, and seeing how far it would go. There is of course much to be said for such an approach. Borrowing a metaphor from Clore and Byrne (1974), attempts to build a road through the murky forest of ignorance that depend on random attempts to start a path here or to fell a tree there make little headway. Real progress is more likely when a group starts in a concerted fashion to work from an agreed base. An acceptable theoretical model or set of postulates can provide such a group of "Paradigm Builders" with both a starting point and a guide (Byrne, 1971). But there is a difficulty. The direction their road takes is likely to be dictated by the tools at their disposal. One group equipped with bulldozers may start on firm ground but be diverted by swamp. Another equipped with pontoons may start through swamp but be diverted by rocky outcrops. Surely, in setting out to penetrate the murky forest, the paradigm builders would do well to use points of vantage, or even a helicopter? Just because paradigmatic research can be so fruitful, it needs access to a descriptive map* so that the extent and limitations of its achievements can be assessed and so that, at each choice point, the course taken can be dictated by the problem as well as by the tools available.

Furthermore, anyone examining the literature on interpersonal relationships cannot fail to be struck not only by the diversity of theoretical and methodological approaches used in their study, but also by the dearth of attempts to integrate them. It may be that some of the

---

*No implication that we can achieve "pure" description is intended. Descriptions are inevitably influenced by the "common knowledge" of the contemporary culture and by pre-existing paradigms (see Chapter 3).

difficulties in the way of integration would disappear if there were adequate means for specifying the limits of applicability of the generalizations that emerge from research findings. Nowhere is this more apparent than in the literature on interpersonal attraction, where much research has been concentrated on what contributes to interpersonal attraction, but much less on the diversity of phenomena embraced by being attracted. This makes the generality of some of the research findings difficult to assess, even within the age/sex categories and cultures for which they were obtained. That views similar to this have been expressed by a number of workers in the field (e.g. Berscheid and Walster, 1969; Byrne, 1971; Levinger and Snoek, 1972; Huston, 1974; Duck, 1977a) does not seem so far to have stimulated attempts to find a way out of the difficulty. Perhaps a search for means adequate to describe and classify relationships will help.

The issue of the importance of a descriptive base for establishing the generality of research findings comes up in another way. An interpersonal relationship involves persons with individually specific constitutions and past histories, living in a particular social network in a particular culture. Multitudinous interacting variables thus affect its course. "Pure" observations or experiments, in which the effect of a particular variable is studied in isolation, are not possible simply because every experiment must involve particular individuals in a particular type of relationship in a particular context and culture (see Tajfel, 1972). The problem is exacerbated by interdisciplinary barriers. Ethologists, psychologists, social psychologists and anthropologists are interested in different sets of variables. Whilst each may pay lip service to the view that there are other variables that interact with the ones in which he is interested, it is not easy to do much about it. In the short term it may help to talk of these variables as existing on different "levels", and to imply that there are some types of human conduct to which one approach is more useful than the others. But in the long term it must be recognized that cultural influences on a relationship do not operate at a different "level" from the influences of individual experience. This is not reductionism; it is merely saying that the properties of a relationship may vary according to the natures of the participants, and these may vary with cultural, with individual-specific experiential and indeed with genetic influences. But interactions between biological, psychological and sociological determinants are ubiquitous. In any given set of observations or experiments we may keep one or two sets of determinants reasonably constant—by working in one culture or subculture, or with physiologically or psychologically normal (whatever that means) individuals. But though constant they will still be there, and we must remember their presence in making generalizations (Tajfel, 1972). If we are to specify the limits of our generalizations, a descriptive base is essential.

There is yet another special reason why description is an important prerequisite for the study of interpersonal relationships. Considering *for the moment* only its behavioural aspects, an interpersonal relationship involves a series of interactions in time. An interaction involves behaviour by two participants. Both interactions and relationships involve emergent properties. Some properties of interactions (e.g. synchrony) are just not relevant to the behaviour of an individual in isolation. Some properties of relationships (e.g. those that depend on the patterning of interactions in time, Chapter 6) are not relevant to interactions. Yet most theory building in the study of relationships has started with propositions derived from studies of individual behaviour. Without prejudging the issue of whether the properties of relationships can be understood in terms of such propositions (see Chapter 23), surely those properties must first be described?

This question of the emergent properties of social relationships is relevant also to another argument which has hindered the development of an integrated study of interpersonal relationships—the argument that psychology is not ready for it. So long as the presumably simpler problems of individual behaviour, of motor skills and visual perception and the like, are not yet solved, is it worth while tackling something much more complex? But such a query rests on the naive view that the more complex phenomena are to be understood as nothing but the simpler elements of which they are composed. As we have seen social interactions, and even more social relationships, involve properties and pose problems which are simply not relevant to the study of individual behaviour. It is of course the case that, in the ultimate analysis, *full* understanding of interpersonal relationships will require understanding of such components as visual perception, motor skills and much else besides. But understanding of the components will not be enough for understanding the more complex phenomena, which have properties of their own. Effort is therefore needed at all relevant levels. To take another example, much is known about learning in spite of our almost total ignorance of the neural mechanisms involved.

Of course a descriptive base is not an aim in itself, nor is it sufficient of itself. We need also theories or at least a series of principles concerned with the dynamics of relationships. Grand theories of broad generality are elusive in psychology, and it is usually necessary to set our sights lower. In some areas we must be content with propositions or principles that can be only loosely sketched and may consist of little more than indications of what matters and how. Such explanatory principles may invoke concepts not present in the initial description of the events to which they apply, and should be coupled with a statement of the range of empirical data to which they are relevant (i.e. which could be deduced from them). Here again, the descriptive base will clearly be essential.

Descriptive statements and explanatory principles must clearly harmonize with each other. Description must be selective, related on the one hand to the real-life problems that, from either a scientific or a practical point of view,* need to be solved, and on the other to the structure we are trying to build—namely the principles that at the moment seem useful. And on their side, the principles also must be related both to the descriptive base and to the problems to be solved. Whilst the usual practice has been to start from "basic" propositions obtained from studies of individual behaviour, to derive principles about interpersonal attraction, interactions or relationships from them, and then to relate those to yet more complex "everyday" phenomena (see e.g. Chapter 16), such a procedure assumes descriptions of the everyday phenomena and an intuitive knowledge of how they can be analysed. It may be more expedient to make the latter explicit, to specify the properties of relationships and then assess how far principles derived from studies of individual behaviour can go in explaining them. Such a procedure may even force us to question whether, or in what sense, individual behaviour is in fact more "basic" than social behaviour with another interacting individual.

The complexity and diversity of relationships between people are such that theoretical pluralism seems at the moment inevitable (Elms, 1975). In some areas theoretical approaches of considerable power are being developed but, in the present state of knowledge, to set theories

---

*Though some have argued that it is wise to maintain a distinction between basic and applied research in the behavioural sciences (Pfaffmann, 1965; Byrne, 1971), basic research can still look to the phenomenon of real life for its material, and will be none the worse for keeping an eye on practical problems as it goes along.

against each other does not seem like a task of top priority. Much energy has been expended by investigators jousting for the honour of their paradigms, but such contests have not always provided an elegant spectacle, and are wasteful of endeavour (cf. Clore and Byrne, 1974). What is needed, within this underdeveloped sub-area of science, is not a mini-revolution, with one paradigm displacing another (Kuhn, 1969), but rather attempts to see *what* is important *when* and *where*. The dangers of eclecticism (Allport, 1964) can perhaps be averted if we focus first on trying to specify where each approach is useful, and then search for ways of relating the explanatory concepts of one group of investigators to those of another, to spot duplications and perhaps, where we are fortunate, to tie groups of principles to a central pillar. And since relating explanatory concepts to each other will often be difficult, it may be worthwhile to keep an eye on the possibility of finding correlations between the phenomena to which each refers and phenomena at a different level of analysis.

It remains the case, of course, that the phenomena of interpersonal relationships pose problems of incredible complexity. This could be special pleading, for every scientist working at the limits of his abilities must believe the problem with which he is concerned to be complex. However there is no need to claim that the problems surrounding interpersonal relationships are *unique* in their complexity (though I may secretly believe that to be the case), but merely to point to the diversity of interpersonal relationships, to the difficulties of describing them adequately and the near impossibility of measuring some of their most important characteristics, and to the multitudinous interacting variables that affect them. (The word "interacting" here requires special emphasis. In a relationship each participant influences the other, each act is in part a response to the past behaviour of the other and may form a stimulus to his future behaviour. The neat distinction between independent and dependent variables, on which so much experimental work in psychology is based, can become elusive). In the face of all these factors, it is not surprising that knowledge in this area is difficult to systematize. But this must not stop us trying. While part of the art of the scientist is to isolate problems which are soluble with the tools that he has or can reasonably fashion (Medawar, 1967), that must not deter him from tackling what seems difficult if it seems also to be important.

And there are, I believe, reasons why the present may well be propitious for attempts to tackle the problems posed by interpersonal relationships. Recent years have seen the gradual demise, within the life sciences, of attempts to build grand theories on an inadequate descriptive base. The epitome of this has been the changing fortunes of learning theories in the thirties, forties and fifties. I do not mean that their achievements should be belittled, but rather that their ambitious goals have perforce been diluted in the face of the diversity of the phenomena confronting them (e.g. Seligman and Hager, 1972; Hinde and Stevenson-Hinde, 1973). Instead there is now a willingness to put observation and description first, to be content initially with short-range generalizations, to build a scientific edifice from the bottom up.

Another hopeful sign is the current willingness to grapple with aspects of human behaviour and experience that cannot readily be reduced to physiological terms and for which physiological explanations seem either a long way ahead (e.g. Bindra, 1976) or perhaps even permanently beyond our reach. This makes it possible to address our endeavours to the everyday events and experiences that we encounter, and to borrow, in a disciplined way, concepts from everyday life to aid in their explication. Other reasons why the time is propitious could be listed—no doubt other workers would take courage from other constellations in the sky. But perhaps the most important issue is that already given, namely that relationships between people are important. Whilst it would be foolish to expend scientific resources in hopeless endeavours, we cannot afford to avoid this problem because it is difficult.

Summary

Our extensive knowledge of interpersonal relationships does not yet constitute an integrated body of knowledge. Some possible reasons for this are: (a) prejudices from outside science that analysis can destroy what is valuable, or that relationships involve intangible properties not accessible to scientific treatment; (b) our beliefs that we know about relationships intuitively, so that the results of scientific enquiry are likely to be trivial; (c) prejudices from within science that such an area of study is not respectable; and (d) the inadequate attention given to the need to provide and use an adequate descriptive base in studying interpersonal relationships.

A descriptive base is held to be important for guiding the course of research, for ensuring that emergent properties are not neglected in the course of analysis, and for assessing the limits of the validity of generalizations. The latter is especially crucial because biological, psychological and cultural variables all affect interpersonal relationships.

In addition to a descriptive base, we need propositions or principles and theories which explain the dynamic properties of relationships. Description and the search for principles must be pursued in relation to each other. Much progress with building theoretical structures has been made, but theoretical pluralism is at present inevitable. "Paradigmatic competition" seems to be a less cogent goal than that of relating different approaches.

2

What Do We Mean by a Relationship?

What do we mean by a "dyadic" or "interpersonal relationship"? We apply the term to husband-and-wife, father-and-daughter, teacher-and-pupil, employer-and-workman, and in many other contexts. Although the way the word "relationship" is used in everyday speech is clear enough, the diversity and complexity of the phenomena involved make any attempt to define precisely what does and does not constitute a relationship inevitably somewhat arbitrary. So before proceeding it is necessary to consider the nature of relationships, and to specify what sort of concepts we shall need to describe and discuss them.

A relationship implies first some sort of intermittent interaction between two people, involving interchanges over an extended period of time. The interchanges have some degree of mutuality, in the sense that the behaviour of each takes some account of the behaviour of the other. However this mutuality does not necessarily imply "cooperation" in its everyday sense: relationships exist between enemies as well as between friends, between those who are forced into each other's company as well as between those who seek it.

In addition, "relationship" in everyday language carries the further implication that there is some degree of continuity between the successive interactions. Each interaction is affected by interactions in the past, and may affect interactions in the future. For that reason a "relationship" between two people may continue over long periods when they do not meet or communicate with each other; the accumulated effects of past interactions will ensure that, when they next meet, they do not see each other as strangers. In such a case, and when we say, for instance that "a separation experience can in some circumstances alter the course of the parent-child relationship", "relationship" refers not to an actual sequence of interactions, but to a potential for patterns of interactions which may be of a certain general type but whose precise form will depend on events in the future.

The nature of the effect of one interaction on subsequent ones will depend not only on what actually happened but also on what each partner thinks about what he experienced during that interaction. While the participants are apart, each may review the course of past interactions, or imagine future ones, in ways that will affect the future course of the relationship. To understand relationships fully, therefore, it is necessary to come to terms not only with their behavioural but also with their affective/cognitive aspects, and to do so whilst recognizing that they are inextricably interwoven.

With this background, we may take up a few points concerning the nature of relationships that will be useful in later chapters.

Relationships as sequences of interactions

At the level of overt behaviour, a relationship involves a series of interactions between two individuals known to each other. By an interaction (or "encounter", in Goffman's (1961) terminology) we usually mean such incidents as individual A shows behaviour X to individual B, or A shows X to B and B responds with Y. Considering, for the moment only, this behavioural aspect in isolation, it is necessary to make a number of points.

(i) There is a degree of arbitrariness in what we call an interaction. Most interactions are much longer than "A shows X to B and B responds with Y". But the question of how long a sequence of social actions could be and still qualify as one interaction need not detain us. Clearly there is no absolute answer, and any decision must be based on what is useful empirically. A useful guide is likely to be the extent to which successive actions have related goals, foci, references or "meanings". But both exchanged "good-mornings" and a long discussion between husband and wife could be treated as one interaction.

(ii) There is a degree of arbitrariness in the distinction between an "interaction" and a "relationship". In general the distinction between an interaction, which involves a strictly limited span of time, and a relationship, which involves a much longer period, is clear enough. To discuss how long we must talk to a stranger in the street before we can properly say we have a relationship with him would not be very constructive. But nevertheless it is important to emphasize that a series of interactions totally

independent of each other would not constitute a relationship. An essential character of a relationship is that each interaction is influenced by other interactions in that relationship. You might talk to the same telephone operator every day for a week, but if you did not know it was the same person, if each conversation was uninfluenced by what you had learned about the operator as an individual on previous occasions, you could not have a relationship with him. A relationship exists only when the probable course of future interactions between the participants differs from that between strangers. Furthermore, whilst an interaction could be defined as having one meaning or "focus", a relationship is likely to have many, each superordinated to those of numerous types of interactions.

(iii) An interaction must involve both partners, and its nature depends on both. This is clear in the case "A does X to B and B responds with Y", though it must be said both that most interactions involve many such sequences, and that there is no implication that social interactions consist solely of chained responses, with each individual responding to what the other just did. Even in the case "A does X to B", A must be responding to stimuli at least broadcast by B, even if they were not specifically directed towards A. The distinction between broadcast signals and those specifically directed is in practice not easy to make (e.g. MacKay, 1972 and discussion thereof). It must also be remembered that B's doing nothing may be an event of great importance to A.

Furthermore it is a proper initial assumption that the nature of any interaction is a product of both partners, even though it appears to be under the control of only one. Both monkey (Spencer-Booth, 1968) and human mothers are liable to behave differently to each of two twins, for instance displaying more "warmth" (see p. 70) to the one than to the other. This maternal warmth is thus a characteristic of the *relationship* of the mother with that twin, and not of the mother as an individual. This point, stressed by Thibaut and Kelley (1959), has frequently been forgotten. Some studies of mother-child interaction run into difficulties through the improper assumption that some of the measures are measures of maternal behaviour or of child behaviour, rather than of the relationship between them (see p. 265).

The issue is equally important in adult relationships. The ability to be consistently kind or consistently sensitive to all others, irrespective of their nature, is found in few real-life individuals, and even the roughest rogues have their tender spots. Of course it is important to maintain a balanced perspective here. There are more or less consistent predispositions that run through the lives of each one of us—tendencies to behave in this way rather than that, to respond warmly, lightly, courteously, self-centredly, and so on. But at the same time social behaviour depends on *both* participants in each interaction, and is thus not exclusively a characteristic of one or the other. Perhaps it is partly for this reason that, although individuals are reasonably consistent from one task to another in intellectual performance, consistency in the personality attributes usually measured by psychologists is rather low (Mischel, 1968, 1973). Much of the behaviour measured in such tests is social behaviour, and may thus depend also on the other interactant, real or imagined (Maccoby and Jacklin, pers. comm.). But, while in the longer term each of us is a somewhat different self in each relationship in which he is involved, and what he is depends in part on the other member of the dyad (e.g. Laing, 1962), it is also the case that a considerable degree of longitudinal and cross-situational consistency exists—as felt intuitively and as demonstrated objectively in adequately designed studies (Block, 1977).

(iv) The behaviour involved in social interactions normally, but not invariably, involves meaning. Here we are concerned with what is included in "X" in the phrase "A does X to B". It is customary in this context to lay emphasis on the distinction between "behaviour" and "action". "Behaviour", according to Weber (1964), is merely reactive, whereas "action" includes behaviour only in so far as the *acting individual* attaches "meaning" to it. A further distinction is made between "social action", guided with respect to the past, present or future behaviour of one or more other individuals, and "non-social action", which is guided without respect to its consequences for others.

These distinctions are valuable as a basis for discussion, but Weber himself repeatedly emphasized that they are not absolute. There are two main issues here. First, "meaning" was not clearly defined by Weber. Whilst it clearly has to do with the functional connections between actions—actions acquire "meaning" through connections with other events—a satisfactory definition has been extraordinarily difficult to find. Using it in an everyday sense, it is still the case that a speaker's words may mean (or seem to mean?) something different from his gestures (see p. 68), so that what he "really" meant is not easy to pin down. Again, what a person says may not mean what he intended it to mean; and the meaning ascribed to an interaction may differ between the participants, or between each of them and an outsider (see John Dunn, 1978).

Second, the distinction between meaningful action and merely reactive behaviour, though analytically valuable, can never be empirically absolute. Whilst it is possible to find almost pure examples of "social action" and of "reactive behaviour", the phenomena of the real world form a continuum between them, and Weber's attempt to distinguish them was in fact an heuristic device to facilitate the classification of their determinants. Weber himself emphasized that, "A very considerable part of all sociologically relevant behaviour, especially purely traditional behaviour, is marginal between the two. In the case of many psychophysical processes, meaningful, i.e. subjectively understandable, action is not to be found at all; in others it is discernible only by the expert psychologist" (p. 128). It is important for many purposes to distinguish between categories of determinants of behaviour/action, but the *dichotomy* of *behaviour* versus *action* itself is dangerous.

While in what follows we shall be primarily concerned with events near the "social action" end of this continuum, and shall frequently emphasize that the actions involved in the relationship between two individuals cannot be studied independently of their meaning (Crick, 1975), there are at least two categories of cases where actions lacking in social meaning for the actor are nevertheless important for a relationship. First, the behaviour of a newborn baby can hardly be said to have social meaning to the baby himself, though it may to the mother. Second, we are inevitably affected by the quirks and ticks of our acquaintances in a way that need have no relation to their social meaning, if any, to those who make them. These examples, which may seem trivial, emphasize the point of Weber's distinction—namely the classification of the determinants of behaviour. We must remember that "meaning" is a slippery concept and that behaviour that is devoid of meaning to one participant may be meaningful to another.

This point is emphasized for a special reason. In attempting to build up a science, in the sense of an ordered body of knowledge, it would be perfectly proper to limit our area of study in any reasonable way. In that spirit, presumably, are to be understood such pronouncements as "It is complex and deliberate actions, unified through their contributions to the meaning of the total act, that constitute the true subject matter of human social behaviour" (Harré and Secord, 1972, p. 40). But if we were to accept such a dictum, we would have to remember that we were dealing with only certain aspects of the phenomena out there in the real world. If our aim is to understand relationships, we must come to terms with "behaviour", and with "actions", and with all their intermediates, as well as with the factors that affect their course, and if we are to do so, we must recognize that theoretical interpretations relevant to only one or the other can be only partial. We shall return to this issue shortly.

(v) Description of an interaction must involve reference to both content and "quality". Behaviour can be described in a number of ways and with varying degrees of precision (e.g. Bateson, 1968; Hinde, 1970a). Were we interested in the physiological mechanisms underlying behaviour, we should need description at a fairly molecular level. In the present context, molar descriptions are more appropriate—though just what level of description is best in any particular case is a difficult problem, to which we shall return later (e.g. Chapter 5).

To describe an interaction it is necessary to describe first what A did to B (and B to A). They may for instance be talking or fighting or kissing. In addition we must specify how they are doing it. Are they talking in an animated or dispassionate fashion? What are they talking about? Are they fighting savagely? Kissing passionately, tenderly or dutifully? Are they involved in what they are doing? To what extent are the different aspects of their behaviour consistent with each other? For instance does the tone of their voices belie the words that they use? The complexity and levels of meaning that may underlie quite brief encounters have been analysed with elegance by Goffman (1959, 1961, 1963, 1967, 1971) and will be referred to again later. For the moment we may refer to such properties of interactions as qualities, without of course any implication that they cannot be subjected to quantitative treatment. It is a matter of everyday experience that the qualities of an interaction can be as or more important than the type of behaviour involved.

It will be evident that, to describe the content of an interaction, we are usually interested in what the individuals are doing or trying to do at a gross level, and fairly crude descriptions may be adequate and even preferable; if A is chasing B it is important to know that both are running, and their relative positions in space, but details of the precise movements of each joint in their legs and arms would cloud the issue. But the level of description that is appropriate for capturing the quality of the interaction is much less predictable. Small expressive movements, such as the slightest raise of an eyebrow, as well as the way in which the behaviour is directed, or the sequencing of interactions within it, may well be important (see Chapter 5).

(vi) Description of the behavioural aspects of a relationship must involve reference to the content, quality and patterning of interactions. A relationship involves a sequence of interactions which is patterned in time. Patterning is used here to refer to their absolute and relative frequencies, when they occur with respect to each other, and how they affect each other. Clearly the relationship between a couple who always kiss after they quarrel will be very different from that between a couple who always quarrel after they kiss, even though the total amounts of kissing and quarrelling are the same in both cases. Relationships thus have properties that depend on the patterning of the interactions, and are not present in the interactions themselves. Research on short-term interactions can thus take us only part of the way towards understanding relationships extended in time. Indeed the significance of interactions to the participants may depend on the content of the relationship in which they are embedded. "It is not what lovers do together but their doing it *together* that is the distinctive source of their special satisfaction" (Blau, 1964, p. 15). And that satisfaction depends, of course, on the particular interaction being seen as one of a series (see Chapter 6 and p. 217).

(vii) Dyadic relationships take place in a social context. There are two main issues here. First, individuals are affected by their past experiences in the group in which they grow up, and by the norms and values prevalent there. This will affect their own dyadic relationships. Second, participants in a dyadic relationship are almost invariably involved in relationships with other individuals, who in turn may have relationships with each other and with other individuals. Each dyadic relationship is in fact nearly always embedded in a social group. The structure of this group provides a further level of complexity. Just as the behavioural aspects of a relationship can be described in terms of the content, quality and patterning of its component interactions, so can the group be described in terms of the content, qualities and patterning of its component relationships (Hinde, 1976b, in press). Problems of social

structure will not be the concern of this book, but it is essential to remember that dyadic relationships can never be fully understood in isolation from their social context (see Chapter 13).

(viii) The extent to which an individual exhibits social behaviour is not indicative of the extent to which that individual enters social relationships. Because some of the most important characteristics of interpersonal relationships lie in the affective/cognitive components (see below), because people's behaviour varies according to whom they are with, and because relationships have emergent properties, studies of social behaviour are not an adequate substitute for studies of social relationships.

Two points relevant to this issue emerged from a recent study of nursery school children. Most previous studies of 3–5 year olds had assumed a dimension of "social participation" (e.g. Parten, 1932), ranging from the child playing on its own (self play), through playing alongside other children (parallel play), to playing interactively with them (group and interactive play). It was supposed that children mature through stages in which each of these types of play predominates in turn. However in a principal component analysis of the data two relevant components emerged, one involving self play and the other ranging from parallel to group and interactive play. In other words, how much a child plays on his own, and how much he interacts with other children when playing with them, are separate issues. Some children showed quite a lot of interactive play but also played freely on their own (Roper and Hinde, 1978).

At the same time the extent to which the children formed relationships with each other was assessed in terms of the consistency with which they had the same neighbours. To summarize the data, "good friends" may be defined as children who sat next to each other on at least 35% of the observations. (The data supported the use of this dependent variable as an indicator of friendship; children who were often neighbours were more likely to talk to each other when together than were children who were neighbours less often). As might be expected, the proportion of children who had at least one good friend tended to be higher amongst those who often showed group or interactive play than amongst those who mostly played in parallel. However the difference was not great, and eleven children with good friends showed much parallel play. Nevertheless these were children who often had the same neighbours even though they appeared not to interact with them very much. There were also a number of children without good friends who often played interactively. And although, again as expected, children who had good friends tended to score negatively on the self play dimension, there were three who had good friends and yet were often alone (Hinde, 1978b). These data show what we all know, namely that you can be constant but not overtly sociable, and sociable but yet promiscuous. Social behaviour does not accurately reflect social relationships.

Affective/Cognitive aspects

If we were concerned only with overt behaviour, we should need some explanatory concepts to account for its changes with time and differences between individuals—motivational and dispositional concepts, for instance. We should also need concepts to help us understand the effects of interactions upon interactions—we could draw here on studies of learning, and perhaps ultimately borrow concepts from physiology. But we have seen that, even if we consider only their behavioural aspects, relationships involve complex influences of interactions upon interactions, that they have emergent properties not present in their component interactions, and that social behaviour does not necessarily predict the formation of social relationships. We have also seen that most behaviour in relationships is to be understood in terms of its social meaning to the actor, and that relationships continue over periods in which the participants do not meet or communicate with each other. Such considerations are alone sufficient to show that an account of interpersonal relationships solely in terms of overt behaviour will not suffice. To most, that will be obvious enough. However accepting that conclusion immediately presents us with important decisions about how much further we should go. If we are to come to terms with the affective/cognitive aspects of interpersonal relationships, and we must surely attempt to do so, we shall need additional concepts. Yet if we are too generous in introducing them we shall find ourselves swimming in a mush with nothing firm to stand on. But if we are too niggardly, we run the risk of missing important phenomena.

The science of interpersonal relationships is too young for us to reach firm decisions as to precisely which concepts will be needed. The problems that arise in studying relationships are diverse, and have been tackled by workers from varied disciplines, with different ends in view. This book is not an attempt at systematic theory building, though it perhaps indicates the shadowy outlines of the shape a theory might have. In keeping with such a purpose, I have been eclectic in my choice of concepts, trying out the tools others have fashioned in the contexts in which they seem useful. Such an approach, however, involves the use of concepts valid at a number of different analytical levels, and in due course it will be necessary to relate them. In the final chapter I have indicated, in informal terms, the way in which this might be done and it becomes apparent that certain issues and concepts have a pivotal importance in the study of interpersonal relationships. In order to establish the level of discourse, these are discussed here.

(i) What A responds to in B is in part a function of what A is. Studies of animals show that individuals respond selectively to the patterns of energy that fall on their sense organs; some features are much more important than others. For example a territory-holding European robin will threaten a bunch of red breast feathers placed in his territory, but not a stuffed juvenile robin which lacks the red breast. Apparently the red breast is more important than all the other characteristics of a robin.* The same principle of "selective perception" is intrinsic to the characaturist's art;

*In a few places it is convenient to illustrate points made by examples drawn from studies of animals, and especially of non-human primates. It can properly be asked whether studies of non-human species, which operate at quite different cognitive and moral levels from us, which have no verbal language and lack the riches of a verbally transmitted culture, and whose relationships show little indication of institutionaliza-tion (see p. 170), could possibly be relevant to the incomparably more complex human case. The point has been well put by Crick (1975); emphasizing that our life is a "semantic fabric", he writes, "if one fails to acknowledge the inherently meaningful nature of the subject matter being considered one simply destroys the nature of the facts being investigated". I should emphasize, therefore, that the few examples from non-human species were selected not through a naive view that monkeys are like man (though current research is demonstrating complexities and resemblances to man that, with the crudeness of our knowledge, had previously been missed), but just because monkeys are *different* from man. Just because they are simpler, just because cultural influences are minimal, some issues stand out more clearly in monkeys than when shrouded in the complexity of the human case. The relevance of these issues to the human case is an empirical matter, to be answered on the basis of data. Previous studies do in fact suggest that, for certain problems and in certain limited ways, a comparative approach can be useful in indicating the way ahead (e.g. Hinde, 1978c). It will I hope be evident that the occasional use of such material does not imply an under-estimate of human diversity or complexity.

he picks out for exaggeration those features on which recognition is based. In all social intercourse, A responds selectively to certain aspects of what B is or does, and what A selects depends in part on A's previous experience. Especially important here, of course, is A's previous experience with B and others like B. The course of the interaction, then, will depend not just on what B is or does, but on A's perception of B, and on B's perception of A. Whilst both people and animals respond selectively, in the case of people it makes sense to talk about A's "perception" of B or A's "view" of B. We can *ask* A how he perceived B, and there is a good chance that A's behaviour to B will be more closely related to how A describes his perception of B than to what B is "really" like. Furthermore, as we shall see, A's behaviour may be affected by his perception of B's perception of him.

(ii) Behaviour is most easily described if we use some concept of anticipation or expectancy. This is even the case with responses to a physical object; as we pick up a stone we tense our muscles to an extent dependent upon its visual properties and our previous experience with similar objects. A's behaviour to B is most easily understood if we invoke expectations in A not merely about B's passive properties, but also about his behaviour. For instance A's initial response may be determined in part by his anticipated need to respond in his turn to the response he expects B to make. And A's expectations about B's response may well be facilitated if A imputes to him (B) expectations about his (A's) initial behaviour—for instance, will A's initiative be a surprise to B? In studies of animal learning, some concept of expectancy has had a limited usefulness as an intervening variable (MacCorquodale and Meehl, 1954; Bolles, 1972). In understanding human interactions it is even more valuable not only because people can tell us (more lucidly than can rats) about their expectancies, but also because people behave as though other people anticipated forthcoming events, and as though other people expected them to do likewise.

It need not be our immediate concern to consider how the phenomena embraced by concepts of expectancy (or indeed other concepts to be mentioned later) depend on lower order mechanisms. In that behaviour depends on the brain, we must presume in principle that such mechanisms are there to be discovered (e.g. Hebb, 1949; Bindra, 1976). We must expect them to be diverse—the tensing of our muscles when we pick up a stone is a different matter from our expectations about a party. The only issue here is that the participants in a relationship do not merely behave to each other in accordance with how each perceives the other now, but in accordance with what they expect each other to do next, next week, or at some indefinite time in the future.

(iii) Behaviour is usually goal-directed. A's behaviour to B may employ one of a number of alternative routes to reach the same end—it is in some sense goal-directed. However the category of goal-directed behaviour involves phenomena of varying degrees of complexity, and some comment is necessary.

First, in discussions of how machines or organisms operate, goal-directed behaviour is usefully contrasted with ballistic behaviour. Once an arrow leaves a bow, no further corrections to its course to the target are possible; its course is determined by its initial velocity and inertia, gravity, air-resistance, and such wind forces as impinge on it, until its flight is brought to an end when it encounters a new situation, such as the ground. When a young baby starts to cry, it usually continues to do so until it is tired out (analagous to the expenditure of the arrow's momentum) or until it encounters a new situation, such as being picked up. Such behaviour is not usefully described as goal-directed (see p. 311).

The minimum requirement for behaviour to be regarded as goal-directed is a feedback loop capable of assessing the discrepancy between the present situation and the goal situation, and of initiating appropriate corrections to the current behaviour. Homing missiles are goal-directed in this sense, their course being corrected to ensure contact with the target.

In practice, the distinction between goal-directed and ballistic behaviour is not so simple as this, even when we are dealing with animals or non-verbal humans (Hinde and Stevenson, 1969). Most mothers would say that a baby a few months old cries "in order to" get their attention, but just when it is reasonable to describe crying in this way is hard to judge. It is easiest to identify behaviour as goal-directed when the actor is both conscious of his goal and can tell you about it. Such behaviour is clearly describable in terms of "plans" (Miller *et al.*, 1960). If questioned, Captain Scott would have been quite explicit about his plans to reach the South Pole. More often, however, the plans are at or just below the threshold of consciousness. For instance, if you

were instructed to stick a pin in the centre of a circle, you would move
the pin gradually, monitoring its distances from a variety of points on
the circumference, until all those distances seemed to be equal, and
then push it home. In this sequence, it must be noted, the first phase is
continuously goal-directed, but the second stage (push it home) is
ballistic. Miller *et al.* would describe the first phase as involving continuous "test-operate-test" sequences, i.e. "test for equidistance from
circumferential points, move the pin, test again", until equidistance is
obtained. Equidistance is the signal to "exit" from that routine, and to
enter the next phase, which may involve another plan or, in this case, a
ballistic move.

Most goal-directed activities involve a sequence of phases. For
instance the above sequence might have involved two earlier phases,
"Find a pin" and "Pick it up". Such sequences can be described in
terms of the master-plan (Stick a pin in the centre of the circle), and
analysed into stages. Three of the latter have their own goals—"Sight
of a pin", "Pin between thumb and finger", "pin oriented to centre of
circle". Each such goal-oriented phase can be described in terms of
rules—"Move the pin until equidistant from all points on the circumference". Sometimes the rules do not involve near-continuous monitoring, as implied by the Miller *et al.* Test-Operate-Test-Exit model, but
instead there is a stop rule: "Rotate the nut until it is tight". Description of such a phase then comes very close to the description of a
ballistic phase.

When we are or can become conscious of our goals, we may label
them as "intentions". Of course our conscious intentions may be
epiphenomena, external to the mechanisms causing our behaviour. Or
we may just be mistaken about our intentions, or retrospectively invent
intentions to explain or cover up what we had done without thinking.
So stated intentions cannot always be used as a "true" guide to the
bases of behaviour. But we behave as if we believed ourselves to be
guided by intentions and, what is perhaps more important, we behave
to others as if they were guided for at least some of the time by their
intentions. Thus for the last reason alone, some intention-like concept
is necessary for the explanation of much social behaviour.

The rules referred to earlier may be explicit verbal rules—for example the goal of motor cycle maintenance might be achieved by following
instructions from a manual. Or, though learned from a manual or from
verbal instruction, they might be well practiced, so that we do not even

say them to ourselves, though we could if pressed. Thus the new recruit learning to use a rifle is instructed to "Place the tip of the foresight in line with the centre of the U of the backsight in line with the lowest central portion of the target", but with practice the words are forgotten, and the stages follow each other or coalesce smoothly; the experienced marksman merely "aims". It is usual to treat such skilled performances as if they were still controlled by a goal-seeking mechanism, and dependent on plans, though the operation of that mechanism is not apparent since the most economical course to the goal is pursued directly. Whether or not this is a correct view is open to question. It is known, for instance, that in some species of birds the early stages of song-learning require that the bird be able to monitor its own performance; deafening disrupts song acquisition. But after the song has been learned, deafening has no effect on song quality (Konishi and Nottebohm, 1969). Whilst singing was goal-directed in its early stages, later it apparently becomes more nearly ballistic.

Some types of behaviour are not usefully described as goal-directed. If we duck on hearing a warning cry, the ducking is essentially ballistic. But even when not usefully described as goal-directed, behaviour may be rule-determined. Following many conventions is habitual, and has at most a rather tenuous relation to the avoidance of disapprobation.

Thus, in considering these types of non-social behaviour, we can recognize four main types—consciously goal-directed and explicitly rule-guided, consciously goal-directed *without* explicit rules, unconsciously goal-directed, and ballistic—with, of course, all intermediates between them. These may be combined in many different ways. For example the whole sequence may be consciously goal-directed, the components unconsciously goal-directed or ballistic; or, and most especially in some pathological behaviour, the whole may be unconsciously directed while the parts are consciously. Furthermore, behaviour of any one of these types may be accompanied by expressive movements which may be consciously controlled to produce an effect, or unconscious and ballistic. When attempting to stick the pin in the circle one may dissemble nonchalance or concentration, or unconsciously protrude the tongue.

Exactly the same possibilities are open in social behaviour. One or both participants may have conscious goals, with each attempting to manipulate each stage of the interaction in a manner that will bring about his goal. Some of Cook's (1977) descriptions of planned seductions are examples. Alternatively one or both participants may not recognize their goals: adults sometimes explain a child's behaviour as "attention-seeking" with a shadowy implication that the child thinks he is doing one thing but is "really", at some unspecified level of consciousness, directing his behaviour to them. Social behaviour may even appear to be ballistic: the conversation of the party bore appears to proceed remorselessly on—though one must allow the possibility that it is successfully achieving the bore's own goals. And in each case the behaviour may be accompanied by expressive behaviour which is either consciously contrived, or unconscious, or purely reflex, or some intermediate between these.

This continuum from consciously rule-guided behaviour at one extreme to ballistic at the other has been recognized by many social psychologists. But the ways in which they have attempted to come to terms with it differ markedly. Garfinkel (1967) assumes that *all* social interaction involves rule-following, and proceeds to seek out the rules. Goffman (e.g. 1969) treats many aspects of social encounters *as if* they involved conscious attempts to achieve a specified goal, or to achieve a specific type of impression on others, and succeeds thereby in casting a flood of light on much everyday behaviour; he is little concerned with the "real" nature of the mechanisms. Harré and Secord (1972) distinguish three types of episode. At one extreme lie "formal" episodes, in which reference is made to explicit rules in accounting for the type and order of the component actions. At the other are "causal" episodes, involving actions linked by causal mechanisms. "Causal" is not clearly defined, but seems to imply either that successive interactions are linked by environmental events or by mechanisms whose physiological nature could in principle be comprehended in the foreseeable future. This might be "behaviour" without meaning in Weber's sense (see p. 18). Between these two lie "enigmatic episodes", whose nature is not immediately clear. Harré and Secord complain that until recently many investigators have sought to interpret such enigmatic episodes on the basis of a causal model, and applaud Goffman and Garfinkel for attempting to interpret them on the basis of the model of formal episodes. They acknowledge, perhaps a little grudgingly, that "adequate understanding may be reached only by an exploitation of both models" (p. 171), and regret our current inability to disentangle and specify the relations between the two approaches (p. 289).

Harré and Secord's distinction between episodes amenable to a rule-following explanation and those for which a causal explanation is more appropriate is of course an heuristic device, and they fully acknowledge that most episodes are "enigmatic" and between the two. However, whilst they underline that most episodes involve individuals as both agents and patients, as acting and being acted upon, they advocate that the student of social episodes should decide whether it is more appropriate to treat them in the one way or the other. But it would surely be more appropriate to emphasize that full understanding requires both. Rather than state that intermediate cases "mark the shadowy boundary between the social sciences and human biology", it is surely better to assume that all cases of human interaction may require both types of analysis. Even their metaphor of the complex "interweaving of the strands of cause and convention" seems to imply that items in social interactions could be teased apart into biological and rule-following items, and that which sort of treatment is more appropriate depends on which predominates. But we must now accept that everything that we learn depends on constraints and predispositions resulting from what we are (Seligman and Hager, 1972; Hinde and Stevenson-Hinde, 1973), and what we learn must include the rules that we learn and most of the rules determining what we learn. Whilst Harré and Secord commend the rule-following metaphor for the analysis of most social episodes, it is more appropriate to emphasize that full understanding will require both.

One further point must be made here. In the preceding discussion we have seen that successive actions in an interaction could be identified as consciously rule-guided, consciously goal-directed, unconsciously goal-directed, or ballistic, and perhaps as hierarchically subordinated to a master-plan. However in theory we need to understand not only the nature of each partner's behaviour in terms of that sort, but also how each perceives the other's behaviour. How A behaves to B will depend on how A interprets B's behaviour. A may see B's cough as a reflex response to a crumb in the throat, or as a deliberate attempt to interrupt him. And which ever was "really" the case, B's further behaviour will be affected by how he perceives A to have perceived his cough.

We must also apply the same considerations to A's own behaviour. At any moment A could interpret his own behaviour as goal-directed ("I am reading a book"), as impelled ("I stumbled" or "I fell asleep"), or as more or less efficiently goal-directed ("I was trying to read but was too sleepy"). In other words, A not only monitors his own behaviour, but he can monitor his own monitoring (Harré and Secord, 1972).

(iv) Behavioural outcomes vary in value. Some of B's possible responses to A will be valued by A more highly than others, while others will be aversive to A. To the external observer, these differences in values to A can sometimes be deduced from the frequencies with which A induces particular types of behaviour from B, and/or from A's responses to the various possible types of behaviour B shows. If the observer can talk with A and B, they may each be able to tell him not only the relative values that they place on each possible type of behaviour the other shows, but also the relative values that they believe the other places on their behaviour. In other words, each behaves as though the other's behaviour was determined by differential values. Furthermore, aspects of their own behaviour and aspects of objects in the external world will have values associated with them. Whilst many of these values have a degree of universality, and are culturally determined or culturally influenced, some are to a degree idiosyncratic.

While a concept of value is clearly necessary, it poses formidable problems of measurement. The values that A places on the various possible outcomes of his behaviour will vary with time, and with other aspects of the total situation, in both absolute and relative terms. (See pp. 219–221 for further discussion.)

(v) People have emotions and feelings. As A behaves, and as B responds, A may have feelings and opinions concerning what both he and B are doing. Whether A behaves because he feels or feels because he behaves, what he feels, or rather what he thinks about what he feels (Valins, 1966), is likely to affect how A behaves to B subsequently. Or at any rate A would say that it did. He might even say that he behaved as he did because of what he believed B to feel. Some reasons why a psychology of individual action must include reference to affective/cognitive states have been reviewed by Harré and Secord (1972): in considering relationships a crucial issue is that each at least imputes such states to himself and to the other, and acts accordingly.

At this point it is pertinent to ask how many different sorts of feelings can be experienced. Ekman and Friesen (1969) take the view that there are a limited number of "primary" emotions—happiness, surprise, fear, sadness, anger, disgust and interest, and perhaps a few others, though the nature of the circumstances in which they are evoked, and the extent to which they are expressed and blended, vary between cultures. On this view the diverse words we use to describe emotions refer to intensity differences or to mixtures of these primary affects. In a more recent book Ekman and Friesen (1975) discuss how the first six of these, and thirty-three different blends between them, are conveyed by the face. The implication is that the various emotions we feel are the consequence of a limited number of distinct physiological mechanisms. A rather different view is taken by Schachter (e.g. Schachter and Singer, 1962), who points out, on the basis of experimental data, that what a person experiences depends both on physiological arousal and on how he labels the situation. Berscheid and Walster (1974a) apply Schachter's paradigm to the emotions experienced in interpersonal relationships, suggesting that these depend on how an individual has learnt to label his feelings in the light of the circumstances he knows to have produced them. On this view there may be as many emotions as an individual learns to distinguish (see also Hinde, 1972b; Candland *et al.*, 1977).

(vi) Experience is stored as symbols which can be manipulated. A's behaviour in an interaction, and the emotions he experiences, are influenced by his past experiences. If asked, he can describe many of those past experiences. Not of course that his description will necessarily be accurate, for it will be both selective and distorted, but it will be related to what actually happened. Furthermore his behaviour and emotions will also be influenced by anticipations about the future. It thus is reasonable to suppose that A's perceptions of the people and situations he encounters, the way he behaves to them and they to him, his thoughts about his feelings and his thoughts about the behaviour and feelings of others, are coded by A and stored in symbolic form (cf. Hebb, 1949; Asch, 1959). This would result in dynamically organized and interrelated schemata of cognitive representations of individuals, events, etc. and of the motivations, intentions and affects characterizing relations between them (Bartlett, 1932; Neisser, 1976). Precisely what is encoded, and the symbols that are used, would of course be culturally influenced. They would also differ between individuals. New experiences would be assimilated to these schemata, which would accommodate accordingly. The symbols might be used to discuss an interaction with a third

party, or to facilitate re-living it after it is over, or to imagine interactions that may never happen. That we know little about the actual mechanisms underlying these postulated schemata matters little for present purposes, though it is possible to produce tentative hypotheses as to their nature (e.g. Bindra, 1976). The only claim made here is that this is a reasonable way of picturing the way people function, and that it is compatible with the manner in which most people imagine themselves, and the people with whom they are interacting, to function.

(vii) Behaviour is constrained by "norms". As a result of these shared schemata, constraints and predispositions will be imposed on A's behaviour, and on his evaluations of the behaviour of others. Where these are shared with others, they are usually referred to as "norms". Thibaut and Kelley (1959, p. 147) define a norm as "a behavioural rule that is accepted to some degree by both members of a dyad"; Tajfel (1972, p. 101) as "an individual's expectations (shared with others) of how others expect him to behave and of how others *will* behave in any given situation". Not only behaviour, and selection between types of behaviour, but also emotions and the values placed on emotions, may be influenced by norms. Even the selection of norms may be influenced by norms.

An individual's behaviour could be described as rule-governed whenever it was consistently constrained to certain paths, or predisposed in certain ways, by virtue of his feelings, values or opinions. To an outside observer, he would be behaving *as if* his behaviour were governed by rules in the same way that a stone falls *as if* governed by the law of gravity. But behaviour is usually described as governed by *norms* only when the rules are more or less consciously recognized and more or less generally accepted by the dyad or group. Norms *need* not be followed, but when they are not, sanctions may operate. We shall later (Chapter 13) find it necessary to consider a continuum between the norms that *must* be observed by people occupying certain positions in society ("roles"), and those whose infringement elicits merely mild disapprobation or unease. We shall also see that norms may be shared by a large group, that they may be worked out within and remain specific to one dyadic relationship, and that they may even be essentially idiosyncratic. The similarities here concern the mode of action; mode of acquisition, sanctions and consequences may differ.

(viii) Individuals as agents. It will be apparent that much of this implies that

individuals operate as agents, manipulating their own environment, with perceptions, intentions and expectations, following rules and choosing between goals. Harré and Secord have provided a detailed exposition of the necessity, for any scientific study of human social behaviour, of treating individuals as agents rather than as mere subjects pushed about by environmental forces. To their argument may be added the simple fact that individuals behave as though other individuals were agents, and guide their own behaviour accordingly: that alone makes necessary to introduce a concept of the individual as agent if interpersonal relationships are to be understood. However this involves no implications, one way or the other, about the extent to which the behaviour of individuals as agents can be understood in terms of lower order mechanisms (see also Bandura, 1977).*

(ix) Relationships exist in time. Finally, although some of the preceding discussion has been written as though social interactions were chain responses, with B's response to A providing the stimulus for A's next response, that is only a device for clarity of exposition. In interpersonal relationships, what A does now may continue to affect B many stages later in the interaction, and even many interactions later. Similarly behaviour now may be affected by goals and expectations of events still in the distant future. The affective/cognitive aspects of interpersonal relationships transcend the behavioural ones. And as a result the relationship acquires an individuality of its own, and may be evaluated or manipulated by the participants.

(x) General. To some, all this will have seemed obvious enough. The constructs introduced are in common use both by the man in the street and by social learning theorists (e.g. Bandura, 1977) and most even by some S-R theorists. Many philosophers would regard the applicability of such concepts as perceptions, intentions, expectancies, values, norms, affective/cognitive phenomena, and organized schemata of symbols as necessary for the recognition of individuals as persons. Harré and Secord (1972) have stressed, on philosophical and psychological grounds, the necessity of accepting that man is a "psychophysiological mix". While their view that the accounts given by the individuals involved must be the main source of data for understanding social

---

*N. Kreitman (pers. comm.) has made the provocative suggestion that the difficulty in handling scientifically the concept of individuals as agents arises because we have no analogies to fall back on in the non-human world.

behaviour is an overstatement, it is clear that those accounts are a source of evidence about how the participants perceive, or think that they perceive, what is going on, and must be taken into account in understanding it.*

Of course nothing that has been said rules out the possibility that the concepts introduced refer to phenomena which are correlated with physiological events. It is legitimate to pursue the view that they are tools temporarily useful for understanding behaviour, which we shall be able to dispense with in due course when we understand what is "really" going on. On this view the implied mentalistic events themselves require causal explanation, and when we have explained them, perhaps we shall be able to regard their causes as the causes of the behaviour, and neglect the mentalistic intermediaries or epiphenomena (Skinner, 1953; cf. Bowers, 1973). But three points must be made here. The first is merely practical. Between the incredible complexity of patterns of neural firing and behaviour we need synthesizing variables such as motivation: prediction via all the physiological intermediaries would be hopelessly cumbersome. Similarly, it may well be that rules, norms, values, etc. are all largely to be understood in terms of past experience and present situation (and/or in terms of patterns of neural firing), but to attempt to account for behaviour in an interpersonal interaction or relationship in terms of all the previous experiences of both participants as well as the present situation (and/or in neural terms) would be a hopeless task. So at the very least we can regard these mentalistic constructs as tools which are essential in practice.

Second, if A interprets B's behaviour in terms of mentalistic concepts, if A treats B as an agent, if A acts on the supposition that he himself is an agent, then we must use these concepts to understand their relationship.

The third point is the most basic. In analysing mechanism we may lose the emergent properties of the whole: analysis and resynthesis must proceed hand in hand (Tinbergen, 1951).

No doubt others will still regard the intrusion of the concepts discussed in the preceding pages as retrogressive, a retreat into mentalism. More specifically, it may be argued that the concepts used lack specificity, that they are too flexible and permit too easy *post hoc*

---

*Agreement on some major issues does not imply that I agree with Harré and Secord's narrow and denigratory view of most behavioural sciences. There is, however, no need to pursue that issue here.

explanations (e.g. Bindra, 1976). Here I would argue that they seem appropriate for the present level of analysis but their refinement at the behavioural and phenomenological levels and their translation into constructs at a finer level of analysis are urgent tasks—the latter a task with which Hebb (1949) and Bindra (1976) have already grappled. But there is no sense in which attempts to treat people as agents directing their own behaviour, when such treatment is appropriate, are less scientific than attempts to treat people as the automata that, at the level of analysis in question, they are clearly not (Harré and Secord, 1972; Bandura, 1976, 1977).

Dynamic aspects of relationships

It is implicit in what has been said that relationships between individuals are seldom static. At the behavioural level, each interaction may affect the course of future ones. The course of the relationship may be affected by the attitudes of the participants to each other, and these may change through the natural processes of growth and development, or as a consequence of events inside and outside the relationship. Thus relationships between individuals are essentially dynamic in nature, and not to be thought of in terms of static dispositions or predilections. We shall return to the issue of dynamic stability in later chapters.

Relationships and the concept of attachment

Whether we regard a relationship as a potential for future interaction at the behavioural level, or describe this in terms of affective/cognitive aspects that transcend the behavioural elements, it is clear that a relationship is much more than the sum of individual behavioural interactions. This is compatible with the view of attachment theorists (e.g. Bowlby, 1969; Ainsworth, 1969; in press) who, though primarily concerned with relationships between one individual and another stronger and/or wiser than he is himself (Bowlby, 1977), see attachment as an organizing construct,* whose value lies in its integrative

*Gewirtz (1976) used attachment in a rather different way for "a complex of an individual's response patterns controlled by cues and consequences from the appearance and behaviors of another". However, unlike Bowlby, he uses the concept with reference to a wide range of relationships.

power (Ainsworth, 1969; Waters, in preparation; Sroufe and Waters, 1977). Sroufe and Waters (1977) define attachment as "an affective tie between infant and caregiver and . . . (as) . . . a behavioural system, flexibly operating in terms of set goals, mediated by feeling, and in interaction with other behavioural systems".* Emphasizing the distinction between attachment and the behavioural items that mediate it, Ainsworth (1972, p. 123) views attachment "as a construct—as an inner organization of behavioural systems which not only controls the 'stable propensity' to seek proximity to an attachment figure, but also is responsible for the distinctive quality of the organization of the specific attachment behaviors through which a given individual promotes proximity with a specific attachment figure".

The distinction between attachment and attachment behaviour is important for attachment theorists, because the attachment behaviour shown, being susceptible to environmental and other influences, may vary while the attachment itself is stable. Critics have attacked attachment theory on the grounds that the several types of attachment behaviour do not show stability over time. In reply Sroufe and Waters (1977) argue "Behaviors may be viewed as exemplars of categories or classes and the manner in which behaviors are *organized* across situations and across individuals may be assessed. From an organizational perspective, assessment involves attending to the 'meaning' of the behavior . . . not simply its occurrence . . . Since multiple behaviors can have similar meanings (serve the same function or have the same equivalent outcome), the prediction becomes not that behavior A will be correlated with behavior A across situations or time, but rather that behavior A, as a member of class X, will predict the occurrence of behaviors in class X in that same context". Such a view is supported by the finding that, while particular types of mother-child interaction show little consistency over time, patterns of reactions assessed as

---

*The concept of behavioural system has been frequently applied in studies of lower species, where it refers to a number of different patterns of behaviour related to each other (directly and/or indirectly) functionally and causally. The relations are of various types. Some patterns may be appetitive to others, some alternatives to others; some may share positive causal factors, others negative (consummatory) ones; some may be mutually facilitatory, others mutually inhibitory. The behaviour patterns themselves may or may not be governed by control systems, and they may form part of higher order control systems. A number of examples have been worked out in detail (e.g. Baerends, 1976). Bischof (1975) used computer simulation of such a system for discussing certain aspects of mother-infant interaction.

wholes show remarkable consistency. To be specific, a child who is rendered anxious by the departure of his mother is liable to be anxious if the same happens six months later, even though the behaviour by which the anxiety is expressed may have changed (Sroufe and Waters, 1977).

While the concept of attachment is compatible with that of "relationship" as used in this paper, it will be apparent from the above quotations that attachment theorists use the term both to refer to the bond between two individuals, and to a behaviour system of one of them (usually the infant). This could lead to confusion (see also pp. 16–17). Furthermore "attachment theory" grew up in the context of studies of the child's tie to his mother (Bowlby, 1969) and, as mentioned already, usually concerns a bond between individuals who are drawn to each other but differ in strength or wisdom. The aim here is much wider. Relationships may of course exist between equals. But also, and this is more important, relationships may exist between individuals who are not drawn to each other, who do not seek each other's company or find pleasure in it, but who interact from time to time through force of external circumstances. I have a relationship with the neighbour who peers into my garden while I am sunbathing, though it is not one I seek to perpetuate. The bonds studied by attachment theorists, then, are to be regarded as one subset of interpersonal relationships; as such, they share properties with the larger category.

Formal versus personal relationships

One other point must be made. The focus in this book is on relationships involving individuals known personally to each other. But we also have relationships with categories of people—we behave as citizens to policemen, drivers to traffic wardens, passengers to ticket collectors: in each case our behaviour is determined in part by previous experience of other individuals in the same category, and in part by knowledge acquired in other ways of the characteristic behaviour of people occupying those positions in society. We even talk about relationships between two or more formal categories of individuals—for instance between students and those in authority, or between the Trade Union officials and Government ministers. Such usages involve extensions of the concept of relationship as applied to two individuals: whilst some of the principles discussed in this book apply to them, they will be mentioned only briefly in the following pages.

In considering relationships that do involve people known individually to each other, it is useful to distinguish between two sources of constraint on the content of the relationship. Much of the behaviour of the participants may be understood in terms of their occupancy of certain positions in the society—we speak of doctor-patient or teacher-pupil relationships, implying that what they do together consists primarily of attempts by one party to cure or teach the other. But the behaviour of acquaintances or friends may depend primarily on their knowledge of each other as individuals, and be relatively little affected by their membership of particular groups or occupancy of particular positions in the society. In most relationships between people, both types of constraint operate. But while the distinction is between the *determinants* of what goes on in relationships, it is often convenient to label *relationships* as (primarily) "role" or "formal" relationships where the former predominate, and as "personal" relationships where the latter are primary (G. J. McCall, 1970, 1974).

Summary

So far as its behavioural aspects are concerned, a "relationship" refers to a series of interactions in time, and to the potential for such a series. Relationships involve both behavioural and affective/cognitive aspects, and their understanding requires that we come to terms with both.

Properties of interactions and relationships are to be seen as properties of the dyad, not as properties of one or other individual.

The behaviour in social interactions usually, but not invariably, involves meaning.

Description of the behaviour involved in an interaction must involve reference to content and quality. Description of a relationship must involve reference to the content, qualities and patterning of the component interactions.

Dyadic relationships always exist in a social context, and cannot be understood without reference to that context.

Social behaviour has a degree of independence from the formation of, or tendency to form, relationships.

The study of relationships must take into account the fact that what

A responds to in B is in part a function of what A is. It will require concepts of expectancy, goal-direction, value, feelings and cognitions, and norms, and must involve the assumption that experience is stored as symbols. It is also necessary to treat individuals as agents, guiding their own behaviour, though this does not preclude the possibility that the behaviour of individuals as agents can potentially be understood in terms of lower order mechanisms.

Relationships are seldom static, and each interaction may effect the course of future ones.

The concept of a "relationship" subsumes that of attachment. It is convenient to distinguish "formal" from "personal" relationships.

3

The Nature and Aims of Description

In Chapter 1 it was argued that any science of interpersonal relationships must rest on a sound base of description and classification. Such a view seems natural to a biologist, since the growth of biology has depended on the natural classification of species. Biologists who study behaviour have in fact placed great emphasis on description, often producing "ethograms" which catalogue the behavioural repertoire of the species they are studying before they analyse any one aspect in depth. A descriptive base has been of equal importance to many anthropologists and some other social scientists. For some experimental and social psychologists the need for description has been less obvious. This was especially the case for those learning theorists who, modelling their approach on that of classical physics, neglected the fact that classical physics dealt to a large extent with everyday phenomena, such as falling apples or the appearance of sticks in water, which did not require description. Where classical physics dealt with phenomena that were not immediately apparent, such as the movements of the planets or the colours produced by a prism, careful description was essential. Of course interpersonal relationships are also everyday phenomena, but whilst we may manage our relationships with moderate success, we are not always adept at pinpointing their special characteristics, describing them to others, or generalizing about them.

The art of description lies in the processes of selection. The beauty of the descriptive work of the great nineteenth century anatomists lay in part in the elegance with which they selected what to describe. In the long term selection is likely to be guided not only by the problems to be solved, but also by the theories thought likely to be useful in solving them. This is a scientifically impure procedure—if carried too far it could lead to theories becoming self-verifying. However such a danger is minimized if we know what we are doing, and if our data selection is guided not just by a pet theory, but also by its competitors.

In the shorter term, the immediate aim of description is to facilitate the identification of differences. An adequate science of interpersonal relationships must be concerned with differences amongst relationships of diverse characteristics, including both close, personal or "primary" relationships (Shils, 1951)—that is, relationships that involve frequent interactions and are usually characterized by warmth, intimacy and commitment—and also formal or role relationships having little emotional content (see p. 38). And it will be necessary to consider differences of two main kinds. First, differences between gross classes of relationships. There are, for instance, differences between parent-child relationships and peer-peer relationships that, as we shall see, have important implications for their dynamics. Second, finer differences between relationships within those gross categories—how does this mother-child relationship differ from that, for example. Characters useful for the first kind of distinction are not necessarily useful also for the second, or vice versa: it is necessary to have means for describing relationships that will cater for either.

Of course it would be nice if we could specify a limited number of unitary dimensions along which relationships differ, and demonstrate their crucial importance. It would in theory be possible to study a wide range of relationships, measure many of their aspects and then reduce the data by factor analysis or some comparable technique to a limited number of dimensions. A number of such attempts have been made, and in many cases the data have been successfully reduced to three principle dimensions, which approximate in everyday terms to dominance/subordinance, love/hate and involvement/detachment (Lorr and McNair, 1963; Becker, 1964; review by Danziger, 1976). But however many measures are used initially, some selection is necessarily involved, and the factors extracted from the analysis are inevitably influenced by that initial selection of data. On the view that we do not yet know just what is important and what is not, and therefore do not yet know exactly what to try to describe or measure, it seems wise to acknowledge the processes of selection. Perhaps it will be as well first to concentrate on what *sorts of* measurements are likely to be useful, that is to specify *categories* of dimensions.

In trying to specify these categories of dimensions it is reasonable not to discard as preliminary guidelines the qualities we notice in everyday life—for instance whether a couple is affectionate, competitive, understanding or selfish in their relationship. It seems likely that we have been shaped to make the sorts of judgements we make about relationships in our culture because those particular judgements are based on characteristics likely to be important to us. Though it is not necessary to the present discussion, a biologist might well go further and support the view that we have been selected in evolution to be aware of some characteristics of relationships rather than others. Osgood (1969) has earlier suggested that language has been selected to communicate good versus bad, strong versus weak and active versus passive features of persons, places and things; and Humphrey (1976) has argued that our intellectual faculties have evolved in adaptation to the complexities of social living (see also Jolly, 1966). Be that as it may, it seems proper not to neglect our everyday predispositions in selecting dimensions relevant for the study of relationships.

However here a difficulty emerges. Our judgements about relationships often have a global character; we label them as "affectionate" or "competitive" without specifying the precise criteria by which we made such judgements. Such ratings based on subjective impressions cannot form the basis of scientific enquiry; we must be able to specify criteria on which the ratings or observations are based.

Consider, for example, the label "affectionate relationship". We might apply this in many circumstances—to peers, parent and child, lovers, or married couples, to mention but a few. But in each of these cases the individuals concerned will be doing different things together, and their "affection" will be "expressed" in different ways. What then are the features that predispose us towards labelling a relationship as affectionate? Here is a possible list:

(a) The partners engage in interactions of a number of different types.

(b) In the absence of the other each partner shows behaviour likely, at least in some circumstances, to restore proximity, real or imagined.

(c) Actions conducive to the welfare of the other are likely to be repeated.

(d) The behaviour of each partner is organized in relation to the ongoing behaviour of the other (meshing—see pp. 61–4).

(e) The anxiety induced by strange objects or situations is alleviated by the presence of the partner (see Bowlby, 1973).

(f) The partners are willing to reveal themselves to each other.

(g) The relationship is seen as likely to be of long duration.

It is not suggested that these are all the properties on which the designation "affectionate" may depend, nor that all these are necessary.* We might wish to add gentleness as a quality of the interactions, or argue that a relationship can be affectionate though of short duration. We shall mention later some less behaviourally oriented dimensions that might well be included. Nor is it suggested that these characteristics are peculiar to affectionate relationships; some of them would also be characteristic of long-standing enemies. Furthermore we might wish to make finer differentiations—for instance between relationships characterized by mutual *liking* and those characterized by *loving* (see e.g. Berscheid and Walster, 1974a; Rubin, 1974; see also pp. 142–4). But the issue here is that while a global assessment of a relationship on a scale of affection may be useful for some (e.g. psychotherapeutic) purposes, this finer level of analysis is more likely to be useful for understanding the dynamics of relationships. The items are such that we could hope to measure them at least on an ordinal scale, and we could use them in, for instance, studies aimed at investigating the conditions conducive to the formation of affectionate relationships, with the hope that other less tangible properties of affectionate relationships may turn out to be associated with them.

It is of course an empirical issue whether separate items of this sort are correlated with each other. We might find couples who were affectionate by other criteria but did not allay each other's anxiety. Indeed a couple who "mesh" well in one context may not do so in another. It is for just this reason that it is necessary to attempt to isolate the characters on which our everyday judgements depend. Identification of the context in which the couple are at cross-purposes, or in which one feels misunderstood (see pp. 121–5), may benefit the relationship. The bases on which we describe relationships as affectionate, competitive, supportive or what have you must be made explicit, and the separate items evaluated in a variety of situations.

There is one danger in this approach which must be recognized—it can be taken to imply that the more superficial or "higher level" categories, such as "affectionate relationships", are of no value if the various measures by which we assess them do not show high intercorrelations. We have already seen an example of the shortcomings of this view in discussing the "attachment" concept in Chapter 2. Particular measures of "attachment behaviour" may show little stability over time, though assessments of attachment as an organizational construct

*See discussion of Wittgenstein's concept of family resemblances by Bambrough (1960, 1961).

do (Sroufe and Waters, 1977). "Affection" may play a similar role even though the several measures of "affectionate behaviour" do not co-vary. One individual may "express" his affection verbally, another physically, and a third in both. Measures of expressed affection may well not co-vary, and might even be negatively correlated.

In practice, then, we may be guided initially by the preconceptions of "higher level" categories we derive from our culture; we must identify the empirical criteria on which those categories are based; we must examine the extent to which, and in what circumstances, those criteria are interrelated; and we must evaluate our higher-level categories both on the intercorrelations between the criteria on which they are based and on their usefulness as organizational constructs.

Descriptions should ideally be made in a language which is independent of any theory that will later be used to explain the phenomena observed. In the interests of scientific purity, therefore, we should attempt to describe first, and then turn to theory language for explanation. But for three reasons that course has not been strictly followed in this book. First, it would make for dull reading. Second, as we have seen, relationships require description at more than one analytical level, and description at one level contributes to explanation at another. And third, the selection of characteristics for description is inevitably influenced by current theory, and it is better to make this explicit. It is hoped that the distinction between data language and explanatory concepts remains clear.

In Chapters 4–10 we shall discuss some categories of criteria that seem valuable for describing relationships. They will be presented in a classificatory system that extends the notion of "content, quality and patterning" of interactions. They concern the properties of the relationship itself, and not the demographic (e.g. age, sex) or personality characteristics of the participants. Each category may contain one or many dimensions, and each dimension may be assessed in terms of one or a number of inter-related measures. The list moves from behavioural measures more useful in differentiating gross types of relationships to those more concerned with thoughts and feelings. It will become apparent that the categories are mutually interrelated, and that many of the dimensions can be applied at a number of levels of analysis. These issues are discussed in Chapter 11.

Summary

Description involves selection. Selection is guided by the problems in hand and the theoretical approaches deemed likely to be useful in solving them. The selection must be such as to highlight the important differences in the phenomena under study.

There is no easy way to know which dimensions of relationships are useful to study. Perhaps it is best to start by describing *categories* of *dimensions* likely to be useful. Intuition may be some guide, but it is important to specify the characters on which intuitions depend.

The data language used for description should ideally not involve concepts used in explanation. However description at one analytical level can facilitate explanation at another.

II

Categories of Dimensions

4

Content and Diversity of Interactions

In this chapter, and in the two that immediately follow, we are concerned with four categories of characteristics of interpersonal relationships that refer primarily to their behavioural aspects. The first two, concerned with what the two individuals do together, are mostly useful for an initial functional classification of relationships within a society. However, all four may also be used to differentiate amongst relationships of a particular functional type.

Content of interactions

The initial categorization of relationships that we make usually refers primarily to what the participants do together. "Teacher-pupil" or "doctor-patient" relationship describes the general nature of the activities of the individuals concerned. Even terms like "mother-child" or "husband-wife" relationship, which may imply the biological characteristics of the participants or institutional aspects of the relationship, still refer primarily to what they do together. We do not necessarily regard a child that has been adopted as having a mother-child relationship with his natural mother, and we speak of couples as "married only in name".

Each such label usually implies a range of types of interaction, not all of which must necessarily occur if the label is to be applied, and which may be accompanied by others not usually implied by it. A mother does not have to feed her child for us to recognize their relationship as a mother-child relationship, nor is the label ruled out if they often play bezique together. Furthermore the ranges of interactions implied by different labels often overlap extensively. Whilst in our culture 100 years ago father-child and mother-child relationships showed little overlap, now many types of interaction may be common to both.

Notwithstanding that flexibility, it is only because there are some regularities in the way in which the various types of interaction are grouped within relationships that is it possible for us to label relationships with such terms as mother-infant or teacher-pupil. These regularities are in part biological; the properties of a relationship involving a child are in part a consequence of the child's immaturity. More important are utilitarian issues and conventions imposed by society. What teacher and pupil, employer and secretary or academic colleagues do together is dictated in part by the initial purpose of their relationship and in part by conventions specifying what is appropriate for people in such relationships. The specification may be inhibitory —limitations on the individuals between whom sexual intercourse may take place are an example. Sometimes the content of a relationship is prescribed quite rigidly but in other cases, as with "friends", only in a much looser sense (Suttles, 1970; Kurth, 1970).

The grouping of types of interaction within relationships raises a question, to which we as yet have no answer, which is especially pertinent to the relationships of a young child (Hinde, 1971). Does it matter how the interactions of a young baby are parcelled up into relationships? We have strong evidence that certain types of interaction have important influences on a child's social development—not just those involved in nurturant care, but also the looking-looking away games that babies play with their mothers (Stern, 1977), the rather more boisterous games that are more common with fathers (Lamb, 1976), the joint looking at representational material (Dunn and Wooding, 1977), the games that develop with peers, and so on. What we do not know is whether it matters how these various types of interactions are distributed amongst the several social companions. For example, if the mother was to take over the father's role in addition to her own, and play boisterous games as frequently and with the same quality as he would have played them, would this make any difference at all to the child's personality development? Or, to put the question in another way, are the differences between children who grow up in one-parent and two-parent families, or between those who grow up with and without siblings, due merely to differences in the content and frequency of the interactions in which they are involved? Or is the way in which those interactions are associated with particular individuals also important? Data on this problem are urgently needed.

It is important to recognize that labels such as "husband-wife" or "teacher-pupil" relationship may be used in two ways. On the one hand, they may refer to the properties of one particular relationship or of a category of relationships in the real world. It could be, for instance, that an anthropologist studying a new society had collected data on 100 married couples and wrote a description of "the husband-wife relationship" in that culture. (Just how such a "typical" relationship should be derived from the actual data is a matter too seldom discussed. For example, should frequency of intercourse be given as the mean, median or mode of the data in the sample?) But such labels are also used in a quite different sense to refer to what participants in such relationships are supposed to do in that society—to their rights and duties. Of course it may be that no couple ever behaves as an ideal married couple is expected to. Either they may strive to, but fail, in which case the institutionalized ideal relationship can be regarded as a goal, and thus as a determining cause, of their behaviour (see p. 170). Or they may just not be interested in behaving that way. Even if they are not interested, the label may affect how third parties treat them, and thus their own relationship. Thus in either case the ideal may be important as a determinant of their behaviour, even though it is likely to be very different from the actual fact (see Chapter 13).

So far we have used the contents of the interactions within a relationship as a means of labelling relationships in ways that are recognized in the society. But within any one such category of relationships, we may differentiate particular ones according to the presence or prominence of certain types of interaction. Thus we are more likely to describe a mother-infant relationship as a warm one if play is frequent than if it is scarce, though of course other criteria also contribute to our judgement. Indeed we may go further and distinguish amongst mother-infant relationships that contain play according to the kinds of play involved—whether or not physical contact is involved, for example. Thus "Content of interactions" may be applied at a number of levels of analysis according to the sort of discrimination at which we are aiming.

As a clinical example, Collins *et al.* (1971) compared the marital relationships of 60 couples in which the husband was receiving outpatient treatment for neurosis with those of 60 control couples. Their work, other aspects of which are discussed later, included an assessment of the contribution of the husband to household duties and child care. Although the patient husbands tended to spend more time about the house than controls, they contributed much less in these areas. (Table 1).

Relative involvement of spouses in housework formed the focus of

TABLE 1

Domestic roles of husbands in 60 marriages where the husband was a neurotic outpatient and 60 control marriages (modified from Collins *et al.*, 1971)

		Regular	Occasional	Never	x^2
Household duties	Patients	16	31	13	$p<0{\cdot}01$
	Controls	32	23	5	
Child care	Patients	10	32	6	$p<0{\cdot}01$
	Controls	26	22	1	

another study in the U.S.A., though here the comparison was between married and cohabiting couples. One might have expected the housework to be fairly equally shared between male and female partners in the latter group, but it was found that the women in both cohabiting and married couples were responsible for the major part. However, in other ways the married couples tended to be more traditional in the performance of household tasks (Stafford *et al.*, 1977).

Finally, while the category of content of interactions has been described as involving what the participants in a relationship do *together*, it must be remembered that this includes competing, fighting and other types of interpersonal conflict. Both competition and conflict may be realistic and direct: for instance the individuals may be arguing or actually fighting. In such cases the occurrence of conflict is clear from the content of the interaction. But they may also be realistic but indirect—for example, the individuals may be competing for something both want, but success in obtaining it may depend on their relationships with a third party. Thus a child may strive to be seen by his parents as better than his or her sibling in order to obtain rewards dispensed by the parent. In such cases the existence of competition may be identified from a number of aspects of the relationship, including the qualities of the interactions (see Chapter 5) and the variation in those qualities with the context (e.g. presence or absence of parent).

Conflict and competition may also be said to be "autistic"—that is, unrelated to specific rewards but stemming from aspects of the personality of one of the participants (Holmes and Hiller, 1976). "Autistic" conflict is likely to be characterized by distrust and misperception (see Chapters 9 and 18), and to affect the qualities of diverse types of interaction in the relationship. Such "autistic" conflict may spread from realistic conflict in one context to embrace many other aspects of the relationship (see p. 252).

Diversity of interactions

A related characteristic concerns the diversity of types of interaction that occur. If a relationship involves only one type of interaction, as for instance a relationship with a drinking companion or business colleague, it can be described as single-stranded or uniplex; if many, as multi-stranded or multiplex. The distinction is of course not absolute, and again depends on the level of analysis. Thus the mother-infant relationship could be called uniplex, involving only maternal-filial responses; or multiplex, involving nursing, playing, protecting, and so on. The important issue is the extent of diversity of behaviour involved, not the dichotomy.

Within a multiplex relationship, interactions of one type may be influenced by those of another. Just because a relationship involves two individuals known to each other, the content or quality of one interaction may be affected by that of any other. This is a common enough observation, and has recently been emphasized in the course of discussions of marital therapy. The sexual components of a couple's relationship affect, and are affected by, the other things that they do together (e.g. Masters and Johnson, 1976; Sager, 1976). Clearly the effects of one type of interaction on others are likely to be richer, the more diverse the interactions in the relationship.

But diversity is important also in another way. The more contexts in which the participants in a relationship interact, the more of their natures can be mutually revealed. In some cases, indeed, actual interaction may not be essential—areas of experience common to both may play an important part in a relationship. Two doctors who work in the same hospital may have much to discuss even though they never meet in the wards, and parent and child may become in some ways closer when the latter marries because a type of experience is shared. Those who have lived for a while in remote places, away from the facilities and constraints of civilization, feel upon their return an urgent need to converse with others who have had a similar experience, and feel a special bond with them (Hinde, 1978d). The category of measures of diversity of interactions is in fact related to Altman and

Taylor's (1973) dimension of breadth, which we shall meet again in Chapter 8.

Summary

The initial categorization of relationships depends on the content of the interactions involved. However, labels such as "husband-wife relationship" may refer either to what a couple actually do together, or to what is expected of people in such a relationship in the culture concerned. Content of interactions can also be used to distinguish between relationships within a major functional class.

A related dimension concerns the diversity of interactions within the relationship—whether the participants share only one type of activity, or many.

5

Qualities of Interactions

Though the bill may be correct and the change exact, it matters how the cashier in the supermarket handles our purchases: a grumpy interaction may not colour the whole day, but it will certainly affect the probability of our return. And the more important the relationship, the more important the qualities of the interactions: use of the label "loving" for a relationship depends on the qualities as well as on the content of the interactions (see pp. 142–3), and there is clear evidence that being a parent is not just doing the right things. For example Schaffer and Emerson (1964), in a study of Scottish children, found that the attachments they formed were determined more by the readiness and intensity with which adults responded to them, than by the amount of time they spent with them. Ainsworth (1979) and her colleagues found that how a mother held her baby (i.e. tenderly and carefully or briskly and awkwardly) was more closely related to properties of the mother-infant relationship, and especially to how the infant responded to close bodily contact, than was how *much* she held it. And Hinde and Spencer-Booth (1971a) found that rhesus monkey infants whose relationships with their mothers could be described as "tensionful" (on the basis of certain specific measures) were more upset after being separated from their mothers for 1–2 weeks than were infants with less tensionful relationships.

In this chapter, therefore, we shall consider various aspects of the "qualities" of interactions. Just how many qualities are likely to be important is quite unknown: perhaps repertory grid techniques (pp. 85–7) could be used to provide an answer. But any such answer is likely to be specific to the particular subculture: what qualities matter, and when, depends very much on the context. Expectations about the quality of interactions with policemen differ between Londoners and New Yorkers, and the perception of gruffness or courtesy by the experienced traveller depends on where he is. Here, however, we shall concentrate on some of the problems of studying the qualities of interactions within a particular cultural context.

The problem of measurement

Some of the qualities we ascribe to relationships, or to interactions within relationships, seem so intangible that any attempt to quantify or scale them might seem hopeless. When we say that this couple have a warm relationship, or even that they kissed each other warmly, it might seem impossible to assess that warmth in an objective manner. But such judgements, if they are of any value, must be made on *some* criteria. Those criteria are often multiple; just as "affectionate" applied to a relationship involves a number of characteristics of the component interactions (see pp. 42–3), so also do qualities of interactions. We may consider four interrelated categories of characters that may be important.

(i) Intensity. The quality of an interaction may be indicated by the intensity of the behaviour shown by the participants. They may whisper, talk or shout, speak slowly or fast, spar or clout each other. Usually but not inevitably related to this, their state of physiological arousal may vary. Of course what matters may be not the physical characteristics of the behaviour, but the meaning attached to it in the context in which it occurs. Whispering may indicate collusion or affection according to whether a third party is or is not present; shouting may mean anger or excitement according to the other expressive movements that accompany it.

(ii) Content and presentation of verbal material. One indicator, and often the most important indicator, of the qualities of an interaction may be the content of the verbal utterances. Categorization of verbal material may not be easy, but considerable progress has been made in some contexts. To mention a few examples chosen for their diversity, Lennard and Bernstein (1960) performed extensive content analyses of tape recordings of psychotherapeutic interviews in a study of their dynamics. Wooton (1974) content-analysed recordings made by leaving tape recorders in homes in order to study class differences in mother-child interaction. The nature of parental control, and the extent to which the child complies, have been studied by Lytton and Zwirner (1975) by categorizing utterances. And using a rather different approach, Brown and Gilman (1960) have shown how, in many languages, the choice of pronoun conveys claims for power and/or solidarity within the relationship.

In interpreting verbal material, it is necessary to recognize that every speech act may have both "locutionary meaning" and also "illocutionary" (assessed from the intended effect of the utterance) or "per locutionary force" (assessed from consequences, not necessarily intended) (Austin, 1962). For example "It's a nice day" has little to do with the weather, but may facilitate the relationship, and the question "May I have the salt?" is really a request. The complexity of the issues involved is demonstrated by Goody's (1978) study of questioning in Gonja. Starting with the view that asking a question not only compels a response, but also carries a message about the relationship between the individuals involved, Goody showed how the precise meaning assigned to the act of asking a question can vary. She classified questions according to two dimensions—one running from requests only for information (e.g. "What time is it?") to rhetorical questions, and the other from control to deference. Questions could be classified in terms of their position on these two dimensions. For example, questions used in greeting ("How are you?") might be rhetorical and with a very small control element, whilst questions asked by a superior to an inferior to set him at his ease and promote social contact would be low in requirements for both information and control. Of special interest here is Goody's description of the mutual influences between social status and the meaning assigned to questions. Where status is not clearly defined, the mode of questioning can help determine the role relationship (see p. 135), but if role relationships are established, constraints are thereby imposed on the meaning assigned to questions asked.

However the relationship between the individuals concerned is only one issue in the interpretation of verbal utterances. Meaning depends also on prosodic (e.g. intonation, stress) and paralinguistic (supporting gestures, etc.) features (e.g. Crystal, 1975). Often such clues as tone of voice and direction of gaze not only facilitate interpretation of the verbal message, but serve as valuable indicators of the quality of the interaction. Thus in interviews about the marriage relationship, the interviewee's tone of voice provides an indicator of his or her view of the warmth of the relationship (Rutter and Brown, 1966). Brown *et al.* (1972) have used such information for predicting relapse from schizophrenic illness after a patient has been released from hospital. Using an "index of expressed emotion" based on the number of critical comments made about the patient by a relative, and also on the degree of hostility and emotional over-involvement (assessed in part from tone of voice), they found that 58% of patients from homes with a high index, but only 16% of those from homes with a low index, relapsed within 9 months. Vaughn and Leff (1976) replicated these findings and also found the index useful for predicting relapse in depressed patients. Gottman *et al.* (1977) have developed a coding system using both verbal content and aspects of non-verbal communication to assess distress in married couples.

Prosodic features have also been used to characterize differences between mother-child relationships involving "normal" and "disturbed" children. Whilst in the former case mothers used a more assertive intonation when expressing approval or disapproval than in neutral situations, mothers of disturbed children tended to do the reverse (Bugental and Love, 1975). A recent review has been given by Fraser (1978).

(iii) Non-vocal communication. Whilst this is of special importance in assessing the qualities of interactions, discussion of recent work in this area is beyond the scope of this book.* Only three points will be mentioned. First, the correct interpretation of expressive movements may depend on previous analysis of their elements, and examination of the ways in which those elements are combined. A simple example is shown in Fig. 1. Second, expressive movements often differ markedly between cultures; for example, humility on the part of one interactant is expressed in the diverse ways shown in Table 1. Conversely, the same or closely similar movements may have different meanings in different cultures: this is shown for the "eyebrow flash" in Fig. 2 (Eibl Eibesfeldt, 1972). For such reasons, cross-cultural study of the qualities of interactions must depend on a sound knowledge of non-verbal communication.

Third, one special difficulty with the study of non-vocal communication in relation to interpersonal relationships must be emphasized. Perhaps as an inevitable consequence of the use of the scientific method, the signals that have been most studied are the stereotyped and culturally accepted ones. These are, perhaps, of special importance in the early stages of a relationship or in interactions between individuals who are not specially intimate with each other. But at least some of the non-vocal communication in an intimate relationship depends,

---

*See for example Ekman and Friesen (1969; 1975), Mehrabian (1972), Hinde (1972), Benthall and Polhemus (1975), Argyle (1975), Danziger (1976).

Fig. 1. Facial expressions as combinations of elements. The figure shows a smile; and two frowns, to show the change in overall impression of effect when the *mouth corners down* combined with different frowns. (Redrawn from Brannigan and Humphries, 1972.)

consciously or unconsciously, on idiosyncratic signals. For obvious reasons, these are more difficult to document (but see Lock, 1976).

(iv) Relations between the behaviour of the two participants. An assessment of maternal warmth might well involve measures not only of how much and in what ways a mother cuddles her baby, but also of how quickly she starts to cuddle him after he comes to her—that is, measurement of the behaviour of one participant in relation to that of the other. Caregivers do in fact differ markedly in their sensitivity to a baby's signals (Sander, 1977).

"Sensitivity" can, of course, be primarily unilateral. But of special interest in the present context are cases in which each participant guides his behaviour in accordance with the ongoing behaviour of the other. On a short time scale, a quality of the interactions of both lovers and boxers lies in the extent to which their movements are directed in accordance not only with the movements of the partner or opponent, but also with his (or her) intended movements. Stern (1977), on the basis of a frame-by-frame film analysis, has shown that about half of Muhammed Ali's left jabs were of shorter duration than the generally agreed fastest visual reaction time of 180 milliseconds. Yet the opponent managed to evade most of them. He could not have done this by

TABLE 1

Cultural differences in ways of expressing humility. From Krout (1942)

Attitude expressed	Behaviour pattern	Culture group
Humility	Throwing oneself on the back, rolling from side to side, slapping outside of thighs (meaning: you need not subdue me; I'm subdued already)	Batokas
	Bowing, extending right arm, moving arm down from horizontal position, raising it to the level of one's head, and lowering it again (meaning: I lift the earth off the ground, and place it on my head as a sign of submission to you)	Turks and Persians
	Walking about with hands bound and rope around one's neck	Ancient Peruvians
	Joining hands over head and bowing (ancient sign of obedience signifying: I submit with tired hands)	Chinese
	Dropping arms; sighing	Europeans
	Stretching hands towards person and striking them together	Congo natives
	Extension of arms; genuflection prostration	Preliterates, European peasants
	Crouching	New Caledonians, Fijians, Tahitians
	Crawling and shuffling forward; walking on fours	Dahomeans
	Bending body downwards	Samoans
	Permitting someone to place his foot on one's head	Fundah and Tonga Tabu peoples
	Prostration, face down	Polynesians
	Pulling palms together for the other person to clasp gently	Unyanyembans
	Bowing while putting joined hands between those of other person and lifting them to one's forehead	Sumatrans

responding to the preliminary stages of the jab. Somehow he must have successfully decoded Muhammed Ali's behavioural sequence in a manner which enabled him to escape the jabs.

To illustrate meshing on a slightly longer time scale, we may consider two illustrations from studies of rhesus monkeys where "behavioural meshing" has been studied quantitatively. As an infant monkey grows up, it spends less and less time on or near its mother, and seems to be becoming more independent of her. However, to describe

(a)

Fig. 2(a). Eyebrow flash. In greeting, the eyebrows are raised rapidly and kept up for about one-sixth of a second. (Drawing by Priscilla Barrett, after a photograph by Eibl-Eibesfeldt, in Hinde, 1974).

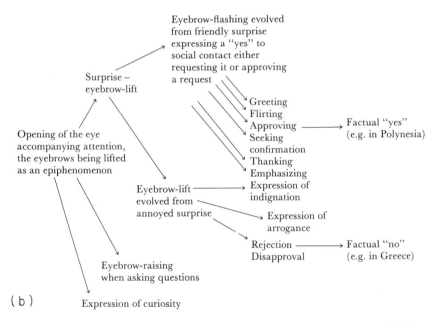

(b)

Fig. 2(b). Diverse uses of eyebrow movements, showing how the eyebrow flash has developed different meanings in different cultures. (After Eibl-Eibesfeldt, 1972.)

the changes in the mother-infant relationship merely as involving increasing independence between mother and infant would be to overlook some of the most interesting aspects. One of these is the way in which the behaviour of the mother and that of the infant become better integrated with each other. One type of evidence for this is as follows. Infant and mother stay in contact with each other for a while, then move apart for a while, and then come together again. Records of which individual was responsible for making and breaking contact were made. During the early weeks, the mother was more likely to break contact during a bout of contact that had been initiated by the infant than she was during one she had initiated herself. Similarly, the infant was more likely to break contact during a bout of contact that the mother had initiated than during one that he had. This implies that, during these early weeks, each partner was liable to initiate contact when the other was not ready for it, with the result that the less willing partner soon broke contact. Once the infants were a few months old, this difference disappeared. Apparently each was then more likely to go to the other when the other wanted it to than had been the case earlier. We can describe this as an increase in "meshing" between the behaviour of mother and infant as the infant developed (Hinde and White, 1974). Perhaps behavioural meshing could serve as an index of "intersubjectivity".

These data were drawn from studies of a number of mother-infant dyads, and were concerned with age trends. Simpson studied the more interesting question of the extent to which mother-infant dyads differed from each other at one age (Hinde and Simpson, 1975). He took as his datum point either the moment when mother or infant broke contact, or that at which they regained contact. In the former case, he showed that after a break in contact some infants were about equally likely to regain contact within five seconds whether they or their mothers had been responsible for the break, whereas others were much more likely to regain contact if the mother had broken contact than if they had broken contact themselves. We could describe this by saying that the former mothers were better at breaking contact when their infants did not want to retain it than were the latter group of mothers.

Of even greater interest are Simpson's findings concerning the events following the moment when an infant made contact with his mother. The data refer to periods in which the infant was leaving the mother to explore and play, returning to her for frequent short visits. Thus most of the visits were terminated by the infant going off again, but some were terminated by the mother. The question arises, therefore, on occasions when the mother brought a visit to an end by leaving, did she do so at a time when the infant was likely to leave anyway? Figure 3 shows data

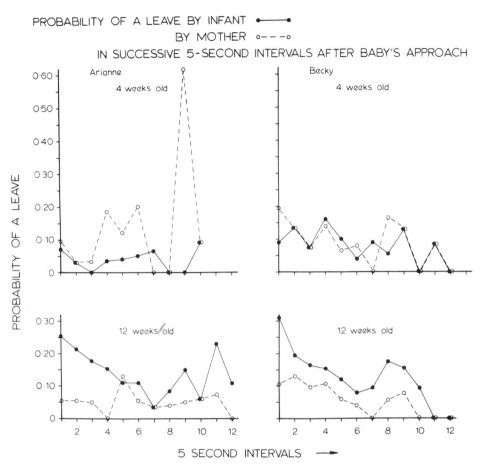

PROBABILITY OF A LEAVE BY INFANT •———•
BY MOTHER o———o
IN SUCCESSIVE 5-SECOND INTERVALS AFTER BABY'S APPROACH

Fig. 3. Behavioural meshing in rhesus monkeys. Probabilities of visits to mother initiated by infant being ended by mother (O – – – – –O) and by infant (●——— ●) after different visit durations. (M. J. A. Simpson, in Hinde and Simpson, 1975.)

for two infants at two ages. In each case Simpson has plotted the probability that the mother and the probability that the infant would leave the other in successive five second periods after the infant had made contact. At both ages, Becky's mother's curve followed Becky's more closely than Ari's mother's curve follows Ari's. When Becky was unlikely to leave, Becky's mother was unlikely to leave, and vice versa. Thus these data indicate that, in this situation, Becky and her mother were better "meshed" than Ari and her mother. It is of great interest that examination of the events after the mother broke contact also indicated that Becky and her mother were the better meshed pair. This raises the possibility, still to be investigated, that good "meshing" may be a common property of many interactions in the relationship.

The presence or absence of phenomena that could be described as behavioural meshing may be of critical importance in many human relationships. Sander (1977) sees mother-infant bonding as the interfacing of two adaptable systems where each partner has attuned his or her behaviour to the "behavioural programmes" of the other. But failure of synchrony between the activities of infant and caregiver, because the infant is in the charge of a number of different caregivers, may result in distortion of the infant's pattern of sleeping and waking (Sander et al., 1970). At a quite different level, and amongst adults, the way in which the participants in a relationship may adjust the lengths of their verbal utterances so that neither holds the floor to the exclusion of the other, could also be called behavioural meshing. This has been documented, for instance, in husbands and wives (Kendon, 1967), and ground controllers and astronauts (Matarazzo et al., 1964). Finally, meshing must be essential for a dyad to behave as a unit in presenting a point of view to others (Goffman, 1959).

Extent of generality of qualities

Qualities may apply to all or only to some aspects of a relationship. Thus they may concern:

(a) All the interactions within a relationship. A couple may behave sensitively or competitively in all contexts. Sometimes the quality of an interaction has reference to the nature of the relationship as a whole, or the desired or intended nature of that relationship, even when it contradicts the content. For instance two people may argue, but express non-verbally that they have an affectionate relationship.

(b) Some of the interactions within a relationship but not others. The distinction may lie with the content of the interactions, a couple behaving passionately in bed but coldly at the breakfast table. Or it may lie in the context; father and son may interact warmly at home but distantly in public, and siblings may be competitive in the presence of their parents but mutually supportive at school.

(c) The behaviour of one of the partners, or of both. Thus it is possible for one partner to behave with sensitivity, and the other not.

However we must be cautious not to presume too easily that a quality concerns one partner and not the other. If one partner behaves sensitively, the other is the recipient of that behaviour, and there is no necessary reason to suppose that all possible recipients would have elicited equally sensitive behaviour. Even where the initiative appears to lie with one partner rather than the other, the quality of the interaction may depend on both. We have already noted that measures of maternal warmth (see Chapter 6), which seem to be a property of the mother, may nevertheless be markedly different between one mother and each of her twins. Whilst many aspects of an individual's behaviour are consistent across contexts, an interaction depends on both participants, and it is usually safer to regard its qualities as properties of the dyad.

Content and quality

Two separate but more or less contemporaneous lines of research, originating in different branches of social science, have emphasized the possibility of dissociation between the content of an individual's behaviour and the quality or style with which that behaviour is expressed (cf. also Austin, 1962, cited p. 57).

We may consider first the approach of Goffman (e.g. 1959, 1961, 1963, 1967), a sociologist who has drawn his material from a wide range of situations but has emphasized public and more superficial relationships to a greater extent than intimate ones. Goffman distinguishes between the expressions an individual *gives* and those he *gives off*. By the expressions an individual gives, Goffman refers to the communication of information in the traditional and narrow sense. Expressions given off are actions that others treat as symptomatic of the actor, the expectation being that the action was performed for reasons other than the information ostensibly conveyed.

It is in the expressions given off that Goffman is primarily interested. He argues that each individual, in communicating, wishes to create a certain impression—to be thought of highly, to be seen as thinking highly of the listener, to be of a certain social class, honest, sly, self-confident, and so on. The others present will seek such information about the speaker in order to "define the situation", enabling them to predict what to expect of the speaker and what he expects of them. It is in the individual's interest to influence this definition of the situation which the others present come to formulate, and he can do this most readily by expressing himself so as to give them an impression that will lead them to accept his plan. To understand how the individual achieves this, Goffman takes a "dramaturgical perspective", treating the speaker as though he was a performer attempting to create an impression in an audience (cf. pp. 28–9). In real life an individual may create an impression deliberately; or he may act more or less unconsciously, perhaps falling in with the conventions of the group; or his behaviour may be totally spontaneous. If the actor dissembles, the listeners may or may not spot what he is up to. If the actor knows that he is likely to be discovered, he may make a false revelation—Goffman emphasizes the potentially infinite cycle of concealment, discovery, false revelation and re-discovery.

Each party to an interaction will be actor and audience in turn, so each will project their definition of the situation, which may or may not be accepted by the other. For the interaction to go smoothly, it is not necessary (or desirable?) that each should candidly express what he feels and honestly agree with the other. Rather each participant conveys a view of the situation which he feels the other will find temporarily acceptable, perhaps concealing some of his feelings behind asserted values to which everyone feels obliged to agree. Each, in other words, must "fit in". But at the same time each individual is allowed to establish tentative rules regarding matters vital to him—for instance to justify his past actions—and allows others to do the same. Goffman describes such a situation as a "working consensus". Since this working consensus is reached progressively, the initial impression made by each party can have a crucial influence on the progress of the interaction. In the same way, the early stages of a relationship may set the tone of later ones: Goffman regards a relationship as arising when an individual plays the same part to the same audience on different occasions.

In this way Goffman analyses a wide range of interactions, ranging from casual encounters to the interactions within intimate relationships, *as if* the individual concerned were playing a part. This involves the individual in projecting a definition of the situation (e.g. "This is my consulting room") and of his self (e.g. "And I am a knowledgeable and competent doctor"). Those parts of the performance that contribute to these definitions are called the "front". The "front" is made up of the physical setting and the personal front, the latter including "appearance", conveying social status, and "manner", concerned with the particular interaction role the performer is playing. There may also be a "back", where the performance is prepared—where, for instance, the doctor instructs his nurse on how to present herself to patients. Disruption of the front may lead to a halt in the sequence of interactions, embarrassment and so on.

Treating social behaviour "as if" it were a performance, liable to be "seen through" by the audience, Goffman provides fascinating insights into what goes on in ordinary social interactions. Of special interest here is his discussion of the extent to which the interactions he describes are in fact performances, and to what extent they are genuine. In the ordinary course of events we treat people as though they were either genuine or dissembling. But status in a social situation is not a material thing, to be possessed and displayed; it is a pattern of appropriate conduct, which must be performed to be realized. Goffman thus regards a performer, who is sincerely convinced that the impression of reality which he stages is the real reality, as being taken in by his own act. Whilst being taken in by one's own act and being cynical about it sound like the extremes of a continuum, Goffman points out that the extremes tend to be more stable than the intermediate regions. In so far as a person is playing a part, that part represents what he would like to be, and in so far as others confirm him in it, he will come to believe that that part is really him. We shall return to this issue in Chapter 9.

A similar initial distinction characterizes the work of a group who have been interested primarily in more intimate, intrafamilial relationships (Bateson et al., 1956; Jackson, 1959; Watzlawick et al., 1967). They emphasize that each message contains, in addition to its explicit content, a command or meta-communicational aspect that defines how the message is to be taken and/or the nature of the relationship between the communicands. For example the words "I'll do it for you", whilst carrying the explicit message that the speaker will perform a task for the recipient, can carry also a whole range of implications about the nature of the relationship. These may range from "I love you and it gives me pleasure to do things for you" to "It is a great nuisance to me, and it is improper for you to put me in a situation in which I have to offer to do it". While the content is the same in each case, the quality is not (see also Fraser, 1978).

As the last example indicates, the meta-communicational aspects of an utterance are often carried by its prosodic features, or by the paralinguistic features that accompany it. They can, however, be carried verbally—"I'll do it for you, if I have to"—just as the content of a communication can be verbal or non-verbal.

Contradictions between the several components of a communication may be especially prevalent in some individuals or in some relationships. For example Bugental *et al.* (1971) analysed video-taped recordings of parent-child interaction in terms of verbal content and two aspects of quality—prosodic (tone of voice) and non-verbal (facial expression) features. Evaluative conflict between channels was more common in the mothers of disturbed children than in the mothers of normals.

The meta-communicational aspects of a message usually carry information about the communicators' definition of himself, of the role identities (see p. 135) he wishes to be included in and excluded from the relationship, and thus a definition of the relationship itself. The importance to the individual of his definition of self is demonstrated most vividly by a technique used in the interrogation of political prisoners. The interrogator aims to deny the prisoner's view of himself and of the situation and to coerce him into adopting his own view (Danziger, 1976).

In ordinary life the extent to which each individual's view of himself is supported within a relationship may be of crucial importance for the future of that relationship. A proffered definition of self or relationship, if not confirmed, may be either rejected, or it may be "disconfirmed". Disconfirmation implies a negation of the reality of the person who suggested the definition (see p. 119). Such disconfirmation may be produced by misunderstanding (intentional or not), inconsistency, a change of subject, and so on. It may involve either the content of the message or its meta-communicational aspect ("contradiction" or "paradox"). In so far as the latter is involved, it may invalidate the claim for recognition or the definition of the relationship made by the originator of the message (Watzlawick *et al.*, 1967).

The double-bind theory of schizophrenia (Bateson *et al.*, 1956), as amended by Watzlawick *et al.* (1967), implies that members of a family are involved in a series of messages that mutually disqualify each other. If this occurs repeatedly in the course of an intense relationship from which there is no escape (and the analogy to the prisoner must be noted), then one or both participants may find themselves in a position in which they have to react to messages, but cannot react appropriately. The individuals cannot confirm the demands in each other's messages concerning the nature of their relationship, or their social identities. Although the double-bind theory has stimulated much research, a great deal of it is of rather dubious quality (Olson, 1972). However the theory as amended by Watzlawick *et al.* (1967), and with an emphasis on the mutuality of the disqualification, which is seen as a product of the relationship rather than of either individual *per se*, continues to receive some support. For example Hassan (1974) found that families with a delinquent or schizophrenic member show minimal mutual validation, apparently as a result of their unsuccessful meta-communication. A recent critical review of family interaction studies is provided by Danziger (1976).

Summary

It is suggested that how people do things may be at least as important for a relationship as what they do. Though there are great problems in measuring the qualities of interactions, these are not insuperable; even the extent to which each participant in a relationship directs his behaviour in accordance with the ongoing goals of the other can be assessed. Qualities may refer to one partner or both; they may be specific to certain interactions characterized by content or context or general to the whole relationship. The quality of an interaction may be closely related to its content, or only distantly related to it. Special consequences follow when content and quality contradict each other.

6

Relative Frequency and Patterning of Interactions

So far we have been concerned with the content and quality of individual interactions. But how people feel about their relationships may depend not only on the separate interactions, but on the relations between them—on the relative frequency of different types of interactions; or on the way in which they are patterned in time. However often the partners kissed, a relationship would hardly be called affectionate unless "affection was expressed" also in other ways. Nor would one partner consider the relationship of his/her partner affectionate if the latter expressed affection only in public, and not in private. An employer may judge his employee's efficiency not by how often he does what is required when asked, but by how often the employee does it in relation to how often he is asked—does he take the initiative and act without an order? Several different issues arise here.

(i) Clusters of co-varying properties. Our assessment of a relationship as affectionate depends on a number of different criteria (p. 42). Many other judgements similarly depend on multiple criteria, and we may be the more ready to apply a label, the more criteria are met. Two examples from studies of rhesus monkeys may be cited.

In one study those rhesus monkey mothers who often took the initiative in establishing ventro-ventral contact with their infants tended, while the infants were young, to be the ones who groomed their infants more than others (Hinde and Spencer-Booth, 1971b). This makes intuitive sense, and it seemed reasonable to subsume these measures under the label of "maternal warmth". It must be noted, of course, that the observation that a mother displays warmth to one infant does not necessarily indicate what she will do to another.

Again, the frequency with which attempts by rhesus monkey infants to gain the nipple were rejected by their mothers was positively correlated with a measure of the part the infants had to play, relative to that played by the mothers, in maintaining proximity to the mother when off her (see pp. 265–271). This again makes intuitive sense, and we might subsume them under the label of "maternal rejectingness".

Intuitive sense must however always be tested against the data. We might have expected dyads high on measures of maternal warmth to be low on measures of maternal rejectingness. This was the case, but the negative correlations between measures from the two groups were not very high and the two dimensions were not just the obverse of each other.

Again, in a later study (Simpson and Howe, in press) on 8 week old infants, the frequency of maternal approaches, the frequency of maternal initiation of close contact with the infant, and the frequency of maternal restraining, all loaded well on a dimension that could be labelled "Mother protects". However there was no tendency for dyads high on that dimension to be low on measures of maternal rejection. Thus the dyads in which positive responses to the infant by the mother are prominent do not necessarily show a low frequency of negative responses. We shall return to this point later.

One point must be emphasized here. Different items indicative of the same quality may be alternatives to each other. We would then expect them to be negatively correlated with each other, rather than positively. Thus one mother might greet her child with physical contact, and another with verbal endearments. A positive correlation between items is not a *necessary* condition for them to be regarded as indicators of the same quality (cf. p. 36).

Another example comes from studies of married couples. Kreitman *et al.* (1971) assessed the qualities of marital relationships by using a semistructured conjoint interview which allowed considerable spontaneity to the subjects. Various items of behaviour were counted or rated. Assessments were based on the assumption, following from the work of Lorr and McNair (1963), of three dimensions of interpersonal behaviour. These were:

(a) Assertiveness-compliance, assessed in terms of over-ruling and contradicting, reprimanding, giving advice or reassurance, interrupting, usurping answers to factual questions, attempts to exclude the partner, aggressive behaviour, unilateral planning for future activities, monopolizing the conversation, and general spontaneity.

(b) Affection-dislike, assessed in terms of complaints about the spouse, expression of concern, declared feelings of affection or dislike, praise or censure of the spouse, pride in spouse's extra-domestic activities, and amount of physical contact.

(c) Intensity of interaction. This proved to be technically unsatisfactory, and need not be discussed.

In the first two cases, each item was rated on a three-point scale, and a total compiled. It will be noted that a reasonably high total on a particular scale could be achieved if the subject was rated highly on a number of items, but does not require that ratings were high on all. Comparing 60 couples in which the husband was receiving out-patient treatment for neurosis with 60 control couples, Kreitman *et al.* (1970, 1971) found no differences in mean assertiveness between the patients and their wives on the one hand, and same sex controls on the other, but the patient-spouse couples showed both greater variation in absolute scores and greater variation in intra-pair differences. The patients, but not their wives, tended to give less affection than the same sex controls. Again the variances for patients and wives, and their range of intra-pair discrepancies, were greater than for the controls (see also Ineichen, 1976).

(ii) Ratio and Derived measures. In assessing qualities of a relationship from the relative frequency and patterning of interactions, relative frequencies of events may be more revealing than absolute frequencies. For example, Fig. 1(a) shows a measure of the absolute frequency per unit time with which attempts by infant rhesus monkeys to gain contact with their mothers were rejected by the mothers. Rejections rose to a peak around the end of the first year and then fell to a low level. Figure 1(b) shows this measure of absolute frequency of rejections expressed as a proportion of the number of times that the infant was in contact or attempted to make contact unsuccessfully. This remained high even when the absolute number of rejections fell. A reasonable interpretation is that the older infants maintained their demands at such a level that a more or less constant proportion were rejected. In the face of more rejecting mothers they could do this only by reducing the absolute number of attempts, and thus of rejections. That the rank order correlations between the absolute and relative measures of rejections remained high is in harmony with this interpretation. Other uses of ratio measures will be described later. The point being made here is that the mother-infant relationship of an infant which tries to make contact 10 times and is rejected 10 times must surely be very different

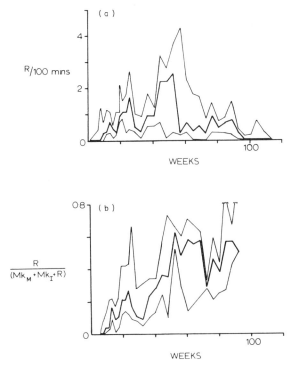

Fig. 1. Mother-infant interaction in captive group-living rhesus monkeys. (a) The rate with which attempts by the infant to gain the nipple were rejected by the mother (R). (b) Relative frequency of rejections, i.e. the frequency with which attempts by the infant to gain the nipple were rejected by the mother (R) divided by the sum of the number of times the infant gained the nipple on its own (Mk$_I$) and the mother's (Mk$_M$) initiative and the number of unsuccessful attempts (R). Abscissa—age of infants. Graphs show median and inter-quartile range. (From Hinde and Simpson, 1975.)

from that of an infant which tries to make contact 100 times and is rejected 10 times. Either we must assess the difference by keeping measures of rejections and contacts in mind simultaneously, or we must attempt to combine them. Further examples are given in Chapter 19.

Many workers are prejudiced against ratio and other derived measures, for two reasons. First they may feel they are too remote from actual behaviour. It can be argued, however, that a ratio may be measuring something more meaningful to the individuals concerned than an absolute measure, or else something that is meaningful in a different way. The above example of the relative frequency of rejections is a case in point. Second, it is argued that ratios can have misleading

properties, and may lead to scaling distortions. This of course is a real
issue, but need not lead to error. In practice data from rhesus monkeys
indicate that ratio measures show at least as much consistency over age
as do the absolute measures from which they are derived (Hinde and
Herrmann, 1977).

(iii) Relations between heterologous interactions. Some properties of relationships
can be regarded as emergent from the relative frequencies of interactions of different sorts. Rhesus monkey data can again be used to
illustrate a relatively simple case. If a rhesus mother frequently rejects
her infant's attempts to gain ventro-ventral contact and never initiates
them, we would describe her as rejecting. (As we have seen, such a
judgement properly applies to the relationship, and not just to the
mother, who might behave differently to a different infant.) If she never
rejects the infant and frequently picks it up herself, we would describe
her as possessive. But if she often rejects and often picks up the baby, or
seldom does either, we would describe her respectively as controlling or
permissive in the context of that relationship (Table 1). These latter
judgements are based not just on one type of interaction, but on both.

TABLE 1

Four properties of mother-infant relationships dependent on the absolute and relative
frequencies of two types of interaction (H=High, L=Low frequency)

	Rejecting	Possessive	Controlling	Permissive
Mother initiates contact	L	H	H	L
Mother rejects infant's attempts at contact	H	L	H	L

Actual data are shown in Fig. 2, where the relative frequency of
rejections is plotted against the proportion of contacts that were initiated by the mother. Dyads whose points lie high on and close to the
ordinate might be described as having a relationship involving a rejecting mother, those lying along and close to the abscissa as possessive.
Assessments of control/permissiveness depend on the extent to which
the two measures are *not* correlated with each other. Data on the
predictive value of such assessments derived from both absolute and
relative measures would be of great interest (Hinde and Simpson,
1975). In so far as we are using the relation between two measures, this

case resembles those discussed under the heading of "correlations between different types of interaction within the relationship" in the previous section. Here however the property in which we are interested is not a property of the individual measures, but of the relation between them.

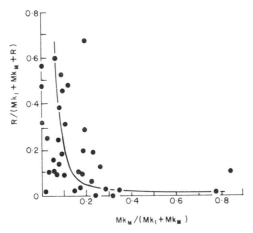

Fig. 2. Mother-infant interaction in captive group-living rhesus monkeys. Ordinate—relative frequency of rejections (as in Fig. 1 (b)). Abscissa—maternal initiative in nipple contacts, i.e. number of nipple contacts initiated by mother (makes, Mk_M) divided by sum of number initiated by mother (Mk_M) and infant (Mk_I). (From Hinde and Simpson, 1975.)

It might be possible to take this sort of approach further and to use objective measures of behaviour to get at the differences in "meaning" of different types of interaction for different individuals. For example, two infants whose attempts to gain contact are rejected by the mother equally often may not be equally frustrated; they may have different needs for contact. Indeed it is reasonable to suppose that, even if all else were equal, infants would differ in the time that they spent off their mothers. Perhaps, therefore, a measure of rejections in relation to the time the individual infants spent on or off their mothers would provide a measure more closely related to the infant's experience than a simple measure of rejection frequency. One could assess, for each infant, the number of rejections experienced per unit time of contact gained. Alternatively one could argue as follows. If differences in frequencies of maternal rejections were solely responsible for differences in time off the mother, there would be an absolute rank order correlation between the two measures. In practice the correlations found, though positive, are not high. This means that an infant ranking lower on rejections than on time off is achieving its contact more easily than would be expected on this hypothesis, and vice versa. Thus the difference between an individual's ranks on the two measures would give an index which would be positive if the infant were rejected frequently relative to time off, and vice versa. In this case the index was found to be slightly less consistent from one age period to another than were the measures from which it was derived, and it was not used. However comparable indices could prove useful in other contexts (Hinde and Herrmann, 1977).

(iv) Patterning of interactions. It is intuitively likely that differences in the patterning of interactions between two relationships can be of crucial importance, even though the frequencies are similar. For instance, a mother-infant relationship in which the mother picks up the baby only when it is crying is likely to have a different course from one in which the mother avoids picking up the baby at such times. One issue may be that the infant's current activity is reinforced by maternal attention (e.g. Brackbill, 1958; Rheingold *et al.*, 1959; Gewirtz, 1961; Brossard and Décarie, 1968). However this may not be the only issue, for data obtained by Bell and Ainsworth (1972) indicate that those babies whose mothers pick them up most readily in any one quarter of the first year are likely to be among the ones who cry least in the next quarter. Of course those mothers who respond quickly to their infants' cries may also differ in many other respects from mothers who are less responsive, so the effect on crying may be indirect. Furthermore latency is only one characteristic of the mother's response; many other features of her response may affect the baby's subsequent crying behaviour (Bernal, 1972; see also Gewirtz and Boyd, 1977) (see pp. 277–8).

Another type of patterning concerns the sequencing of positive, neutral and negative outcomes provided by one partner for the other. For example it is often suggested that courtship is more likely to be successful if the potential lover does not show complete devotion from the start but rather changes from a neutral or even negative attitude to one of admiration. Experimental data are in harmony with this view. Aronson and Linder (1965) arranged that students, who believed themselves to be engaged in interviewing a second student who was actually a confederate, should hear intermittent evaluations of themselves from the interviewee. These evaluations were either consistently positive, consistently negative, or changed from initially negative to positive or initially positive to negative. It was found that the subjects were attracted to the interviewee, or agreed with her opinions (Sigall and Aronson, 1967), most when they had received negative evaluations changing to positive, next most when the evaluations had been consistently positive, less when the evaluations had been consistently negative, and least when they had changed from positive to negative. Since the total number of positive and negative evaluations received in the two changing conditions were similar, it is clear that the sequence matters.

Such data are of course open to a number of interpretations. One possibility is that negative evaluations changing to positive are preferable to consistently positive ones because the positive ones reduce the dissatisfaction induced by the earlier negative ones, and that the reduction in dissatisfaction is rewarding. Another possibility is that evaluations that are consistently positive or negative are regarded as lacking in substance and insufficiently related to the subject's behaviour, whereas evaluations that change are interpreted by the subjects as directed to them personally. The latter explanation would account also for the fact that the positive-negative sequence engendered less attraction or tendency to form similar opinions than the all-negative sequence, even though the latter contained a higher total number of negative evaluations (Gergen, 1969).

Summary and conclusion

The properties of relationships depend not only on the properties of the several types of interactions, but on their relative frequency and patterning. The simplest case is where a property can be ascribed to a relationship the more readily, the greater the correlation between different measures of either the frequency or quality of interactions. Maternal warmth or rejectingness have been cited as examples. Sometimes ratios between measures reveal more than, or reveal something different from, the measures themselves. And some important properties may depend on lack of correlation between two measures: only because, in the example cited, maternal initiative in making contact and maternal rejectingness were not perfectly negatively correlated did a dimension of control (high on both) or permissiveness (low on both) make sense. Qualities may emerge also from temporal relations between the activities of the two partners (e.g. latency to respond) or their temporal patterning (e.g. sequence of positive and negative responses).

In this chapter, more than any other, it has been necessary to draw examples from non-human species. This is because I am not aware of many examples of applications of this approach to human interpersonal relationships. Yet it seems merely to make explicit the processes underlying our everyday use of such terms as warm, controlling, competitive or frustrating. We would hardly describe a spouse as sexually frustrated by a partner if he or she never attempted to make love; the frustrating quality of the relationship depends on the ratio of successes to attempts. (That sexual frustration may be caused by facets of the individual's own personality, rather than by the partner, is not the issue here.) It would seem that the quantitative application of such measures to the human case might be revealing.

In man, however, a further issue may arise. Adults, at least, monitor their own relationships (see pp. 29–30). Each of us applies labels of the type mentioned to our own relationships. We also attribute enduring properties to the partners in our relationships. But our monitoring is selective and can be biased, and may be influenced by past experience. Having experienced some warm or some frustrating interactions, we may look for such properties in others, seeing the whole relationship in similar terms. Such perceptions can become self-fulfilling. This issue, which applies equally to the dimensions discussed in other chapters, will be taken up again later.

7

Similarity versus Difference; Reciprocity versus Complementarity

One important aspect of interpersonal relationships concerns the extent to which the behaviour of the two participants is similar, and the extent to which it is complementary. That is our starting point in this chapter. But similarity or complementarity in behaviour could be based on similarity or complementarity in personal characteristics. A considerable amount of research has in fact been concerned with assessing the importance, for interpersonal attraction or for the growth or stability of relationships, of similarity on the one hand and complementarity on the other. Not surprisingly, neither is ubiquitously important, and the more recent research findings point to the need for finding out which is important where. An important aspect of complementarity, involving control of one partner by the other, will be considered in Chapters 18 and 19.

Reciprocity versus complementarity

Relationships differ in the extent to which the interactions are reciprocal (or symmetrical) or complementary. A reciprocal interaction is one in which the participants show similar behaviour, either simultaneously or alternately, whereas in a complementary interaction the behaviour of each participant differs from, but complements, that of the other. Thus when two children engage in rough-and-tumble play they may alternately chase and be chased, push and be pushed, as first one and then the other takes the initiative; the sequence of interactions is reciprocal. But when a mother interacts with her baby, she shows maternal behaviour and the baby shows filial; each interaction is complementary. In male-female sexual behaviour the part taken by each is complementary to that taken by the other. Dominance-subordinance interactions are by definition complementary.

In part because the individuals in any dyad usually differ in some way, whether in potential for achieving dominance or giving advice or whatever, relationships in which all interactions are reciprocal are probably rare. But some relationships, such as those between peers, colleagues or drinking companions, approach this condition. By contrast, relationships in which all interactions are complementary are common. For instance the formal relationships in hierarchically arranged organizations like armies and businesses are of this type. In such relationships, the status difference is likely to be in the same direction in all contexts: in a traditional army it is difficult for an officer not to be in the "boss" position even during off-duty hours. Indeed individuals may feel discomfort if their rank relationships in different contexts are not similar, and will attempt to maintain congruence between them (Homans, 1974). The implication is that it is better to be clear about who has the higher status, for uncertainty promotes anxiety (though see Runciman, 1967).

However, in the more sophisticated personal relationships there *need* be no congruence in the direction of complementarity in different aspects of the relationship. One partner may take the lead in some contexts, and the other in others. Indeed the interactions within relationships may show complex patterns of reciprocity and complementarity, with idiosyncratic patterns of imbalance. It is then not possible to characterize a relationship as a whole as either reciprocal or complementary, but only the constituent interactions.

Further complexity arises from the fact that complementarity may occur with respect to many different properties—dominance/subordinance, maleness/femaleness, nurturance/succorance (Henderson, 1974), achievement/vicariousness, etc. It is important to note that such labels are valuable only in so far as each applies to a property common to a number of interactions. Consider the relatively simple case of dominance/subordinance as applied to monkey dyads. If we observe merely that A bites B and C bites D, it does not add anything to say that A and C are dominant over B and D respectively. But if A threatens B, bites B, and has priority to food and water over B, whilst B avoids A and grooms A more than A grooms B, and if a similar position is found in the direction of interactions between C and D, dominance/subordinance is useful in a descriptive and even in an explanatory sense. If for instance the participants who threaten more are usually the ones that are avoided more, receive more grooming, and hold their tails highest, we may "explain" all these aspects of the relationship in terms of the dominance/subordinance of the participants (Hinde, 1978a). This issue is of course a general one. Whilst there is no need for the directions of complementarity with respect to any property to be congruent in different contexts, labels such as dominant/subordinate or nurturant/succorant are the more useful, the more contexts to which they apply.

Thus reciprocity and complementarity are properties of groups of interactions rather than of a relationship as a whole. But on occasion different complementary properties may even be present in one interaction—a sexual partner could be female, dominant and nurturant simultaneously. And we shall see later that complementarity may even change during the course of an interaction (Berne,1967, cited p. 108). However these complexities do not detract from the importance of the issues.

Similarities versus differences in personal characteristics

Common experience suggests that the pattern of reciprocity/complementarity will have crucial importance for the dynamics of a relationship. Some needs* (used in the rather general sense of Murray, 1938) can be satisfied only by someone with a similar need, others only by a partner with a complementary one. A child wanting to play searches for another like himself, but a merchant with goods to sell seeks a customer who needs to buy, not another merchant.

In forming close personal relationships, most people have a complex pattern of needs, which could best be met by someone with some similar and some complementary characteristics. However much of the earlier research in this area was concerned with establishing that either one or the other was important.

*It would be equally easy to use the language of "role expectations", each partner having a series of "role expectations" with respect to his or her own future behaviour and that of the partner (Kerckhoff and Davis, 1962; Murstein, 1967a; G. J. McCall, 1970). Compatability of role expectations might involve either reciprocal or complementary behaviour from the partner. Complementarity would be more important in relationships involving marked "role" differences, such as traditional marriages and work teams involving diverse skills.

Similarity

SIMILARITY AS A FACTOR IN AFFILIATIVE RELATIONSHIPS

People tend to make friends with, or to marry, others who are in some way similar to themselves. Thus a number of studies (mostly conducted in the U.S.A.) have shown that married couples tend to come from similar backgrounds, and to have similar religions; to have had similar family relationships; to be of similar stature, appearance and attractiveness; and to be of similar habits (e.g. Burgess and Locke, 1960; Berscheid and Walster, 1969, 1974b; Kerckhoff, 1974; review Byrne, 1971; Webster *et al.*, 1978). Comparable data are available for adolescent friends (Kandel, 1978).

Friends and married couples tend also to be similar in various measures of attitude,* or at least to perceive each other as more similar than do less closely related individuals (Tharp, 1963a; Byrne, 1961a, 1971; Pierce, 1970; Murstein, 1971a, c; Duck, 1973; Griffitt and Veitch, 1974; Clore, 1977).

Evidence for similarity in personality* between friends and spouses is, however, rather less substantial. Some studies found no relationship, whilst others obtained a positive result (e.g. Byrne, 1971). There is, however, evidence that similarity in personality is more likely to be found in stable marriages than in unstable ones (Cattel and Nesselroade, 1967; review Byrne, 1971). One reason why similarity in personality, as revealed by personality tests, might not be apparent amongst people attracted to each other in real life lies in the nature of

---

*Attitude and Personality. "Attitude" is used here to refer to a more or less stable system of beliefs, usually with evaluative component, towards an object or concept, or towards a set of such objects or concepts. Attitudes are usually considered as involving affective, cognitive and behavioural components. They may be assessed by self-report questionnaires, observational techniques, performance in specified tasks, or by physiological responses to standard stimuli or situations. The tests discussed here all refer primarily to the first of these. (See Jaspars, 1978, for detailed discussion of the concept.)

Personality is used to refer to more or less stable dispositions to respond in specified ways in a variety of situations. Thus personality "traits" or characteristics are postulated or deduced variables inferred from behaviour. Again a wide variety of assessment techniques are used, including projective tests, subjective assessments, and observation of behaviour. But the tests discussed in this chapter again involve primarily self-report questionnaires, the answers to which are usually subjected to some form of factor analysis. It will be apparent that the distinction between attitudes and personality traits is not always sharp.

the tests; the relation between scores on many traditional personality tests and behaviour in everyday situations is not strong (Mischel, 1968; but see Block, 1977). Another reason (see pp. 294–301) is that different types of tests may be appropriate for different types of relationships or different stages in the formation of a relationship.

Yet another form of similarity that has proved to be important in interpersonal relationships concerns the way in which individuals encode their experience, the "constructs" they use to make sense of the world about them, and the manner in which those constructs are related to each other (e.g. Kelly, 1955). Similarities in "construct systems" seem to become more important as friendship advances (e.g. Duck, 1977b). The technique used to assess such issues ("repertory grid") is discussed in the next section.

METHODOLOGY—TWO IMPORTANT TECHNIQUES

Before going any further, it is necessary to describe two techniques. One has been much used in laboratory studies of the effect of attitude similarity on interpersonal attraction, the other is used to assess similarities and differences in the way people construe the world.

Attitude Similarity and Interpersonal Attraction

Much of the experimental work in this area concerns not on-going relationships or even interactions, but the extent to which one individual is attracted to another on the basis of certain limited types of information. Often the issue is the extent to which one individual says he would like another, given evidence about the similarity/dissimilarity in attitudes between them. An experimental technique commonly used involves first asking subjects to complete attitude questionnaires. Later they are asked to rate another person (the "stranger"), from his answers to the questionnaire, on a scale of six seven-point items. This "Interpersonal Judgement scale" contains two items concerning how much the subject believes he would like, and enjoy working with, the stranger. Often the questionnaires, with which the subjects are presented, come from "bogus strangers", having been falsified in each case to agree or disagree to a given extent with the subject's own. The proportion of similar attitudes is usually found to be significantly positively correlated with the two rating scale items concerned with attraction (e.g. Byrne, 1961a, 1971; Byrne and Nelson, 1965a, b). Not surprisingly agreement on issues held to be important has more influence on "inter-personal attraction" than agreement on less important issues (Griffitt, 1974).

Although most of the experiments have been carried out with North American college students and have involved the assessment of inter-personal attraction as a result of attitude similarity, Byrne and his colleagues have extended these findings in a number of directions. Comparable data have been obtained for younger and older subjects in a variety of cultures. Other methods of presentation and other measures of the attraction response, verbal and non-verbal, have been used. The findings appear to be uninfluenced by a number of personality variables in the subjects, though need for affiliation, social avoidance and distress may play some role. The effects of stimulus characters of the stranger on attraction interact with those of attitude similarity in predictable ways (review in Byrne, 1971).

One possible reservation about these studies is that they are largely concerned with the subject's response to a stranger in a highly artificial situation, with no interaction possible. This was in fact part of a deliberate policy, an attempt to find consistent cause-effect relations in a laboratory setting. However it is important that comparable data had earlier been obtained by Newcomb (1956, 1961) in a more natural situation. Newcomb assessed the opinions and values of male college students at various points over a sixteen week period. The students were initially strangers, but lived together throughout the experimental period. Those whose pre-experimental opinions and values were similar tended to become friends later on, but not necessarily straight away. Since opinions and values did not change substantially, one issue could be that friendships formed gradually as individuals discovered others similar to themselves (see also p. 184).

Personal Construct Analysis

We are concerned here with a self-report technique which can be used to assess how individuals see themselves, others, and the world. It can thus be applied to assessing how far people encode their experience in similar ways. Its use in this way has so far been limited to relatively few studies, but there are promising indications that it reveals issues of considerable importance in close personal relationships, especially in relationships at a moderately advanced stage. Before describing the technique, it is necessary to sketch aspects of the theory on which it is based.

The basic assumptions are derived from G. A. Kelly's (1955, 1970) Personal Construct Theory. Kelly focusses on man's attempts to make sense of the world that he encounters, and to test that sense in terms of its ability to predict the future. Each of us construes events in the world about us differently, and each of us develops our own system of *constructs*, or differentiations between elements of experience, to help us make sense of the world. They may concern objects, values, opinions, attributes, etc. These constructs are interrelated in innumerable but personally idiosyncratic ways, in part by interdigitated hierarchies. Thus "hens" may be subordinated to "birds" and then to "animals" in one hierarchy, and to "potential food" in another. The constructs themselves are seen as bipolar—"intelligent—stupid", "happy—sad". Even "hens" may mean "not ducks". The use of a construct to classify aspects of experience involves excluding some items as well as including others.

Although it is necessary to use verbal labels to discuss constructs, they are not themselves necessarily verbal or dependent on verbal labels. Any discrimination that can be made can provide a construct, but constructs do not merely refer to discriminations made in the past. They are valuable for ordering past experience, but also, and more importantly, for making sense of current events and for predicting the future. Each individual's personal construct system is seen as continually under test by experience, and as continually elaborated through experience. It embraces all that has been learned, the individual's goals, intentions and values. Kelly emphasizes that interpersonal interaction depends on some degree of mutual understanding, on the extent to which the individuals construe each other's construct systems correctly.

This approach is put into practice through the repertory grid technique, which attempts to assess the patterning of a person's constructs (Ryle and Lunghi, 1970; Bannister and Fransella, 1971; Fransella and Bannister, 1977). For example, an individual might be asked to name 20 or 30 people important in his (or her) life. Then three of those people would be selected, and the individual would be asked to specify one way in which two of them differed from the third. He might answer that two were sensitive and the third was not. He would then be asked to extend this distinction to all the other people in the list. Then another triad would be selected, and he would be asked again to say how any two differed from the third. This time two might be honest and one dishonest. This distinction also could be applied to all people on the list. Repetition of the procedure would generate a matrix with people along the top and (bipolar) constructs down the side. The entry in each cell would specify how the construct applied to the individual concerned. Each entry might be in the form of a yes/no answer, but more usually a rating of how far the constructs applied or a rank ordering of the individuals in terms of the construct is used. In practice, 20–30 constructs seem to suffice for most individuals.

Factor analysis of such a matrix can show to what extent the constructs are in fact similar to each other and thus redundant and to what extent they are genuinely different. Comparison of the columns will show how far the subject perceives the various individuals as similar to each other. If the subject himself is included, then comparison of his column with others will show how far he sees himself as like particular others, and how far different from them.

In the above example the items in the grid were individuals, but they could equally well have been events, possible choices of action, dyadic relationships, or whatever suited the case in hand. And while the comparisons are usually made in terms of constructs that the subject himself supplies, some can be supplied by the investigator or therapist. These could be, for instance, "like me", "as I'd like to be", or "like I used to be". The factor analysis then shows the relation of these supplied constructs to those supplied by the subject. As an example, a grid derived from the matrix made by a patient who had lost a leg in an industrial accident is shown in Fig. 1. In this grid, constructs close together are alike in meaning. The axes, derived from the factor analysis, are deliberately unlabelled. It will be seen, in this example, that the patient tended to rank the same people as high on "like me" as he ranked low on "understanding". This implies that he did not see himself as an understanding person. Although the patient's difficulties appeared at first sight to stem from his accident, the grid suggests they may have been more longstanding. Thus the position of "like I used to be" was a long way from "as I would like to be", and the latter was closer to "understanding" and "good mixer" than to "good worker".

Kelly argued that similarities between the construct systems of two individuals would facilitate social intercourse between them. Two

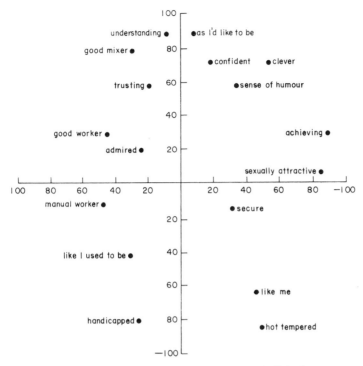

Fig. 1. Relationship scores along two axes for supplied and elicited constructs. (From Bannister and Fransella, 1971.)

individuals can communicate more fully if each has some grasp of the way in which the other works, of how he sees the world. The more each shares the other's view of reality, the more can be left unsaid, and the more easily does communication extend beyond superficialities. Extending this view, Duck (1973a,b) has argued that similarity in construct systems is likely to facilitate friendship formation in two ways. First, it will facilitate communication and understanding. Second, and perhaps more important, each construct system will provide an external validation for the system developed by the other. Duck did in fact find that, in a repertory grid test, subjects tended to generate constructs that were relevant to their friends, though such constructs might of course apply also to others. (To be precise, friends accounted for more first factors in the factor analysis and it was assumed that the first factor extracted from such an analysis is the more important and central for the individual.)

In this case Duck concentrated on the *structure* of the constructs generated by his subjects. In later experiments he used their *content* to compare the utility of Reptests with those of tests of attitudes and values in differentiating between established friends and non-friends. In these cases subjects were simply asked to generate constructs, and were not required to complete grids. More similar constructs were generated by friends than by non-friends, while the attitude tests failed to differentiate between them.

These tests were concerned with friendships which were already firmly established. Duck (1977b) also compared the value of a personality test (California Personality Inventory) with that of content similarity of constructs in Reptests for recently acquainted subjects and established friendship groups. The CPI predicted attraction in the former, but not in the latter. The Reptest predicted the established friendships in the second group. Thus Duck argues that construct similarity is important for the development and maintenance of friendship at moderately advanced stages of friendship formation (see also pp. 298–300).

We shall see later that this technique can be used also to assess how individuals see the relationships in which they are involved, and how they assess them relative to other relationships.

WHY IS SIMILARITY ATTRACTIVE?

We have seen that like tend to associate with like in real life, that laboratory experiments demonstrate a relation between attitude similarity and interpersonal attraction, and that similarity in construct systems seems to be important for established friends. Of course such findings do not mean that an influence of similarity on attraction is ubiquitous—we shall return to that issue later. But in the meanwhile, how are these findings to be accounted for? We may consider a number of possibilities, not with the presumption that one or more is right and the others wrong, but in the expectation that some will be right in some cases and others in others.

Propinquity

People may tend to encounter others like themselves for reasons that have nothing to do with their personal preferences. They may live near each other, perhaps because they share social characteristics of wealth, race, class, etc. They may encounter each other because they go to the same school or college or have similar occupations (e.g. Kerckhoff, 1974). Room-mates may be attracted to each other even though very dissimilar from each other (Newcomb, 1961). Proximity allows individuals to exchange resources with less cost than is possible for individuals living far apart (Thibaut and Kelley, 1959), and increases the possibility of their being familiar with each other.

Social Pressures and Social Norms (see p. 32)

Choice of friend or spouse is often constrained by social pressures. Pressures towards marrying a partner of the same race, religion and social class, whilst not so strong as they were, are still potent in many sections of western societies. These social pressures may be internalized, so that liaisons within the group come to be preferred, and similarity to self becomes a desirable attribute in another. Kerckhoff (1974) reviews evidence that such social norms are most likely to be flouted by those least likely to lose thereby.

Such social pressures are particularly potent over matters of race, religion and social class. Marriages between spouses of different status tend to show less marital happiness, stability and value consensus than marriages between spouses of similar status. In reviewing evidence on this issue, Pearlin (1975) emphasizes that negative consequences probably follow only when someone who thinks status important marries someone of lower status. Of course many marriages between persons of different race or status involve conscious rejection of social prohibitions against such liaisons, and the resulting interpersonal commitment may strengthen the bond.

Inherited Predispositions

Biologists, finding that strangers tend to elicit aggression whilst members of the same group tend to elicit affiliative responses in a wide range of species, have suggested that this may also be true of man (e.g. Tinbergen, 1968). This could supply a basis for in-group affiliations. While this is a reasonable view, hard evidence is obviously difficult to come by. In any case it is in no way contradictory to the theory of internalized social pressures put forward in the previous paragraph, for

social learning could occur under the influence of inherited predispositions to differentiate between group members and outsiders (e.g. Hinde
and Stevenson-Hinde, 1973).

Similarity faute de mieux

Another possibility is that like associates with like not because, if given
a free choice, each would prefer someone like himself, but because each
assumes that the costs of obtaining someone better would be too great
(see Lewin *et al.*, 1944; Walster *et al.*, 1966; Homans, 1974). This view
rests especially on studies of the choice of dating partners in North
American colleges and universities, the main attribute discussed being
physical attractiveness.

Walster *et al.* (1966) suggested that the choice of a dating partner
depends on balancing the possible gains against the costs. Individuals
tend to assume that it would be more difficult to date an attractive
partner than a less attractive one because attractive partners are more
sought after and therefore will have other offers. The perceived probability of acceptance thus decreases with increasing attractiveness of
the chosen partner. On the other hand, the greater the attractiveness
of the chooser, the lower the probability that anybody he asks for a
date will reject him. Thus the more attractive the person looking for
a date, the more attractive should be the dating partner that he or
she will select. However, there are costs in being rejected—embarrassment, the ridicule of one's friends, unhappiness, and so on. These
costs will depend on various aspects of one's situation and also
on one's own opinion of oneself. The higher the costs, the less risk is
the chooser likely to be willing to run. If the chooser balances the
gains of the more desirable partners against the costs of possible
rejection, he or she is likely to choose someone more or less like
himself.

The subjects were students at a dance who thought they would be
paired by a computer on the basis of questionnaires they had completed. As predicted the more attractive the student, the more desirable
he expected an appropriate partner would be. In fact the students were
paired at random. They were asked, during an intermission, how much
they liked their partner and whether they would seek to prolong the
acquaintance. Here the data showed little influence of the physical
attractiveness of the respondents (rated by independent judges) on

their own responses. All subjects, whatever their own attractiveness, were prone to like attractive partners.

Other studies have provided some support for the matching hypothesis for opposite sex couples (e.g. Murstein, 1971c), but the evidence has been on the whole rather weak (Stroebe *et al.*, 1971). Most data indicate that subjects prefer dates with individuals of high attractiveness and desirability, regardless of their own attractiveness (Berscheid and Walster, 1974b). Even though some of the studies showed that a person's own attractiveness affected his selection of a dating partner, the individuals selected were far above the chooser's own level of attractiveness (Stroebe, 1977; Moss, cited Byrne, 1971). Interestingly, in one study the subject's estimate of his or her own attractiveness was found to provide better evidence for matching than attractiveness as assessed by an independent rater (Stroebe *et al.*, 1971), and in another study to show a closer relationship with the subject's assessment of the probability that he would be accepted by the stimulus person (Huston, 1973).

Some additional support for the matching hypothesis is claimed from a study by Kiesler and Baral (1970). Students whose self-esteem had been lowered by the experimenter behaved more romantically with a female confederate who was only moderately attractive, whereas students whose self-esteem had been raised behaved more romantically with an attractive one. It has also been suggested that individuals will choose the most attractive partner from amongst others whom they have already met, but tend to choose someone more like themselves if they are to be responsible for initiating contact (Berscheid *et al.*, 1971; Walster *et al.*, 1978); however the evidence is not clear (Stroebe, 1977).

In these studies, almost the only independent variable considered was physical attractiveness. Murstein (e.g. 1971e) has argued that, in the early stages of courtship, couples will assess each other on a whole series of dimensions, of which physical attractiveness is but one. On this view individuals are likely to be attracted to others whose *overall* attractiveness is similar to their own, though that attractiveness may involve assessment of status, background, professional potential and so on as well as physical characteristics. Some evidence in support of this view is available (see Murstein, 1971c; Walster *et al.*, 1978a).

It is worth noting that a comparable mechanism has been suggested for certain aspects of the patterning of relationships in non-human primates. Within a group the individuals are often arranged in one or more dominance hierarchies. As is well known, monkeys spend a lot of time grooming each other—an activity which may have some cleansing function, but is certainly more important in social communication, and has been regarded as an analogue of "social approval" (Hinde and Stevenson-Hinde, 1976). A number of workers have found that, within any dyad, the subordinate monkey tends to groom the more dominant one more than vice versa, and that individuals tend to direct their grooming more towards others close to them in the dominance hierarchy than to ones much higher or much lower than themselves (e.g. Lindberg, 1973; Oki and Maeda, 1973; Simpson, 1973; Seyfarth, 1976). Seyfarth (1977; Seyfarth *et al.*, 1978) has suggested that this can be accounted for on two assumptions—that high-ranking individuals are more attractive than others, and that access to preferred partners is restricted by competition, the results of which can be predicted from the dominance hierarchy. Thus high-ranking females, who meet little or no competition, interact with others of high rank; middle-ranking females, who meet competition from those higher in the hierarchy, "compromise" by grooming others of middle rank; and low-ranking females can interact only with each other. Seyfarth (1977) simulated the field data in a computer model which was able also to accommodate other influences on grooming interactions, such as the degree of genetic relatedness between individuals and the special attractiveness of newly parturient females.

Acquisition of Similarity

Another possibility is that similarity of attitudes or personality are a consequence rather than a cause of mutual association. Were this the case, one would expect that married couples would tend to resemble each other more, the longer they had been married. The evidence on this issue is equivocal (Berscheid and Walster, 1969), and one must conclude that an effect of association on similarity, if it exists, is not strong. Even if the evidence were there, it may be noted, it would have to be interpreted with care; similarity could be enhancing the longevity of marriage rather than being produced by it.

However some longitudinal studies are of special interest. E. L. Kelly (1955) found that husbands and wives did not tend to show more attitude similarity after 18 years of marriage than at the time of engagement. However Uhr (cited Barry, 1970) divided these couples into those happily and unhappily married. The happy couples showed more attitude differences at engagement, but became more alike, whereas the unhappy ones became more unlike. The changes were most marked in the happily married wives, who had changed to become more like their husbands, and in the unhappily married husbands, who had changed away from their wives.

Supporting evidence comes from a cross-sectional study by Ferreira and Winter (1974). These authors used a questionnaire to assess the extent to which married couples would show "spontaneous agreement" (i.e. agreement before discussion) on a wide range of problems. The couples were divided into normals and abnormals, the latter having had at least one family member (parent or child) with emotional problems or having been involved in psychiatric therapy, delinquency or a criminal offence. In spite of the crude criteria for separating the groups, a clear difference was found, with the normals showing more spontaneous agreement than the abnormals. However this difference was not present amongst couples that had been married for three years or less; the degree of spontaneous agreement increased with length of marriage amongst the normals, but did not amongst the abnormals. Thus amongst these couples normals showed more spontaneous agreement the longer they had been married, and the abnormals did not. The authors acknowledge the difficulties in interpreting cross-sectional data of this sort, but the results strongly suggest an increasing tendency for couples to share more opinions with time.

Another group of characteristics in which husbands and wives may show increasing similarity with time includes symptoms of neurosis. A number of studies indicate that married couples show greater than chance similarity in neurotic status. This could be due to assortative mating. Murstein (1967b), for example, found that college students tend to become engaged to others similar to themselves in this respect. Another possibility is that couples whose members resemble each other in this respect are more likely to marry, whilst couples who do not are more likely to separate. In the same study, Murstein showed that dating couples who did not progress towards marriage showed a negative correlation on an index of neuroticism, whereas couples who progressed showed a positive correlation.

However there is also evidence for the acquisition of similarity during marriage. Kreitman *et al.* (1970) studied 60 married couples in which the husbands were receiving outpatient treatment for neurosis, and 60 control couples. The patients' wives tended to be more disturbed than the control wives. The evidence was against assortative mating; early in marriage the patients' wives did not differ on any measure of disability from the controls, but later they came to do so. It thus seemed likely that interaction during marriage led to the disturbance in the patients' wives. Speculating that this might be associated with more face-to-face interaction in the patients' marriages, and poorer extra-marital social relationships in their wives, Nelson *et al.* (1970) sampled the activities of the couples in both groups. Both hypotheses were confirmed.

Similarity per se *is Reinforcing*

A number of authors has suggested that interaction between similar persons is rewarding *per se*, and thus likely to be continued. There are a number of reasons why this should be so. At an everyday level, it could be because they share similar values or ways of looking at the world, and this fosters communication and minimizes tension (Kelly, 1955, see p. 85). Or it could be that norms placing a high value on similarity in others are internalized early in life (Lewis, 1975).

Another explanation that has received much attention is that similarity in attitude is reinforcing because it provides confirmation of the subject's actions or opinions (Byrne, 1971; Clore and Byrne, 1974; Clore, 1977). On this view every individual needs to assess social reality correctly, and his perception of reality can be validated only by others (Festinger, 1954). We thus need "consensual validation" of our world by others. If we find that others share our attitudes we are attracted to them, it is suggested, because we believe that they will confirm our social beliefs. This would perhaps be even more probable if they construed their experiences of the world in the same way as we do (see pp. 85–6). To be more precise, it is suggested that similarity, in providing consensual validation, produces positive affect, and is for that reason reinforcing. Byrne did in fact find that it is reinforcing to be agreed with (see also Kelvin, 1970). Further studies were cited on pp. 83–4.

Predicting from this that the attractiveness of similarity would increase with the need for consensual validation, Byrne *et al.* (1966) compared the effects on attraction of similarity over unverifiable beliefs with those of similarity over verifiable facts. As expected, similarity was associated with attraction more in the former case than in the latter. A number of other experiments indicate that the more uncertainty there is about an opinion an individual holds, the greater the attractiveness of individuals who offer support (Wheeler, 1974).

Byrne and Clore (1967) likewise predicted that subjects who were themselves temporarily confused would be more attracted to a bogus stranger who appeared to have attitudes similar to their own. Accordingly they gave subjects various kinds of confusing experience, such as viewing meaningless films, before testing them in the above manner. Moderate disturbance increased the effects of similarity on attractiveness, though high disturbance did not. Other experiments have given even more clear-cut results (e.g. Byrne and Griffitt, 1966).

One finding of special interest was that a subject's attraction to another (assessed as indicated on pp. 83–4) may be affected not only by the number of agreements on elements within an attitude scale, but by the way in which those agreements were structured. To exemplify the meaning of structure here, Tesser (1971) compared two cases of 50% agreement on a 10 item scale in which the first five items concern interrelated issues and the second five, another set of interrelated issues. Agreement on the first five and not on the second would imply agreement on structuring, whereas agreement on items 1, 3, 5, 7 and 9 and disagreement on the others would not. In general, for interrelated items, structural similarity will be greatest at 0 or 100% attitudinal similarity, but least at 50%. For unrelated items, structural similarity is of course not possible, and only attitudinal similarity could affect attraction. Tesser did in fact find attraction was a linear function of attitude similarity on independent items, whereas both linear and curvilinear components were found with interrelated items. This study is given special mention because it provides an interesting link with the work on similarity in construct systems, discussed on p. 88.

Similarity and Being Liked

Yet another explanation for an effect of attitude similarity on liking is that attitude similarity indicates that liking is likely to be reciprocated. On this view, the attractiveness of similar others would be related to the desire to be liked (Walster and Walster, 1963). Subjects who were confident of being liked would be less likely to chose to interact with similar others than subjects who did not expect to be liked. This prediction was confirmed; indeed subjects who had been assured that they would be liked preferred dissimilar others to similar ones, whilst subjects who expected not to be liked preferred similar others. In this same experiment, some subjects were instructed to interact with others who would like them. Such subjects tended to interact with similar others.

These results therefore raise the possibility that the relation between attitudinal similarity and liking in the bogus stranger experiments is not due to similarity enhancing attractiveness directly, but to its affecting beliefs about the probability of being liked. In those experiments almost the only thing the subject knows about the bogus stranger is the extent to which he answers a set of questions similarly to himself. If the answers are similar, this may lead the subject to believe that the stranger would like him, and thus predispose the subject to like the stranger. It is in fact found that if the subject is also given knowledge of whether the (bogus) stranger does or does not like him, the effect of attitude similarity *vs* dissimilarity on attraction is either absent (Aronson and Worchel, 1966) or much smaller than that of like *vs* dislike (Byrne and Rhamey, 1965; Byrne and Griffitt, 1966). Positive or negative evaluations have an even greater effect on attraction than does similarity or dissimilarity of attitudes on impersonal topics.

Similarity and Role Satisfaction

In the later stages of courtship, individuals assess each other for comparability on a wide variety of dimensions. Using role to refer to "the norms for a particular relationship, and for particular situations", Murstein (1971c, p. 118) has suggested that the extent to which people will find role satisfaction with partners perceived overall as similar to themselves, or with individuals they see as different, will depend on individual personality characteristics. The argument depends on the view that the partner chosen is likely to be perceived as similar both to the chooser's ideal spouse and to his or her ideal self. However individuals differ in the extent to which they are satisfied with themselves. An individual who is satisfied with himself (i.e. where there is a close correlation between his perception of himself and that of his ideal self) is likely to choose someone like himself, but one who is dissatisfied with himself will choose someone close to his ideal self and ideal spouse, who will therefore be unlike himself.

Murstein asked each member of 99 university dating couples to complete a modified version of the Edwards Personal Preference Schedule on behalf of his or her self, ideal self, fiancé(e) and ideal spouse. The results showed that the subjects with high self-acceptance chose partners perceived as more like themselves than did those with low self-acceptance.

In a related study, Bailey *et al.* (1974) predicted that individuals who thought well of themselves would select friends similar in intelligence to themselves, whilst individuals not satisfied with their own intelligence would select a partner complementary to themselves. However the data did not support the attractiveness of similarity in either case. The authors explain their findings as follows. For those with high self-acceptance there was no relation between their actual ability and their perception of their own intelligence. Therefore, it is suggested, they selected a friend less bright than themselves to maintain their own unrealistic view of themselves. The low self-acceptance subjects were more realistic in their self-estimates, but tended to chose friends nearer to their ideal—perhaps in order vicariously to fulfil that ideal.

Similarity per se *versus the Establishment of Positive Beliefs*

The immediately preceding hypotheses have involved two rather different views. One is that perceived similarity of a stranger produces an affective response more or less directly, the other that perceived similarity produces positive beliefs about the likelihood of being liked or of finding role satisfaction. Byrne, though suggesting a relatively direct effect via "consensual validation", has been careful to emphasize that, while experiments on interpersonal attraction can often be *described* in simple stimulus-response terms, cognitive intermediaries may well be involved. "Human beings . . . are actively engaged in remembering, informing, expecting, inducing and deducing even in the limiting confines of an experimental situation" (Byrne, 1971, p. 255).

In practice the bogus stranger situation by its very nature minimizes any attraction arising from possible beliefs about future interaction. This was highlighted in an experiment designed to test the common-sense prediction that agreement or disagreement on sexual matters should be influenced by the sexual identities of the individuals concerned. With the prediction that similarity *vs* dissimilarity of sexually relevant attitudes would have a greater effect on attraction towards someone of the opposite sex than to someone of the same sex, subjects were given sexual and achievement items from the Personal Preference Schedule. Whilst subjects were more attracted to bogus strangers who gave responses similar to their own, there was no confirmation of the initial prediction. Byrne *et al.* (1974a) suggest that differential attraction to a member of the opposite sex as a result of agreement on sexual issues would be found only in a situation in which further interaction was anticipated. Consensual validation can be provided by a member of either sex in the absence of further interaction, but similarity would be important in facilitating the subject's goals only if the stranger were of the opposite sex and future interactions were anticipated.

Most of the stimuli used in experiments on interpersonal attraction can be regarded as having two components, information and affect. The former could involve positive or negative evaluations, but without implications for the perceiver. Affective stimuli, however, have evaluative or other emotive significance for the perceiver. Clore (1977, p. 30) gives the example "the observation that Mary is angry at John would convey information to any perceiver, but for John himself, such information engenders an affective reaction as well". Stimuli can thus be seen as varying along two dimensions, one concerned with information and the other with affect. Use of adjectives such as "intelligent" or "stupid" to describe a third person would exemplify the extremes of the former, whilst extremes of pleasure and pain would define the affective dimension. Most stimuli used in studies of interpersonal attraction have both informational and affective components. Experiments have been designed to separate the effects of affect and information with some success (e.g. Byrne and Rhamey, 1965, Byrne *et al.*, 1974b, Wyer 1965).

Thus Byrne and Clore argue that similarity *can* augment attraction by producing consensual validation, but in addition acknowledge the possibility that both similarity and dissimilarity can affect attraction by inducing beliefs about future rewards. Ajzen takes a more extreme view —namely that there is no need to suppose that similarity is attractive *per se*, for it is so only when it leads to the establishment of positive beliefs about the other person (Ajzen, 1974, 1977). This view is based on the supposition that information is actively processed, some items being accepted and others rejected, and that the whole is evaluated according to the past experience of the subject (e.g. Bruner and Tagiuri, 1954). It is then argued that, if attribute desirability and attribute similarity are separated, similarity may have little effect on attraction—a view which also receives experimental support (Fischbein and Ajzen, 1975; Ajzen, 1977).

There is in fact considerable evidence that similarity is often important in so far as it indicates that the other person is likely to provide benefits (see also Coombs, 1966; Johnson and Johnson, 1972). Furthermore the evidence that the effectiveness of similarity is related to a desire to be liked (see above; also some support in Layton and Insko, 1974) or as promising role satisfaction can be seen as concerning special cases of perceived similarity inducing positive beliefs. Ajzen (1977) cites a number of studies showing how somewhat contradictory data on the effects of similarity can be reconciled on the view that similarity is attractive when it leads to the formation of positive beliefs.

It is important to stress that similarity can also provoke dislike—a finding not easy to accommodate on anything but an information processing approach. For instance, the perceived similarity of another may reduce one's own feeling of being special (Fromkin, 1972; Rubin, 1973). Indeed, paradoxically, interaction with someone different from oneself can be important just because it provides evidence for the differentiation of the individual and confirms his personal integrity: perhaps such an effect can occur only in a relationship that is already close and positive (see also Tajfel, 1978b), with respect to small groups).

On this view, then, the importance to an individual of the perceived similarity of a real or bogus stranger lies in the beliefs engendered. In the case of attitude similarity, this could be important because it validates the individual's view of the world and enables him to deal with it more competently (Byrne and Clore, 1967). But similarity in attitudes or in other characteristics is important primarily because of concomitant predictions about future benefits—for instance, similarities in interests or outlooks and lack of friction from gross disagreements (e.g. Lott and Lott, 1974). Similarities might predict desirable qualities of interaction, greater potential for meshing, or similar viewpoints on how much meshing matters.

At this point it is proper to emphasize that the attractiveness of similarity is not ubiquitous. For example, a later replication of Newcomb's field study of students gave only weak support for a role of attitude similarity, except where attitudes to self were considered (Curry and Emerson, 1970). Izard (1960) gave a personal preference schedule to an entire freshman class. Six months later subjects were asked to name the three individuals they liked most and least in their class. The personality profiles were similar for subjects and their friends, but not for subjects and those they liked least. So far so good, and the study was later replicated. But a later study with college seniors did not show any relationship between similarity and attraction. Izard (1963) speculated that similarity in one's friends might become less important with maturity.

Again, in a simulated naturalistic study, Griffitt and Veitch (1974) assessed attitude similarity by a questionnaire method, and friendship choices, amongst men living together in a crowded shelter for 10 days. Although attitude similarity was significantly greater amongst those who became friends than amongst those who did not, the difference was not very great, amounting to agreement on about 4% of the attitude items. Thus even if attitude similarity was a factor in friendship choice, it does not seem to have been a very important one.

In another study of college couples, those who remained together over a two year period were no more similar to each other in attitudes than those who broke up, though they were more similar in age, intelligence, and educational aspirations (Hill et al., 1976; see also Levinger et al., 1970).

But such findings are not difficult to reconcile. Whether or not attitude similarity is important in providing consensual validation early in an acquaintanceship, it does not necessarily engender positive beliefs. Some similar attitudes may augur well for the future of a relationship, whilst others are irrelevant, and in other areas differences may be preferred. And as a relationship progresses, similarity may well become less important, and differences along some dimensions relatively more.

Thus in real-life relationships the effects of similarities and differences are closely interwoven. A philosopher may be attracted to other philosophers, but bored by those who think exactly as he does and excited where a limited difference of opinion bodes fruitful and enjoyable debate. The very fact that most people choose to live with someone of the opposite sex shows that complementarity over some issues is also important though, as we shall now see, attempts to generalize about patterns of complementarity in marriage are fraught with difficulties.

Complementarity

COMPLEMENTARITY AS A FACTOR IN AFFILIATIVE RELATIONSHIPS

Apparently contradictory to the view that similarity is attractive, there is also evidence that people are attracted to those with needs complementary to their own. Clinically, the importance of need complementarity has long been apparent (e.g. Kubie, 1956). Winch (1958; Winch *et al.*, 1955) provided one of the first detailed tests of this view. He focussed on 12 needs—abasement, achievement, approach, autonomy, deference, dominance, hostility, nurturance, recognition, status aspiration, status striving and succorance, and the personality traits of anxiety, emotionality and vicariousness. A number of young married couples matched for their general life circumstances were studied, their needs being assessed by interview and questionnaire techniques, and by a Thematic Apperception Test.

Winch looked for complementarity of two sorts. On the one hand, two individuals could have needs similar in kind but yet complement each other because their needs differed in intensity. For instance one might be high on a need for dominance and the other low. The Parsons and Bales (1955) model of marriage fits this type, with the husband primarily instrumental in the extra-familial world and secondarily expressive, and the wife the reverse. On the other hand, needs could be similar in intensity but different in kind. An individual with a high need for abasement might complement one with a high need for dominance.

Winch claimed that couples tended to have needs which complemented each other's in a higher proportion of cases than would be expected with randomly matched couples. Using a variety of data reduction techniques, he suggested that most of the marriages in his study fell into four groups distinguishable along the dimensions of dominance/submissiveness and nurturance/receptivity, as shown in Table 1. Winch was able to associate properties of other types with some of the categories—for example wives with marriages falling in the two lower cells in Table 1 tended to have dominant mothers whom they disliked. However he recognized that not all marriages fall into one of these types.

Some later studies have produced further evidence that complementarity is important in the initiation or maintenance of relationships. For instance schoolboys (but not girls) were found to choose friends who

TABLE 1

Dimensions and types of complementary marriages as described by Winch (1958)

Dominant-Submissive	Nurturant-Receptive	
	Husband-nurturant	Wife-nurturant
	Wife-receptive	Husband-receptive
Husband-dominant	Ibsenian	Master-Servant Girl
Wife-submissive	Carl-Clare	Earl-Edith
Wife-dominant	Thurberian	Mother-Son
Husband-submissive	George-Grace	Adam-Alice

were complementary in a variety of ways as assessed by the Rorschach test and other techniques (Hilkevitch, 1960). Again Stewart and Rubin (1976) cite evidence showing that power-motivated men tended to seek alliances with weaker subordinates, and to have wives who were dependent and submissive (see also Wagner, 1975).

But Winch's analysis has been sharply criticized on methodological grounds by Tharp (1963a, b), and later studies of the part played by complementarity in friendship and marriage have produced conflicting results. Many indicate that complementarity plays no, or at most a minor, part (e.g. Schellenberg and Bee, 1960; Izard, 1960; Murstein, 1961; Pierce, 1970; Seyfried, 1977). Winch (1967), in accepting some of these criticisms, argued that complementary needs must be compatible with group norms. For instance a passive husband/domineering wife relationship is likely to be less satisfactory than the reverse. But in general, while the concept of need complementarity makes intuitive sense, studies attempting to show that complementarity across the board is important have not been successful.

But we have already seen that complementarity in all aspects is not to be expected in sophisticated interpersonal relationships. Each partner is likely to have many needs, some demanding reciprocity and others complementarity of different sorts. A husband may take the lead in some contexts, and the wife in others (e.g. O'Rourke, 1963; see also Seyfried, 1977). Furthermore, as Winch recognized, some needs may be satisfied outside the relationship (see also Levinger, 1964).

A further issue arises from the fact that needs as assessed in a laboratory or clinical setting may be a poor guide to need satisfaction in a real-life relationship. Need gratification can be delayed, and a relationship may work because the partners' apparently incompatible needs are satisfied at different times. The reconciliation of diverse needs may be facilitated by the development of norms (see p. 224) which regulate the synchronization of activities, permit turn-taking, reduce differences of opinion, and so on (Thibaut and Kelley, 1959). Furthermore one type of behaviour may satisfy more than one need; making love can express many aspects of the personality.

In any case, compatibility does not involve only the potential for appropriate reciprocity or complementarity in particular types of behaviour. For one thing, compatibility over who initiates change in activity is also necessary. Two people who both like to be initiators are likely to be at odds. And if we are really to understand a relationship, we must ask not only "Who takes the decisions in this context and in that?" but also "Who decides who should take the decisions?" and even perhaps "Who decides who decides who should take the decisions?" (see p. 106).

Yet another possibility was suggested by Winch (1958) and also by Cattell and Nesselroade (1967)—that individuals may be attracted to others who possess characteristics that they lack themselves. This need-completion view differs from need complementarity in that emphasis is laid not on interaction between subject and potential friend, but on psychological completion. Although these investigators found little evidence for their hypothesis, there are data showing that individuals often perceive their friends as having traits that they admire but lack themselves (Thompson and Nishimura, 1952; see also Bailey *et al.*, 1974, cited p. 97).

In view of such considerations, it is clear that we should not expect to understand most relationships in terms of simple patterns of reciprocity and complementarity. However, studies designed with due respect for the complexities of real-life relationships give hope for progress.

For example Schutz (1960) postulated three types of "compatibility"—originator compatibility, or agreement on who should initiate interactions; interchange compatibility, or agreement over how much interaction should occur; and "reciprocal" compatibility, or compatibility (reciprocal or complementary in the present terminology) between the types of behaviour the partners like to show. Schutz further suggested that these types of compatibility could be found in three categories of need—need for inclusion (i.e. to interact and associate with others), for control, and for affection. He investigated the relation between the three types of compatibility and the three needs in a group of students. The students answered questionnaires measuring their needs within these three categories, and also answered a sociometric questionnaire indicating which three others they would select as room-mates and which three they would select as travelling companions on a long car journey. The nature of compatibility differed between the two role relationships: room-mates showed all three types of compatibility at more than chance level, but travelling companions only reciprocal and originator compatibility. Furthermore, for room-mates affection was most important, whilst for travelling companions control was. Whilst the legitimacy of Schutz's three categories of need, and thus his detailed conclusions, may be questioned, his general conclusion that different types of role relationships require different types of compatibility makes sense (see also Rychlak, 1965). Kerckhoff and Davis (1962) found complementarity on the Schutz scales amongst dating couples to be predictive of permanency in the relationship (see p. 296).

Another study of interest here was designed to assess the effects of personality differences between the individuals concerned (Hendrick and Brown, 1971). Subjects were assessed for introversion-extroversion on the Maudsley Personality Inventory. They were then presented with the answers to the questionnaire of two (bogus) strangers, one answered in a predominantly extraverted and the other in a predominantly introverted way. The subjects were then asked how they thought they would get on with these people in a variety of contexts. The contexts were chosen to cover a number of different role relationships. Extraverts rated the extravert higher as reliable friend, party-goer and leader, but had no preference between extravert and introvert in the role of honest and ethical person. Introverts, however, preferred the extravert as a fellow party-goer and as a leader, but the introvert as a reliable friend and as an honest and ethical person. Thus whether or not the subjects preferred a stranger similar to or unlike themselves on this dimension depended on their own personality and on the context in which they expected to interact with him.

These experimental studies demonstrate that research that attempts to take note of the complexity of real-life relationships, and aimed at finding out "what is important to whom and when", has a lot of promise. We shall meet further examples in Chapter 21.

Weiss (1974) has adopted a rather different approach. Impressed by the loneliness of individuals who were parents without partners, and by the loneliness of a rather different sort experienced by married couples living in a strange neighbourbood, Weiss used his clinical experience to draw up a list of "provisions" or needs which are normally met in relationships with others. His list was:

(1) Attachment, providing a sense of security and place.

(2) Social integration and friendship, providing shared concerns.

(3) Opportunity for nurturance, as when taking care of a child provides a sense of being needed.

(4) Reassurance of worth, provided by relationships which attest to a person's competence.

(5) A sense of reliable alliance, usually provided by kin, and involving a sense of dependable assistance if needed.

(6) Obtaining of guidance, important to individuals in stressful situations.

Weiss conjectured that a satisfactory life organization would make available a set of relationships that would furnish all these provisions. He pointed out that these different provisions may be incompatible to some degree within any one relationship—the assumptions of friendship, for example, may be incompatible with the provision of opportunity for nurturance.

Weiss regarded his list as "a framework for thinking, lightly filled in with observations and conjecture". It has however been used as the basis for an "Interview Schedule for Social Interaction" (Duncan-Jones, in press). Individuals are asked about the relationships from which they obtain attachment, nurturance, etc. and the extent to which they are satisfied. In this instrument "social integration" is divided into acquaintance and friendship, and "obtaining guidance" has been dropped. Opportunity for nurturance has also been dropped as it was found not to fit into any of the mathematical models developed from the data; it is suggested that this was because it is only salient at certain points in the life cycle. Further work along these lines should prove of considerable interest, but much depends on the initial selection of needs.

Thus we must expect relationships, and especially marital relationships, to be built upon complex patterns of needs in the two partners, needs which affect each other and are satisfied in varying ways in reciprocal and complementary interactions inside and outside the relationship. What is important is not reciprocity or complementarity over large areas of the relationship, but compatibility, involving either reciprocity or complementarity, appropriate in nature and direction, in each content area within the relationship (e.g. Murstein, 1967a; review Seyfried, 1977). Furthermore we shall see later that what is important may change as a relationship develops (Chapter 21).

Having recognized the possible complexity of patterns of reciprocity and complementarity, it is important also to remember that there are likely to be limits on the complexity that exists in any one case. Just because each interaction within a relationship affects and is affected by others, complementarity along such dimensions as dominance/subordinance or nurturance/succorance is likely to have at least some generality from one type of interaction to another. As we have seen, dominance/subordinance relations are not confined to the barrack square or the office, but obtrude in interactions off-duty or after hours. The processes by which such spread occurs will limit the complexity of the pattern of dominance/subordinance even in close personal relationships. And in so far as each participant has traits or is believed to have traits consistent from one behavioural context to another, and the other accommodates him or herself to them, complementarity is likely to have *some* degree of consistency across contexts.

We may consider a case in which the role of complementarity has been successfully assessed in a clinical sample. Kreitman and his colleagues (Collins *et al.*, 1971) investigated the relative roles of 120 married couples—60 in which the husbands were neurotic patients and 60 controls. They concentrated on certain family functions—child-rearing, choice of dwelling, financial arrangements, maintenance of social relationships, holidays and entertainments. In studying the roles of husband and wife in these areas they distinguished three levels of activity—executive (what is actually done), executive decision-making (deciding what is to be done), and how responsibility for executive decisions in each area is determined. For example, a husband might actually make the holiday booking, the wife might decide where they should go, and the husband insist that she should make the decision and accept responsibility for it. In this study attention was concentrated on executive decision making. By an interview technique each area was scored in terms of eight categories: five of these referred to degrees of husband or wife domination (the mid-point here being joint decisions), one was used for where husband and wife were divided and acted in opposition, one for "not applicable" and another for not known cases.

The data prompted a division of marriages into those where one partner dominated the other, and those in which neither dominated. The latter were split into those where each partner collaborated cooperatively (cooperative marriages) and those where each partner was more or less equally active, but distinct areas were demarcated for each spouse (segregated marriages). The distribution of the marital types is shown in Table 2.

TABLE 2

Distribution of marital role patterns in patient and control couples. Modified from Collins *et al.* (1971)

	Dominated marriages	
	Husband-dominated* (at least 2 areas mainly the husband's province, and not more than one the wife's)	Wife-dominated* (at least 3 areas mainly the wife's domain, and none the husband's)
Patients	14	10
Controls	6	14
	Non-dominated marriages	
	Cooperative (at least 4 areas scored as joint)	Segregated
Patients	16	20
Controls	29	11

*Husband and wife dominated marriages were defined differently because the areas chosen for examination tend to reflect the wife's activity more than the husband's.

It will be seen that the patient-spouse marriages showed more husband-dominated and segregated marriages than the controls, and fewer cooperative marriages. Joint decision making was less common, the more severe the husband's pathology. The divided role category was found in at least one role area in only 12 of the patient-pairs and 5 of the controls. It tended to involve child-raising more often than any other area.

The authors raise two interesting possibilities. One is that the role pattern of the wife in the neurotic marriages may not be of her own making, and may therefore be conducive to the increasing neurosis which is seen in the wives of neurotics (see p. 93). The other is that the wives' role patterns could serve as a protective device for the wives: perhaps with an irritable and self-absorbed husband it is actually easier for the wife to assume certain roles herself and leave others to the husband, rather than live in continuous strife (see also Ovenstone, 1973).

ACCEPTANCE OF THE PATTERN OF COMPLEMENTARITY BY THE PARTNERS

Kreitman's study raises another important point. It is not only the pattern of reciprocity *vs* complementarity within a relationship that is important, but the extent to which both partners recognize the pattern for what it is and accept it. Dominance between married couples is often measured by questionnaires given to both participants. Thus in Ryle's (1966) marital patterns test members of couples are each asked questions of the type "I cannot win an argument with her" and "She cannot win an argument with me", being required to answer "True", "Untrue" or "Uncertain". On its own such a test provides a measure of how each participant sees this aspect of the relationship, and thus how far they agree, but not of how far their pictures resemble reality, or of how far they accept their perception of the relationship. We shall return to this issue in Chapter 9.

In ordinary life lack of acceptance of the pattern of reciprocity *vs* complementarity may become evident by disqualificatory replies by one partner to the meta-communicational aspects of the other's communications (see pp. 67–8). A related issue arises from Berne's (1967) distinction between three "ego states"—Parent, Adult and Child. These are seen by Berne as coherent sets of feelings, accompanied by appropriate behaviour, potentially present in all individuals. Normally only one takes charge. The ego state that is dominant can be inferred from the current behaviour and feelings, and the terms are self-explanatory. Thus the Child is innocent, spontaneous and fun-loving; the Adult mature and orientated towards reality and the Parent authoritative. The parent state may be either directly active, when the person responds as his own parent did, or indirectly active, when the response is of the type the person's parent would have wanted. Similarly the child may behave as he would have done under parental influence—for instance precociously or compliantly, or the child may involve a spontaneous expression, for instance of rebellion and creativity.

Berne suggests that transactions between two individuals can be analysed according to the ego states involved at the time of the interchange, though these may change from moment to moment. The nature of interactions depends on which ego state of the initiator addressed which ego state of the respondent, and which replied. For instance, if a patient asks for a glass of water, and the nurse brings it, the child of the initiator has addressed the parent of the respondent, and the parent of the respondent has replied. Or if a man says to his friend "It is a nice day", and the friend replies "Yes it is, I was thinking of cutting the lawn", the transaction is adult to adult with adult replying. Berne classifies such transactions, in which the ego state of the respondent addressed by the initiator is the ego state that replies to the initiator, and where that reply goes to the ego state of the initiator that addressed it, as "complementary".* In "complementary" transactions each partner is attempting to cooperate with the other, and the interchange is likely to continue. However the respondent may reply with a different ego state from that addressed, and/or reply to a different ego state from that which initiated the interchange. The remark "Where are my cuff links?" is directed from adult to adult, but the reply "You always blame me for everything" is a child to parent reply. Such transactions Berne describes as "crossed". With crossed transactions, communication is likely to be broken off. The reply disqualifies the claim, latent in the initial remark, for a relationship of a particular type.

Berne introduces a further complication in describing the manner in which transactions can be conducted at two "levels" simultaneously —an overt social level and a covert psychological one. A salesman addressing a customer at an overt adult-adult level may be in reality appealing to the child in him.

This transactional analysis is concerned in the first instance with the course of interactions, but Berne has applied it also to the course of long-term relationships. For instance he describes a married couple in which the husband was dominant and forbade the wife certain activities in which she was actually afraid to indulge. At the overt social level the husband's parent was addressing the wife's child, but at a covert psychological level the transaction was between the wife's child and the husband's child, the husband's dominance being a cover for his

---

*This terminology is of course different from that used elsewhere in this book. "Complementary" in Berne's sense has therefore been placed in quotation marks.

own insecurity. Berne describes this as a "game", and has developed a
taxonomy of "Games people play".

Berne's model of the three ego states is to be regarded as an "as if"
model, which provides a convenient way of describing interactions and
the rituals, games and so on built up from them. His taxonomy of
games is not to be taken too seriously, though it provides a useful
way for conceptualizing the multiple levels at which relationships
operate.

Conclusion and summary

This chapter started with the observation that relationships differ in
the extent to which the component interactions are reciprocal or complementary. The pattern of reciprocity *vs* complementarity may be
dictated by the nature of the relationship; in formal relationships, such
as those between employer and employee or between nurse and patient,
who bosses whom or who behaves nurturantly to whom is inherent in
the nature of the relationship. Nevertheless understanding of the pattern of reciprocity *vs* complementarity in such relationships will be
essential if we are to come to terms with their dynamics.

Close personal relationships may involve complex patterns of reciprocity *vs* complementarity, with idiosyncratic patterns of imbalance.
The pattern in any one relationship, though influenced by cultural
norms, is worked out by the participants. The pattern which emerges
will depend in part on the characteristics of the partners, and in part on
how they perceive and accommodate to each other.

There is considerable evidence that spouses and friends are likely to
resemble each other in a variety of sociological and psychological
characteristics. Furthermore attitude similarity, and to a lesser degree
similarity in personality, may be conducive to interpersonal attraction.
A number of suggestions as to why this should be so have been made.
Those likely to have the widest applicability are that perceived similarity is associated with consensual validation, that it facilitates communication, and that it leads to positive beliefs, perhaps in holding
promise of rewarding interaction in contexts demanding reciprocity.

Differences can also contribute to the building of interpersonal relationships. They may be important in involving complementary needs,
the two partners thereby satisfying each other, or (and here the evi-

dence is much less substantial) because each partner sees the other as completing his own personality.

However the suppositions, prevalent in the earlier literature, that either overall similarity or difference along one or more dimensions, assessed in tests outside the relationship, is of major importance for friendship choice or for the development of a personal relationship is an over-simplification. There are several reasons for this. First, similarities of some sorts do not contribute to interpersonal attraction in any of the above ways, and may even have the opposite effect. Some types of interaction require similarity and reciprocity, others difference of a complementary sort. Incompatibility between partners can involve the lack of opportunity either to do things together as equals, or to behave in a nurturant, succorant, dominant or some other complementary fashion. We shall also see later (Chapter 21) that similarities and differences of different sorts may be primarily important at different stages in the development of a relationship.

Second, needs as assessed in standard non-interactive tests have a variable relevance to real-life situations. And third, but related to this, in the dynamic interchanges of a real-life relationship there are considerable opportunities for the partners to accommodate to each other's needs, or to satisfy some needs elsewhere.

The conclusion that the issues are complex is of course banal. It certainly fails to do justice to the considerable skilful experimental work in this area. It is important to remember that much of that work, and especially that on the effects of similarity on interpersonal attraction, was carried out as part of a deliberate policy of isolating variables and determining their effects. The experimenters were of course well aware that the information acquired in a laboratory experiment on attraction differs from that which would be acquired in a natural meeting, and that it is acquired in the absence of any natural context, often without possibilities for interaction (see e.g. Byrne, 1971; Clore and Byrne, 1974; reviews by Huston, 1974; Duck, 1977a). Indeed attempts have been made to explore the effects of such complexities systematically. However it is an always present possibility that this basically sound scientific procedure *can* lead to a neglect of interactions between variables, and to a belief that a variable important (or unimportant) in one context is ubiquitously so. There is thus also a need for studying real-life interaction, and especially real-life long-term relationships, in spite of their complexities. It would seem that adequate methodologies are now beginning to emerge, and there is considerable hope that a marriage between experimental and observational techniques will be even more fertile in the future.

Two other issues are implicit in the preceding discussion. The first is the importance not only of what the participants in a relationship do together, but of what they need or want to do or be. This includes not only needs to receive specific rewards, but also needs to see themselves or to be seen as persons of particular types (Kelley, 1979). The extent to which those needs or wants are satisfied is of course a crucial determinant of the future course of the relationship. The problems involved in the assessment of individual behavioural characteristics, attitudes, needs, etc. and the extent to which they are context dependent, is beyond the scope of this book and will not be discussed further. But the second point is related to it—the extent to which the relationship works is going to depend in part on how accurately the partners attribute characteristics to each other, and how far they can reconcile their needs and provide satisfaction each to the other. These in turn will depend on how well they know each other. This forms the starting point of the next two chapters.

8

Intimacy

Whilst discussing what the participants in a relationship do together, and how they do it, we were mostly concerned with the interactions within a relationship seen as separate units by an external observer. In considering the frequency and patterning of interactions, and the pattern of reciprocity *vs* complementarity, the focus was not on the individual interactions, but on the relations between the parts within the whole sequence of interactions. Already a number of non-behavioural concepts, such as expectations and social norms, have been invoked. In the next three chapters we shall pursue these paths even further. In considering intimacy, interpersonal perception and commitment we shall be concerned even more with properties of the relationship as a whole, and we shall focus primarily on affective/cognitive aspects.

The issues that we shall discuss here are not equally important in all relationships. For some formal relationships they would be irrelevant, for some personal relationships crucial. Although there are of course all intergradations among the latter, the extremes of the continuum are emphasized by Kurth's (1970) distinction between "friendly relations", referring to an uncommitted pleasant association derived from role-governed interactions, and "friendship" as an intimate personal relationship involving each individual as a total person. Perhaps even more pertinent is Bernard's (1964) distinction between two general patterns of husband-wife relationships. In the "parallel" pattern, the wife's satisfaction is assessed by the extent to which the man is a good provider, sober, kind to the children, and so on, and the husband's by the extent to which the woman is a good housekeeper, cook, sexual partner and mother: beyond that, each lives his or her own life in a primarily male or female world. In other words, the marriage is defined primarily in terms of the socially prescribed content of the interactions between the partners. By contrast, in the pattern described by Bernard as "interactional", though he uses that term in a sense different from that in this book, much more is demanded; companionship and recognition of personality are regarded as essential characteristics of a happy marriage. Such couples are more sensitive to the individual personality of the spouse, as distinct from the extent to which the functions of a spouse are fulfilled.

Whilst this distinction between relationships differing in "depth" is commonplace, "depth" is often treated as a unitary variable (see e.g. Levinger cited in Chapter 21). But introspection alone is sufficient to show that a number of different aspects of relationships contribute to judgements of "depth". Here we shall consider these in three categories—intimacy, interpersonal perception and commitment.

Intimacy

The extent to which the participants in a relationship are prepared to reveal all aspects of themselves, experiential, emotional and physical, to each other is a crucial dimension of many relationships. At the behavioural level, it may determine what interactions are possible. Thus in relationships with a potentially sexual component, physical intimacy demands a willingness for some degree of self-revelation. More generally important is the extent to which the participants reveal all aspects of their history, aspirations and desires, strengths and weaknesses to each other. Through these each may build up a knowledge of the other as a total person—knowledge which will extend far beyond the interactions between them and with the potential for affecting the quality of those interactions in a fundamental way.

Intimacy, or degree of self-disclosure, is not an easy thing to measure, but a number of techniques have been developed. Jourard, in a number of pioneering studies (e.g. 1971), has used a Self-Disclosure Questionnaire containing 60 questions in each of six content areas—attitudes and opinions, tastes and interests, work, money, personality and body. Subjects were asked to respond by indicating on a three-point scale to what extent each type of information had been revealed to father, mother, same sex best friend and opposite sex best friend.

The primary aim of such an instrument is to characterize individuals along a scale from "disclosers" to "non-disclosers". It is perhaps not surprising that it does not accurately predict self-disclosure to strangers in an experimental situation—intimacy depends on the relationship and on the context. It is, of course, possible to improve the instrument's predictive value for a particular relationship and context by asking subjects what they would be willing to reveal in that context.

Of more interest here is a method used by Altman and Taylor (1973) to assess the self-disclosure that has occurred in specific situations. Their approach is based on a picture of the personality as the "systematic organization of the individual's ideas, beliefs, feelings and emotions". This organization involves the arrangement of items into areas such as sex, family or work. For heuristic purposes, they find it convenient to picture the personality as an onion, composed of successive layers of skins. The above areas are defined on the surface, where relatively superficial items, such as specific biographical facts, are located (Fig. 1). The inner layers contain progressively fewer more

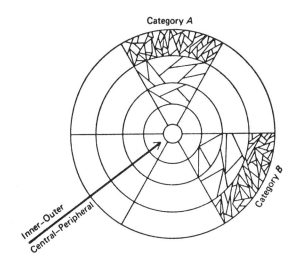

Fig. 1. Altman and Taylor's (1973) analogue of personality structure. Categories A and B refer to topical or substantive areas of personality at each of several levels.

fundamental items, involving "basic core feelings about life, trust in others, and the nature of one's self-image" (p. 17) (see also Levinger and Snoek, 1972). These more central areas may affect numerous peripheral areas, but they are more vulnerable than the external layers and less accessible to others. Such a view is in harmony with the models of personality structure suggested by a number of other theorists (e.g. Lewin, 1964; Polansky et al., 1961).

Intimacy between two individuals can thus be assessed in terms of breadth—that is, how many of the other's surface areas each contacts—and depth, how far penetration proceeds. As a relationship develops, each individual exposes more areas to the other, and penetration in each area becomes deeper. To pursue the onion analogy, as a relationship grows, many wedges are cut into the onion, each becoming wider and deeper.

To assess degree of intimacy in a quantitative way, Altman and Taylor collected 671 items relevant to self-disclosure, either by taking them from existing tests or by inventing them intuitively. These items were rated by one group of judges for intimacy, while another classed them into a priori topical categories. Thirteen categories were identified, including "own marriage", "family", "Love-dating-sex", "Relationships with others" and so on. Each item acquired an intimacy scale rating from one to eleven based on the judge's ratings.

On this basis, two aspects of breadth could be measured. Breadth category was simply the number of categories (out of 13) the individual revealed about himself. Breadth frequency was measured either by the total number of items revealed, or by the number per category. Various temporal measures, such as "total time talked per category", were also possible. Measures of intimacy were obtained from the intimacy scale values of the statements used in interaction—for instance, their overall mean value, or the average value for a previously chosen list of items, according to the problem in hand. Of course, the scaling of the items in such an instrument is liable to change with time and to differ between sub-cultural groups. It must thus be used with caution.

Using techniques of this general sort, it has been possible to document the manner in which intimacy between college room-mates (Taylor, 1968), or between sailors confined together for 10 days (Altman and Haythorn, 1965), increases with time. In experimental situations it has been possible to show, for instance, that social approval contingent upon self-exposure augments further intimacy (Taylor et al., 1969).

Such relatively objective methods for determining degree of intimacy are important because members of established couples may perceive intimacy to be greater than is actually the case. In a study of the disclosure between husbands and wives, Levinger and Senn (1967) found high correlations between perceived disclosures given and received, but much lower correlations between independent measures of each partner's disclosure to the other. It seemed that each partner tends to overestimate the degree of reciprocity in the relationship.

Social norms (see p. 32) may be crucial in determining the level of intimacy appropriate in a relationship. There is good reason for this if continuity (see p. 154) in the relationship is necessary for social reasons, for matters likely to be disruptive to the relationship may thereby be avoided. While we can agree to disagree with others on issues that seem to us minor, we often find it difficult to get on with people with whom we disagree on major issues. So when we have to get on with others with whom we might disagree on important issues, it is perhaps better to avoid controversial topics such as religion or politics and to use "polite conversation" which implicitly acknowledges the relationship but avoids those topics on which disagreement might be disruptive. The assumption often seems to be that if you have to be colleagues or neighbours or acquaintances, or have to eat together in the same college, it may be better not to know each other's opinions in case disagreement on issues not relevant to the context of the relationship should be a cause of friction.

In such a case, a move towards greater intimacy would be met by withdrawal. More usually, however, intimacy breeds intimacy—a matter to be discussed in Chapter 20. Which happens depends, as might be expected, on the content and on the meaning ascribed to the move towards intimacy by the individuals involved.

Intimacy is always limited. Even in the most intimate relationships, there is likely to be something that is held back (cf. Goffman, 1959). This may be because disclosure would bring costs to the discloser—perhaps secret desires that would only bring hurt if shared—or because disclosure would offend the partner, such as private opinions about a mother-in-law. Or it may be that areas of privacy have a special value of their own (see p. 302).

Studies of physical intimacy, as indicated by physical proximity, contact etc. run into a similar issue. Some studies suggest that changes in physical intimacy elicit compensatory responses, such that a preferred level of overall "intimacy" is maintained. For instance, increased proximity may lead to decreased eye contact (Argyle and Dean, 1965). Other studies indicate the opposite—for instance, touching by a confederate elicited increased self-disclosures from a subject (Jourard and Friedman, 1970). Patterson (1976) suggests that such apparently contradictory findings can be reconciled on the supposition that changes in perceived intimacy produce changes in arousal levels, which may be evaluated as positive or negative emotional states. Negative emotional states then produce compensatory behaviour tending to restore the initial level of intimacy, whilst positive emotional states produce reciprocal behaviour leading to greater intimacy. (That the concept of arousal is used uncritically here, and seems redundant, does not affect the general argument.)

In this chapter some factors influencing the degree of self-disclosure in a relationship have been mentioned. (For others see the discussion on pp. 301–3). Because of the diversity of factors affecting intimacy, Altman and Taylor (1973) quite rightly emphasize the need to study such factors as privacy, the length of time people are together, and opportunity to leave the situation "as determinants of the social penetration process". At the same time, however, this reveals a basic weakness in their position—the implication that intimacy is the sole issue involved in the depth of a relationship. This would be a very narrow view. An extreme case is the confidante—someone with whom a person is very intimate, but with whom he may never interact in other ways. If interactions with a confidante do occur in other contexts, such interactions may yet proceed awkwardly in spite of (as well as, perhaps, because of) the intimacies exchanged.

Summary

Some methods for assessing the intimacy of a relationship are discussed.

The degree of intimacy in a relationship may be overestimated by the participants. There are limits to intimacy in any relationship, some of which are set by social norms.

9

Interpersonal Perception

This chapter is concerned with the relations between the views held by the participants in a relationship about themselves, about each other, and also about objects and people outside their relationship. We shall ask, for instance, whether A sees B as the sort of person B sees himself as (i.e. does A understand B?), and whether B feels that A sees him as he "really is"—that is, whether B feels that A sees B as B sees B (does B feel that A understands him?). Such issues are also closely related to the question of "satisfaction"—is A's view of B close to A's view of his ideal partner in the relationship in question?

The way in which each partner in a relationship sees the other is important in a very fundamental way. Mead (1934) and Cooley (1956) have argued that our view of ourselves can develop only from the way in which others behave to us. We can evaluate ourselves only through the ways in which we perceive others to respond to us. Each individual's perceptions of other people's views of him are incorporated into his view of himself. Thus what we are depends on the views about us held by our partners in the relationships in which we have participated—and presumably most especially on the views of the members of our family of origin and of others with whom we have had important relationships (see also Laing, 1962). There is a real sense in which we are those we love and have loved. We have already mentioned the possibility that rejection or disconfirmation by a partner of the self we believe we are may have dire consequences.

Beyond this the extent to which partners agree about the external world, and the extent to which each sees the other as he is, or as he sees himself, may have many effects on their relationship. At the lowest level, behavioural meshing (see pp. 62–3) would not be possible unless each partner's views of the other were reasonably close to reality. Their feelings about each other may affect and be affected by the extent to which they agree about the rest of the world (Chapters 7 and 14). And if B believes that A's view of him is different from his (B's) own view of himself, he (B) will feel misunderstood. Thus various aspects of interpersonal perception may be of vital importance for the dynamics of a relationship.

Misperceiving others

There are in fact many reasons why we may perceive others incorrectly. At a global level, our own notions about how people function, our so-called "implicit personality theories", may blind us to the way in which individuals actually behave (Bruner and Tagiuri, 1954). An example from a study of nursery school children was salutary to the author. As discussed previously, the older views that children mature through stages of predominantly self play and parallel play to showing predominantly group and interactive play, and that a given group of children can be ranged along a dimension of social maturity according to how much of each type they show, was not borne out by a principle components analysis of observational data. Yet in answering a questionnaire containing items concerned with the children's social behaviour not only the teachers but also the observers (who had not yet analysed their data) answered as though the children could be arranged along such a dimension. For instance children who were noticed often to engage in group or interactive play were scored as seldom showing self play, when later examination of the observational data showed that that had not necessarily been the case. The present author was one of the observers (Roper and Hinde, in press)

At another level, we may misperceive others because we see them as concealing their "true" attitudes, dissembling, or constrained by social pressures, attempts to please us and the like (e.g. Mettee and Aronson, 1974; Stroebe, 1977). Important as such issues are, we shall not pursue them here.

Of more interest in the present context is the possibility that individuals misperceive others unwittingly without intending to do so. One example has already been mentioned—each member of a couple may see the other as revealing more intimate details of himself than is actually the case. As another example, Byrne and Blaylock (1963) obtained ratings for husbands and wives on a scale for dogmatism, and also assessed each partner's view of the other on the same scale. The results showed that each saw the other as more like him or herself than the other really was. Similarly Murstein (1967a), studying a sample of

99 University couples (engaged or going steady), found that the self-perceptions of the two members of each dyad were not significantly more similar than those of randomly selected couples. However the subjects perceived more homogamy than was the case when the separate perceptions were examined. And in a later study of dating couples Murstein (1967a, 1971a) found that there tended to be more similarity between an individual's perception of his (or her) partner and his ideal spouse than there was between the ideal spouse and the partner's perception of herself (or himself). Such misperceptions are important for the progress or stability of the relationship (Murstein, 1971c), Levinger and Breedlove (1966) found that spouses who scored high on a marital satisfaction index tended to overestimate their similarity, while spouses who scored low tended to underestimate it. The relations between interpersonal perception and interpersonal attraction are considered in Chapter 14.

Assessing interpersonal perception

It is difficult enough to find out how A behaves in his relationship with B, and it might seem even more difficult to assess reliably what A thinks about B, and what B thinks A thinks about B. At this point it may be useful to review a few of the methods available. A more extensive review, concerned also with other aspects of interpersonal relationships, is provided by Cromwell et al. (1976).

One group of methods involves self-reports in an imposed situation which are subjected to projective interpretation by a therapist. For instance a couple may be given a conjoint thematic apperception test, and the resulting stories then diagnosed. Such methods will not be considered further here.

Of more interest are methods in which each member of the dyad answers a questionnaire and the responses to the test items are taken at their face value and used as data. Objective scoring is thus possible. A number of instruments have been standardized, e.g. the Interpersonal Checklist, Marital Communications Checklist, Family Relationships Inventory, etc. (references in Cromwell et al., 1976).

The most interesting data have been obtained when individuals are asked to fill in a questionnaire from more than one stance. In an early example of this approach, Dymond (1954) asked each partner from 15 married couples to answer a true-false questionnaire made up of 115 items from the Minnesota Multiphasic Personality Inventory. Each individual was then asked to fill out another copy as he or she predicted his or her spouse would complete it. Thus each item was answered as True or False four times, as indicated in Table 1. Since predictions

TABLE 1

Hypothetical set of answers to MMPI items used in assessing interpersonal perception and marital happiness (from Dymond, 1954)

	Items	1	2	3	4	5
(1)	Husband's answer	T	T	F	T	F
(2)	Husband's prediction of wife's answer	T	F	F	T	T
(3)	Wife's own answer	F	T	F	T	T
(4)	Wife's prediction of husband's answer	T	T	T	F	F

could reflect the ability to predict not the answer of the spouse but those of most of the subjects' acquaintances, all items marked similarly True or False by more than 66% of the group were dropped. From these answers, scores were obtained for *similarity* by comparing rows 1 and 3 (3 out of 5 in the Table); for *understanding* by comparing rows 2 and 3 or 1 and 4 (3 out of 5); and for *assumed similarity* by comparing rows 1 and 2 and rows 3 and 4 (3 out of 5 and 1 out of 5 respectively). The couples were divided into happy and unhappy ones—in part on their own assessment and in part on that of the experimenter. The data indicated that the happy couples had more understanding of each other, and were more like each other in their self-descriptions, than the unhappy ones. There was no indication that assumed similarity was related to happiness, but there was a difference between unhappy and happy couples in the sort of errors made. Unhappy spouses tended to assume the spouse to be similar when he or she was not, rather than assuming differences where none apparently existed. With happy spouses the two types of error were more or less equally frequent. These results were based on a small sample, and later studies do suggest that assumed similarity is related to happiness (see p. 124). However this provides an example of the method.

As another example, we may consider Drewery's (1969) interpersonal perception technique. This is based on a standardized instrument for assessing personality traits, the Edwards Personal Preferences Schedule, designed to measure 15 traits by a questionnaire method. The subject is presented with 255 paired statements, and required to select one from each pair. The two statements in each pair are equated for social desirability, but concern different traits. The pairings are such that a statement about each trait is combined with one about each other in two pairings. Thus if the statements concerning a particular trait were selected every time, that trait could score a maximum of 28 points, and no other traits could score more than 26. When used for studying a dyadic relationship, say that of a married couple, each member answers the schedule three times—on one occasion describing her or himself, on another describing the spouse, and on yet another describing how she (or he) believes the spouse perceives her (or him). Thus the pair completes six schedules in all, as indicated by the letters in Table 2(a).

TABLE 2

Drewery's use of the Edwards Personal Preference Schedule. (a) The six schedules. (b) The correlations used by Drewery and Rae. (See text)

Husband's protocol	Respondent asked to describe	Wife's protocol
A	Myself as I am	B
A_1	My spouse as I see him/her	B_1
A_2	Myself as I think my spouse sees me	B_2

(a)

Husband's expectations	Wife's expectations
$B\ vs\ A_1$	$A\ vs\ B_1$
$B_1\ vs\ A_2$	$A_1\ vs\ B_2$
$A\ vs\ A_2$	$B\ vs\ B_2$

$A\ vs\ B$

(b)

A number of comparisons between these protocols can be made. Thus Drewery and Rae (1969) calculated seven correlation coefficients for each couple, as shown in Table 2(b). The size of these coefficients indicate, for example, whether the husband sees himself as the wife sees him (A-B_1), or whether the wife sees herself as she thinks her spouse sees her (B-B_2). In a comparison of marriages having an alcoholic member with non-psychiatric marriages Drewery and Rae (1969) found that the correlations for patients were consistently, and usually significantly, lower than those for the controls. For example, the correlation for A vs B_1 was 0·26 for controls and −0·32 for patients. Normal men's views of their wives accorded only poorly with their self-descriptions (A_1 vs B, $r = 0·48$), but the wives did rather better (B_1 vs A, $r = 0·64$). Another finding concerned the socio-sexual roles of the partners. Spouses in the non-psychiatric marriages shared a clear concept of masculinity, but partners in the alcoholic marriages tended to lack this consensus, showing a conflictful interplay of dependence and independence needs. How far the quantitative side of such questionnaires can be pushed is an open issue, for there may be problems concerning the degree of independence between the items. But it is clear that the method has a degree of validity.

Using a basically similar approach, Laing (1969; Laing *et al*., 1966) has tackled further complexities. It is necessary to say a few words about his system. Laing explicitly emphasizes how relationships are experienced by the people involved. He thus uses the term "relationship" in a rather different sense from that used elsewhere in this book. For a dyadic relationship (in our sense) between A and B, Laing distinguishes between A's relationship with B and B's relationship with A. Both A and B will have views of each of these. Furthermore, A has views about his (or her) relationship with himself (or herself), and about B's relationship with himself (or herself), and similarly for B. Thus at the level of Direct perspective there are 8 possibilities, A's views of A's relationship with A, of B's relationship with B, of A's relationship with B and of B's relationship with A, and similarly for B.

Now A will also have a view on, for instance, B's view of A's relationship with A, etc. This is the level of meta-perspective. For example, I may feel disappointed with myself for giving a poor lecture. If one of my colleagues knows that I am disappointed with myself, that is meta-perspective. But beyond that, I may know that my colleague knows that I am disappointed with myself; that is the level of meta-meta-perspective. It will be apparent that, for each of the four possible views of A at the level of direct perspective, B may have a view at the level of meta-perspective. For each of those A may have a view at the level of meta-metaperspective.

Laing has used this sort of analysis of "interpersonal perception" to examine the extent to which:

1 The two participants agree at the direct level (e.g. does A's view of the relationship (AB) agree with B's view of (AB)).
2 They are aware of and understand the other's point of view (e.g. does A's view of B's view of (AB) correspond with B's view of (AB)).
3 They feel understood (e.g. does A's view of B's view of A's view of himself (AA) agree with A's view of himself).
4 Each realizes that the other understands him (e.g. does A's view of B's view of A's view of himself correspond with B's view of A's view of himself).

This leads to a number of possibilities. For example A and B agree about, let us say, A's relationship with B at the direct level. But while A may understand B's view of A's relationship with B, B may not understand A's. And if A does understand B's view of A's relationship with B, B may or may not realize that he does.

Whether the level of meta-metaperspective is useful clinically is an open issue. Laing has attempted to evaluate agreement, understanding and realization of understanding in six areas of interpersonal perception—it will be apparent that this is a not inconsiderable task. However it is claimed that this sort of analysis is useful for localizing the trouble spots in intimate relationships. Alperson (1975) has shown that Boolean algebra can provide a rigorous language for interpreting this and other comparable tests.

We may now consider the question of the extent to which the partners feel satisfied with the relationship. A number of attempts have been made to assess the relation between each partner's hopes or expectations about various aspects of the relationship, and how he actually sees it. For example Tharp (1963b) developed a Marriage Role Questionnaire aimed at assessing the discrepancy between an individual's expectations about his role in a relationship, and his perception of that role. Half of the questions concerned expectations about marriage, and the other half the extent to which the subject saw those expectations as fulfilled in his own marriage. By a mixture of factor analysis and common sense the data were reduced to five clusters—Internal Instrumentality, Division of Responsibilities, Solidarity, External Relations and Sexuality. The Questionnaire was found to discriminate between a group of psychiatric out-patients and their

spouses and a group of married college students. However later data
suggest that this type of approach is less sensitive than a questionnaire
aimed at assessing the degree of satisfaction with the emotional relationship, perhaps because it focusses on the content rather than the
affect of the relationship (Quick and Jacob, 1973).

Murstein (1972a) used an even more elaborate technique. College
pre-marital couples received 76 questions in a "Marital expectation
test". Each subject answered the questions under eight different "sets",
distinguished by the object of perception—self, ideal self, ideal spouse,
boy (girl) friend, how boy (girl) friend sees you, how boy (girl) friend
sees his (her) ideal spouse, how boy (girl) friend sees him (her) self, and
how boy (girl) friend sees his (her) ideal self. Murstein predicted that the
couples whose courtship made progress would be those who earlier had
confirmed their partner's self and ideal self-concepts, and also had accurately predicted them. The hypotheses were essentially confirmed, though
it seemed as though the men were more important as perceptual targets
than the women (see also Murstein 1971c; Tharp, 1963a; Barry, 1970).

Several studies (reviewed Chadwick *et al.*, 1976) show that the extent
to which the partner is seen to fill the desired marital role is a usual
correlate of marital satisfaction later on. These authors regard the
frequent finding of a correlation between marital happiness and social
status as a special case of this, for a high status husband is more likely to
be seen as successful in an instrumental role. In their own questionnaire study Chadwick *et al.* found that agreement about marital roles
and the performance of those roles were the most significant correlates
of perceived willingness to marry the same spouse again.

Personal construct analysis

In Chapter 7 we saw how the technique of personal construct analysis
could be used to assess the importance for friendship of similarity in the
ways in which individuals see the world. The technique can also be
used to assess how individuals perceive their relationships.

First, we may consider a study which provides evidence that the
nature of an individual's construct system may be predictive not of the
formation of particular friendships, but of social adjustment in general.
Hayden *et al.* (1977) studied 30 emotionally disturbed boys. To obtain a
grid, the experimenters used 10 photographs of an 8 year old boy doing

a difficult task. Each child was first shown three of these photographs, and asked to say in which two the child was thinking and feeling most similarly. The child was then asked to explain how the thoughts and feelings of the child in the third picture differed from those in the other two. Ten triads were used in this way to elicit the constructs, repeated constructs not being permitted. The subject was then required to rate each photo on each construct on a seven-point scale. The complexity of the subject's construct system was assessed from the variance explained by the first factor in a principle component analysis, large variance implying a simple construct system. The number of the rating points used by the subject provided a measure of the differentiation capacity of the constructs. The social adjustments of the boys was assessed from ratings of specified aspects of their behaviour by members of the hospital staff. Their capacity to predict social behaviour was assessed from their ability, in a subsequent test, to arrange the photographs in their correct sequential order. It was found that the behavioural assessments were significantly related to the complexity and differentiation of the construct systems of the subjects, and with their accuracy in arranging the figures. The data thus provide some support for the view that social adjustment is related to the nature of the subject's construct system and to his power of prediction in social situations.

Of special interest in the current context are repertory grids in which the elements are relationships between individuals. For example, Ryle and Breen (1972) studied heterosexual couples, some of whom were known by independent criteria to be maladjusted. Lists containing a number of constructs (e.g. Is affectionate to, Is submissive to, Is dependent upon) were made up, some being supplied by the experimenter and others elicited from the subjects. The experimenters, in consultation with the subjects, also selected a set of dyads of importance to the subject—e.g. self to partner, self to father, father to mother. Each member of each dyad was then presented with two grids, the constructs being arranged along one edge and the dyads along another. They were asked to rate each relationship for each construct on a seven-point scale, first according to their own views, and second as they predicted that their partner would do it. The construct space provided by the first two factors from a principle components analysis of the resulting scores was then plotted. The closeness of two elements (dyads) in the construct space then implies perception of role similarity. When two lines joining a dyad are parallel, this represents a similar role relationship. The data showed that the maladjusted couples were more likely to see their relationship with their partner as like their relationship with a parent, and their own role as like that of a child, than were the controls; and that when the relationship was going badly they perceived their own role as more child-like, while that of their partner became less parent-like (see also Ryle and Lunghi, 1970).

A related example is provided by Ryle and Lipshitz's (1975, 1976) use of a "reconstruction grid" to plot the course of marital therapy. A list of 18 constructs describing behaviour of one partner to the other and 15 describing feeling towards or about the other was presented to the couple. The couple were asked to rate these 33 constructs on 11 occasions, giving each item two scores, one representing the relationship of husband to wife and the other that of wife to husband. The resulting 33×22 grid was then subjected to a form of principle components analysis. The progress of the therapy could be seen by plotting every second (to save congestion) occasion on a plot of the two principle dimensions to emerge. Figure 1 shows the successive positions that the couple occupied.

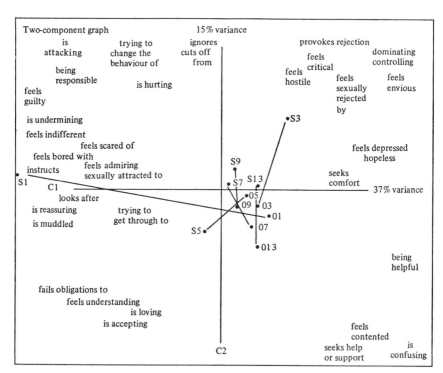

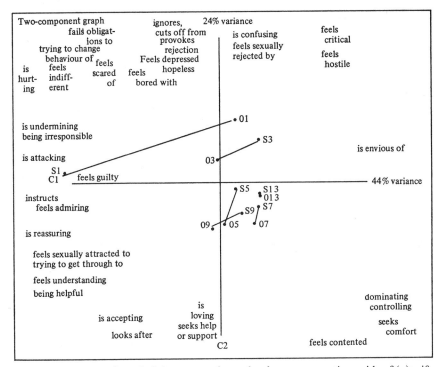

Fig. 1. The course of marital therapy as shown by the reconstruction grids of (a) wife and (b) husband in terms of the first two components. Every second occasion is recorded. S is self-to-other; O is other-to-self. (From Ryle and Lipshitz, 1975.)

In the wife's reconstruction grid . . . it is seen that she-to-him moved initially from being extremely, but ambivalently, negative (bored, indifferent, scared of, but also reassuring and respecting) to being rejected, rejection-provoking, dominating and hostile on the third occasion. Thereafter she moved towards the seeking comfort and reassurance and being contented and accepting area. She saw less change in him-to-her than in herself-to-him, locating him in the more accepting, helpful and confusing quadrant throughout. The husband's reconstruction grid followed a similar pattern in that he saw himself as moving from an ambivalently attacking and undermining position though being hostile, anxious, depressed and critical to a final position in which self-to-other and other-to-self are both in the contented but also dominating quadrant. By the end of therapy, therefore, they agree in seeing their relationship as much more similar than had been the case before treatment (Ryle and Lipshitz, 1975, p. 42).

Conclusion and summary

Finally, it must be stressed that the issues discussed in this chapter will matter to very different extents to different individuals and in different relationships. It may be very important that a doctor sees a patient as he "really" is, and even that a doctor should see the patient's view of himself correctly. But it may not matter whether the patient sees the doctor as he really is, or as he sees himself.

Our beliefs about how others see us, and their relation to how we see ourselves, are crucial to our integrity as people. The relations between how the partners in a relationship see each other and see themselves will have an important influence on the course of their relationship.

Some methods for assessing various aspects of interpersonal perception and satisfaction are described.

10

Commitment

One of the most important aspects of some relationships, but the one least studied, concerns the extent to which the participants are committed to it. Although the seeds of commitment can be seen in relatively trivial relationships, as in loyalty to a particular bank cashier, it becomes of special importance in relationships in which the participants see themselves as a dyad, differentiated from other dyads. Lovers and married couples provide the most obvious, but by no means the only, examples.

Before commitment can be adequately studied some analysis of what the concept implies will clearly be necessary. The situation may be compared with that of love discussed on p. 42, and even more appropriately with that described by Coke Brown (cited Harré and Secord, 1972) for the concept of "involvement". Brown demonstrated that "involvement" is used in different ways in different studies, and even within particular studies, and that this has hindered the course of research. In general, Brown listed twelve reasons for identifying an individual as involved (Harré and Secord, 1972, p. 301):

> We are more likely to describe an individual as being involved and we are more likely to describe one individual as being more involved than another if that individual: (1) takes direct action in regard to the topic or object; (2) presently spends or devotes a large amount of time to the object or issue; (3) is knowledgeable concerning the topic; (4) has maintained an interest in the topic over a long span of time; (5) is not easily distracted from the topic when discussing it; (6) says that others should be interested in the topic and downgrades those who are not interested or who do not agree with his position; (7) expresses strong emotion or concern when discussing the topic; (8) reacts strongly or changes his behaviour dramatically at critical periods of success or failure (i.e. is despondent when his candidate loses); (9) maintains his position against strong opposition; (10) has a well-defined position on the topic; (11) is a member of one or more groups which are concerned with the issue; or (12) relates the topic or his position on the topic to a large portion of his life space.

Several of Brown's points about "involvement" are relevant also for "commitment" (e.g. 1–5, 7, 9, 12), and it is clear that a comparable analysis for "commitment" will be essential for its further study.

Lacking such an analysis, the term commitment is used here in a general sense to refer to situations in which one or both parties either accept their relationship as continuing indefinitely or direct their behaviour towards ensuring its continuance or towards optimizing its properties. This immediately raises two points. First, commitment is concerned with the course of a relationship over time, and we must dissociate two aspects of the relationship (see also Chapter 12)—first its content and quality; and second its continuity, implying continuing interaction of unspecified content. The relative importance of these differs with the nature of the relationship. In many formal relationships, and in less intimate personal relationships, continuity may be assumed to imply consistency in content and vice versa. So long as I go to the same doctor, we shall have a doctor/patient relationship, though this does not absolutely preclude our relationship developing in other ways. I should feel entitled to an explanation if he suddenly refused to treat me, and if I suddenly went elsewhere he would feel the same. However commitment to continuity may also be conditional upon change in content, as when a lover continues to woo only so long as he sees his courtship is progressing. And in intimate personal relationships the emphasis may be on continuity, no matter how the content may change. Even Ruth's promise to Naomi—"Where thou goest, I will go . . ." involved a willingness to change with her, and even to share her grave.

Second, it is useful to distinguish exogenous commitment, where continuity (and often also content) is imposed from outside, from endogenous commitment, where it is sought from within. Exogenous commitment may be part of the *a priori* definition of the relationship: blood relatives and, in some societies, the partners to arranged marriages must remain such throughout their lives, though the content of their relationship may change to a degree that is largely culturally determined. Endogenous commitment may of course lead to exogenous commitment, as when courtship leads to binding ties supported by public sanctions; and exogenous commitment to continuity may lead to endogenous commitment to consistency.

Commitment may have diverse effects depending on its nature and the other properties of the relationship. If continuity is assured, the parties may accept the costs of the relationship yet strive to optimize its mutual rewards; or they may cease to do so, perhaps feeling that it "needn't be worked at". Commitment is of course especially important when it is endogenous and continuity is desired but not assured. Here the relationship as a whole becomes a goal, with the outcomes of interactions subgoals to that end. One aim must be to ensure adequate rewards for the partner in case other relationships should appear more attractive; this may transcend short-term personal satisfaction (see p. 215).

Of course commitment is not limited to positive relationships. It is possible to be committed, endogenously or exogenously, to a relationship with a rival or enemy, with dedication to his undoing. Even relationships that are on the whole positive may, by virtue of their continuity, have elements of this. Such a tendency can be seen, for instance, in sibling rivalry.

Whilst personal commitment by a participant in a relationship reflects, and if acknowledged determines, many aspects of his behaviour, of even greater importance in close personal relationships is faith in the partner's commitment. First, expectation of continuity is essential if each partner is to provide rewards now in the hope that they will be reciprocated in the future (see pp. 221–2). Second, self-revelation involves exposing oneself to hurt, so progress towards greater intimacy depends on confidence in the partner. Faith in the partner's commitment brings belief that he (or she) would not exploit opportunities for harm, in part because to do so would weaken the viability of the relationship that he (or she) also wishes to preserve. And third, an individual's personal growth is likely to involve some change in the relationships most important to him (or her); faith in the partner's commitment to the relationship's continuity may include faith that the relationship has the flexibility to accommodate growth.

Just because commitment may have diverse consequences, the questions of how it can be measured, and of how many dimensions are involved, are quite open. Here we shall concentrate on its development in positive personal relationships: it seems profitable to classify the processes involved into three categories.

COMMITMENT INHERENT IN THE DEVELOPMENT OF THE RELATIONSHIP

There are a number of reasons why a current relationship might seem preferable to a novel one:

(a) Interaction with a partially predictable partner may be preferable to interaction with someone less predictable—a tendency interpretable either in terms of minimizing dissonance (Chapter 14) or in terms of maximizing rewards and minimizing costs (Chapter 16). The known *modus vivendi*, with its accepted norms, may seem preferable to working out a new relationship.

(b) Aspects of the relationship, and the maintenance of its norms, may be secondarily rewarding by association with past happiness.

(c) Association with another individual involves the investment of resources in the relationship. As discussed later, this investment may be made against an expectation of unspecified future gains, and thus involves trust in the partner. In so far as the resources are not easily replaceable, they represent powerful forces to maintain the goal of prolonging the relationship.

This also can be described in terms of dissonance (Chapter 14). Any aspect of the relationship that turns out to be uncongenial, or that fails to come up to expectations, is inconsistent with the memory of the effort that was put into building the relationship. The resulting strain would be reduced if the uncongenial aspects were disregarded, or the expectations seen to be unreal. It would be increased if the relationship were to be severed. Thus the greater the effort put in, the greater is the commitment likely to be.

Because of this investment, each partner will have something to gain by staying within the relationship, and must therefore attempt to ensure that his partner does likewise. This may require further provision of benefits to the partner without concern at least for current, and perhaps for ultimate, reciprocity (see also Chapter 20).

The Private Pledge

Commitment to a relationship is often symbolized by an overt act, like the gift of a ring. But a degree of commitment develops not only in relationships seen as culminating in marriage, but also in many more mundane relationships. Even in heterosexual relationships the ring is usually a symbol of commitment which has developed in the absence of overt acknowledgement, though of course the mutual acknowledgement of that commitment can have a profound influence on the future of the relationship (see above). The private pledge is thus best seen as rooted in the processes described in the preceding paragraphs, developing gradually, and culminating only in some instances in an overt act of acknowledgement.

Two theoretical languages are available for analysing the development and properties of the private pledge. The first is that of symbolic interactionism discussed in more detail in Chapter 14. It is necessary that the partners in a relationship should define that relationship similarly. The definition must involve agreement about the content of and priorities within the relationship, and have implicit reference to some or all of the characteristics of the relationship described in the preceding chapters. It may involve agreement not only about what the participants in the relationship should do together, but also what they should not do together, and perhaps about what each should and should not do with outsiders. It will involve rules of conduct, and rules concerning which rules of etiquette or civil proprieties, potent in the society at large, do and do not apply within the relationship (Denzin, 1970). Most of the difficulties in the earlier stages of a relationship, even with primarily formal relationships such as that between secretary and employer, can be seen as involving the reaching of an acceptable agreed definition of the relationship. Many of the traumatic aspects of the relationships between parents and adolescents stem from the difficulties of changing the definition of the relationship—that is, of maintaining continuity but changing content.

The definition is usually worked out progressively as the relationship develops—not necessarily explicitly, but at least as each accepts or denies the claims the other makes in each interaction (see pp. 65–6). The process can be regarded as involving change in the "role identities" of each partner in accordance with the support provided by the other. The dynamics of the relationship will come to depend in part on idiosyncratic conventions concerned with what is done and when it is done, with turn-taking, with communication and so on. It may involve increasing intimacy, but it need not do so—indeed it may involve agreement about areas of discourse which will be excluded. As each adjusts to the other, he may become progressively less able to find the support he needs elsewhere.

Each step in this process can be regarded as contributing to a private pledge to continue the relationship. Any sign by one partner that he or she is adapting his "role identities" or changing his behaviour to suit the other may be taken by the latter as a sign of commitment.

The processes whereby commitment becomes conscious and/or

explicit are diverse, and may involve not only genuine expressions of feelings but also manipulative attempts by one partner to induce commitment in the other. They may include, for instance, the use of the pronouns "we" and "our", attempts to differentiate the relationship from others by the sharing of secrets, or the elaboration of private signs and mutual rights (e.g. Goffman, 1959). Major issues are the performance of activities costly to the performer but rewarding to the partner, and the acknowledgement that there is pleasure in "doing it together" no matter what *it* is (Blau, 1964).

A second theoretical language, which may provide additional insights into the nature of commitment, comes from the psychology of groups, of which the dyad is the smallest possible representative. Tajfel (1978) uses the term "Social identity" to refer to that part of an individual's self-concept (i.e. that part of A's view of A) that derives from his knowledge of his membership of social groups, together with the value and emotional significance attached to that membership. In the case of the dyad, not only the rewards which the participants exchange but also the membership of the dyad may have an important influence on their behaviour towards each other and towards outsiders. As they become committed, members of a dyad may come to favour each other over outsiders, to show a united front to outsiders and even to differentiate less amongst outsiders than they had done previously. Furthermore, recognition of the dyad as a unit by the participants and by outsiders will affect the future course of the relationship. In so far as each participant perceives that dyad membership contributes positively to the way he sees himself and brings him other rewards, he will act to further the existence of the dyad as a unit. Social situations that force the participants to act as members of the dyad will enhance the extent to which they identify with it, and the more they identify with it, the more they will perceive social situations as requiring them to act as a dyad. The possibilities for positive feedback are considerable (see Tajfel's (1978) discussion of the processes of differentiation between groups).

None of this implies that commitment to one relationship necessarily involves the exclusion of others. In some cultures, for some types of relationship and for some individuals, increasing commitment to build up one relationship may be seen as implying a willingness to forgo others, and there may be practical reasons why that should be so, but that is not a necessary implication of the term "commitment" as used here. Of course where it is regarded as important by the individuals concerned, that importance may be paramount.

The Public Pledge

In the case of personal relationships, commitment developed privately may be symbolized by public acts, such as doing something in public together, or by the giving of a ring or brooch. An essential characteristic of such acts is that they involve others.

Involvement of others becomes even more important in the rituals and ceremonies which, though not ubiquitous, accompany marriage in most cultures. They may involve not only commitment by the marriage partners, but also by members of their families. Such ceremonies may not only provide powerful social forces for the maintenance of the relationship, but may cause the partners to believe that their bond is blessed, divine, or in some other way likely to succeed (Rosenblatt, 1974a).

Of course rituals signifying commitment to a relationship are not limited to marriage. "Blood brotherhoods" are of this nature, and one consequence of many initiation ceremonies is a commitment to one or more interpersonal relationships. In such cases, public commitment may occur in the absence of any personal attachment.

Such public ceremonies are of course of major significance in those cultures where husband and wife are unacquainted with each other at the time of their marriage, and thus have no personal ties to bind them together. Even in Western Europe and North America, engaged couples may know relatively little about each other. Murstein's (1971a) data on this have already been mentioned. Each member of 99 University dating couples was asked to fill in a modified version of the Edwards Personal Preference Schedule (see p. 123) on behalf of self, ideal self, fiancé(e) and ideal spouse. Although in the eyes of each partner individually the partner was quite close to the ideal spouse, there was a near zero correlation between the self-concept of one member of the couple and the ideal spouse of the other. One may wonder how such relationships are viable, and it seems likely that commitment to each other, and to playing the role of the engaged couple, provides a necessary glue in the early stages. Murstein predicted that after marriage the self-concept should move closer to the ideal desired by the partner, as the individual strove to meet the aspirations of the partner and as the partner lowers his ideal to approximate more closely to reality (see pp. 126 and 135). Some disappointment is likely to occur, but private and public commitment may be important in keeping the couple together during the development of their relationship. And with regard to later stages, there is likely to be a positive feedback relationship between culturally held conventions about the immutability of the marriage contract and the incidence of divorce. An increase in divorce will affect the plausibility of the conventions and thus the perceived immutability of the contract, and thus the incidence of divorce.

Public commitment is important not only because a pledge is made public, but also because outsiders may then contribute to the relationship. The mutual interdependence for role support will involve the maintenance of each other's role identities not only in their own eyes, but in the eyes of third parties. And to the extent that the partners treat themselves as a dyad, outsiders will do so too and thereby contribute to their commitment.

Summary

Commitment, one of the most important aspects of many personal relationships, is at the same time the least studied. Commitment may concern continuity of the relationship, its content, or both. It may be imposed from outside the relationship (exogenous) or develop within it (endogenous). The consequences of commitment vary with its nature and with that of the relationship. Faith in the partner's commitment is of special importance.

Forms of commitment inherent in the development of a relationship give rise to increasingly explicit private pledges. Public pledges may or may not be associated with prior attachment, and help to stabilize relationships.

11

The Nature of the Descriptive Categories

In the preceding chapters, various categories of dimensions of relationships have been discussed. Division of relationships by content has usually been regarded as primary because of its social relevance—we ordinarily classify relationships according to what people do together. For many purposes, the subsequent categories can therefore be regarded as qualifying the initial labelling on the basis of content—"How intimate is this marital relationship?" or "How bossy is your employer?". In other contexts it might be convenient to start with a quite different type of categorization, and there is no suggestion that these categories are the only ways of classifying or assessing relationships. But while any taxonomy of relationships may well be useful for some purposes and not for others, one which starts with the socially recognized categories based on content is likely to be most valuable.

However, there must be no misunderstanding about the nature of the categories of dimensions discussed in the preceding chapters. They are in no sense absolute, but merely a convenient way to pigeon-hole data. In many cases the precise characteristics that will prove useful, and the precise ways in which those characteristics can be measured, remain to be worked out. A number of general points relating to the nature of the categories must now be mentioned.

Is the level of analysis appropriate?

Describing relationships includes a process of analysis. Since every relationship differs from all others, we must seek for aspects that we can compare along dimensions valid for a range of relationships. But in doing so we must not forget the whole. The question arises, are the categories of dimensions we have discussed concerned with phenomena at a level of analysis appropriate to the problems that those interested in the dynamics of relationships wish to solve? The answer must surely be that we do not know, and only future research can tell.

In general, the dimensions are at a finer level than the more superficial blanket judgements made in everyday conversation (Are they loving, understanding, competitive, etc.?). Sometimes, of course, the use of such higher order characteristics is inevitable. A third party may be in no position to observe the interactions that most interest him, and have to rely on overall evaluations of sections of the relationship. And even when we are not forced to use data of that sort, they can provide us with useful short cuts.

Sometimes, indeed, overall judgements have a special importance, arising from the fact that people evaluate their relationships. What matters to the participants in a relationship are aspects of its overall character: individual interactions are significant only in so far as they are symptomatic of the whole. And evaluations by the participants can affect the relationship's future course. If a growing relationship is seen by one partner as involving increasing dependence, or if the partner is seen as bossy, this will affect future behaviour.

But in using higher order characteristics we should always ask what they depend on. Can we identify the particular characteristics on which they are based? This is not a question of seeing whether the diverse adjectives we use about relationships can be reduced to three or four (see p. 41), but of identifying the bases of the judgements themselves. Only if we do that can we fully understand how the characteristics under study contribute to the dynamics of the relationship, and only then will we be able to understand the significance of correlations, or departures from correlation, between characters.

In any case, in using more or less global ratings of a relationship, made either by a participant or by a third party, it is important to remember that they may be specific to a limited number of contexts within the relationship. One example has already been cited: Schutz (1960) found that for relationships involving close interaction for a short period, satisfactory dominance relationships are seen as necessary, but for room-mates compatibility with regard to affective needs is more important (see p. 103).

Furthermore, properties may interact. An example is available from the experimental literature on heterosexual attraction. Heterosexual couples were required to work at a task together, with the male in the dominant role. Competence at the task and interpersonal attraction were assessed. Women liked competent partners more than incompetent ones, but the mode of dominance (physical or verbal) interacted with competence. Physically dominant and competent males were liked most and physically dominant and incompetent ones least (Touhey, 1974).

While the categories listed in the preceding chapters are at a finer level than those most often used in everyday conversation, they focus on issues rather more complex than the characteristics usually used in, for instance, studies of non-verbal communication. This is probably reasonable, for the use of characteristics at too fine a level of analysis is likely to involve both redundancy between highly correlated characters and complexity which would obscure the important issues. Furthermore, analysis can lead to the neglect of emergent properties (e.g. Chapter 6). However further research may require some movement towards finer levels of analysis. Aspects of non-verbal communication have been mentioned as indicators of the quality of interactions (p. 58), and comparable characters of both non-verbal and verbal interaction have been used to good effect to characterize patterns of family interaction (e.g. Ferriera and Winter, 1968). A greater dependence on finer level categories is especially likely as the category of "qualities of interactions" is studied further, for understanding of the dynamics of relationships must ultimately involve understanding of the course and nature of the component interactions. The dividends to be reaped from studies of sequences of behaviour are indicated by Patterson's (1975) studies of aggression within families (p. 200), and by numerous studies of the mother-infant relationship (Chapter 22).

Whether or not the categories of dimensions suggested here are at an appropriate level of analysis, it is important that those studying interpersonal relationships should be constantly aware of the dilemma. Of course we sometimes wish to evaluate the extent to which a relationship is "affectionate", "caring" or "competitive", but our evaluation will depend on characteristics at a finer level of analysis, and it is an open issue how far characteristics from the different categories of dimensions listed in the preceding chapters will be intercorrelated. Uncritical overall evaluations of relationships are likely to hinder understanding of their dynamics, and analysis is therefore necessary. Yet analysis may allow emergent properties to escape, lead to neglect of issues which matter to the participants, and result in too great a mass of detail.

Are the categories sufficiently inclusive?

A second question is whether the categories are sufficiently inclusive. The reader may already have thought of aspects of relationships that do not fit readily into any of them. Some of the properties that appear to be omitted are perhaps so intangible that hope of even a crude attempt at measurement seems as yet too far beyond our grasp; one hopes that such items will prove to be correlated with others that can be assessed more readily.

But the main point here is that, as emphasized in Chapter 3, the aim of description is to be selective, not all-inclusive. What we must aim for is a series of dimensions adequate for the tasks in hand. For most specific problems, we shall not need all those discussed in the preceding chapters. Perhaps in the future problems will arise which need assessments that would not fall easily into any of the categories of dimensions considered. However, the issue is not whether description is complete, but whether at the moment it is adequate.

Some of the items that may appear to be omitted are, I believe, multidimensional. We may consider, by way of example, some of the positive labels applied to relationships. Some of the criteria conducive to labelling a relationship as affectionate were mentioned on p. 42: it is for those lower order criteria, which may or may not be correlated with each other, for which these categories of dimensions are intended. Criteria for most of the further distinctions made between types of affectionate relationship can be accommodated within the categories of dimensions discussed. For example esteem and respect are usually one-sided and less personal than liking or loving; their presence would be revealed in the qualities of interactions and in aspects of complementarity.

With regard to liking or loving, the questionnaire items used by Rubin (1974) to differentiate between them are shown in Table 1. It will be noted that nearly all the items on the liking scale refer to perceived properties of the other person, and not to the relationship: the only exceptions are 1, which refers to quality of interactions (meshing); and 7 and perhaps 12, which are concerned with interpersonal perception. Rubin (1973) in fact indicates that the scale is related to "respect" as much as "liking". In the love scale, most items refer to feelings about the other which could be translated into the content and quality of interactions that would occur in certain circumstances (e.g. 1. *If* B were

TABLE 1

Self-report scales for loving and liking used by Rubin (1974). Items 1, 3, 5 and 11 of the Love scale, and items 1, 7, 8 and 10 of the liking scale, were subsequently dropped.

Love scale

1. If _____ were feeling badly, my first duty would be to cheer him (her) up
2. I feel that I can confide in _____ about virtually everything
3. I find it easy to ignore _____'s faults
4. I would do almost anything for _____
5. I feel very possessive toward _____
6. If I could never be with _____, I would feel miserable
7. If I were lonely, my first thought would be to seek _____ out
8. One of my primary concerns is _____'s welfare
9. I would forgive _____ for practically anything
10. I feel responsible for _____'s well-being
11. When I am with _____, I spend a good deal of time just looking at him (her)
12. I would greatly enjoy being confided in by _____
13. It would be hard for me to get along without _____

Liking scale

1. When I am with _____, we almost always are in the same mood
2. I think that _____ is unusually well-adjusted
3. I would highly recommend _____ for a responsible job
4. In my opinion, _____ is an exceptionally mature person
5. I have great confidence in _____'s good judgment
6. Most people would react favorably to _____ after a brief acquaintance
7. I think that _____ and I are quite similar to one another
8. I would vote for _____ in a class or group election
9. I think that _____ is one of those people who quickly wins respect
10. I feel that _____ is an extremely intelligent person
11. _____ is one of the most likable people I know
12. _____ is the sort of person whom I myself would like to be
13. It seems to me that it is very easy for _____ to gain admiration

feeling badly. . .; 4. I would do almost anything for B *if* circumstances arose). The exceptions are 3 and 9, which might refer also to interpersonal perception; and 2 and 12 which refer to intimacy. It is interesting to note that the love scale was predictive of courtship progress only when one or both partners also scored high on a romanticism scale—indicating that they subscribed to the ideology implied by the questions.

Within the category of love, Maslow (1954) distinguished between deficiency ("D") love, in which A loves B for what B can do for or with A, from "B" love, or love for the other's being. The latter is related to Sullivan's (1953) emphasis on the caring aspect of love and Fromm's (1957) on loving as giving. It will be apparent that these distinctions would be reflected in differences in the content, quality and reciprocity *vs* complementarity of the interactions.

Fromm (1957) distinguished four basic elements in love—care, responsibility, respect and knowledge. *Care* he epitomizes as most evident in a mother's love for her child, and would be apparent in the content, quality and complementarity of interactions. By *responsibility* Fromm apparently means care between equals, with care for the other's psychic needs being especially important. This would be apparent in aspects of content and interpersonal perception. So also, would *respect*, which Fromm describes as the ability to see a person as he is, to be aware of his unique personality. And *knowledge*, as described by Fromm, involves both intimacy and interpersonal perception. Fromm also cites Sullivan (1953) as emphasizing that intimacy permits validation of all components of personal worth.

The use of the label "passionate love" depends, according to Berscheid and Walster (1974a), in part on the extent to which an individual is aroused physiologically, and in part on the way in which he has learned to label his feelings. The former will be immediately reflected in the content and quality of the interactions shown, the latter in a number of the other dimensions, especially perhaps the quality of the interactions, intimacy and commitment.

In a similar way, it is suggested, the criteria on which other overall assessments of relationships are based may be accommodated in these dimensions.

Some omitted issues

Having said that, there are still some issues whose omission calls for more extended comment. An obvious case is the omission of any specific reference to overall interpersonal evaluations and attributions. Clearly, beliefs about the characteristics of the participants play a crucial role in the dynamics of close personal relationships (Kelley, 1979). We attribute the behaviour of our partners in relationships to enduring dispositions. These attributions may or may not be accurate (see Chapter 9), but they help determine the behaviour we show. We also attribute characteristics to ourselves, and attempt to behave in ways which we believe will impress others in ways we deem appropriate. Thus attributions about individual characteristics play a crucial role in the dialectic between personality and relationships. And we also assess our relationships, to see whether we have been able to behave in ways that meet our hopes or expectations.

But several points must be made about such attributions. First, there are many ways of loving (see above) and hating, and the proper understanding of the dynamics of relationships demands analysis.

Second, such judgements are made on the basis of particular interactions. It is quite possible to like a person in one context but not in another. A might love B in the one-to-one role of a confidant, but be irritated by the way he shows off in public. Indeed, global assessments are valid only to the extent that assessments made in the several content areas of a relationship are consistent.

Third, judgements applicable to specific content areas are implicit in many of the dimensions we have discussed already. There are some things we are unlikely to do with people we dislike, others we do only with those we esteem or love. Evaluations of the partner are likely to be apparent in the qualities of interactions—we are unlikely to behave gently to someone we believe to be a bully, or warmly to someone we despise (but see below). The beliefs one partner has about another affect many aspects of interpersonal perception. That a friend should appreciate you implies that he should share your (positive) beliefs about you. High intimacy and high commitment usually demand a degree of mutual esteem.

The important issue, therefore, is whether one partner's attributions about the other affect the relationship in ways that would not be captured by dimensions in any of the categories listed. But the issue of *overall* evaluations must, of course, remain open. They have been avoided here, not because the overall feelings that one person has about another are thought to be unimportant for their relationship, but for the merely practical reasons that it seems better to assess them in separate content areas rather than for the relationship as a whole, and that the categories of dimensions so far described may then prove adequate.

A second and very important issue concerns the extent to which the categories of dimensions listed succeed in penetrating to the meanings behind actions. Although I have referred to the possibility of dissociation between the overt content of behaviour and the quality with which it is expressed, between the explicit and the meta-communicational aspects of messages (pp. 67–8), I have not devoted space to the extent to which one partner may be dissembling or deceiving the other. It remains to be seen whether or not the issues are adequately covered by the qualities and patterning of interactions, interpersonal perception and so on. The borderlines between deliberate and unconscious dissembling, and indeed between dissembling and straightforwardness, are in any case notoriously difficult to draw (see p. 66). However the point that the behaviour of one participant in an interaction may have different meanings for the actor, for the other participants, and for an outside observer is a crucial one. Perhaps the most important part of a clinician's skill lies in disentangling them. It may be that the best initial clues come from considerations of the total situation—the past histories or long-term aspirations of the individuals concerned. The test, however, must surely be in the content and quality of the interactions (Freud, 1914).

This brings us to three groups of variables that may have a crucial influence on the dynamics of a relationship but lie outside any of the categories mentioned so far.

The first of these concerns the actual (as opposed to the perceived) characteristics of the participants. At a gross level, their absolute and relative cognitive and moral levels (e.g. Kohlberg, 1976) will have a major influence on the nature of the relationship (e.g. Lickona, 1974, 1976). Just because of the gross difference in cognitive and moral levels, there are limits on the sort of relationship you can have with your dog; and the mother-child relationship, often regarded as the source of all relationships, is highly peculiar in this respect (see Chapter 22). An individual's conception of love must certainly be related to the cognitive and moral levels at which he operates.

Full understanding of relationships will require detailed understanding of the dialectic between personality and relationships. How the participants behave, and how they assess the relationship, depends on their personalities. But here the focus is on relationships: this is not a book about personality. In any case, attempts to relate the course of relationships to the characteristics of the participants have not so far proved outstandingly successful. In the marital relations literature, a few studies have demonstrated a prognostic value in individual personality characteristics: for instance male-female relationships involving a male high in need for power are likely to break up (Stewart and Rubin, 1976). Some studies indicate that similarities or differences in attitudes or personality are conducive to the formation or continuation of relationships, but the results, for personality at least, are not impressive

(Chapter 7). One reason for this is that the relative importance of attitude and personality characteristics changes with the stage of the relationship (see Chapter 21). Another is that the aspects of personality studied have often been insufficiently sophisticated (see Chapters 7 and 21). A third issue, perhaps most important, is that it is in the nature of a relationship that each individual seeks out particular aspects of the personality of the other (see p. 135). Some recent approaches to personality have emphasized the extent to which it is context dependent (e.g. Mischel, 1973), and this is nowhere more evident than in interpersonal relationships. If each participant exposes to the other only a selection of his possible role identities, context independent assessments of personality are unlikely to be relevant.

A second issue concerns the temporal aspects of relationships. The characteristics of relationships discussed in the preceding chapters must of necessity be assessed over a limited span of time. But the dynamics of a relationship, and its prognosis, may depend on events outside the span within which it was assessed. In so far as personality characteristics are relevant, they may have been determined long previously. And since the influence of past experiences may be exerted in some contexts and not others, it may be undetected during the period in which the relationship was assessed, but potent later. An obvious case is early parent loss, a potent contributor to depression in adulthood in the presence of other precipitating life events (Brown *et al.*, 1975). Furthermore hopes for the future may be crucially important for the current dynamics of a relationship: expectations that the partner will provide benefits in the future are basic to some relationships (see Chapter 16; Tedeschi, 1974).

A third issue concerns the social context. Description of a dyadic relationship may involve isolating it from the social context in which it occurs. Every relationship is in part culturally determined, and is enmeshed in a network of other relationships, and may be affected by them. For example, an individual seeing himself as "falling in love" may see this as involving increasing dependence on his partner. The extent to which he does so, and the way in which he evaluates it, will depend on cultural conventions as to the desirability of "dependence", and the extent to which his needs could be met in other relationships in which he is or might be engaged. The nature of his evaluation may in turn affect the quality of his interactions. These issues are discussed further in Chapters 13 and 16.

McCall's list of dimensions

The only other comparable list of dimensions of interpersonal relationships of which I am aware is provided by McCall (1970).* His list is
related to the present discussion as follows:

(1) Intimacy. This was discussed in Chapter 8.

(2) Duration. This was referred to on p. 147.

(3) Formality, i.e. the degree to which the relationship is structured
by some role relationship between the members (see Chapter 13).

(4) Embeddedness, i.e. the extent to which it is embedded within a
larger organization, such as a family or school (see Chapter 13).

(5) Actuality. The degree to which the relationship is manifest in
concrete encounters, or remains on a symbolic plane. An example of
relationships on a *purely* symbolic plane might be a relationship with
a deceased person, or with a deity. Such relationships have been
mentioned only briefly here. They clearly differ in many respects
from concrete relationships in which each individual can affect the
other, though their study could well throw light on real-life relationships. The importance in any relationship of A's view of B is of course
fully recognized here (see Chapter 9).

(6) Reciprocity. By this McCall refers to the extent to which commitment is reciprocal (see Chapter 10).

(7) Differentiation. The degree to which members are distinguished
from each other with respect to affect, status, power, authority,
leadership, communication and conformity. These issues are discussed here in the context of Reciprocity *vs* Complementarity (Chapter 7).

Independence of the categories

The value of any of the categories of dimensions discussed in the
preceding chapters would be much diminished if dimensions within it
were predictable from those in another. In practice those mentioned
are all independent in the sense that specification of all relevant characteristics within one category does not imply the specification of those in
another. There are, however, a number of cases in which certain
configurations of characteristics in one category imply a predisposition
for particular characteristics in another.

*See also Kelley, 1979, pp. 33–42.

First, specification of the content of the interactions often implies specification of a number of other characteristics. A relationship involving A teaching B necessarily involves complementary interactions, one involving psychotherapy involves one-sided intimacy. Furthermore many socially recognized role-relationships, defined by content, are subject to social constraints in other ways (Marwell and Hage, 1970; see p. 173). Second, if specification of the content of the interactions has reference to only one type of interaction, then the relationship is uniplex and the category of properties emergent from the relative frequency and patterning of interactions is necessarily irrelevant. The latter is true also if diversity is specified as uniplex. Third, the categories of intimacy, interpersonal perception and commitment are often interrelated in that specification that the relationship is high or low on one of these dimensions may have implications for the others. Thus intimate relationships are likely to be high on interpersonal perception and commitment, though this is not necessarily the case. Again, relationships in which the behavioural interactions are high on meshing are likely also to be high on intimacy and commitment, though this is not necessarily the case. There is of course room for discussion on these issues, but it is clear that only some of the categories are interdependent and that that interdependence is at most partial. It is also clear that dependency between the categories is not reciprocal—for specification of content as involving nurturance necessarily implies complementarity, but specification of complementarity does not imply nurturance.

However although the categories of dimensions only overlap to a limited extent, they do interact. Characteristics of one type may affect the meaning ascribed to characteristics of a quite different kind. For instance the meaning of the words "Well done" will vary with the content, quality, and intimacy of the relationship between hearer and speaker. Goody's analysis of the influence of social position and context on the meaning ascribed to questions was mentioned in Chapter 5.

Summary

This attempt to categorize some dimensions of interpersonal relationships that may be useful in understanding their dynamics is not an attempt to provide a scheme for their comprehensive description. The categories imply description at a level of analysis intermediate between overall ratings and the examination of details of interactions: some reasons for choosing this level are discussed, but the issue is still open. Description is, properly and inevitably, selective. There are some omissions. Some of these, including the personalities of participants, their past experience, the relationship's past and possible future, and external social forces, are important for the dynamics of relationships.

III

The Dynamics of Interpersonal Relationships

12

The Study of Dynamics

In the preceding chapters we have surveyed a series of categories of dimensions of relationships. These involved what the partners do together, how many different things they do, the qualities of their interactions, overall properties of the relationship dependent on the absolute or relative frequency and patterning of the interactions, the pattern of reciprocity *vs* complementarity in the interactions, and aspects of intimacy, interpersonal perception and commitment. But description is only a means to an end; our long-term aim is to reach understanding of how relationships work, of their dynamics.

STABILITY AND CHANGE

The first need here is to come to terms with what we mean by stability and change in interpersonal relationships. By the definition we have used, relationships exist over time, and each interaction within a relationship may be influenced by past interactions as well as by expectations of future ones. Just because the history of previous interactions is different for each interaction that occurs, relationships are likely to change with time. In addition, and perhaps even more important, the participants in a relationship are likely to change with time, either through natural processes of growth, development and decay, or as a consequence of events within the relationship, or as a consequence of events outside it, the latter including interactions in other relationships in which they are involved. All this implies that relationships are seldom static, that a changing pattern of interactions is likely to be the rule rather than the exception, and that such stability as they have is essentially dynamic in nature.

If it is unusual for the properties of a relationship to remain constant over time, what do we mean by a "stable" relationship? Most relationships change progressively, or vary whilst remaining within certain limits, or change from one temporarily more or less constant state to another. Such changes or variations may be anything from trivial to so great that the new relationship has little in common with the old. An example of the latter would be a parent-child relationship. This starts with one set of interaction types, marked complementarity related to the gross differences in moral and cognitive levels, and gradually changes to something more like a peer-peer relationship with a different set of interactions, more reciprocity and even reversed complementarity, and much greater similarity in moral and cognitive levels. Clearly, then, stability is a relative matter, and how much change we allow without describing the relationship as a new one is an arbitrary matter.

Furthermore we must distinguish two types of stability—consistency, implying constancy of content, and continuity, in the sense of continued association. For many of the relationships in which we are involved, continuity is assured by external factors. We may have little choice but to visit the grocer at the end of the street, or may live in an institution and be powerless to determine who lives next door. In such cases continuity is not an issue, but consistency will be, for each interaction will affect the nature of future interactions. Institutions in the sociological sense may play a similar role: in societies where marriages are arranged and divorce impossible or unthinkable, continuity is unlikely to be an issue for marriage partners. In other cases continuity may be at issue, but consistency of little importance because the nature of the interactions is in large measure pre-determined: there may be two grocers along the street.

Whilst for Darby and Joan consistency and continuity were synonymous, for some close personal relationships they are almost incompatible. If courtship is to progress, the nature of the relationship must change, so there must be continuity without consistency. And even where continuity is assured, personal growth may demand changes in content or other properties; the growth of an individual who cannot change the relationships most important to him may be stifled. The conventional dominated wife or bachelor son of a demanding mother seem to be cases in point, but it must be remembered that their tragedy resides in the fact that inability to change the relationship is a product of *both* parties. The costs to wife or son of breaking or changing the current relationship might well include damage to their own integrity, and be severe (cf. Black, 1975).

In discussing the stability of relationships, it is useful initially to make some gross distinctions between different types of stability, and control systems analysis provides some guidelines (Hinde and Stevenson-Hinde, 1976). Where the "state" of the relationship tends to approach a goal or ideal no matter what the current parameters may be, the situation can be described as involving *global stability*. Thus marriage partners may strive towards an ideal relationship, and parents may try to build an ideal relationship with their children. Such ideals are often encapsulated in the so-called norms which govern behaviour within given roles in the society. Of course some goals may be peculiar to the dyad, differing in some degree from those held appropriate for the corresponding "formal" relationship (see pp. 51 and 176)—husband and wife may strive for goals that differ from those of the ideal marriage in their society. Indeed husband and wife may strive for different goals, at any rate at first; but the durability of a relationship depends in part on the partners reaching reasonable agreement as to how they "define the relationship". This must include not only what they will do together and how they will do it, but also what they will do with outsiders and what will be private to the relationship (cf. McCall, M., 1970).

Usually, however, the partners strive only so long as the ideal seems attainable, or only so long as the present state is within certain limits: marriage partners may strive towards an ideal marriage only so long as their relationship retains certain properties. If commitment is lost, the relationship almost inevitably becomes more distant. Such cases, in which the state heads for a goal only when it is in a specifiable region near the goal, can be described as involving *asymptotic stability*. The greater the availability of divorce, the more do marriages depend on asymptotic and the less on global stability.

In both of these cases, a goal must be postulated. We have seen that these goals are often determined in large part by the culture: the participants may seek to build a marriage or a parent-child relationship which their society will view with approval. But in many relationships stability seems to depend not on seeking for an ideal, but rather on the opposite—the active avoidance of undesirable states. One can then postulate a *stability boundary*, as when marriage partners retreat from states that make divorce a real possibility. Another example, on a shorter time scale, is the avoidance of excessive escalation in parent-infant interaction. Such a mechanism could permit considerable flexibility in the content of the relationship. For example, relationships between parent and adolescent child sometimes seem to depend on the avoidance of interactions that could terminate the possibility of future interactions, and not on consistency of content.

Many relationships in our societies involve acknowledged goals or boundaries of these types. As indicated above, one aspect of the term "commitment" is the acceptance of such goals and/or boundaries. But it is not necessary that they be either culturally determined or consciously recognized. For instance, individuals may be so constituted as automatically to avoid states in which aggression between them is probable.

Furthermore, mechanisms involving goals or boundaries are not the only means whereby the stability of relationships is maintained. The constituent interactions may maintain stability, in the absence of any long-term goal (see Chapter 20). We shall see that the interactions within a mother-infant relationship may be such as to maintain stability even in the case of rhesus monkeys, where striving for an ideal relationship seems unlikely. Furthermore each relationship is set in a nexus of other relationships, and is inevitably affected by them: powerful social forces may contribute to the stability of individuals' relationships.

This introduction to the problems of stability and change has emphasized mechanisms that promote stability in the face of changes in the participants and forces external to it. But it must not be assumed that stability is always a goal. In most types of teacher-pupil relationship, for example, change in content, and even in continuity, is itself a long-term goal, or is at least seen as an inevitable consequence of the short-term goals of the participants. The aim of courtship is a long-term change in the nature of the relationship, and the same is true of interactions in the initial stages of almost any relationship.

THE STUDY OF DYNAMICS

To understand the stability of relationships we must therefore come to terms both with how relationships are preserved in the face of internal changes and the buffetings of the external world, and also with how they may change progressively, again as a consequence of factors internal and external to them, and yet preserve their integrity. These two aspects of dynamic stability are, of course, interdependent. In the following chapters we shall consider some approaches to understanding the factors affecting the course of relationships.

Now much scientific advance has come from pitting theories against each other. Observations or experiments that are compatible with this theory but not with that bring us a little nearer the truth. But it may be that there are also times when it is more profitable to survey the current scene, to assess the range of applicability of the theoretical approaches current at the moment, to see how far they overlap and how far they are intertranslatable. Whilst this book does not proceed very far with any of these tasks, its aim is to prepare the way for such survey work, rather than to assess one theoretical approach against another. In keeping with that aim, I have not attempted detailed expositions of particular theoretical approaches. Instead I have attempted to convey their flavour—inevitably with some, but I hope not too much, distortion.

In general, it would seem profitable to search for explanatory principles (theory is an over-used word) in a few areas. The first involves social and other extra-dyadic influences; included here are the influences from other relationships in which the individuals are involved, and the social norms and values they acquire from the subcultures in which they live (Chapter 13). The second concerns the ways in which the partners perceive themselves, each other, their relationship, and also their ideal selves, partners and relationships. Theories of cognitive dissonance and balance are discussed in Chapter 14: I have drawn on attribution theory, also of basic importance for understanding dynamics, where relevant rather than in a separate chapter. Third, it is necessary to consider how interactions affect subsequent interactions: here we shall consider a selection of learning theories, and review briefly the way in which they have been used in exchange theories (Chapters 15–17 and part of Chapter 18). Finally, taking a longer view, it is necessary to consider the means whereby relationships accommodate to external stressors or to changes in the participants, and the circumstances in which the effects of change become progressive (Chapters 19 and 20).

It will become apparent that these areas overlap. Some of the phenomena usually discussed in the context of balance theories can equally be explained in terms of reinforcement. The influences of social norms are exerted in part through the effectiveness of different situations as rewards. Long-term changes in relationships depend in part on the patterning of the availability of rewards in time.

Throughout the coming chapters it will be repeatedly emphasized that what is important for one relationship may not be so for another—the explanatory principles for which we search must be closely related to the descriptive base.

Summary

Two types of stability are distinguished—continuity, implying continued association, and consistency, implying constancy of content. A variety of mechanisms may contribute to stability—attempts to achieve an ideal (goal) relationship, avoidance of undesirable states, feedback effects of the sequential interactions and social pressures.

13

Social and Other Extra-Dyadic Influences

A comprehensive examination of social influences on interpersonal relationships is far beyond the reach of this book. It would properly start with social influences on perception (Tajfel, 1969), on values and norms; it would have to include discussion of cultural differences in the relationships that are recognized, in what is expected within those relationships, and in the influences of relationships on relationships. Implied by all these is an important influence of socialization practices: full understanding demands knowledge not only of the values and beliefs individuals bring to a relationship, but also of how they were acquired. However such issues would take us too far afield, and discussion must be limited to a few aspects. Even more than elsewhere in this book, the aim is to make contact with the relevant bodies of knowledge, rather than to provide an exhaustive survey.

Influences from the physical environment

That relationships between individuals may be affected by their physical environment is well illustrated in the clinical literature. For instance a family's life circumstances and social class have consistently been found to be associated with the incidence of psychiatric disorders (e.g. Kolvin *et al.*, 1971). In a U.S. sample depressive symptoms were more common in low income groups (Schwab *et al.*, 1976), and Richman (1974, 1977) found that women living in flats in London were more prone to depression and loneliness than women living in houses. In some of these cases, at least, there were strong reasons for believing the external factors to be causal.

Whilst crowding can engender or augment negative feelings (e.g. Schiffenbauer and Schiavo, 1976), a number of field studies have demonstrated the importance of propinquity in the formation of relationships (see p. 88). The influence of physical space on the formation of friendships has been studied also in the context of house and class-room design (Byrne, 1961b).

In the shorter term, the availability of an appropriate environment (Hall, 1966) or the precise arrangement of physical features may affect the course of interactions. For instance it has been claimed that interaction is more likely between individuals sitting on either side of the corner of a table than in other positions; that people in a competitive interaction chose to sit opposite to each other (Sommer, 1959, 1965); and that subjects forced to sit close to others or to intrude on their space respond more negatively than controls (Dabbs, 1971). Goffman (1959) has provided a penetrating analysis of the manner in which aspects of the physical environment, as well as of the person himself, are used as "fronts" to help define the situation.

In a multiplex relationship, the physical and behavioural context may influence the content of the interactions that occur, and differences in the context may serve to insulate interactions that would otherwise be incompatible. For example Harcourt (1977), studying groups of mountain gorilla, noted that the adult males competed for females primarily during those parts of the day spent in travelling and feeding. Affiliative behaviour between them occurred mostly in midday rest periods. Harcourt suggests the analogy of the friendship of competing sportsmen, and one thinks also of the sport of competing businessmen.

Barker (e.g. 1963, 1965, 1978) has embraced and extended many of these issues in his loose but potentially useful concept of "behavior settings". These are "ecological" units, including both human and physical components, and embracing a number, often a large number, of "behavior episodes". "Behavior episodes" are molar units of behaviour with the "attributes of constancy of direction, equal potency throughout their parts, and limited size range".

The examples given by Barker vary greatly in scope. One involves a child looking at another's ladybird beetle, and includes a series of events initiated by one child walking round with the beetle and terminated by the other child pulling the possessor's arm down so that she could see the beetle better. The limits of the "behavior setting" in which this occurred could be defined in terms of physical space and its temporal beginning and end.

As another example, Barker describes the physical and human components of the lecture theatre in which he was speaking, including the lights, chairs, etc. each ordered in particular ways. A third example is a baseball game, with players, spectators, field and implements. Barker points out that the same people behave in different ways in different "behavior settings", and different sets of people behave in similar ways in the same setting. For example, academic communities incorporate different and idiosyncratic individuals, year after year, into the characteristic patterns of their several "behavior settings". Barker cites Rausch *et al.*'s (1959) study of a therapeutic community as finding more variation on the hostility-friendliness and dominance-passivity dimensions in the behaviour of the same boys in different settings than there were with different individuals in the same setting.

On the basis of such data Barker argues, perhaps not completely justifiably, that "behavior settings" are "strongly self-regulated systems". Although the concept of behavior setting is not a very tight one, Barker uses it to good effect to compare, for instance, students in a small and a large high school. The former had fewer students in each "behavior setting" than the large one, and the students "were more strongly motivated, engaged in more varied activities, and were more responsibly involved than the students in the large school" (see also Barker, 1978).

Relationships affect relationships

Each individual has relationships with many others, and each relationship he has will be affected by the other relationships that he has and the other relationships that his several partners have. This fact of everyday life barely requires illustration, though many individuals live with the myth that their many relationships can remain insulated from each other. There is both the possibility that a relationship may be diverted if one participant enters another, and the fact that its very viability may depend on other relationships in which the partners are involved.

Such influences from outside the relationship may take many forms, only some of which can be mentioned here. But it is important to emphasize from the start that they include not only the *actual* influences of third parties or other relationships, but also their potential influences as seen by the participants in the relationship in question. Suppose, for instance, that A and B could interact in many possible ways. Some of those which were most beneficial to A might involve heavy costs for B.

Those heavy costs might be such that they would cause B to prefer a relationship with C. For that reason, A might be well advised to avoid those interactions that otherwise might have been most beneficial to him (Thibaut and Kelley, 1959).

Just because one's first tendency is to think of external influences as detrimental to a relationship on the "Two's company three's a crowd" model, it is important to emphasize that precisely the opposite may be the case. A relationship may be strengthened by recognition from third parties, or maintained because its continuation ensures rewards outside it. Murstein (1977) has likened courtship to a slowly accelerating conveyor belt leading to matrimony, in order to convey the potency of the social pressures that make it progressively more difficult to get off. Furthermore, attempted interference with the progress of a relationship by an outside party can have the effect of strengthening it. Correlational evidence suggests that parental interference can strengthen the relationship between an engaged couple though, as the authors point out, other explanations are possible (Driscoll et al., 1972; Rubin, 1974). Such a finding could be understood in terms of Brehm's (1976) generalization that individuals act to protect their freedom of action. On this view, if an option is threatened the individual becomes more likely to exercise it. Such a course of action is more probable, the more important the option is to him.

The importance of influences external to the relationship can be illustrated by data on the effects of relationships on relationships within and between families. First, the classic study of 20 families by Bott (1957) showed that the extent to which husband and wife shared activities, interests and decisions was related to the social network in which the family was embedded. Families in a "close-knit" network, in which the various friends and relatives knew each other, tended to have segregated husband and wife roles. Where the network was "loose-knit", with friends and relatives not knowing each other, husband and wife tended to depend more on each other and to have joint roles. This generalization has subsequently received support in other studies (Gluckman in Bott, 1971).

Within the family, a number of workers have studied the effects of children on the nature of a marriage. Though there are differences of opinion as to the generalizations that can be made, it is clear that the effects are profound (Slater and Woodside, 1951; Fletcher, 1966; Rosenblatt, 1974b; Glenn, 1975; Humphrey, 1975; Miller and Newman, 1978; Cowan *et al.*, 1978). Once children are born, the parents' behaviour to the children is correlated with the nature of their marriage. Thus Kemper and Riechler (1976) found that children were rewarded more and punished less by parents satisfied with their marriage than by less-satisfied parents. Of course such correlational studies (see also Matteson, 1974) leave open the question of the direction and nature of the causal links, but such a criticism applies less forcibly to studies showing that temporary absences of the father may affect the mother's attitude to the children (Marsella *et al.*, 1974), that the sex of the first child may affect parental attitudes to the second (Cicirelli, 1975), and that the arrival of the second born may affect the parents' relationship with the first (Dunn and Kendrick, in prep. a, b).

This last case may be used to exemplify the complex ways in which a relationship may be affected by a third party. Dunn and Kendrick studied 41 families in Cambridge, from the mother's second pregnancy until the second child was about 18 months old. With the birth of the sibling, there were changes in almost all aspects of the mother-first born relationship. At the behavioural level, the diversity, quality and relative frequency and patterning of the interactions all changed—in part because the mother was busy, preoccupied and often over-tired, and in part perhaps because she saw the new baby as having the greater need. Confrontations between mother and first-born became more frequent, and the latter tended to regress in some respects. At the same time there were often signs of increased maturity and self-awareness, negative and positive changes often going together. The first-born's response to the new sibling involved care, interest and concern on the one hand and hostile behaviour or teasing on the other.

Clearly, changes in the mother-firstborn relationship at many levels were involved. These could include changes in the self-perception of the first-born. Dunn and Kendrick suggest that "the arrival of the new sibling would involve a new dimension of self-awareness, a re-categorization of self, on the part of the first child. Now he is the big one, not the small; the elder, not the younger; the boy, not the girl, and so on". At the same time, however, the first-born may be comparing his lot with the baby's, the maternal attention he receives now with that he used to receive. No doubt much depends on the mother's sensitivity to the changes in the first-born's life resulting from the baby's arrival. On the one hand she may succeed in bringing him in as a partner in coping with the baby, so that he sees himself as "the big one" and on the mother's side. Or the contrast between his and the baby's relationship with the mother may alienate him, and he may even use the baby as a model and regress. The changes that occur will of course depend on the first-born as well as the mother and will certainly be complex.

Of course this only just scratches the surface of the problem. The new baby is likely also to have direct effects on mother-father and father-firstborn relationships, and these also may have ramifying secondary consequences. Within a family containing one or more older children, any triad is liable to differentiate into a pair of allies and an isolate, and this may be crucial in the development of family relationships (de Schazer, 1975). The ramifications of the effects of change in one focus on the rest of the family is perhaps best shown by Burton's (1975) study of the consequences for the family of a chronically sick child (see also Gath, 1973).

Parke *et al.* (1979) have recently set out a scheme for conceptualizing influences within a family triad which can encompass both face-to-face interactions and influences exerted over time. Figure 1 shows the possible types of influence exerted by A on B and C. Single arrows represent behaviours or cognitions involving or directed at

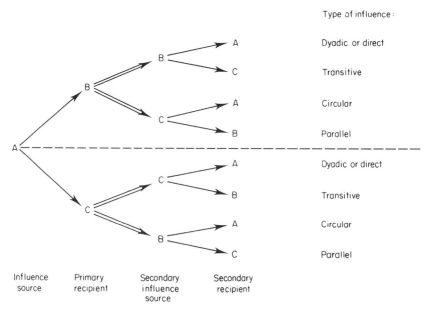

Fig. 1. General model of influence patterns within a triad. A is the individual whose influence is being studied (From Parke *et al.*, 1979).

another individual. For example, $A \rightarrow B$ could represent the attitude of A to B, a specific item of behaviour directed by A to B, or the style of A's interaction with B over a period. The double arrows indicate the consequences of such directed behaviours or cognitions. So a direct influence $A \rightarrow B \overset{\rightarrow}{\underset{\rightarrow}{}} B \rightarrow A$, represents a situation where the consequence of A's actions or attitudes to B is an action or attitude of B to A—for instance a mother smiles at her infant and the infant smiles back. Transitive influences involve mediation by one individual of an influence on another—for instance, the father kisses the mother and the mother then nuzzles the infant. In a circular influence the same individual initiates the sequence and is the secondary recipient after mediation by the others—for instance father tickles infant, infant vocalizes and then mother smiles at father. Finally, in a parallel influence the primary and secondary recipients are the same individual—for instance the father tickles the infant and then the mother imitates him by tickling the infant, or the father ignores the infant's vocalization and so the mother responds to it in an exaggerated fashion.

Although the examples given all involve short-term interactions, the categories have much wider applicability. Thus an example of a circular influence might be the finding that boys in mother-dominant families are more likely to imitate their mothers than their fathers ($M \rightarrow F \overset{\rightarrow}{\underset{\rightarrow}{}} I \rightarrow M$). Parke *et al.* illustrate their scheme with numerous examples drawn from family interaction patterns. Although, as the authors point out, it has some difficulties with family members' perceptions of relationships between other family members, or of the family as a unit, the scheme undoubtedly represents a useful way of picturing the effects of relationships on relationships.

This last point, family members' perception of the family as a unit, requires a rather different sort of approach. A promising conceptual scheme is provided by Wertheim's (1975a,b,c) treatment of the family as an open system, including its individual members as subsystems and itself embraced within supra-systems, such as the community. The family is seen as having a degree of stability, but also an ability for adapting to changes in the intra- and extra-familial environment. Of special interest in the present context is Wertheim's analysis of family patterns in terms of hierarchies of rules. First, "ground" or "first-order rules" refer to concrete action and contain specific behavioural prescriptions, such as "In our family, we don't fight". These are governed by "meta-rules", or rules about the ground rules. These reflect the moral code of the family, regulating behaviour accordingly. Different meta-rules might lead to different sorts of stability and/or change in the family structure. "Family members should never quarrel" implies a rigid, unchanging system (described as intra-systemically enforced family stability or morphostasis). "If people are angry, it's best to talk it through", involves more flexibility to meet a threat (intra-systemically negotiated morphostasis). And "If people don't get on, it's best to get advice from someone more experienced" implies the possibility of change as a result of outside intervention (induced morphogenesis). Meta-rules may be guided by meta-meta rules, such as "Only kinfolk have to be protected, there is no loyalty to strangers", and these to an even smaller number of meta-meta-meta-rules, and so on. (There is a similarity here to Thibaut and Kelley's (1959) analysis of the behaviour of dyads and groups in terms of "norms" and "meta-norms", the latter specifying the domains of applicability of and priorities between norms.)

Wertheim emphasizes that the degree of family integration can be assessed only at the level of meta-rules. For example, the ground rule "In this family everyone comes and goes as he or she pleases" may be qualified by a meta-rule such as "A family should enable its members to develop fully as individuals". Individuals can then "come and go" only so long as this is seen by everyone to be conducive to individual development. Thus each individual rule derives its meaning from the network of systemic rules of which it is part.

Wertheim suggests that the organization of these rules can be understood in terms of two principles—the principle of hierarchical linkage, as outlined above, and the principle of functional linkage. The latter defines functional connections within and between the structural levels. These circuits contain major rules and sub-rules, with the latter at either a similar or lower level in the hierarchy (see Fig. 2). It is suggested that intellectually and psychosocially adequate family systems differ from inadequate ones in having a reasonably complex, differentiated, integrated and internally consistent rule network.

Further consideration of Wertheim's use of concepts from systems theory to throw light on the mechanisms involved in maintaining a balance between morphostasis and morphogenesis would take us far beyond the subject of dyadic relationships. But her conceptual scheme is important here in indicating a possible objective method for tackling the way in which relationships may be affected not only by third parties

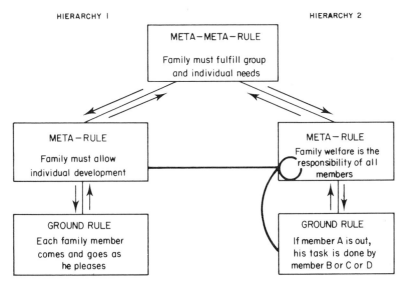

Fig. 2. Structural and dynamic features of systemic rule networks, as suggested by Wertheim (1975c). A possible rule circuit is shown by the thick line; the circle indicates the major rule for this circuit connected to two sub-rules.

or other relationships, but by larger structures of which the relationship in question forms part. Furthermore, within the dyad the application of the model of a hierarchy of rules to the problems posed by interpersonal commitment seems likely to be profitable.

The dyad as a unit within a group

Outsiders may affect the dynamics of a dyadic relationship in another way—namely by causing the participants to feel and/or behave as a unit, distinct from and in some cases set in opposition to the others. Here we are concerned with dyads in which mutual commitment has some importance. To the extent that the dyad has a structure of beliefs based on the idea that the formation of alternative liaisons is undesirable, difficult or impossible, it can be considered as a (minimally sized) group. Such a dyad may behave as a unit to others, treating them as though they were in some degree outsiders (Tajfel, in press).

The dyad as a unit vis-à-vis other units is exploited in some types of group therapy, where a number of couples attend with the aim of exploring different marital systems (Kreitman, pers. comm.).

Socio-Cultural influences

Every human relationship is influenced in fundamental ways by the culture in which it develops. In so far as the participants share cultural norms, the basic structure of their relationship will be determined by those norms. They will agree that theirs is a relationship of a particular type, and expect it to have certain properties. But they are likely also to have been subjected to different influences by virtue of class, wealth, religion, opportunity or peer-group, so that the premises and expectations they bring to the relationship are far from identical. Some degree of negotiation as to the "definition of the relationship" (see pp. 135 and 189–192) will then be essential. In this section we shall consider the nature of some of these cultural and sub-cultural influences.

CULTURAL INFLUENCES ON EMOTIONS

Processes of socialization may permit or inhibit certain properties of relationships by influencing the sorts of emotions that individuals feel. On the one hand it seems probable that certain "primary emotions" are potentially distinguishable physiologically and find expression in patterns which do not depend on social experience (e.g. Eibl Eibesfeldt, 1972; Ekman and Friesen, 1969). Even here, there may be cultural differences in the extent to which these emotions are expressed or inhibited, and in the context in which they are elicited. But beyond that there is considerable circumstantial evidence to indicate that the diversity of emotions experienced is largely due to cultural factors. Berscheid and Walster (1974a) have suggested, for example, that when a child hears his mother say "Don't be shy" he learns that the emotion one feels in the presence of strangers is called "shyness". In general, it is suggested, an adult identifies his emotions in part by physiological cues and in part from associations with the concomitant situation—associations that are in large part acquired during socialization.

Applying this line of argument to the issue of "passionate love", Berscheid and Walster point out that the phenomenon of passionate love is not universal, but emphasized much more in some cultures than in others. It appears to be a poorly articulated emotion, and adolescents have only vague notions as to how it should be identified. Whether or not they label their feelings as "love"—and furthermore, one may add, whether they act out the role of romantic lovers—will depend on the cultural climate. The more the culture idealizes the lover, the more will they be rewarded for labelling their feelings as love and for acting as lovers are expected to act. Furthermore, in a culture that emphasizes the value of particular attributes, such as physical beauty, manliness or docility, for inducing love in an opposite-sexed partner, an individual will be the more likely to seek out such a partner and the more likely to label his feelings as love and to act as a lover when he finds one. There may also be sex differences, probably culturally induced, in the experience of love—in one study men were found to be more idealistic and more cynical but less pragmatic than women (Dion and Dion, 1975). The culture will thus affect the emotions individuals feel or express, and thus the sorts of relationships they form. Furthermore, Berscheid and Walster (1974a) suggest that the ways in which culture decrees that we label feelings, and thus the nature of the relationships in which we are involved, may depend in part on contextual cues. It appears, for instance, that young adults are more likely to use "romantic love" to refer to relationships with the opposite sex that are in progress, but "infatuation" for those that have been terminated: if this is so, the distinction can be made only in retrospect.

ROLES

The term "role" has had a confused history in the social sciences, and has carried a wide spectrum of meanings (Linton, 1936; Newcomb, 1952; Banton, 1965; Sarbin and Allen, 1968; Hinde, 1978a). The narrow usage, in which "role" refers to the rights and duties imposed on the incumbents of certain positions within a society, characteristic especially of the anthropological literature, grades into a much wider usage among some social psychologists. In this section we shall first consider its narrower usage, though later in the chapter we shall be concerned with its wider (and looser) implications. Even here, however, it is necessary to make some further terminological points.

The term "role" is usually used in relation to behaviour (or expectancies about behaviour or criteria relevant to behaviour, Kelvin, 1970) associated with a position or status in the society. We may speak of the role of Prime Minister, doctor, traffic warden or good neighbour. The behaviour in question is that normally or ideally shown by the diverse incumbents of the position, and does not refer to their individual idiosyncrasies. The behaviour is usually described in terms of certain of its effects on others—the rights and duties of the incumbent.

"Role" is thus not a category at the data level with absolute properties, but a concept that may or may not be useful in coming to terms
with specified problems. It is usually used with respect to two problems—(a) that of the determinants of behaviour in the individual and
(b) that of the way in which individual behaviour contributes to the
structure of relationships, groups or societies. As I shall use it, "role" is
linked closely to the concept of "institution". Thus "marriage" is an
institution, "husband" and "wife" are roles; "sovereignty" is an
institution, "king" and "subject" roles. An institution involves one or
more positions with recognized rights and duties: "role" can refer *either*
to determinants of the behaviour of the incumbents of these positions, *or* to the manner in which their behaviour contributes to the
institution.

If the role concept is to be useful with reference to the determinants of
social action (i.e. the factors because of which this social action differs
from that), it must differentiate one set of determinants from the many
others that affect behaviour. That set must surely be the goals and
limits that individuals set themselves in relation to their position in
society. For example, the difference between the behaviour of boys and
girls can be regarded as due to interactions between differences in their
biological make-ups (biological constraints and predispositions), in the
way in which others treat them (social constraints and predispositions), and in their own ideas about the behaviour that is appropriate to
the sex they see themselves as having (goal constraints and predispositions). It need hardly be said that the important word here is "interaction"—biological factors affect social ones, and social ones biological;
and the subject's own goals are derived from those of other individuals,
and influence and are influenced by how he is treated by others. Within
all this complexity, the role concept is usefully applied to a subset of
determinants—namely those that constitute the goals (conscious or
unconscious) of the subject defined in respect to the relevant real or
imagined effects of his behaviour on others.

On this view, not all the determinants of social behaviour can be
described in role terms. A baby's behaviour is determined not at all by
his own concept of how a baby should behave—he has not yet reached a
stage of development where he could have one. Furthermore his
behaviour only gradually comes to be shaped by those around him; the
role concept is irrelevant to the determinants of his behaviour. In the

same way the behaviour of invalids, or old men, is to be understood only partially in role terms: inherent constraints on behaviour are more conspicuous than those that arise from their socially determined roles. With healthy adults the latter are usually more conspicuous (cf. p. 172). The behaviour of the king, *qua* king, can be described to a considerable extent in role terms. But even a king acts out his role in an idiosyncratic way: if it were possible to place two individuals in the same throne at the same time, they would carry out their duties differently. Thus to attempt to account for all the behaviour of a king while acting as king in role (*sensu stricto*) terms would be a mistake; other determinants not necessarily wholly compatible with the kingly role, such as personal ambition and indigestion, may also operate. This does not imply a confusion between paradigm and empirical fact (cf. Harré and Secord, 1972), but merely an emphasis on the multiple determinants of human behaviour. Both the extreme sociological view epitomized by "we act despite our feelings" (Harré, 1975), and those extreme psychological ones which neglect role factors altogether, must be rejected. Not only are both relevant most of the time, but they interact. Many of our actions are rooted in feelings derived from role prescriptions which thereby regulate many of our interpersonal relationships.

The use of the role concept in reference to the socially relevant *consequences* of behaviour may be quite unrelated to its use with reference to determinants. Thus a baby plays a large role in the family even though the determinants of its behaviour are not usefully considered in role terms. The structure of relationships within a hospital is determined in part by aspects of patients' behaviour the causation of which cannot usefully be described in role terms (i.e. in terms of the goals or limits patients set themselves). And much of the behaviour of individuals in organizations may be determined by factors, such as personal ambitions, quite different from their role in (= consequences for) the organization. The determinants of the actions of a soldier in battle may be related not at all to the strategic plan of the commander-in-chief. The soldier may be ignorant of that plan, and yet the consequences of his actions play a crucial role in it. Again, role as a determinant of behaviour may involve goals that are never attained. Parents may strive to create a parent-child relationship of the type most valued in their culture, but the consequences of their behaviour may never match up to the goals they set themselves.

While roles as determinants of behaviour and roles as consequences of behaviour are thus in principle separable, in practice they are often closely linked. This comes about in two ways. First, the goals which act as determinants often are closely related to the consequences which result. If a chairman successfully guides a discussion to a sound decision acceptable to all, the most important determinant of his behaviour, namely the goal towards which it was directed, and its consequences, are identical. Second, when the social goals are not achieved, social sanctions may result. Anticipation of such sanctions may form an additional determinant.

Now social roles are usually defined in terms of the content of the interactions involved. Thus husband, mother, doctor, manager and employee are necessarily involved in certain relationships, and their "rights and duties" in those relationships are defined in terms of the content of at least some of the interactions. Some of these rights and duties concern interactions that are to be included in the relationship, others those that are to be excluded.

Some such labels for relationships refer to only one type of interaction, or to a small group of related interactions. To be a manager, it may be necessary only to manage in a certain limited range of contexts; to be an employee it may be necessary only to do certain kinds of work. But more usually rights and duties are multiple. The explanatory power of the role label will of course increase with the extent to which that is the case. If the only difference between other ranks and commissioned officers in an old-fashioned army was that the former saluted the latter we would have no need for a concept of commissioned rank, though we might usefully classify soldiers into saluters and salutees (cf. pp. 80–1). In practice, individuals occupying different ranks were obliged to interact in some ways, for example by condescension/obedience, and not to interact in others, such as eating at the same table. Furthermore the diversity of interactions between them was limited, certain qualities of interaction were proscribed, their interactions were by definition complementary, and their intimacy was likely to be limited. Thus a difference in rank implied both that some interactions were possible, and that they would have certain properties, whilst other interactions were not.

Both the number and the nature of recognizable roles differ between societies. For instance, in many societies a male has a special relationship with his mother's brother (Goody, 1959), but such a relationship is not so emphasized in our own. Conventions also influence the sort of individual to be preferred in most of the role relationships specified in the culture.

Conventions may also decree which role relationships are (more or less) indissoluble, and which can be vacated at will. This has important influences on the dynamics of the relationships. If either partner can opt out at will, there is always the possibility that other relationships will seem more attractive: it therefore behoves each participant to ensure that the relationship remains sufficiently attractive to the other to ensure that he remains within it (Thibaut and Kelley, 1959). But to some role relationships, the participants are inevitably committed. Kinship ties, for instance, are a part of life, and must be accepted. This has two consequences. First, it makes possible the unlimited exploitation of one partner by the other. This is one argument against social practices imposing permanence on relationships of particular types (see p. 154). But second, it may also facilitate the development of trust: each partner may be the readier to dispense rewards now, knowing that the other will be there to help in the future (see p. 134).

ROLE—NON-OBLIGATORY RIGHTS AND DUTIES

We have seen that some relationships, like that between commissioned officer and soldier, involve diverse obligatory rights and duties, specifying many or all dimensions of the relationship. In other cases, however, some may be obligatory, and others merely expected. For instance, in the husband-wife relationship (public) commitment is, in most societies, part of the definition of the role. In addition certain types of interaction may be obligatory. But other aspects of the relationship, such as the degrees of intimacy and the pattern of reciprocity *vs* complementarity, will, to extents that differ between societies (Rosenblatt, 1974a) and even between different locations in one society (Kerckhoff, 1974), be expected rather than obligatory. Again, a teacher is obliged to teach, but there may be considerable latitude in the degree of control/permissiveness expected of him. Even "friendship" has societally recognized properties, including a degree of deviance from societal norms (Suttles, 1970): such properties may guide the course of friendship, but are not obligatory. Within any society the various types of role relationship differ in the extent to which the partners' behaviour is regulated by external forces (Marwell and Hage, 1969).

The term "role" is thus sometimes extended to cover a wide spectrum including both obligations and expectations, and the distinction between the two can never be a precise one. But the continuum can be traced by the extent to which sanctions are imposed. For instance, in a study of changing family roles in the U.S.A. Nye (1974) identified the existence of roles by asking both whether a person occupying a given position (e.g. husband or wife) has a duty to enact the role, and whether there are sanctions if he did not. But sanctions could involve little more than disapproval. Perhaps the minimum requirement is that, if rights are infringed or duties unfulfilled, the injured party may appeal to the convention, and the transgressor shows guilt (cf. Thibaut and Kelley, 1959).

Non-obligatory role expectations have been studied especially in the mother-child relationship. Whilst interactions within that relationship that are closely related to the infant's basic biological needs are relatively invariant across cultures, other aspects of the relationship vary considerably. For example Caudill and Weinstein (1969) compared the mother-infant relationships in 30 families in the U.S.A. with those in 30 Japanese ones. They found that the U.S. mothers had a more lively and stimulating approach to their babies, as indicated by a number of variables, and their babies were more happily vocal and active, and explored more. The Japanese mothers did more lulling, carrying and rocking, and tried harder to soothe and quiet their babies. The investigators felt their data to imply that the mothers tended to rear the babies they wanted, the babies learning even in the first 3–4 months to behave in culturally appropriate ways.

Such modulatory influences may be very persistent. Connor (1974) found similar differences between U.S. families and Japanese families which had lived in the U.S.A. for three generations. Comparable inertia in the face of pressure for change was found by Geest (1976) in a study of marital roles in the Kwatu area of Ghana. Though she may wield considerable social power, the wife is traditionally deferent to her husband. Schoolchildren's answers to questions showed that they evaluated positively the possibility that a man should eat together with his wife, and that he should help her grind fufu. But in spite of these expressed preferences amongst the young, role segregation was still considerable.

The influence of social expectations differs between societies, and changes with time in any one society. For example, thirty years ago

Komarovsky (1946) found that girl students interacting with men tended to play down their academic qualities: they tried to adopt the persona which at that time was believed to be most attractive to men. They were in fact behaving towards a stereotype of the male student as they saw him. Again Peplau (1976) compared women with "modern" and "traditional" sex role attitudes when in a competitive situation. The latter performed less well when competing against their boy friends than when working with them. For women with more "modern" attitudes the reverse was the case. The difference in attitude affected the relationship even in the artificial test situation.

However it is probably usual for changes in behaviour to lag behind changes in role attitudes. On the basis of questionnaire data obtained from 1154 married men and women, Araji (1977) believed that many showed incongruence between their attitudes and behaviour. Both men and women had egalitarian role attitudes which were not reflected in behaviour.

As these examples suggest, each individual brings to his relationships presuppositions derived not only from the society as a whole, but also from many overlapping categories to which he (or she) sees himself (or herself) as belonging within the society. "I am a girl (or a boy)", "A modern woman", "A member of the younger generation", "Liberal", "Academic" and so on. Actions are fundamentally influenced by perceived membership of such categories, and by the perceived structure of relations between them: in appropriate contexts category members are differentiated from outsiders; and the outsiders, and even the members, are seen as stereotypes. And both what individuals expect from their relationships, and how they behave within them, will be affected by the promises and expectations they have acquired from, and associate with, these various overlapping sub-divisions of the society as a whole (cf. Tajfel, 1978).

At this point it is necessary to refer back to the earlier anthropological use of the term "role" to refer to behaviour associated with a position or status in the society. Each such "role" is associated with specific rights and duties, and involves "norms" (see definition on p. 32) deviations from which provoke sanctions. Such a concept is appropriate when we are concerned with differences between societies—for instance how the recognized rights and duties of the Head of Government, or of Wives, in the relationships relevant to their positions differ between this society and that. But from that we have gone on to consider differences between sub-cultures within a society—between Japanese and Caucasian families in California, for instance. Once again norms, enforced by sanctions of some degree, operate. And beyond that, each individual belongs not to one but to many groups within the society, deriving expectations from each of them with respect to certain types of relationship. Norms by definition are shared with others, but while some are common to a large society, others may be shared only by small sub-groups within that society, and be subject to constant re-negotiation between those sub-groups. Now, having moved as it were from anthropological to sociological and social psychological usage, we must go one step further and consider expectations about behaviour more or less specific to individuals within a relationship. Since each individual may belong to many sub-groups, his repertoire of norms could in theory be almost idiosyncratic. And individuals also have idiosyncratic *specific* expectations as a result of their own life histories. One aspect of this is discussed in the next section.

CULTURAL AND SOCIAL INFLUENCES IN THE DEVELOPMENT OF PARTICULAR
RELATIONSHIPS

The determinants of "personality" characteristics are beyond the scope of this book, but one aspect of personality must be mentioned—the properties of relationships of different types seen as desirable by the individual in question. Just because cultural conventions are acquired by individuals especially from others significant in their lives, it is often difficult to draw a line between those properties of relationships that are seen as desirable through general cultural conventions and those seen as desirable through the influence of one or more others significant in an individual's life. While the general nature of each type of role relationship may be assimilated from the culture, the particular way in which an individual behaves in each role that he occupies is idiosyncratically coloured by the significant others with whom he has interacted (Lewis, 1975). For example Teevan (1972) found norms and values relating to premarital sexuality to be much influenced by the peer group. The attitudes of young married students to their roles as husband and father are similarly influenced by important figures in their lives (Hutter, 1974). Such influences may not be consciously recognized. As another example Toman (1971) has suggested that adult social relationships have more chance of success, the more they resemble early intrafamilial ones. To be more specific, he suggests that sibling positions tend to determine "role" preferences in later social contexts. Thus, considering only two child families, an elder brother with a younger sister would be used to a senior position and to close interaction with a girl, and a younger sister with one elder brother would be used to the junior position with an elder brother. Such a couple would on this thesis be deemed compatible. By contrast a boy with a younger brother would be incompatible with a sister with a younger sister. A survey of 2300 families and 108 divorced couples provided some support for this view.

The quality of a woman's relationships with her various family members provide further evidence for this principle. Uddenberg *et al.* (1979) compared the descriptions of their parents given by 69 women with their reports about their partners and children, and with independent data from the latter. The women's relationships with opposite sex partners and sons, but not with daughters, were related to their perceived relationships with their fathers. Thus the father-daughter relationship appears to influence the daughter's way of relating to other significant males.

Whilst in these cases the influence of particular others affects behaviour in relationships of certain types, there are of course more general influences which affect most or all of the individual's relationships. The distinction between the relationship-specific characteristics of an individual's behaviour and his more general personality traits is hard to draw—hence some of the current dispute in personality theory.

An interesting example is provided by the influence of the given name. Ashanti children are given, as one of their names, the name of the day of the week on which they were born. Amongst male children, particular personality types are traditionally associated with being born on particular days. In particular, Monday boys are supposed to be retiring, quiet and peaceful, and Wednesday's boys to be quick-tempered, aggressive trouble-makers. Jahoda (1954) compared the frequency distribution of the day-names between the boys in a school and the delinquents in the law courts. Monday children were markedly under-represented in the latter sample. For offences against the person, Wednesday's children were over-represented. This is in harmony with the view that Ashanti beliefs influence the course of social development.

In like vein, there is some evidence that nicknames or assumed names of children (Harré, 1975) and adults (Seeman, 1976) can influence the personality of the person concerned.

NORMS OF BEHAVIOUR IN THE DEVELOPMENT OF RELATIONSHIPS

Norms of behaviour will also affect the various moves in the development of a relationship. As we have seen in Chapter 10 each partner must work out with the other an agreed definition of the relationship. In doing so, each will make use of symbols, whose meanings are the result of a consensus of opinion within the society. Often an essential contribution to a definition of the situation comes from preliminary moves such as those involved in greeting. Greeting ceremonials or specified sequences of behaviour are an essential preliminary to further interactions in many contexts in human (e.g. Goody, 1973; Kendon and Ferber, 1973; Harré, 1974) and non-human (e.g. Kummer, 1975) societies. In the longer term there may be socio-cultural rules about the steps to be followed in establishing a relationship. In heterosexual relationships, for instance, there are cultural and sub-cultural differences in who should take the first step, and in the significance of asking the partner to one's home (e.g. Cook, 1977). And there may be special rituals for cementing relationships, such as having a beer together, or for maintaining a degree of distance in a relationship whose continuity is enforced, such as cutting (e.g. Harré, 1977). Many of these micro-sociological issues have been documented by Goffman (e.g. 1963, 1967), Argyle (e.g. 1975), Harré (1977) and others. Finally, as the relationship develops, the partners will develop their own "norms". Each will come to expect the other to behave in particular ways, and deviances will demand explanation.

GENERAL

Thus the social influences on the behaviour of an individual in a given relationship come from (a) expectancies concerning obligatory properties of the type of role-relationship in question. In some formal relationships these may be all-important, in some personal relationships much less apparent. They may be shared with all other members of the society, or with more limited sub-groups within it; (b) expectancies concerning similar but less obligatory properties; (c) social influences from significant others affecting behaviour in a limited range of relationships; (d) social influences from significant others affecting more general personality factors and (e) experiences in earlier stages of the relationship, themselves affected by social conventions. Thus the norms that determine behaviour within relationships must be seen as varying along (at least) two dimensions—the extent to which they are obligatory, and the extent to which they are shared with others. Such a view, implying a continuity between dyad-specific and culturally general norms, is in harmony with Berger and Luckmann's (1966) view of how such norms develop.

ROLE CONFLICT

Every role is complementary to some other role or roles. Husband and wife, doctor and patient, trawler skipper and crewman, each occupy complementary roles, and each has legitimate expectations about the behaviour of the other to him or her. These expectations will include culturally valued norms of reciprocity and fairness (Blau, 1964). It will be apparent that conflict may arise in a number of ways. One may not live up to the expectations of the other. Or the participants may hold different views about the behaviour expected from people in such a relationship. Or one or both may fail to understand how the other interprets his role, or the extent to which he or she believes that he adequately fills it. The consequences of such role conflict may be apparent in nearly all dimensions of the relationship.

The consequences of role conflict are likely to differ from those of conflicts arising from other sources. For example, a husband who did not earn his living would in many circles be considered not to be fulfilling his role, but a husband who could not play badminton would not, however frustrating this might be to his wife. Studies of perceived marital roles, and the extent to which spouses see them as being fulfilled, have been reviewed by Tharp (1963a, b) and Barry (1970).

The term "role conflict" has been used deliberately broadly here, to embrace all causes of conflict caused by departures from role expectations (Sarbin and Allen, 1968). Role conflict can of course also occur within an individual who finds himself in situations where he has to face up to two or more conflicting expectations simultaneously.

HOW DO SOCIAL FORCES AFFECT THE INDIVIDUAL?

Finally a fundamental issue, implicit in the preceding discussion, must be made explicit. How are we to relate the cultural forces, the social institutions that shape the nature of relationships, to the psychological forces guiding the behaviour of the individual? We have seen that the whole problem not only of socialization but of personality development is involved here. For some purposes "definition of the situation" and "definition of the relationship" (see pp. 65 and 135) are useful conceptual tools. Individuals perceive and define situations in terms determined by their past history. In seeking to reach mutually agreed definitions of their relationships they are influenced by their past history, including the norms they have acquired, and by the current situation. Many influences from their past history will be shared with all or most other individuals growing up in the same culture. Others will be specific to the individual.

The definitions of the situation and of the relationship will include expectancies about how the individual and others should behave. It will involve specification of the relative rewarding values of different possible outcomes, which may lead to the formulation of plans of action, and thus determine subsequent behaviour. Thus the way in which the actor defines the situation and in particular the relative values he has acquired, form a link between the social and the psychological forces determining the nature of relationships (cf. Stebbins, 1969; Tajfel, in press).

However if the concept of the "definition of the situation" embraces diverse expectations and values placed on different types of behaviour within a relationship, we must ask at what level of analysis it should properly be applied. Is it just the sum of its component parts, or does the concept imply the existence of emergent properties, or of a whole whose perception as such is an important determinant of the behaviour of the participants? Such concepts are useful in part because of their flexibility, but they need to be given edges before much further progress can be made.

We have seen that the course of a relationship may be affected by influences from the physical environment, by the immediate impact of other relationships, and by a variety of cultural and social influences. In conclusion it must be emphasized that, if we wish to describe these influences in any detail, assess their distribution or estimate their potency, we must do so against a background of an adequate description of the relationships themselves.

Summary

The following extra-dyadic influences on relationships are discussed:
(a) Influences from the physical environment.
(b) Influences from the other relationships in which the participants are involved. This includes some discussion of the complex network of relationships within a family.
(c) Cultural influences on the emotions shown in social situations.
(d) Social norms, with obligatory or expected rights and duties, shared with other members of groups or sub-groups in the society.
(e) Individually-specific experiences, including those from significant others in the individual's life time.

14

Dissonance, Balance and Related Issues

Dissonance and balance

We have seen in Chapter 7 that it may be rewarding to find that others share our views. The suggestion was that people need to assess social reality correctly. Our social beliefs can be validated only by other people, and when others provide confirmation of our views ("consensual validation"), we may feel positive affect and be attracted to them.

But what if we discover that a colleague we think highly of holds opinions different from our own on an important matter? The immediate outcome is likely to be experienced anxiety—anxiety which may choke or disturb the relationship at that point (Sullivan, 1953). Apparently our beliefs and attitudes not only require validation from the external world, they also need to have some degree of consistency with each other. Of course we may not recognize inconsistency, but if we do, it must be put right. We may decide that we do not think so highly of our colleague after all, or change our own opinion, or disbelieve the news—"he can't really think *that!*"

A number of related theories involve this general view. Items of knowledge, opinion or belief that individuals have, if not irrelevant to each other, will be either consistent or inconsistent with each other. For example, how we see ourselves behaving towards another person may affect our feelings towards him (e.g. Festinger, 1957). An individual who harms another may convince himself that the victim deserved what he got. He is more likely to do this, the more highly he thinks of himself (Glass, 1964), perhaps because it is then more "dissonant" for him to accept blame himself. Of course these are not the only escapes open to the harm-doer; he may accept responsibility and attempt compensation, deny responsibility, minimize the harm he has done (Brock and Buss, 1962) and so on.

Again, belief that a man is a scoundrel and news that he has recently wronged a friend would be consistent, whilst the same belief would be inconsistent with news that he had helped a friend at great personal sacrifice. In the latter case, tension will be felt and some change is likely to occur. We might change our view of the individual in question, or disbelieve the news (e.g. Heider, 1958; Newcomb, 1961; Kelley, 1971).

Some of the theories in this area lay emphasis on consistency between cognitive elements (attitudes or beliefs), others on consistency between attitudes and behaviour, and yet others on consistency between attitudes and the self-image (e.g. Aronson, 1969). In so far as what is important about an actor's behaviour is what he believes himself to have done, and in so far as the self-image involves beliefs about the self, we need not, for present purposes, be too concerned about the differences between these approaches. Let us consider how the extent to which we share opinions with others may affect our feelings about them, or vice versa.

Newcomb (1961) supposed that individuals form positive and negative attitudes towards objects (physical and social) in the world. If two individuals like each other and perceive each other to have similar attitudes towards an object, a state of balance will exist. However imbalance occurs if they like each other but see each other as having dissimilar attitudes, or dislike each other and see each other as having similar attitudes. In such a case, if they expect their relationship to be a continuing one, one or both will change either his feelings towards the object or towards the other individual. The object concerned may be external to the dyad. Thus A, who likes watching football, is more likely to like B if he perceives that B likes watching football. Furthermore A will like B the more, the more important watching football is to him. This could be because A looks forward to enjoyable discussions with B about football, but it could also simply be because positive views about another football-lover are consistent with his own positive views about himself—"He must be another good chap, like me." Alternatively, if A likes B but perceives that B does not like football, he may decide that after all watching football is a waste of time. It has been shown experimentally that subjects are more likely to change their views to accord with those of a liked partner than with a disliked one, and more likely to change their views to differ from a disliked one (e.g. Sampson and Insko, 1964).

In other cases the "object" may concern characteristics of one of the individuals involved. A, who is proud of his badminton skills (i.e. who likes A in this respect), is more prone to like B if A perceives that B appreciates his (A's) skill (i.e. if B also likes A in this respect). Alternatively, A, liking B, might come to believe that B appreciated his skill at badminton or, knowing that B was uninterested in badminton, that badminton does not matter all that much anyway.

In his classic study, Newcomb (1961) studied students, initially strangers to each other, living together in a house near the University campus. At the start of term, the students were given several attitude and personality inventories, and their values in a number of important life areas were assessed. At intervals during the study the students were asked to estimate the attitude of other students, various measures of friendship were taken, and a few simple experiments were conducted. It was found that the students were attracted to others with the same values and to others who liked the same people as themselves. Agreement on attitudes led to the gradual development of friendship. And as friendships developed, agreement between them increased. Experiments employing an outside stooge also showed that attraction increased agreement. All these findings are in accordance with balance theory.

One result of special interest concerned the effect of the personality of the subjects on the way balance was obtained. The students had previously been assessed on a scale for authoritarianism. Since authoritarian individuals are more rigid than non-authoritarian ones, and tend to interpret the world in terms of their own preconceived notions, they would be expected to be less good at perceiving other peoples' attitudes. This was the case. So, although both groups were equally likely to achieve balanced relationships, they did it in different ways. Non-authoritarians became attracted to people who agreed with them, whilst authoritarians achieved balance by misperceiving other peoples' attitudes.

In a similar vein, Byrne and Wong (1962) found that white subjects scoring high on prejudice on a desegregation scale assumed greater attitude dissimilarity (see p. 83) between themselves and a black stranger than between themselves and a white stranger. They also assumed greater dissimilarity between themselves and a black person than did subjects low on prejudice.

Balance theories have been applied to many other aspects of interpersonal relationships. For instance they would predict that perceived similarity in a positively affiliative relationship would be greater than the actual similarity as measured by the differences between the partners' self concepts (e.g. Murstein, 1967a, cited pp. 120–1). Again, balance theories have been cited in relation to the view that relationships are seen as better, the more effort that is put into them. Shortcomings of the relationship are inconsistent with the effort put in, and will be minimized, whilst desirable qualities will be consistent, and therefore maximized—"I must love him if I have looked after him all these years". Similarly, personal commitment (see Chapter 10), as well as depending on a positive evaluation of the partner, is likely to enhance it. Once A is committed to B, negative qualities in B will be inconsistent and positive qualities consistent; attention will be focussed on the latter, and the former may be seen in a more favourable light.

Of course, within a dyadic relationship, balance may exist for A but not for B. A may perceive that B's attitudes towards object O are the same as he has, but B may perceive A's attitudes to differ from his own. It must also be remembered that balance depends on perceived, not actual, similarity: A and B may like each other and perceive each other to have similar attitudes or personalities, when in fact their attitudes differ. As we have seen, this is probably common, since engaged and married couples see each other as having attitudes more similar to their own than is actually the case.

In the earlier balance theories it was assumed that an individual's attitudes to other people and his attitudes to objects have similar properties. However Newcomb (1971) has pointed out the limitations of this view; A's attitude to B is affected by his view of B's attitude to A, an issue which does not arise with A's attitude to a non-social object. Newcomb argues also that different balanced states are not equivalent to each other; there are differences between balanced states when A likes B and balanced states when A does not like B. The latter are more unstable, and involve less marked tendencies towards balance. Newcomb ascribes this to the intrusion of forces other than those towards balance—for instance, ambivalence about both positive and negative reciprocation from a disliked person, and the limited involvement of A with a person for whom he has no regard. If A likes B he is likely to assume that B likes him, but if A dislikes B he may neither assume that B dislikes him nor care whether he does.

Early balance theories also tended to be over-simplistic in their dependence on overall assessments of "attraction" or "liking". As argued here in a number of contexts (see p. 42, 140), such global assessments may have been useful tools for some laboratory experiments, but distort reality. Newcomb (1971) takes up this issue in reply to a previous criticism of balance theory—its apparent inability to cope with the case of the triangle Joe loves Ann, Ann loves Harry, does Joe like Harry? Balance theory suggests that he should, but if Joe sees Harry as a rival, commonsense suggests that he will not. Newcomb argues that attraction is not unitary, and will vary with the role perceptions (see p. 135) of the individuals involved. Joe may perceive Harry sometimes as a male friend and sometimes as a rival: it is a commonplace that we can be attracted to a person in some contexts and not in others. On this view a tendency towards "balance" is not ubiquitous (see also Murstein, 1971b), but a principle which provides a handle on certain aspects of interpersonal relationships.

Indeed, it is important to remember that imbalance depends on how the participants perceive the total situation (e.g. Abelson, 1959). Agreement with someone we do not expect to meet matters much less than agreement with a person we shall see shortly (Insko et al., 1974). Imbalance matters only if it is thought about: we accept but neglect some features in our friends that we would find unpleasant in others. And a friend's discordant view may be seen as based on sound motivation (e.g. friendly criticism), or "understood" as part of other more desirable characteristics ("the defects of his qualities").

As these examples indicate, one of the qualities, and one of the defects, of balance theories is their flexibility. Although theories of dissonance and balance have been stated much more precisely than this brief summary might indicate, it is clear that, if used descriptively, they could rather easily be used to explain almost anything.

Furthermore, alternative explanations of some of the phenomena are possible. For example Bem (1967, 1972) suggested that people generally do not know their own attitudes, but infer them from their behaviour. Thus while dissonance theory postulates that an unpleasant motivational state arises from dissonance between attitudes and behaviour, and that this state can be reduced by an attitude change, Bem argues that a person's attitudes come to be compatible with his behaviour because they are inferred from it. It appears to be very difficult to design a definitive experiment to decide between the two views (Bem and McConnell, 1970), and it may be that they have distinct areas of applicability (Fazio et al., 1977). But such difficulties do indicate that we should regard balance theories as most useful tools.

There is also another problem. We have seen that balance theories would predict that A would be attracted towards another individual B who had attitudes similar to his own not only about objects in the external world, but also about himself. And this should hold for both positive and negative evaluations—we should be attracted not only to others who recognize the good points that we know we have, but also to others who perceive the weak ones (Deutsch and Solomon, 1959). In his classic studies of the formation of relationships amongst students, Newcomb did indeed obtain some evidence that a student tended to be attracted to another whom he saw as seeing him in the same way as he saw himself, even where undesirable characteristics were concerned. However, balance theory generally receives less support in situations involving dislike than it does in situations where the feelings to the other person are positive. In the former type of situation it seems that a need to be liked by others, however poorly one may view oneself, overrides the effect of consistency or balance.

Deutsch and Solomon (1959) gave subjects false information about their own performance on a task, and an evaluation from a team mate of their performance. The subjects then had to express their feelings about their evaluator. Those who thought they had done well liked a positive evaluator more than a negative one, while subjects who thought they had done poorly had no consistent preference. The results were interpreted in terms of two biases—one to prefer positive evaluations over negative ones, and another to prefer ones consistent with the subject's own views. These would cancel each other for the subjects who thought they had done poorly. Data from other studies provide strong support for the view that people are attracted to those who evaluate them highly, especially if they initially have low self-esteem. Of course positive evaluations from others are subject to the effects of a variety of qualifying influences, including the subject's perceptions of the validity of the evaluation and of the evaluator and his intent, the subject's need for positive evaluations, and the nature of preceding interactions (Mettee and Aronson, 1974). By contrast, the view that people are attracted to those who evaluate them as they evaluate themselves is generally supported only where the evaluations concern specific attributes of the subject rather than global assessments (Stroebe, 1977; see also Curry and Emerson, 1970).

Because of these reservations, it is clear that we should use theories of dissonance and balance with circumspection. However they do provide a valuable framework for thought and their achievements show that assessments of whether B sees O as A sees O, and whether A believes that B sees A as A sees A, are likely to be of crucial importance for understanding A's feelings about B.

Secord and Backman's interpersonal congruency

Secord and Backman (1974) have attempted to pull many of these findings together in a theory of "interpersonal congruency". This embraces many predictions of dissonance theory and balance theories, and also the views of those who emphasize the importance of reciprocity or complementarity (see Chapter 7).

Emphasizing the role of cognitive processes rather than need gratification, they present their theory as concerned with the manner in which individuals maintain a stable interpersonal environment. In any particular instance, they consider three components—an aspect of A's self, A's interpretation of his behaviour relevant to that aspect, and his beliefs about another person's (B's) behaviour and feelings to him with regard to that aspect. They suggest that A tries to maintain a state of congruency between these three components such that the behaviour of A and B imply a definition of self that is congruent with the relevant aspects of his self-concept.

Congruency may take a number of forms. In congruency by implication, A perceives B as seeing him to possess a characteristic corresponding to an aspect of his self-concept. A girl who feels she is beautiful perceives that someone else admires her. In congruency by validation, B calls for behaviour from A that corresponds to his self-concept. An individual who sees himself as nurturant is able to behave in a nurturant way with someone who is succorant (thus, it will be noted, the concept of need complementarity becomes unnecessary: congruency of self-concepts suffices). And in congruency by comparison, the behaviour of B suggests by comparison that A possesses a particular component of self. Thus A considers himself clever, and convinces himself that this is true by mixing with less clever people.

Secord and Backman suggest that individuals maximize congruency by a number of techniques:

(1) Cognitive restructuring. The individual may misperceive how others see him or misinterpret his own behaviour, or else he may restructure the situation in order to change the evaluation of his own

behaviour. For example, a number of studies have illustrated the manner in which information about the self is distorted to produce greater congruency with the individual's view of himself (see above and Harvey *et al.*, 1957). We have already noted that, when an individual acts in a manner of which he might feel ashamed, he restructures the situation so that the act is seen either as no longer bad (see (2) below) or as beyond his own control (Scott and Lyman, 1968).

(2) Selective evaluation. Here A increases congruency by altering his evaluation of self, behaviour or the other person appropriately. Thus he may evaluate highly those who behave congruently to him, or minimize incongruency by devaluing others to whom he behaves in a manner incongruent with his self-concept. Such processes are illustrated by, for instance, a study of a sorority where the individuals most liked by a member were those whom she perceived as having the most congruent view of her and who actually had the most congruent view (Backman and Secord, 1962).

(3) Selective interaction. A elects to interact with those with whom he can most readily establish a congruent state. It will be noted that this can lead to a choice either of a partner who responds in a complementary fashion, as when one who sees himself to need succorance chooses a close friend with a need for nurturance; or of a partner who responds in a reciprocal fashion, as when one seeing himself as having high intelligence chooses another of comparable intelligence who will value his own.

(4) Response evocation and self-presentation. A person may maintain congruency by developing techniques that evoke congruent responses from others. For Goffman's analysis of the ways in which this may be achieved see p. 65.

(5) Congruency by comparison. Incongruency may be partially resolved through comparison. Thus if A knows that he has an undesirable characteristic, he may exaggerate the extent to which other people are similar, or select others high on that characteristic with whom to compare himself (see also (3) above).

Symbolic interactionism

In Chapter 7 we saw that the course of a relationship was likely to depend not only on what A and B do together, but also on the extent to which each sees his needs as satisfied in the sundry reciprocal and complementary interactions that occur. We also saw that the smooth course of the relationship might well depend on the extent to which each adjusted to the other, and accommodated to the other's needs. The extent to which A can accommodate to B must depend in part on whether A sees B as B sees himself, and the related issues discussed in Chapter 9. We may now return to the question of how he achieves satisfaction. What we are concerned with here is not just the satisfaction of particular needs in particular interactions, but also longer-term fulfilment in the course of the relationship—does A's view of B approximate to A's view of his ideal partner. A consistent language to handle such issues is necessary. One possible language emerges from Goffman's use of the dramaturgical perspective (see p. 65). Here we may make a slight digression to see how that can be applied to the present context. Defining a "character" as a person with a distinctive organization of personal characteristics, and a "role"* as a plausible line of action truly expressive of the personality of a character (see also Goffman, 1959), McCall (1970, 1974; McCall and Simmons, 1966) regards "role identity" as "a person's imaginative view of himself, the way he likes to think of himself as the occupant of a particular social position". Each person may have many "role identities", which are seen both as emerging as a consequence of interaction and as having a causal function in his behaviour, providing both plans for action and the criteria by which action is evaluated. They also provide a means for interpreting the world of objects and people he encounters in terms of their meaning for him.

A person's "role identities" are seen as hierarchically organized, with some more prominent than others. The less prominent "role identities" may be called into temporary prominence by special circumstances, especially those relating to their potential relative rewards and costs (see p. 211). In each encounter with another individual, a person endeavours to display a selection of his "role identities", and these will constitute the character he there assumes. The other party may, however, give differential support to the several "role identities" displayed, and thus play a part in determining their relative prominence.

The consequent interactions involve bargaining between two indi-

---

*Note this usage differs from that on p. 169, so quotation marks are used.

viduals. A tries to perceive the character underlying the set of "role identities" that B displays, and devises a "role" for himself that can best make use of B's "role" and character. This of course is a two-way process, and continuation of the interaction demands some mutual accommodation such that each improvises a "role" roughly in line with that of the other.

Thus while in purely formal relationships (see p. 37) (role relationships in the usual sense, p. 169) each participant fits the other's requirements almost as a matter of definition, personal relationships require a fit in each of the "role identities" involved. Most relationships have both formal and personal (idiosyncratic) aspects, and whilst the requirements of the former may be met relatively easily, those of the latter may not. The social roles of husband and wife may fit quite smoothly, but the personal conceptions of two individuals as husband and wife may clash (cf. p. 179). Development of the relationship may then require suppression or distortion of some "role identities", and development of others, according to the "role support" received from the partner (G. McCall, 1970; M. McCall, 1970).

Such improvisation demands that each party presents one or more of his "role identities" to the other, and also communicates to the other what he takes his "role" to be (Goffman, 1959). These communications may fail, but if a relationship is to be established they must lead to selection by each participant from amongst his "role identities" those which can be incorporated into the relationship. Each must reach a compromise both with his own differential priorities amongst his own "role identities", and with the differential priorities amongst the other's. The process can be described as a negotiation as to who each person is.

Whether or not a relationship continues will, in McCall's view, depend on how reliably each provides the other with the rewards he needs or desires, and at what costs. But amongst the most important of these needs, in many cases, is that of providing "role support"—that is, confirmation of each person's "role identities". In McCall's view this involves more than support for the particular place in society, with its attendant rights and duties, that the other wishes to occupy (see p. 169), and more than social approval or esteem. The important issue is that it should tend to confirm the person's individual view of himself and of how he should behave. There is a link here with the G. A. Kelly/ Duck view that similarity in construct systems may facilitate friendship because each partner provides the other with confirmation of his view of himself and of the world (see p. 87). Even more important is the parallel with H. H. Kelley's emphasis on the importance of each individual's ability to express his own preferred dispositions, and of the extent to which he facilitates or inhibits the expression of his partner's (see pp. 144–5 and 217–18).

The symbolic interactionist approach is not yet well buttressed by empirical data. It is perhaps better seen as a way of describing how relationships work than a theory of their dynamics, and it has already been suggested (p. 180) that the concepts used require more rigid specification. However it emphasizes an important issue—the need for the two participants in a relationship not only to have compatible views about themselves and each other, but to see their relationship, present and future, in a similar way. An individual's satisfaction with a relationship will depend on the difference between how he sees the behaviour of his ideal self and of an ideal partner in that relationship and how it works out in actuality. His view of the behaviour of an ideal partner will depend in part on his view of himself. All four perceptions —of himself, of his ideal self, of the ideal partner, and of the actual partner, may be modified in the course of the relationship.

Summary

In this chapter several rather different approaches to the study of the interpersonal relationships have been discussed. Dissonance and balance theories, though more diverse than this discussion indicates, are concerned with the consequences of inconsistencies between an individuals beliefs about himself, others, and objects in the outside world. Secord and Backman have attempted to synthesize these with views about the importance of reciprocity/complementarity in a theory of interpersonal congruency, and elements of all three are combined in the approach known as symbolic interactionism, which itself has points of contact with personal construct theory and with H. H. Kelley's theory of social interdependence. Balance theories have the advantages and disadvantages of flexibility: the latter are even more apparent in symbolic interactionism, which nevertheless calls attention to important aspects of the relationship as a whole.

15

Learning Paradigms and Processes

Any science of interpersonal relationships must involve a close liaison with learning theory. But the day when that will be possible is as yet a good way off: the understanding of interpersonal relationships requires so much hard work at the descriptive level that the forging of precisely defined links with learning theories, except either in a rather general sense or in certain narrowly defined contexts (see e.g. below), is not yet possible. However just because such links are so desirable, it behoves the student of interpersonal relationships to survey the shore, even if he cannot yet reach it.

In this chapter, therefore, we shall first discuss briefly three models of learning used in laboratory situations, considering how far they are applicable to real-life situations. We shall also consider briefly two types of theory of the process of learning, and review the relations between the laboratory paradigms and the theories of process.

The three learning paradigms—exposure learning, classical conditioning and operant conditioning—are useful in that they provide a convenient framework for diverse examples of learning. They are distinguished in terms of the operations involved (see below). It is therefore not necessarily the case that different examples of any one paradigm involve precisely the same processes at a finer level of analysis, nor that examples of different paradigms necessarily involve different processes. We shall see later that the "pure" learning paradigms, based on laboratory studies, can usefully be given more flexibility with additional concepts if the complexity or diversity of the situations in which they are to be applied demands it: this has the effect of blunting their precision but extending their range of usefulness.

Exposure learning

This refers to changes in behaviour that result from an individual being exposed to an object or situation, under circumstances in which no consistent response apart from investigatory or exploratory behaviour is elicited by that situation, and with no obvious reward. The label "exposure learning" has been applied to the results of a variety of types of experiments with animal and human subjects, and the mechanisms involved are certainly diverse.

In some cases, the change in behaviour consists simply of a reduction in investigation of the object concerned. Such learning is usually studied in the context of "habituation" (Hinde, 1970b). Investigatory behaviour is characteristically directed more towards novel than towards familiar objects, and decreases as the object "becomes familiar".

Another consequence of exposure learning is that as a stimulus becomes familiar it also becomes more easily discriminated from other stimuli. Gibson et al. (1959) found that, if stimulus shapes cut out of metal sheets were placed in rats' home cages, then the rats learned a discrimination involving those objects more quickly than rats which had not been exposed to them in their home cages.

Exposure learning can also promote a preference. Bateson (1964) found that chicks reared in pens whose walls were painted with vertical stripes subsequently followed models painted with vertical stripes more readily than models painted with horizontal stripes, and vice versa. The testing was, of course, carried out in a situation initially strange to the chicks, though the preference was self-perpetuating and continued as the situation became familiar.

Similar ideas have been applied to inter-individual attraction in man. Homans (1951, 1961) postulated that how much two people like each other was likely to increase with the frequency of their interactions. Newcomb (1961) found that students who were room-mates tended to express preferences for each other from the very beginning of term, and a number of other studies have demonstrated the importance of propinquity (e.g. Yoshioka and Athanasiou 1971), especially early on in acquaintanceship. Brockner and Swap (1976) showed that frequency of exposure had an effect comparable to that of attitudinal similarity on interpersonal attraction as measured by disclosure and by the Interpersonal Judgement Scale (cf. p. 83). Zajonc (1968) has reviewed much of the experimental literature indicating that frequent exposure of a stimulus enhances its attractiveness. Not all of these writers see the effect of frequent interaction on interpersonal attraction as a consequence of exposure *per se*. Homans (1961), for instance, explains it in terms of frequency of reward and minimization of cost.

But not all apparent effects of familiarity on attraction can be explained in terms of classical conditioning, or as the result of a cognitive set, or as an artefact. There is evidence that it occurs even in coercive situations, and a reinforcement explanation of all cases of exposure learning easily becomes tautological (see also Harrison, 1977).

Familiar objects are also often comforting in anxiety-provoking situations. Another possible consequence of exposure learning, therefore, is that the object or situation acquires anxiety-reducing properties. For example, a chick which has been reared in groups of other chicks for seven days gives frequent "distress" calls if placed alone in a strange pen, but its calling is reduced if a mirror is present, presumably because the mirror provides some of the visual stimuli with which it had become familiar. With a chick reared in isolation for seven days the mirror tends to have the reverse effect, presumably because the stimuli it provides are in this case strange (Kaufman and Hinde, 1961). The comforting influence of maternal presence for a rhesus monkey infant or human child in a strange situation (Harlow and Zimmerman, 1959; Bowlby, 1969; Ainsworth, 1969) could be partly due merely to familiarity, though it can also be argued that this effect depends on classical conditioning (see below).

Another group of cases that fits the exposure learning paradigm, though clearly involving different processes, is more usually classed as "modelling". This involves exposure of the subject to another individual showing a particular type of behaviour, and subsequent reproduction of that behaviour by the subject. Students of animal learning (e.g. Thorpe, 1963) usually recognize three distinct categories here—"local enhancement", where the subject is merely attracted to the stimulus to which the model was responding, and then shows behaviour that resembles that of the model only because it is elicited by the same stimulus; "social facilitation", where the behaviour in question is already in the subject's repertoire, as with "infectious" yawning; and true imitation, where the subject subsequently produces behaviour resembling that of the model but new to his own repertoire, as in song-learning in birds (Thorpe, 1961). In man the nature of "modelling" can be even more complex, its precise nature varying between instances (Berger and Lambert, 1968; Bandura, 1977). Reinforcement received from another individual may affect the probability that that individual is taken as a model (e.g. Grusec and Mischel, 1966). Reinforcement probably acts not only "Backwards", to increase the probability that the imitative response will be repeated, but also facilitates the attentional, organizational and rehearsal processes that lead to the imitative response in the first instance. Thus the probability of modelling may be enhanced vicariously, by the perception that the model is rewarded. Whilst some imitative behaviour of children may be evoked directly and immediately by the model's actions, most modelling behaviour occurs after a delay, and implies the involvement of cognitive intermediaries (Bandura, 1971, 1977).

Studies concerned with "conformity" should perhaps also be mentioned here. Asch (e.g. 1952) has clearly demonstrated, in experimental situations, the great influence on the judgements an individual makes of a tendency to conform with those made by others. From a theoretical point of view, such cases fit even less comfortably into the exposure learning paradigm than does "modelling", and it would certainly not be difficult to suggest rewards contingent upon conformity, or costs on its absence. But in real-life situations modelling and conformity may be closely related.

At this point the obvious danger of grouping such heterogeneous examples as "exposure learning" should be emphasized—we may come to regard them as sharing a common mechanism. Clearly the influence of propinquity on attractiveness between people living in the same housing unit may involve opportunities to meet and a feeling of shared experiences—quite different issues from the perceptual learning shown by chicks or rats, or from the modelling by an adolescent of an admired adult. The paradigm is merely descriptive of the operations involved.

It is also important to note that the demonstration of an effect of exposure on attraction does not necessarily mean that such effects are normally important, nor that increased exposure always increases attractiveness. Indeed there is also evidence that increased familiarity may in some circumstances diminish attractiveness. In quail, Bateson (1978) has shown that potential mates who are slightly novel are preferred to more familiar ones. In man, whilst mates are usually of a similar race, social class, religion, etc. (see p. 82), there is also some suggestion that very familiar individuals are less attractive than moderately familiar ones. Although much of the evidence here is not watertight, it is of interest because of its possible relevance to incest taboos. In Taiwan, child marriages in which the bride-to-be lives in her husband's family were less stable and less productive of children than when husband and wife had been less well known to each other before marriage (Wolf, e.g. 1970). Although alternative explanations are possible—for instance the women concerned were often of inferior status (Kirkpatrick, 1972)—more recent work makes them improbable. Wolf (cited Demarest 1977) has shown that the younger the husband was when the wife was adopted, the higher the proportion of marriages ending in divorce. The evidence that childhood association leads to disinterest is thus considerable. Comparable evidence comes from Israeli kibbutzim: marriages between members of the same peer group are extremely rare (Shepher, 1971).

Furthermore, familiarity within a relationship can produce a change in its quality. "Passionate" love, for example, tends to diminish with time—though it may be replaced with other varieties. The data suggest, then, that whilst familiarity may increase attractiveness, and that it may enhance the ability of another individual to provide comfort in anxiety producing situations, there is also something attractive about limited novelty.

Classical conditioning

This involves the pairing of a so-called "unconditioned stimulus", which already elicits a response, with a (to be) "conditioned stimulus", which does not initially elicit that response. After one or more pairings the conditioned stimulus, even if presented on its own, comes to elicit a response closely similar to that initially elicited only by the unconditioned stimulus. For example, if tactile stimulation elicits relaxation in an infant, it is possible that visual and/or auditory stimuli associated with this event (e.g. sight and voice of parent) will come to do so on their own. Clearly, such a paradigm can readily be applied to emotional responses. Thus Mowrer (1960) postulated that, through a classical conditioning paradigm, conditioned stimuli can elicit emotional states (e.g. hope, disappointment, fear and relief). He then used an operant conditioning paradigm (see below) to describe behaviour directed towards (or away from) these conditioned stimuli.

An early study in which the classical conditioning paradigm was applied to interpersonal attraction involved groups each of three children. Each group played a game in which one or more members were rewarded whilst others were not. Each child was then asked which two children he (or she) would like to take with him on their next family holiday. Children who had been rewarded were more likely to choose members of their three member group than children who had not been rewarded. Lott and Lott (1960, 1974) explained their findings in terms of the reward being associated with other members of the group.

Lott and Lott (e.g. 1960, 1972, 1974) relate their use of a classical conditioning paradigm closely to Hullian learning theory. Their basic hypothesis is that we tend to like a person if we experience reward in his or her presence. This may occur because that other person has characteristics (e.g. beauty) such that his or her mere presence provides pleasure; or because he or she behaves positively towards us, for instance by smiling at or praising us, or by helping us, or is merely consistently present in pleasant circumstances. Lott and Lott treat liking as a positive attitude which could be related to the (implicit) anticipatory response of Hullian theory. On this view experience of reward produces an observable or a covert response to it, and this becomes conditioned to other stimuli present at the time, including (other) people, and can subsequently be elicited by them. Furthermore feelings produced by the situation may be attached to people present, who will then be liked or disliked the more as a consequence (e.g. Griffitt and Veitch, 1971). Thus a person present at the time of a pleasant experience will be able to evoke the same response, either completely or in an incomplete and anticipatory form. It is thus suggested that the processes by which a person may acquire attractiveness are similar to the processes by which stimuli acquire secondary reinforcing properties. In this way Lott and Lott seek to embrace interpersonal attraction within the general framework of S-R theory. They stress, of course, that the effectiveness of a given experience in evoking liking may depend on the motivational state of the individual concerned—being asked for a date is more likely to lead to a woman's evaluating highly a male confederate of the experimenter if her self-esteem has just been lowered than if it had been raised (Walster, 1965). Whilst acknowledging that the meaning of the experience is crucial, they interpret this in terms of the motivation of the subject, and tend to regard the use of cognitive, information-processing terms (see below) as unnecessary.

A conditioning paradigm has also been used extensively by Byrne (1971; Clore and Byrne, 1974). They suppose that positive and negative reinforcements elicit differential affect, and that affect may elicit attraction towards an individual associated with that affect.

Clore and Byrne (1974) review evidence that:

(1) Stimuli associated with reinforcements (punishments) are liked (disliked). For example, after a joint experiment subjects liked their partners more if they had received extra credit for their research participation in his presence than if they had not. Other experiments showed that stimuli associated with reinforcement, whether animate or inanimate, tend to be liked.

(2) Stimuli that influence attraction are reinforcing. Here a variety of types of experiment show that evaluative stimuli alter the probability of any response with which they are associated.

(3) Stimuli associated with positive affect are liked, and vice versa. One experiment cited here showed that when discussion with a stranger occurred under conditions in which the subject was experiencing discomfort (raised temperature or crowding), the stranger was liked less than when the exchange took place under comfortable conditions.

(4) Stimuli that influence attraction elicit affective responses. Both self-reports and physiological measures indicate affective responses to agreeing/disagreeing or similar/dissimilar strangers.

Byrne has used this reinforcement-affect model to make quantitative predictions about attraction, on the basis that attraction is a positive linear function of the sum of weighted positive reinforcements associated with the stimulus person (number × magnitude) divided by the total number of weighted positive and negative reinforcements associated with him (Byrne 1971).

As we have already seen, Byrne uses the conditioning paradigm to explain the attractiveness of attitude similarity between strangers, with similarity as the unconditioned stimulus. The experimental situation he used (see p. 83) is very different from that used in the classical situation by Pavlov and other experimentalists studying learning in animals, and it is clear that many other variables may mediate between stimulus and response. Indeed people may learn little from repeated paired experiences unless they perceive the events as correlated with each other (e.g. Bandura, 1977). This does not lessen the value of the classical conditioning paradigm at a descriptive level. As discussed previously, Byrne has not been averse to acknowledging the role of cognitive intermediaries although this involves moving quite a long way from the Pavlovian dog learning to salivate to a tone whilst strapped in a harness. Thus Clore and Byrne's attitude to the conditioning paradigm is important. Although they feel that confirmation or disconfirmation of the model is not possible, they do find it useful in integrating data, generating research and making predictions.

Operant conditioning

The emphasis here is on the manner in which responses are shaped and maintained by their environmental consequences. If a stimulus event which is contingent upon a response increases the future probability of that response, the stimulus is called a reinforcer. If reinforcement has occurred in a particular situation, then that situation will set the occasion for the repetition of that response.

For example, Gewirtz (1961) used the reinforcement concept to describe the development of an infant's attachment to its mother. Assuming that relationships are made up of behaviour systems directed to and maintained by reinforcers, Gewirtz argued that an infant will form an attachment with the person "who mediates most of the important environmental consequences of his behaviours" (Gewirtz, 1961, p. 237).

Another important example of the application of operant principles to real-life situations, is provided by the work of Patterson (e.g. 1975). This involved a study of behaviour problems amongst children in natural family situations. First he identified a group of "coercive" types of behaviour which were found with high frequency in aggressive children and were used by them to control family members— for example, Disapproval, Negativism, Non-compliance, Physicaı Negative, Tease and Humiliate. Variations in the frequency of the coercive skills during dyadic changes between family members were then studied. Patterson identified two kinds of stimuli that appeared to be important in determining the appearance of these types of behaviour—those associated with the initiation of coercive behaviour, and those associated with its maintenance. Of course the effectiveness of these stimuli was influenced by other variables, such as hunger or fatigue. The effectiveness of some of them was proved in laboratory experiments, and a detailed analysis of one case proved their predictive power.

Although Patterson's analysis is primarily concerned with the immediate precipitants of undesirable behaviour, it also has important implications concerning the longer term relationships between family members. Comparing "problem" families with controls, he assessed the frequency with which "hostile" behaviour from a child was followed by a response from another family member likely to induce another hostile response. Such sequences were five times more common in the problem families.

Principles of operant conditioning have usually been applied to interpersonal relationships in the context of "exchange theories": these will be considered in the next two chapters. We shall see that whilst the operant principles on which such theories are based have been derived from studies of animals in simple situations, in real-life rewards may act in a number of different ways. They may act directly, for instance by virtue of their own physical properties; they may have symbolic value; they may take the form of approval or esteem from others, which perhaps carries the promise of more tangible rewards at a later date; or they may involve enhanced self-satisfaction or self-regard. Furthermore it must be remembered that social actions (or indeed the perception of the actions of others) may have consequences in addition to affecting the future probability of the behaviour itself—there may be informational or incentive-motivational consequences which affect many types of behaviour (e.g. Bandura, 1977).

The perceptual-motivational view of learning

With classical conditioning, a response comes to be elicited by a conditioned stimulus, by virtue of pairing that stimulus with an unconditioned stimulus. With operant conditioning, a response increases in probability by virtue of a reinforcing event being made contingent upon the response.

Many of the experiments on both classical and instrumental learning involve very simple stimulus situations: with the more complex stimulus situations operating in real life there is a good deal of evidence to indicate that both are normally associated with exposure or observational learning, for the individual learns "about the stimulus" as well as how to respond to it (e.g. Lawrence, 1950; Thorpe, 1963; Sutherland, 1966). However even with this addition, neither paradigm is adequate to account for all cases of learning (Bindra, 1976).

It has in fact been suggested that not only both stimulus-stimulus contingencies and response-reinforcement contingencies form the basis of learning in real-life situations (e.g. Skinner, 1938; Mowrer, 1960), but that exposure learning is involved as well (Thorpe, 1963). For example, motivational arousal could be affected by conditioned stimulus—unconditioned stimulus contingencies, and shaping of the response by response-reward contingencies. Bindra (1976, 1978) has criticized this view on three main grounds.

(a) Such a view fails to explain how the motivational arousal produced by the conditioned stimulus and the reinforcement-induced response shaping are appropriately integrated.

(b) It requires that the acquisition of a new instrumental response should not be possible without the occurrence of that response: there is however evidence that learning without responding can occur (Solomon and Turner, 1962).

(c) It requires contingency between the instrumental response and reinforcement, and thus cannot account for auto-shaping (Jenkins, 1973) or latent learning (Thorpe 1963).

We may note in passing that: (a) The first of these objections is based on the assumption that "motivational arousal" is completely general, rather than specific to one response or response system: in an extreme form such a view is difficult to uphold (Hinde, 1970a; Andrew, 1974; Fentress, 1976). (b) The occurrence of learning without responding has been explained in terms of the elicitation of central drive states by reinforcement-linked conditional stimuli (Solomon and Turner, 1962). (c) The occurrence of latent learning has hitherto been understood in terms of exposure (observational) learning, normally forming part of instrumental conditioning (e.g. Thorpe, 1963); and auto-shaping may be taken to demonstrate the operation of classical conditioning within situations involving a "directed" operant response (e.g. Jenkins, 1973; Moore, 1973).

Bindra (1976) has produced a perceptual-motivational view of learning that brings these issues together. He takes the ethological view that motivation depends on both current stimulation and internal conditions, and supposes that learning consists essentially of stimulus-stimulus (not stimulus-response) associations. If one of the stimulus complexes has hedonic or incentive properties (i.e. is a potential reinforcer in operant terms), it will generate a central motive state, and the association between the stimulus complexes will then empower the other stimulus to elicit the same central state, and thus any response related to that state. While this resembles classical conditioning, Bindra emphasizes that it involves more than mere response-substitution, for the new (conditioned) response is not the same as the old one, but determined by the motivational state generated by the conditioned stimulus and the total situation.

Bindra describes the learning in terms of the activation and linkage of "pexgos", standing for *p*resently *ex*cited *g*nostic *o*rganizations. This theoretical concept is related to Hebb's (1949) "cell assembly", and provides a potential basis for links with neurophysiology. It is thus a theory about the processes of learning rather than an experimental paradigm. It embraces the three paradigms of exposure learning (including modelling), classical conditioning and operant conditioning not so much by using new principles, but by emphasizing processes, such as the association of stimuli controlling a central state with the to-be-conditioned stimulus, which were previously discussed but insufficiently emphasized by learning theorists. It would seem to have potential in the study of interpersonal relationships in that it could more easily handle the rather intangible reinforcers/incentives, such as social approval or loving glances, which are of crucial importance in inter-personal situations but not linked to specific responses (see Chapter 17).

Information-Processing and other cognitive models

Bindra's model of the learning process is couched in terms potentially translatable into the language of neurophysiology. This, however, is not a necessary characteristic of such a model. Cognitive theorists, laying emphasis on the acquisition of knowledge about the world, also attempt to model the learning process. But in doing so they postulate transformational processes or structures within the organism that are not necessarily or even potentially linked to known physical entities. "Schemas", "filters", "stores", "categorizing systems" are examples of such constructs. One variety of cognitive theory, the "information processing" approach, involves an analogy with communication net-works, in which the brain is seen as subjecting information to a series of transformations involving "filtering", "coding", etc. The processes are ascribed to hypothetical operators—"memory retrievers", "com-parators", etc.—defined in terms of their supposed functions. Although relating the postulated structures, processes and operators to neurophysiologically specifiable structures or processes is not a central aim, and current neurophysiological knowledge is little used in theory construction, there is of course nothing incompatible between an information-processing approach and studies of brain function, and where links can be suggested, information theorists are glad to do so. A variety of theories have been developed, many possessing great sophistication and predictive power (e.g. Broadbent, 1958, 1971).

Most information processing approaches depend to a large extent on laboratory experiments, in many of which stimuli are "presented" to passive subjects. Neisser (e.g. 1976) has the same sort of misgivings about such experiments on perception as were expressed earlier (see p. 84) about some laboratory experiments on interpersonal attraction—"A satisfactory theory of human cognition can hardly be established by experiments that provide inexperienced subjects with brief opportunities to perform novel and meaningless tasks." (Neisser, 1976, p. 8).

Instead of postulating a sequence of operations on the incoming information Neisser, arguing in part from real-life situations, emphasizes that even perception involves essentially cyclic processes in which the perceiver constructs anticipatory schemata that enable him to accept the incoming information, which in turn modifies the schemata. He rejects mechanistic models which treat the mind as a fixed capacity device for converting discrete and meaningless inputs into conscious percepts, emphasizing that perception and cognition are transactions with the world that do not merely inform but transform the perceiver. This emphasis is entirely in accord with the conception of ongoing dialectic between the personality of the individual and the relationships in which he is involved (see Preface and p. 326).

The social learning theorists (e.g. Bandura, 1977) take a similar approach, but are even more free with cognitive concepts. Bandura invokes, for instance, symbolic coding, cognitive organization, symbolic rehearsal, motor rehearsal, self-observation, vicarious reinforcement and other possible processes in the explanation of exposure learning. In a similar vein, he describes "reinforcement" as conveying information about the appropriateness of responses, directing attention to environmental cues, creating expectations that motivate actions, creating attraction or antipathy to persons, places and things, and altering peoples' self-evaluations in ways that affect their subsequent willingness to engage in conduct that is discrepant with their self-attitudes. While such an approach makes a great deal of intuitive sense, and provides an appealing way of describing everyday behaviour, the language becomes so elastic that its explanatory power would seem to diminish. It must be said that it is extremely difficult to escape from this difficulty.

Like all other theorists, information processing theorists must explain why some things are learned and not others. "Anticipatory schemata" may be given a crucial role here—we perceive what we are prepared to perceive. Beyond that, as with the operant paradigm, some form of Law of Effect is usually used—it is held that whether an action is likely to be repeated when circumstances recur depends on its outcome. But, as indicated above, emphasis is laid not so much on the outcome *per se*, as in learning paradigms, but on its information value—a reinforcement signals which conditions are the desirable ones. On this issue Bindra's incentive-motivational theory and cognitive theories are not too far apart.

Since cognitive theories are concerned primarily with the ways in which human beings acquire and use new knowledge, they are potentially more directly relevant to the study of interpersonal relationships than the others we have considered so far.

Theories of learning—Overview

In the preceding pages we have sketched three learning paradigms and two approaches to the study of learning processes, one potentially relatable to neurophysiology and the other less easily so. We may consider here some relations between them and their potential value for the study of interpersonal relationships.

The merit of the learning paradigms lies in the fact that the thousands of learning situations that have been studied in the laboratory, with humans and a wide variety of animal species as subjects, can be described in terms of only a few learning paradigms (Kling, 1971). In the laboratory these paradigms can be used in a precise way, quantitative laws can be based upon them (e.g. Byrne, 1971), and such laws have the advantage of being in principle falsifiable.

But when we move outside the laboratory, and study the relationships of sophisticated adult human beings in real-life situations, the issues become more complex. There are then obvious dangers in using tools derived from relatively simple laboratory experiments, though those dangers lie not so much in the tools themselves, as in how they are used. In situations that are limited and can be reasonably clearly defined, they can still be used in a quantitative way (e.g. Byrne, 1971, Byrne and Patterson, 1975, discussed on p. 98 and 199). And beyond that, they are still of value descriptively, to show up similarities between apparently different situations and to order the data obtained from diverse experiments or observations.

Of course the fact that several learning paradigms can be distinguished in terms referring primarily to experimental procedures in laboratory situations does not mean that they occur separately in real life. Even in many experimental situations they may be closely interdigitated (Thorpe, 1963). This has been demonstrated with particular elegance in studies of the imprinting of the following response of nidifugous birds (Bateson, 1971). It is well known that if young chicks or ducklings are exposed to an object for a while during a "sensitive period" within their first few days of life, they will follow that object with great tenacity if it moves away from them. The learning processes are usually referred to as "imprinting". It will be apparent that the procedure for imprinting follows the paradigm for exposure learning—a period of exposure to the stimulus, followed by a test to see what has been learned (e.g. Gibson et al., 1959; Bateson, 1964). Whilst a chick can become imprinted on practically any reasonably conspicuous object within wide limits of size, shape and colour, as it does so the particular object on which it is imprinted becomes more effective in eliciting following than any other. This can be described in terms of classical conditioning (James, 1959). And dark-reared chicks will perform a response (stepping on a pedal) with increased frequency if that response produces a conspicuous object, which they in turn approach (Bateson and Reese, 1969). The operant paradigm is also therefore applicable. Thus each of the three paradigms can be applied to the imprinting situation.

If the learning paradigms are applied to real-life situations, it is important to remember that one is dealing with paradigms, and not with processes. Even though learning in diverse situations by diverse species can be described in terms of a few paradigms, the learning processes may well differ. Such differences often become apparent through the necessity of building additional concepts around the paradigms. For example, Schachter and Singer (1962) used a classical conditioning paradigm to study emotional responses. Epinephrine (unconditioned stimulus) was administered to elicit physiological arousal (unconditioned response) in different situations (conditioned stimuli). However they found that the subjects' emotional responses depended not only on these experimental manipulations, but also on what the experimenter had told the subject would happen as a result of the injection. Schachter (1964) therefore went a step beyond the classical conditioning paradigm to propose that what a person actually experiences will depend not only on his physiological state but also on how he labels the situation (see p. 168 for discussion of romantic love).

In general, as we have seen, it is not profitable to attempt to describe the learning involved in interpersonal relationships without recourse to cognitive concepts—the effectiveness of rewards and punishments are influenced not merely by motivational variables, but by the expectations that individuals have concerning the outcome of interactions, and their perceptions of their own intentions and those of the other interactant. Their expectations may be affected by assessments of what is "fair", assessments which may be both culturally influenced and more or less specific to the individual involved. That the classical conditioning paradigm as used by Lott and Lott (see above) must be buttressed by additional concepts in real life is shown, for instance, by the finding that rewards or punishments provided by another must be perceived by the receiver to be purposefully administered if they are to affect the giver's attractiveness (Pepitone and Kleiner, 1957). The interactional and long-term nature of real-life relationships inevitably strains concepts derived from a rigidly S-R theory of learning. Experiences within a relationship affect not only the probability of particular responses but also, for instance, probabilities of categories of responses conditional upon other aspects of the context (see below).

In Bindra's perceptual-motivational theory of learning, and in cognitive (e.g. information processing) theories, additional concepts can more readily be incorporated. Both are intended to deal with process, and both are designed to accommodate, and in their own ways explain, processes and aspects of processes known to occur in the real world. While the paradigms are applicable to only limited ranges of phenomena, and permit quantitative and falsifiable laws within their respective ranges, these process theories have a broader scope. In principle, most process theories could be falsified by a demonstration that a particular phenomenon is better explained in a way other than the theory suggests, or by a demonstration of internal inconsistency, or by new phenomena that the theory cannot accommodate. However falsification is improbable, since they have been constructed on a broad base with intent to embrace very wide areas of human and animal behaviour, and can accommodate additional or modificatory concepts with little difficulty. This lack of falsifiability, which can be a major obstacle to scientific progress, is perhaps less of a problem in the case of Bindra's theory, which in principle could also be falsified by neuro-physiological evidence.

Such flexibility and relative unfalsifiability in approaches to the study of learning could pose severe difficulties for a science of interpersonal relationships which must in some degree depend on them. As we shall see (Chapter 16), theories for understanding interpersonal relationships are in fact still built on the more general statements of the learning theories of three decades ago, with cognitive concepts added as necessary. Do they not need a more satisfactory foundation? The problem is exacerbated by the facts that perceptual-motivational and cognitive theories themselves have many critics (see e.g. discussion following Bindra, 1978), and are in any case but two examples of many process theories. Indeed they have been chosen for mention here in part because they are so far apart in many respects—perhaps I should apologize if they feel themselves to be strange bed-fellows. With flexibility in choosing theories, and flexibility in any one theory once chosen, how can a science of interpersonal relationships be built?

Of course it is very easy to point to shortcomings in current learning theory approaches to real-life problems, and very difficult to suggest anything better. But perhaps even awareness of our shortcomings is a step forward. And it does seem that none of the theoretical approaches have yet come to grips with many of the complex phenomena that really matter for the understanding of interpersonal relationships. Consider a father, coming home after a long day, greeted lovingly by his young daughter. If he were asked what he valued in his life, he might well place his daughter's greetings high on his list. But attempts to treat the greetings as reinforcers (using the term in a strict operant sense) are clearly inadequate. They do not make him come home more often, and while they may affect other parameters of his behaviour just before reaching home, this is not the important point. The greeting does not just influence immediately preceding behaviour, nor the nature of the behaviour he shows to his daughter as she greets him or subsequently, it has affective consequences that influence a large section of his life, including his attitudes to all members of his family and even his behaviour during the working day (cf. Byrne *et al.*, 1973, for a related argument). Operant theorists could advance the concept of response generalization, but it would surely bend under the load it was asked to carry. It would be nearer to say that the experience influenced a behaviour system (see p. 36) or motivational state (see Bindra, cited above), and nearer still that it influenced a system of cognitive schemata, but here we are again back with the problem of unfalsifiability. The difficulty lies not so much with the inadequacies of the learning theories—process theories are potentially capable of going a long way to meet it—as with our inadequate knowledge of the structure of actions. Scientific method has given priority to understanding the products of analysis, the elements of action, and as yet we know too little about the relations between the elements: for that reason it is difficult to predict the repercussions of such a simple experience.

As perhaps this example shows, in one way the controversies surrounding learning theories could be an advantage, at any rate for the moment. We are so far from a science of interpersonal relationships that rigid links to studies of individual learning and discussion in terms of particular learning paradigms is possible only in very limited areas. So much of the subject matter still needs to be mapped, that the precise nature of the learning theory or theories it demands is not yet apparent. Indeed it may be just as well that there is no generally accepted process theory of individual learning, for then a science of interpersonal relationships might be shackled to it. If Humphrey (1976) is right in supposing that our more complex abilities were evolved primarily in social contexts, it could even be the case that information will flow the other way, and that an understanding of social phenomena will facilitate the study of learning.

Perhaps, then, it is best that we remain with the more general statements, employing the learning paradigms where they seem useful and buttressing them, albeit in a disciplined way, with further concepts where it seems necessary. Elsewhere in this book, therefore, I have felt free to move from one approach for understanding the facts of learning to another, as seemed most appropriate to the phenomenon under discussion. This may well be only a temporarily valuable strategy—application of modern cognitive approaches to the phenomena of social relationships would seem to offer some hope for the future. But for the moment, provided it is accompanied by reasonable discipline in the additional concepts employed, a flexible approach seems best.

The catholic nature of such a procedure demands immediate clarification on one terminological issue. In practically every situation the production and modification of behaviour depends on stimuli that give pleasure or pain. Such hedonic stimuli may affect, directly or indirectly, the future probability of actions similar to that just performed. In laboratory studies of learning, stimuli that alter the probability of recurrence of a response are usually referred to as "rewards" or "reinforcers" (Kling and Schrier, 1971). Of the two terms, "reinforcer" is generally preferred because it carries no necessary implication that it is pleasant to the recipient. Exchange theorists, concerned with interactions between adult human beings, more often use "reward", and this is in keeping with its generally looser and less sophisticated usage, and with the fact that the primary emphasis is on the perception by the recipient that it is valuable or pleasant. Where the opposite is the case, the term "cost" is often used. Other terms have been used in particular theoretical contexts and will be retained here where appropriate. Thus we have seen that hedonic stimuli may also act as incentives by inducing a particular motivational state and thereby facilitating a wide range of future actions. Where the main emphasis is on the motivating action of a stimulus, we shall use the term incentive as appropriate.

Summary

Three learning paradigms (exposure learning, classical conditioning and operant conditioning) and two approaches to the study of learning process (Bindra's perceptual-motivational theory and cognitive approaches) have been discussed briefly. If the former are to be applied to social situations, they must usually be supplemented by cognitive concepts. Process theories are usually flexible, and for that reason not easily falsifiable. All process theories are in some degree controversial, and depend on experimental studies of individual learning whose adequacy to cope with social behaviour has not been fully tested. It is suggested that an attempt to base a formal theory of social relationships either on one or two paradigms or on any particular process theory would not be timely.

16

Exchange and Interdependence Theories

The most influential attempts to apply learning paradigms to human interpersonal relationships can be grouped under the general heading of exchange theories. That these are diverse will become apparent shortly, but they share the assumption that social behaviour is in large measure determined by the rewards or expectations of rewards consequent upon it. That is not necessarily to say that *all* social behaviour is to be seen in terms of exchange, though theorists differ in how widely they cast their nets. Most exchange theorists emphasize that the interactions and relationship between two individuals cannot be seen as the mere sum of reciprocal giving and receiving of rewards, but have additional properties resulting in part from the fact that the giving and taking constitute an exchange occurring in time and within a social context.

Definitions

The present discussion has the limited aim of establishing the place of exchange theories within the general framework presented in this book.* It is first necessary to introduce, in terms sufficiently broad to permit general discussion, a few concepts used in most variants of exchange and interdependence theories.

(a) Reward. The use of this term was discussed on p. 210. In social interactions, B may reward A not only directly, but also by making rewards available from others.

(b) Cost. The extent to which an activity is punishing, including the extent to which its performance results in alternative rewards being foregone. Included here are physical or mental fatigue and embarrassment or anxiety etc. incurred through the behaviour. (It may be noted that minimization of costs may form one basis for attraction.

*Recent reviews are given by La Gaipa, 1977; Chadwick-Jones, 1976; Simpson, 1976.

Thibaut and Kelley (1959) cite the case of a stutterer who said she liked a friend because the latter thought stuttering cute.)

(c) Resource. This is sometimes used as synonymous with reward (e.g. sometimes by Foa and Foa (1974), cited in Chapter 17). More usually it refers to the attributes by virtue of which P *could* modify the rewards and costs experienced by another person. This may include material goods that he possesses, skills and expertise, and social characteristics (sex, age, etc.) which he brings to the situation and which may be valued by the other. The skills and social activities are often referred to as his investments, in the sense of "that with which he is invested".

(d) and (e) Value and Dependency. A given resource is not of equal value to all individuals: indeed its value to any one may vary with time and situation. The value of a given resource to B is usually spoken of in terms of the need for or dependency of B on A or on the particular resource in question.

(f) Profit. The rewards less the costs for engaging in a certain activity.

(g) Alternative sources of reward. The extent to which A can influence B will depend not only on the value to B of A's resources but also on the alternative sources of such rewards available to B.

Within these broad definitions, the emphases are placed rather differently by different theorists. As examples we shall consider briefly certain aspects of the classic approaches of Homans and of Thibaut and Kelley. We shall then examine the basic propositions of Equity theory, derived from these and from the work of Adams (1965) and more recently formalized by Walster *et al.* (1976). We shall then be in a position to consider some of the problems faced by, and the limitations of, exchange theories.

Homans

Homans (1961, 1974) attempted to build up a logical theory by deriving hypotheses to explain actual behaviour from a small number of explanatory propositions. The initial propositions were intended to be closely related to those of operant theory (cf. p. 200), reward being used in much the same way as reinforcement (see p. 210). They concerned stimulus generalization (stimuli similar to stimuli associated with behaviour that was rewarded increase the probability that the behaviour will appear again); value and frequency of reward (the more and the more often behaviour is rewarded, the greater the frequency with which it will appear); and satiation (rewards become less valuable with repetition). In addition Homans introduced a concept of distributive justice (see below), suggesting that an individual expects to receive rewards in relation to his costs, and will show anger if he does not. From his basic propositions Homans derived additional propositions and corollaries with which to explain everyday behaviour.

A central issue, both in Homans's theory and in other comparable theories, concerns the manner in which individuals assess the rewards and costs they obtain. The Law of Distributive Justice describes the manner in which individuals expect to receive rewards commensurate with the costs incurred in an interaction and a profit in line with the investments they bring to it. What counts as an investment is to a large degree culture-specific, though such things as age, maleness, beauty, seniority, wealth, wisdom and acquired skills contribute in many societies. People appraise the rewards they receive and the costs they incur in relation to those received and incurred by comparable others in comparable situations. As Homans (1961, p. 76) puts it, "For with men the heart of these situations is a comparison". If the rule of distributive justice is not seen to be met, Homans postulates that the individual concerned will show anger. In his (1976) view, what is compared is not the subjective values and costs of the rewards and contributions, but rather the outward and visible amounts of the rewards and contributions, as perceived by all the parties concerned. "Thus workers in a factory compare their earnings but not how much these earnings 'mean' to each of them" (1976, p. 232). It is implied that a party to a dyadic relationship will see justice to have been done if he perceives the ratio of his rewards to his costs to be similar to those he perceives his partner to obtain, and to those he sees comparable others to obtain in comparable situations.

Homans also discusses the problem of choice, suggesting that the decision between alternative actions depends in each case on the product of the value of the outcome and the probability of getting it. Probable outcomes may, of course, be assessed over a long time span, and there is no implication that the individual will be necessarily right in his assessment.

Thus Homans has attempted to demonstrate the possibility of arriving at a rigidly deductive scheme, defining his concepts reasonably precisely and discussing the extent to which the variables could be measured. The latter, as we shall see, poses great difficulties, especially when it comes to measuring "value" and comparing the values of different resources (e.g. Abrahamsson, 1970). Though setting out from a Skinnerian position, Homans employed, especially in relation to the notion of distributive justice, cognitive and emotional concepts such as value, anger and choice. While some have argued that such concepts reduce the elegance of his scheme, they enormously increase the possibility of providing plausible explanations of real-life social behaviour. Some have argued that Homans did not go far enough in this direction (e.g. Stebbins, 1969; Davis, 1973). However Homans's aim, restated recently (Homans, 1976), is to derive principles of social behaviour from more general propositions valid for social and non-social behaviour.

Thibaut and Kelley

Thibaut and Kelley (1959; Kelley and Thibaut, 1978; Kelley, 1979) have emphasized social interdependence rather than mere exchange. Like Homans's, their approach was based in learning theory, but they lay even more emphasis on the cognitive operations that guide each participant's choice of action, supposing for instance that each individual maintains a "set" or plan of action which is evaluated in terms of the outcomes produced. They stress especially the interdependency inherent in any relationship (cf. Lewin, 1964). This interdependency arises from each partner's ability to influence the behaviour of the other by determining his rewards and punishments. Successful interaction must involve the continuity of the relationship, and this depends on the satisfaction of both parties concerned. In effect, this emphasis on interdependency involves a greater recognition of the continuity of the relationship in time. For A to maximize his outcomes he must consider not only the rewards and costs to him that are consequent upon his actions, but also the consequences for B: A must try to maximize B's profit as well as his own, or B may opt out of the relationship (see also Asch, 1959; Kelley, 1979).

Thibaut and Kelley also emphasize that every relationship is embedded in a network of other relationships, both actual and possible. The participants compare their outcomes within the relationship with the outcomes they have experienced in the past, and with those they might expect in other relationships, by means of two comparison levels. One is the minimum level of possible outcomes that A feels he deserves (actor's comparison level), and is based on the average value of past outcomes in relation to the actor's present situation, qualifications, and so on. The second is A's view of the alternative outcomes open to him in other situations or relationships (alternatives comparison level). Thibaut and Kelley suggest that A evaluates the outcomes he actually receives in a relationship relative to these two levels. Comparison with the actor's comparison level determines his satisfaction with the relationship, while comparison with the alternatives comparison level determines his dependence on it. Some concepts of this sort are clearly essential if the approach is to be applied to real-life situations, and inevitably cognitive concepts are required to augment the basic learning theory.

Much of the research to which Thibaut and Kelley's work has given rise has involved outcome matrices in game-like situations (e.g. Rapaport, 1969; Gergen, 1969; Kelley and Stahelski, 1970a,b,c; Kelley and Thibaut, 1978). The most frequent used is Prisoner's Dilemma. The game consists of a series of choices made by each partner in the absence of any knowledge of the partner's current choice. The outcome each gets depends both on his own choice and on that of his partner. In Fig. 1a each player has a binary choice. The outcome for B for each combination is shown in the upper right triangles, and that for A in the lower left triangles. Each is told the results of his own and his partner's choice but, in the classic form of the game, they are not otherwise allowed to communicate. Since, on every turn, each partner has to predict his partner's choice as well as making his own, data on how cooperative each perceives the other to be, how accurate each is at predicting the other's moves, and what each does when he believes his partner will cooperate, are available.

The variance in an outcome matrix of the type shown in Fig. 1a can be analysed into three components. One, termed "reflexive control", concerns the extent to which each partner can influence his own outcomes. The second, "fate control", concerns the extent to which the outcome of each partner is controlled, irrespective of what he does, by the partner's choice. And the third component concerns the extent to which their outcomes are determined by the combination of their actions—"behaviour control". For example one partner might have better outcomes if he matched the behaviour of the other, or vice versa. In general, if A shows behaviour x, B may do better to show p rather than q; but if A does y, B may do better to do q (see Fig. 1a). Depending on the nature of the matrix, the two individuals may have similar or different ("correspondent" or "non-correspondent") preferences for joint actions. The "fate control" and "behaviour control" components

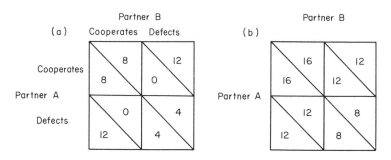

Fig. 1. (a) Given matrix for Prisoners' Dilemma. (b) Effective matrix, after transformation for maximizing joint outcomes. In (a) Choices to maximize own outcomes (right column and lower row) yield each an outcome of only 4. In (b) Choices shift to left column and upper row, giving better outcome (8) in given matrix (a). Many other transformations (e.g. maximize others' outcomes, own relative outcomes, etc.) are of course possible (Kelley, 1979).

represent the interdependence properties of the matrix. In general terms, they represent the extent to which each may take decisions to do what is rewarding to the other, and the extent to which they may cooperate to obtain mutually rewarding outcomes.

Many variants of the outcome matrix shown in Fig. 1a are possible. The values in the cells can be varied, so that the temptation to defect changes: for example in "Chicken" the values in the bottom right-hand triangles could be -4. The participants may be allowed to communicate only by the moves they make, or by non-verbal or verbal means. Again, one of the participants may be bogus, passing pre-programmed responses to the subject. By using such games to study the processes of exchange and negotiation in a two-person situation, Thibaut and Kelley and others have attempted to abstract laws of general validity. It is argued that real-life relationships can often profitably be seen as posing to each participant the problem of choosing a course of action in order to maximize long-term profit, when which choice he should make depends in part on the choice being made by the other, and in part also on the other's probable outcomes.

Whilst there has been some dispute over the extent to which specific research findings derived from this approach can be generalized (e.g. Chadwick-Jones, 1976; Eiser, 1978a), the use of outcome matrices has been extraordinarily productive of ideas about the course of social interaction, the nature of power, negotiation, etc. Of course, as Thibaut and Kelley point out, people do not always assess situations dispassionately or act accordingly. Furthermore, people do not act solely to maximize their own outcomes in the given matrix, but take account of the other person's as well. They may direct their behaviour so that their joint outcomes are maximized, or to do their partner down at some cost to themselves, or in many other ways.

Such strategies can be conceptualized as transformations of the given matrix. For instance, decisions to maximize the joint outcomes of both participants in Fig. 1a yields the matrix shown in Fig. 1b: in this case the use of such a transformed matrix by both participants would yield greater given outcomes. Many types of decision would of course be possible—for instance to maximize one's own relative outcomes, or the difference between own and other's outcomes. The outcomes yielded would depend on the decisions made by *both* partners.

Such decisions can be regarded as in part the consequences of dispositions to be cooperative, competitive, loyal, and so on. Each partner attributes such dispositions to the other on the basis of his observed behaviour, and such attributions may or may not be reassuring about the future of the relationship. But beyond that, while each partners' decisions will be influenced by his own nature, they will also be affected by the dispositions he attributes to his partner, so that each partner's actual and perceived dispositions will affect the direct outcomes each obtains. In addition to the direct outcomes as specified in the given matrix (e.g. Fig. 1a), an individual may obtain (and affect his partner's ability to obtain) symbolic, abstract outcomes from displaying dispositions (for instance, to be cooperative) that he likes to see himself as having (cf. p. 192). Conceivably satisfaction at the dispositional level can compensate for poor outcomes at the direct level. However if living up to principles involves poor direct outcomes the relationship may be impractical, while adequate direct outcomes obtained with poor dispositional ones may be unfulfilling—as when a competitive individual gets what he wants too easily (Kelley and Thibaut, 1978, Kelley, 1979).

Equity theory

In studies of the relationships between individuals, vigorous growth is at present taking place in the context of equity theory. Whilst having much in common with the two preceding approaches, this was applied initially by Adams (1965) and his colleagues in situations where rewards and costs could be measured with reasonable objectivity. Adams, like Homans and Thibaut and Kelley, emphasized the importance of processes of social comparison in perceived equity. A person perceives an interaction or relationship to be equitable provided that he sees his rewards to be proportionate to his costs, in comparison with his partner or with comparable others. The more A sees himself as putting into an activity, in comparison with what he sees another to put in, the more he feels he should receive in return. Inequity can arise if A finds the ratio of outcomes to inputs to be too small in comparison with B, in which case A finds the situation to be unjust, or too great, when he experiences guilt.

More recently an attempt has been made to extend equity theory into a general theory of social psychology by relating it to the theory of social norms, and to dissonance theory, and by formalizing it in a series of propositions (Walster et al., 1976; Walster et al., 1978). The first proposition merely states that individuals try to maximize their outcomes. However, it is pointed out that if everyone did this, chaos would result and all would suffer. Groups must therefore work out compromise systems for "equitably" apportioning rewards and costs among members, and for inducing their members to accept such systems (Proposition IIA). This will generally be achieved by rewarding those who treat others equitably and punishing those who do not (IIB). In assessing equity, outcomes (rewards—costs) are defined as the consequences a scrutineer perceives the participant to have incurred, where the scrutineer may be either one of the participants or an outsider. Scrutineers need not agree.

Further propositions state that individuals finding themselves to be participating in inequitable relationships become distressed (III) and will then attempt to restore equity (IV). Restoration of equity can be achieved in a number of ways. First, "actual equity" can be restored by appropriate alteration of the participant's own outcomes by manipulation of either rewards or costs, or those of the other participant. Alternatively a participant can restore "psychological equity" by appropriately distorting his perception of his or his partner's outcomes. Here equity theory assimilates dissonance theory.

These principles can be illustrated from research on the relationship between harmdoers and their victims. Applied in this context, the principles indicate that a harmdoer may either compensate a victim, or he may convince himself that the victim deserved what he got, or did not really suffer, or that he (the harmdoer) was not really responsible. At this point, equity theorists are obliged to predict which course of action will be taken when. In practice it is possible to classify the response of a harmdoer as involving either compensation or justification, and then to work out the variables which predispose towards one or the other. Considering not only the harmdoer but also the victim and outside agencies, Walster *et al.* (1976) have summarized research on the variables affecting the steps taken to restore equity.

Equity theory, originally applied primarily to business relationships, thus here finds application to exploitative relationships within or outside the business sphere. Similar principles have been applied in studies of the variables influencing altruistic behaviour (see e.g. Walster *et al.*, 1976; Adams and Freedman, 1976). Applications to the study of more intimate relationships are discussed later in this chapter.

General issues

Since the present aim is not so much analysis (see e.g. Chadwick-Jones 1976) as synthesis, these brief summaries will perhaps suffice to indicate the general nature of the principal exchange theories influential today. We may now discuss some general issues relevant in greater or lesser degree to all exchange theorists.

THE PROBLEM OF MEASUREMENT

The problem of measuring the rewards exchanged and costs incurred in real-life situations is crucial for exchange theorists. If they are to proceed beyond a qualitative approach to real-life problems, they must find a way of assessing profits and costs. The matrices used by Thibaut and Kelley and other theorists may be filled with numbers that are useful for illustrating theoretical points, but the actual measurement of values in real life is, except in certain very limited areas, a very difficult problem. For some types of relationship, such as that between employer and employee, it is possible to assess the several rewards and costs involved (wages, hours of work, fringe benefits) against a common yardstick. It was for just this reason that equity theorists first concentrated on monetary exchanges. But if one is dealing with personal relationships where social approval, understanding or intangible services are at issue, how can one make measurements adequate for scientific enquiry? The problem is exacerbated by the facts that the value of a particular reward is different for different individuals, and changes with time for any one—not just as a consequence of satiation, but through changing contextual factors.

Furthermore profits and costs must be assessed in relation to their meanings to the individuals concerned. For instance the value of social approval, or of gestures of affection and love, depend on their being seen as genuine and not too freely given (Blau, 1964) as well as on the context. And a given item may vary in value according to who gives it and who receives it. As discussed in Chapter 17, money has the same value no matter who gives it, but a kiss does not.

In addition, an emphasis on rewards minus costs implies equivalence between an activity bringing high rewards with high costs and another bringing the same profit with less effort. In practice, however, high rewards and high costs seem likely to be associated with conflict, in a psychological sense, and thus to require qualitatively different treatment.

But there is yet hope for limited progress if we do not aim too high. For many purposes an equal interval scale is not necessary—we need only one in which the rewards and costs can be ordered in degree of effectiveness. This will enable us to say that an individual will show behaviour that will bring him reward X in spite of cost Y, or that he will show behaviour to obtain reward X in spite of cost Z, though we shall not then know whether he would show X if the costs were Y + Z. If we aim to make limited comparisons, rather than to build grand theories, ordinal measurement may be enough. Each of us is all the time making decisions (not, of course, necessarily conscious decisions) that rewards are greater or less than costs, and that this reward is greater than that. One could therefore use the behaviour of individuals to assess rewards and costs on ordinal scales, valid at least for particular moments in time.

And the very fact that it is the meaning of the rewards and costs to the individuals concerned that matters can be turned to good advantage—one can *ask* people what they feel about their outcomes and inputs, what rewards they feel they have received and provided, and so on. Walster *et al.* (1978) provide examples of some scales. The problem of measurement, though formidable, can be seen as making difficulties for the exchange theorist in practice rather than one necessarily bringing defeat in principle (see also Kelley, 1979).

HOW DO INDIVIDUALS ASSESS WHAT IS FAIR?

As we have seen, in answer to this question Homans invoked the "law of distributive justice", and Thibaut and Kelley used two "comparison levels", the first concerned with satisfaction with the relationship itself, and the other with dependence on it. Since for Homans the costs of engaging in an interaction include the rewards forgone by not engaging in other possible interactions, his proposal and that of Thibaut and Kelley are in fact very similar (Homans, 1974). In neither case, of course, is there any necessary implication either of conscious decision, or that justice implies equality. But many difficulties arise. For one thing, the participants are likely to have different values and different standards about what is fair. In so far as "fairness" requires that A should see not only his own outcomes as fair, but also those of B, this involves considerations of interpersonal perception (see p. 119). Another point, recognized by Homans, stems from the fact that relationships are extended in time. What is considered "fair" nearly always involves expectations about the future, so that assessment at any one time is bound to involve a degree of arbitrariness.

This problem of uncertainty has been emphasized especially by Blau (1964). He took the view that social exchange differs from economic exchange in that it does not necessarily involve attempts to obtain the greatest material profits and in that it entails unspecified obligations. When an individual buys a house, a precise sum of money is paid. But if A does a kind turn for B he creates a diffuse obligation to reciprocate without specifying precisely what would be a fair exchange. In Blau's view this is not a mere methodological problem, but a substantive fact. "It is not just the social scientist who cannot exactly measure how much approval a given helpful action is worth; the actors themselves cannot precisely specify the worth of approval or of help in the absence of a money price" (Blau, 1964, p. 95).

Nor, often, can they bargain about the returns to be made—a norm of trust is essential. The fact that we can and do specify how much gratitude we expect for a service rendered, albeit only in round terms, is not the issue here; such thanks can be seen as acknowledgement of unspecified future indebtedness. Indeed "intrinsic" rewards can often not be separated from the extrinsic ones: one may gain friendliness from an interaction as well as more tangible rewards. In any case love, respect and many other social rewards are spontaneous expressions of feelings, and cannot (in Blau's view) be said in any meaningful way to be used in bargaining.

Given that some standard operates, other workers have distinguished a variety of criteria for "fairness". Lerner (1974) emphasizes that, in any one society, a number of different rules of justice may develop. These are applicable in different situations. Sometimes notions of *equality* or parity prevail—everyone deserves equal outcomes. In others equality is subordinated to *equity*—each person's outcomes should be related to what he has put in—either to his costs in the endeavour in question, or to his investments, where the latter includes also the skills, expertise, social status etc. with which he is equipped. Disproportionate outcomes may be aversive to both parties, even though one is receiving a high level of rewards in relation to his costs (e.g. Walster *et al.*, 1978). Several studies have been concerned with the factors that determine whether equality or equity will prevail. There is some evidence that equality is paramount amongst younger children and that equity increases in importance with age (e.g. Leventhal and Lane, 1970). Lerner (1974) suggests that equality is more likely amongst close friends, but admits that the evidence for the view is rather weak (Benton, 1971).

A third form of justice, so-called *"Marxist" justice*, encompasses the view that each deserves outcomes in proportion to his needs. Lerner suggests that this is most likely to apply when the subject identifies in some way with the needy other. This happens especially inside families. Outside the family it is perhaps most often found in cases where people have been hit by unavoidable catastrophe ("It could have been me"), and when they are seen to have deserved better than they have got. In the latter case, considerations of equity also enter. It would seem that, almost by definition, "Marxist" justice is most likely to apply in the context of complementary interactions.

Another form of justice discussed by Lerner (1974) is the justice of *"legitimate competition"*. This seems most likely to apply when resources are limited and A has negative or neutral feelings for B.

In the context of the present discussion, it will be apparent that the special importance of Lerner's approach lies in his emphasis on the way in which participants' definitions of the nature of the relationship may determine what is considered fair. For this purpose, he suggests, relationships can be seen as varying along two dimensions. The first concerns its closeness—do the partners identify and empathize with each other, do they merely have a less close bond involving similar circumstances or some degree of promotive interdependence ("unit relationships"), or are they in an antagonistic or competitive relationship. The second dimension concerns whether the other person is seen as an individual person or as the incumbent of a position in society. Table 1 (Lerner *et al.*, 1976) shows the types of justice associated with

TABLE 1

Forms of justice in different types of relationship. Modified from Lerner *et al.* (1976). (For explanation, see text)

		Perceived relationship		
		Identity	Unit	Non-Unit
	Person	Perception of 0 as self	Perception of similarity with or belonging with 0	Perception of contrasting interests
				Law
		Needs (Marxist)	Parity (Equality)	Darwinian Justice
Object of relationship	Incumbent	Perception of self in 0's circumstances	Perception of equivalence with 0	Scarce resources, with equally legitimate claims
		Entitlement Social obligations	Equity	Justified self-interest

relationships of each of the possible six types. A positive personal bond favours justice determined either by needs or by considerations of equality according to the closeness of the relationships, whilst a role relationship favours some form of equity (see also Walster *et al.*, 1978a).

This is clearly an important step forward though, as Homans (1976) points out, it still involves some over-simplification. While parents may allocate resources amongst their children according to need, the children may be quick to spot departures from equality in their outcomes. Again, a teenage daughter seeking an advance on her allowance from her father might stress her needs, thereby favouring "Marxist" justice, whilst the parent might ask what she had contributed to the relationship, favouring equity. Or different rules may be followed in different types of interaction within the relationship. Husband and wife might operate on equality over food delicacies, but "Marxist" justice over the use of the joint resources for clothes.

An important reservation concerning equity theories, recently voiced by B. Caddick (cited Tajfel, 1978), must be mentioned here. Most of the support for such theories comes from face to face interactions between experimental subjects, or from data obtained within a more or less homogeneous social group. Furthermore in experimental work inequity is nearly always created by the experimenter, and not by the intentional behaviour of the participant who stands to gain from it. Tajfel points out that, in such experiments, no social differentiations, apart from being advantaged or disadvantaged as individuals, exist between the subjects. But equitable treatment of others, while it may apply to in-groups, does not extend to out-groups: history is full of examples of depersonalization or dehumanization of out-groups. Thus equity theory may require considerable modification if it is to be applied outside groups which can be regarded as socially homogeneous.

Another issue involves the development within a relationship of "norms"—that is, of behavioural rules that are more or less accepted by both members. As we have seen, norms may be shared with other members of the society, but they may also be more or less specific to the dyad. These may regulate not only what the participants do and how they do it, who takes which decision and how conflicts are resolved, but also what are to be counted as rewards and costs, what values are to be placed on various types of behaviour, and what ratio of rewards to costs is to be accepted by each partner. If the norms are agreed upon and adhered to, conflict may be reduced and reward/cost ratios improved. Of course the two partners may favour different norms. If one is weaker than the other, he might benefit from norms of fair-sharing of incomes, while the stronger would benefit from a norm of loyalty which would prevent the weaker from withdrawing from the relationship. Such an agreement by each party to abide by norms that benefit the other can itself be regarded as a form of exchange (Simpson, 1976).

None of this should be taken as implying that, within any relation-ship, fairness of one sort or another is bound to prevail. Because the participants strive to maintain a balance between their inputs and outputs there will be a tendency towards fairness, often described as a "strain towards reciprocity". But because each also strives to accumu-late a balance in his favour there will also be a "strain towards imbal-ance" (Blau, 1964). In Blau's view this may be true even of the relationship between two lovers, for each may, for example, act in order to obtain credit or to avoid debt in the future. But the tendency of each participant to maximize his gains must be weighed against some need to help the other involved in the relationship (Thibaut and Kelley, 1959). A detailed example, concerning the relations between a trawler skipper and his crew, has been worked out by Barth (1966).

Finally for a number of reasons, most of which have been mentioned already, the continuation of a relationship does not *necessarily* depend on each partner believing that the other is providing him with as much or more than he deserves (Thibaut and Kelley, 1959; Murstein, 1977). For one thing, neither member is likely to dissolve the relationship unless a more viable alternative exists. For another, a relationship may bring rewards, or its dissolution costs, from sources other than the partner: an employee may continue to work for a disliked boss because he likes his workmates. Third, rewards may be accepted, although of small immediate value, as symbols of future rewards. Fourth, members of the couple may be governed by attempts to emulate an internal model, or by prior commitment (see pp. 131 and 217). There is thus need to specify not only where the various possible types of justice are involved, but also where justice is of secondary importance.

WHY DOES FAIRNESS MATTER?

We must ask not only what is considered to be fair, but also why fairness matters. Some tendency towards reciprocity may come from each partner's tendency to reward the other in order that the partner should provide rewards in his turn. But beyond that, why should the participants in a relationship think that fairness matters?

A number of answers are possible, but most involve the view that individuals expect to be rewarded for being fair. On this view the rewards stemming from an exchange which is seen to be fair are greater than those inherent in the exchange itself, for there is also a reward in being fair. The latter can be taken as an assumption, or derived from more basic postulates. Thus if failure to achieve equity brings anger (see p. 213) or distress (see p. 218), and if it is rewarding to avoid these states, fairness will be sought in addition to the reward itself. Equity theory suggests that society offers rewards for fairness. If these are internalized in the course of socialization, fair exchange may bring high self-regard. Kelley's (1979) views on this issue were mentioned on p. 217.

Of special interest here is Lerner's (1974) suggestion that belief in a just world is necessary for adequate social functioning. If we all believed that rewards and punishments arrived randomly, we should be incapable of effective action. Lerner thus pictures individuals as making, in the course of socialization, "Personal Contracts" with themselves to give up immediate rewards in their own longer term interests (Lerner, 1974). Present-day costs are seen in the first instance as an effective route to future rewards. But individuals are also seen as recognizing a degree of equivalence between themselves and others. That being so, if an individual perceives that others do not get what they deserve, he may regard this as a threat to his getting what he sees as his own just desserts. He is therefore motivated to behave with justice to others as a means of maintaining the premises on which his own personal contract was founded. On this view, then, exchange of resources with another is seen not so much as important in its own right, but as a means of maintaining a personal contract that is essentially independent of the current relationship.

NATURE OF DISTRESS

Whilst equity theorists have postulated that inequity results in anger or "distress", little effort has been put into the study of this state. Adams and Freedman (1976) point out that an attack on the nature of this supposed state, an investigation of the extent to which it should be pictured as varying along one, two (guilt and anger), or more dimensions, the nature of its determinants, and the effectiveness of various measures in reducing it, would be important avenues for extending existing knowledge.

As we have seen, equity theorists are trying to forge links with sociology by their treatment of fairness as a socially induced norm (see p. 218) and with dissonance theory by suggesting that injustice can be either rectified in fact, or misperceived (see p. 219). But further links with studies of interpersonal perception must be forged. If a relationship is to continue, each participant must direct his behaviour in such a manner that the other sees himself to be fairly treated. If A is to achieve this, A's view of B's view of the relationship must resemble B's view of the relationship. And beyond this, at least in personal relationships, B's behaviour, for instance his tendency to leave the relationship, will be affected by his assessment of A's intentions. If B perceives himself to be unfairly treated, but believes that A was genuinely misled in believing that B felt himself to be fairly treated even though B did not, he will be much less likely to leave or seek reprisals than if he believes that A was deliberately profiting at his expense.

RELATIONS TO PERSONALITY THEORY

Individuals are likely to differ in their views not only of what constitutes rewards and costs, but also of what sort of justice, if any, should prevail in what sorts of relationships. Thus some relation between exchange theories and personality theories is essential. Some work in this direction has been started—for instance Walster et al. (1976) cite studies of the effect of self-esteem and other personality variables on the response of a harmdoer. (I have already mentioned, on p. 184, an earlier study involving the use of personality variables in relation to balance theories. In so far as individuals select roles and select between norms within roles, some interaction between personality and role theories is also needed.) However the difficulties may be considerable because a given individual will deem different types of justice to be appropriate in different types of relationship, and because assessments of personality are influenced at least in part by the context, and context can mean here the types of relationship to which they are relevant. Thus balance, role and exchange theories must be related not only to personality theory but also to a scheme for describing relationships. A given research finding needs to be located on a grid specifying both the personality characteristics and relationship characteristics for which it is valid. This, of course, is looking a long way ahead.

ALTRUISM AND INTIMATE RELATIONSHIPS

One of the most difficult issues that the exchange theorist has to face is the fact that social exchange sometimes is, or at least has the appearance of being, altruistic. Individuals often provide others with rewards with no expectation that those others will reciprocate. This principle is exemplified equally by the uncountable little acts of kindness performed daily to strangers as by the dramatic acts of heroism in war or peace-time rescues. Friends and family members do not always seek to maximize their gains from a narrowly egocentric point of view (Levinger and Snoek, 1972).* Experimental studies on the readiness of strangers to provide help ranging from the gift of a dime to a bone marrow transplant have been reviewed by Berkowitz (1972). As he stresses, "Many persons do help their fellow men even when there are no obvious material benefits to be gained from this action" (p. 67). While the possibility that hope of some future reward operated cannot be ruled out from field data, it is minimized in many laboratory studies (Berkowitz, 1972; Staub, 1974).

It will be apparent that exchange theories can cope with such cases. Homans (1961, 1976) argued that the profit gained depends on what people value. They may value the success of their children or their view of themselves as self-sacrificing humanitarians (see Kelley, 1979, cited p. 217). Lerner's "personal contract" is clearly also relevant here. The usual approach is to suppose that people follow rules internalized in childhood in order to avoid guilt feelings or social disapproval. Thus such behaviour is seen as controlled by internal factors rather than by the hope of external rewards. Here two difficulties arise. First, whilst the concept of "self-reinforcement" can be treated in a hard-headed fashion (e.g. Bandura, 1976), it is also easy to use it loosely. Great care is needed to ensure that "empathic reinforcement"

---

*Sociobiologists (e.g. Wilson, 1975) would not expect family members always to behave selfishly with each other. Their explanation of altruism would concern the manner in which the consequences of altruistic behaviour contributed to inclusive (genetic) fitness. But in the present context we are concerned with its proximate causes.

does not become an explanation that will explain anything (cf. p. 208). Second, the importance of internalized influences is not static and constant, but depends on a host of situational determinants. These may affect "the extent to which the individual is aware that someone is dependent upon him, recalls the pertinent social ideals, believes that this dependency is proper or improper, and is willing to accept the psychological costs of being helpful" (Berkowitz, 1972, p. 106). The variability in the effectiveness of supposed internalized moral stan- dards is clearly liable to detract greatly from their explanatory value (see also Asch, 1959).

Another approach is to argue that altruistic behaviour is not really incompatible with exchange theory predictions because it usually leads to hostility, humiliation and alienation (Walster *et al.*, 1978). Whilst the evidence that both benefactor and recipient *may* feel ill at ease in relationships involving altruism is considerable, it is of course impos- sible for the exchange theorists to prove that ambivalence is always present, or for their opponents to prove that it is ever absent.

At this point it might be reasonable to question the limits of usefulness of exchange theories (see p. 217). Are they to be seen as potentially ubiquitously applicable, unifying all aspects of social interactions and relationships? Or is their scope more limited? On the basis of data of the type given in the last paragraph, it could be argued that attempts to apply them too widely will only detract from their value. Such is Blau's (1964) view. Men may be physically coerced to act, they may act for fear of supernatural beings or of other men, for conscience, or perhaps altruistically: in these areas the concept of social exchange is not useful. It is valuable only between the area of *economic* transaction where profit and loss can be calculated precisely and these other areas where it is not applicable. Berkowitz's (e.g. Berkowitz and Friedman, 1967) postula- tion of a norm of social responsibility also places limits on the value of a traditional exchange theory approach (see also Schwartz, 1977; Hoffman, 1975). However Kelley's emphasis that it can be rewarding to behave in ways that confirm the characteristics we attribute to ourselves goes a long way to meet the difficulty: rewards are obtainable at the dis- positional as well as the direct level (see p. 217).

The relevance of the world of rewards and costs could be questioned not only in the context of altruistic behaviour. Walster *et al.* (1978a) list some of the difficulties of applying equity theory to intimate relation- ships. They point out that equity theorists have usually concerned themselves with casual, short-term interactions, from which intimate relationships differ in ways which hinder consideration of rewards and costs. This is not only a matter that the participants like or love each other and share intimacy, so that what is equitable is more difficult to assess, but also that they are likely to interact over a long period, so that perceived inequity can be tolerated as impermanent. Furthermore the resources exchanged include less concrete and more particularistic resources (cf. p. 240), and the participants are more ready to exchange resources of different types. And perhaps most important of all, participants in a really intimate relationship see themselves as a couple: the rewards and costs of the individuals are no longer the issue; it is the *couple's* inputs and outcomes that are important. One's gains are no longer the other's losses. To these issues may be added, in the case of romatic love, the importance of fantasy; fantasied rewards may be as or more important than real ones (Berscheid and Walster, 1974).

Nevertheless, some support for the application of equity theory to close personal relationships comes from studies arising from the Walster *et al.* (1966) matching hypothesis (p. 91), though that hypothesis must cope with many complexities in real life situations, and some other studies of intimate relationships appear not to support predictions from equity theory (e.g. Walster *et al.*, 1978b). However Walster *et al.* (1978a) claim not that equity theory is adequate to explain all aspects of intimate relationships, but that it can provide important insights. In a balanced discussion, they acknowledge possible limitations of their theoretical approach for relationships of this type.

It will be apparent that the approach of Kelley and Thibaut (1978; Kelley, 1979) meets many of these difficulties. As we have seen (pp. 214–18), they focus on the interdependence of the two partners over time, rather than short-term exchange. Each partner responds to a *pattern* of outcomes, and to his predictions about the nature of that pattern in the future: these predictions depend in part on attributions he makes about his partner. Furthermore each individual is responsive not only to his own outcomes, but also to the other's. This is a function not only of the need to keep the partner involved, but of the acquisition of potential rewards at the dispositional level—each partner may seek to see him or herself and to be seen as a considerate, tender, forgiving etc., lover, as well as obtaining immediate rewards.

EXCHANGE THEORIES OF THE DYAD, AND THE SURROUNDING GROUP

It is important to stress here again some of the issues mentioned in Chapter 13. Whilst in this chapter exchange theories have been discussed in relation to the dyad, exchange theorists have pointed out that equity may be achieved in a transrelational manner—if A finds his relationship with B to be inequitable, and cannot restore balance in that relationship, he may compare himself also with another individual C, or with other people in general, so overall he feels justice to have been done (W. Austin, cited Walster *et al.*, 1978).

Beyond that, Blau (1964) has emphasized that the dynamics of the dyad can often not be understood without reference to the group. This is not merely that the investments and needs of each individual may be affected by his position in the group, nor that each member of the dyad has other relationships, interactions or potential interactions which may affect his dependency on the other. Intra-dyadic interactions may be affected also by the manner in which one member *sees* the other interacting with other individuals. Extra-dyadic interactions by the partner may elicit admiration, disgust or jealousy. Furthermore we have seen that intra-dyadic exchange may depend on group norms. As an obvious example, norms may prevent competitive interactions between the workers in a group. More important, norms of obligation to members of the group may permit unbalanced exchanges within dyads: an individual may give more than he gains in one relationship, but be compensated in other relationships or through membership of the group as a whole (Blau 1964; Thibaut and Kelley, 1959).

Summary

In this chapter three varieties of exchange theory—the classical theories of Homans and of Thibaut and Kelley, and also equity theory as recently formalized by Walster *et al.* (1978a)—have been sketched briefly. The discussion has centred round a number of issues more or less common to all of them—for instance the problems of measurement, of how individuals assess what is fair, and of why fairness matters. Equity theorists have already begun to establish links with balance theories and role theories, but much further work along these lines is needed. The precise limits of applicability of exchange theories remains an open issue, but Kelley and Thibaut's use of the concept of the transformation matrix, and their emphasis on the possibility of obtaining rewards at the dispositional as well as at the direct level, demonstrate that considerations of reward and cost can profitably be applied to close personal relationships. It is clear, however, that the relative importance of the two levels varies with the type of relationship: any theoretical approach must thus be related to a descriptive base.

One problem, related to this need for an adequate description of relationships, and fundamental for exchange theorists, has been glossed over so far. Does everything that is exchanged have similar properties? This is discussed in the next chapter.

17

The Categorization of Rewards

Any attempt to understand the roles of learning phenomena in interpersonal relationships must sooner or later employ a concept of reward, reinforcement or incentive. The exchange theories discussed in the last chapter inherited much of their structure from Hullian or from operant theory. But the concept of reinforcement, although used in a hard-headed way in laboratory experiments is, as we have seen, liable to be somewhat diluted in studies of complex human actions (Chomsky, 1959). In this chapter we must consider how some of the difficulties that arise can be met.

Reinforcement in learning theory and real-life rewards

In so far as exchange theories are descended from learning theories, they inherit a system based primarily on experiments in which food was used as a reinforcer for hungry animals. Many laboratory experiments on learning use animals whose body weight has been lowered by starvation; they are therefore highly motivated. Furthermore we know that, within limits, the effectiveness of food as a reinforcer varies with the period for which the animal has been deprived of food. It is therefore possible to control motivation rather precisely.

But food is relatively rare as a reinforcer in interpersonal relationships. Even in the early mother-infant relationship, where food was earlier thought to be critical, it is now apparent that its importance was over-rated (Harlow and Zimmerman, 1959; Bowlby, 1969). And whilst there are still unfortunately exceptions in some classes and some societies, food as such is usually important in adult relationships in the western world more as a symbol than for its need-reducing properties. The rewards important in interpersonal relationships are in fact diverse, ranging from tangible goods and services, through items primarily of symbolic value like money, to the expression of intangible emotions such as love.

We must therefore ask whether the properties of these varied types of social rewards are necessarily similar to those of food. Could we be misled in attempting to apply a theory drawn from studies of the effects of food on hungry animals to the subtleties of interpersonal relationships? In particular, are we dealing with individuals as highly motivated for, say, social approval as a pigeon starved to 80% of its body weight is motivated to feed? And can we assume that changes, of the sort that occur in the effectiveness of food with deprivation, occur also with other rewards?

We may consider these questions in the context of work on "social approval", a category of reward frequently used in studies of social interaction and interpersonal attraction. That social approval is a potent reward was demonstrated by the classic studies of Verplanck (1955). Individuals, who did not know they were being used as subjects for an experiment, increased the rate at which they made statements of opinion when these were followed by social approval from the experimenter, and decreased the rate when approval was withheld (see also Greenspoon, 1955; Hildum and Brown, 1956).

But this does not mean that all subjects need social approval in the way that a partially starved pigeon needs food. In fact people differ markedly in their long-term need for social approval. This need has been measured in a variety of ways, one of the more usual being a questionnaire consisting of items which can be answered in a more or less socially desirable way. Individuals who give socially desirable answers are supposed to have a high need for social approval. Such individuals did indeed respond to approval from the experimenter—for instance by increasing the frequency of plural nouns used when these were followed by an approving "mm-hmm" and a nod of the head from the experimenter. Subjects who scored low on the questionnaire showed only a transient increase in the use of plural nouns (Crowne and Marlowe, 1964). In other words, social approval resembles food as a reinforcer in that it is more effective with subjects having a high need for it (assessed by an independent means), but not all subjects do have a sufficiently high need for social approval of this type to maintain its effectiveness. If we accept the validity of such findings, they pose the further question of the basic difference or differences between people who have high and low needs for self-approval. A commonsense point of view might be that those with a high need for self approval had low opinions of themselves, but this seems not to be the case (Hewitt and

Goldman, 1974). While there are possible methodological weaknesses in this study (Stroebe, 1977), it would seem that need for social approval, at least as revealed by questionnaire methods, is far from simple.

Turning to the question of whether short-term deprivation influences the effectiveness of social rewards in the same way that hunger influences that of food, some doubt is cast on the general proposition by studies of sexual responsiveness. Sexual behaviour depends on physiological mechanisms about as well known as those of feeding, and, by virtue of its "biological" nature, one might expect sexual rewards to have more in common with food than many other social rewards. But it is well known in animals that sexual motivation may have a complex relation to time since previous sexual activity (e.g. Beach and Jordan, 1956; Beach et al., 1966). It is likely that the same is true in man, for the arousal elicited by pornographic films is said to show little correlation with the length of preceding sexual deprivation (Larsen, 1971).

In the case of social approval, some evidence suggesting that preceding satiation or deprivation can influence its effectiveness as a reinforcer has been brought forward. For example Gewirtz and Baer (1958) found that approval was a more effective reinforcer for children who had received no social approval during a pre-experimental period of over 20 minutes than for children who had (see also Landau and Gewirtz, 1967). However other studies show that the effectiveness of social reinforcers depends much more on longer-term needs for social rewards than on the immediately preceding conditions of satiation or deprivation (e.g. Zigler, 1964). Berg et al. (1976) found that social reward given one or two days earlier had a greater influence on the effectiveness of social reward in a preference learning task than did social reward immediately before the task. Furthermore, even if deprivation/satiation of social rewards does influence their effectiveness for children, it may not do so in adults. Walters and Parke (1964) found that social isolation had a greater effect on the responsiveness of children to social reward than on that of adolescents. Whilst this issue remains unresolved (see Mettee and Aronson, 1974, for a further review), intuition strongly suggests that the independent variables influencing the effectiveness of social rewards are very different from those operating in the case of food. For instance the distrust engendered by excessive social approval is surely different from the disgust produced by excessive food.

The power of the reinforcement concept in the laboratory depends also in part on our ability to predict which events will and will not have reinforcing properties. In non-social learning situations such predictions are often possible, but it has now been recognized that a given event may be reinforcing for one response but not for another, and that the effectiveness of potential reinforcers is influenced by a variety of constraints (Seligman and Hager, 1972; Hinde and Stevenson-Hinde, 1973). In social institutions the problem is of course many times worse (e.g. Firth, 1965; Heath, 1972). The effectiveness of "social approval", for example, varies enormously with the social situation, and depends on its being accepted as genuine, and on the frequency with which the individual in question is known to bestow his approval (Blau, 1964; Stroebe, 1977). It may even be aversive in some contexts.

But if we cannot predict in advance which events will have reinforcing properties and which will not, explanations of behaviour based on the reinforcement concept will be circular. There is a danger that rewards will be postulated *ad infinitum* and thus explain anything. The situation here is just that which bogged down instinct theory 50 years ago: instincts were postulated to explain each type of behaviour observed, and therefore explained nothing. This issue has been much discussed (e.g. Burgess and Akers, 1966; Blau, 1964). It is of course here that a proper integration of personality theory with studies of interpersonal relationships is most needed: specification of what is reinforcing in what circumstances demands understanding of the differences between individuals.

The classification of rewards

But another path towards surmounting these difficulties might be to categorize the rewards under study. Perhaps, if we could divide the rewards into classes, we should be able to distinguish between the properties of the members of those classes. This might even help us to predict when particular events would or would not be rewarding by reference to the class to which they belong. It is in fact the case that different exchange theorists have concentrated on exchanges involving different types of resource (La Gaipa, 1977). Homans (1974) and Blau (1964) were concerned largely with exchanges involving social approval and information relating to skills and expertise, Altman and Taylor (1973) with information of a more personal kind, Adams (1965) with pay or money. La Gaipa (1977) points out that this has affected their theorizing, in that different mediating variables tend to be postulated to explain reciprocity—exchanges of goods and services are said to be based on "obligation", but exchanges of "information" on "liking".

Homans did in fact recognize differences between physical goods and other social rewards, but saw this as no obstacle to theory building. Blau went a good deal further; his classification of social rewards, mentioned incidentally previously, used primarily three dimensions. First he divided rewards into those that are:

(a) *Intrinsic.* These are concerned with the characteristic of the individual or with the fact of interaction rather than with particular activities. Expressions of affection may be valued from one individual but not from another.

(b) *Extrinsic.* These are not specific to a particular relationship Services rendered or approval given may be equally acceptable no matter where they come from.

The second dimension concerns the spontaneity of the rewards:

(a) *Spontaneous evaluations.* These cannot be bartered in exchange, because they depend on spontaneous rather than calculated reactions. Approval of one's actions may be rewarding only if it is seen as not involving a calculated attempt to please.

(b) *Calculated actions.* Here the fact that the action is intended as an inducement does not detract from its inherent value as a reward. It is given in anticipation of future rewards.

Finally, rewards that can be reciprocally supplied are distinguished from those that are necessarily complementary (or *unilateral* in Blau's terminology).

Thus pleasing physical characteristics might be (mainly) spontaneous and intrinsic, but A giving B the feeling that he is welcome would be calculated and intrinsic. Amongst extrinsic rewards, an actor's calculated performance might evoke spontaneous applause. Some examples are shown in Table 1.

Though the distinction between spontaneous and calculated is not easy to make in practice, it again calls attention to a shortcoming in the label "exchange theory", namely that social rewards are very different from economic ones (see also p. 229). Blau further points out that, while some rewards are clearly detachable from their source, this also is a matter of degree. Many extrinsic benefits, such as advice, assistance

TABLE 1
Blau's classification of rewards. (Modified from Blau, 1964)

| | Reciprocal | | Complementary |
	Intrinsic	Extrinsic	
Spontaneous evaluations	Personal attraction	Social approval	Respect— prestige
Calculated actions	Social acceptance	Instrumental services	Compliance— power

and compliance are both valuable in their own right and valuable because they come from a particular other. This is yet another reason for distinguishing social from economic exchange—"The impersonal economic market is designed to strip specific commodities of these entangling alliances with other benefits . . ." (Blau, 1964, p. 96).

More detailed suggestions for the classification of rewards come from the work of Foa and Foa (1974), and it is to their scheme that we shall give most attention. Using data drawn primarily from questionnaires given to adult subjects in a variety of cultures, and also ideas arising from developmental and other studies, these authors have constructed a far-reaching theory of the "structure" of the mind. By emphasizing "structure" they call attention to the need not merely to distinguish dimensions, but also to understand the relations of those dimensions to each other. Here we are concerned with only one aspect of their theory—their treatment of the resources used in interpersonal exchange. It will become apparent that the types of argument and the nature of the data used by Foa and Foa are very different from those discussed elsewhere in this book. And we shall see that further research may require many modifications to the scheme they propose. But their conclusions appear to provide a basis on which it will be profitable to build. Let us consider those conclusions first, and return to the difficulties later.

Foa and Foa suggest that the resources used in interpersonal exchange can conveniently be classified into six categories:

(a) Love or positive affect—that is, expression of affectionate regard, warmth or comfort (e.g. "your company is pleasant"; "you are charming").

(b) Status—evaluations conveying prestige, regard or esteem (e.g. "well done"; "I am honoured by your presence").

(c) Information—opinions, advice, instruction, etc. (e.g. "It is five o'clock").

(d) Goods—tangible objects.

(e) Services—activities that affect the body or person of another.

(f) Money.

These classes are classes of meaning assigned to actions, so that each class covers numerous actions conveying resources of the same general kind. In recognizing these categories, Foa and Foa emphasize that the distinctions between them are not absolute; indeed we shall see that their thesis depends in part on the view that some of these categories are more closely related to each other than are others.

Considering the categories first from a developmental viewpoint, they argue that an infant at first receives an undifferentiated bundle of love and services: differentiation between them becomes possible only when he can do some things for himself, so that the mother can give him the one without the other. Subsequently the child differentiates goods from services and status from love. The former is possible only when the child realizes that some objects disappear (e.g. "dinner all gone"), whilst others can be used again and again. The differentiation of status from love depends, of course, on the development of language. Finally money is differentiated from goods and information from status. Money is at first treated merely as an object, its exchange potential being realized only gradually. Information from parents, or requests for information from parents, are initially closely associated with praise from the parent, and praise is one form of giving status; only later does a child encounter other criteria for status, such as physical strength. Thus the Foa's view of the gradual differentiation of resource classes can be illustrated as in Fig. 1. Though based largely on anecdotal impressions, the sequence seems reasonable. It is important since differentiation is not necessarily complete, and the "permeability" of the boundary between any two categories will depend on the sequence. Thus Foa and Foa argue that resources that are close together in this sequence are more related, are more likely to occur together, and will tend to be perceived as more similar than resources remote from each other. They suggest that services and status are more closely related to love than is money, while services and money are more closely related to goods than to status. On these latter points they present evidence of quite different kinds, to be mentioned in a moment.

If the resources are to be ordered with respect to their similarity, it is proper to ask, similar in what respects? Two dimensions are of special importance. The first, which the Foas call particularism, concerns one aspect of the context defining the effectiveness of the resource in question. The value of love depends on whom it comes from, but the value of

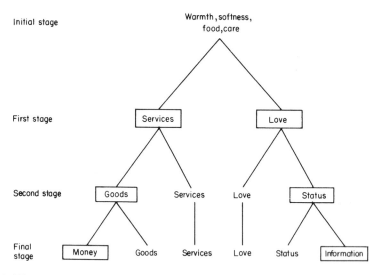

Fig. 1. The ontogenetic differentiation of resource classes. Newly differentiated classes are indicated by a box (Foa and Foa, 1974).

money does not (see also Blau, 1964). In operant terms, this dimension concerns "the extent to which variables associated with the agent of reinforcement are important discriminative stimuli affecting the salience of the reinforcer" (Foa and Foa, 1974).

The second dimension is concreteness. Services and goods are regarded as concrete. By contrast status and information, typically conveyed by verbal or non-verbal behaviour, are typically symbolic. Love and money, so the Foas argue, are exchanged in both concrete and symbolic forms and thus occupy an intermediate position on this coordinate. The argument here depends on the view that the classes are not discrete, the boundaries are permeable, so that actions in one class may have more or less affinity with those in neighbouring classes. A verbal expression of love resembles the conveyance of status rather than services, and tends towards the "symbolic" end of the continuum, whilst kissing and touching are closer to services than to status, and are regarded as more concrete (in the current sense) ways of expressing affection.

Thus these two dimensions provide the structure of resource classes shown in Fig. 2. It will be noted that the order of the classes is the same as that given by developmental considerations.

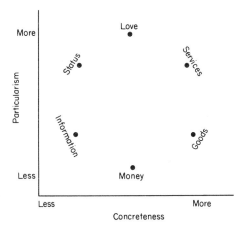

Fig. 2. The cognitive structure of resource classes. (Foa, 1971. Copyright 1971 by the American Association for the Advancement of Science.)

Another approach adopted by the Foas was to test the perceived similarity between the resource classes empirically. Subjects were given a series of messages each of which represented a particular resource class (e.g. Money: "Here is your pay"; Services, "I repaired it for you"; Love, "I care about you".) They were asked to return, from a selection provided by the experimenter, the messages that they considered most similar to (or most dissimilar from) the one they had been given. At each trial they were provided with five messages from which to select their answers, one from each resource class other than that of the message given to them on that trial. Table 2 shows the percentage frequency with which the various resources were returned as most like the resource received. The order of resources given in Fig. 2 would predict that the highest frequencies should lie nearest to the diagonal: with few exceptions, this is the case. The predicted pattern of the smallest percentage near the diagonal was likewise obtained in nearly all cases for the most dissimilar resource.

In a second type of test, concerned with the degree of boundary permeability between resource classes, subjects were presented with a situation in which they were supposed to be providing a resource to another individual, and asked which resource they would prefer to

TABLE 2

Percentage frequency distribution of resource returned being *most like* resource received (Foa and Foa, 1974)

| | | | Resource returned | | | | |
		Love	Status	Infor-mation	Money	Goods	Ser-vices	All resources
	Love	—	65	10	0	2	23	100%
	Status	62	—	20	10	3	5	100%
Resource	Information	17	34	—	11	24	14	100%
Received	Money	0	16	8	—	60	16	100%
	Goods	6	5	21	55	—	13	100%
	Services	41	18	7	16	18	—	100%
	All resources	21	23	11	15	18	12	100%

receive in exchange. For example the subject might be told "You convey to a person that you enjoy being with them (*sic*) and feel affection for them" (Love), or "You are helping a person by providing certain services for them" (Services). Examples of the items to be rated as desirable in return are "The person gives you some merchandise" (Goods) or "You receive affection from the person". The results are presented in terms of intercorrelation matrices, of which one example is given. Table 3 shows the relation between the preference for receiving

TABLE 3

Intercorrelation among *preferences for status* when *different resources* are given (correlation coefficients multiplied by 100) (Foa and Foa, 1974)

Resource given	Love	Status	Infor-mation	Money	Goods	Services
Love	—	61	40	29	46	52
Status	61	—	52	26	54	45
Information	40	52	—	42	56	51
Money	29	26	42	—	66	57
Goods	46	54	56	66	—	69
Services	52	45	51	57	69	—

status when various resources are given. For example, the figure of 0·61 indicates the correlation between the desire to receive status when love is given and the desire to receive status when status is given. The prediction is that resource classes postulated as close together in the structure in Fig. 2 should receive higher intercorrelations than those that are more distant. The relative sizes of the coefficients are in line with this prediction.

A further important difference between the resource classes must be mentioned. The Foas argue that, if one gives money to another, one is simultaneously taking it away from oneself. However this is not necessarily true of all resources. At the other extreme, they suggest that if one gives love to another, one simultaneously increases the amount one has oneself (see also Blau, 1964). Similarly, if an individual takes love away from another (e.g. quarrels with him), he simultaneously reduces the amount he has for himself. They propose in fact that the structure of resource classes also indicates the relationship between giving to other and what is left for self. For love, and to a lesser extent for status, this relationship is positive. Giving information to another usually does not affect the amount possessed; in some circumstances it may increase it, as when teaching increases understanding, and in others it may diminish the value of the information possessed. Giving money or goods reduces the amount possessed by the giver. For services the relationship is also negative.

What we have here is an attempt to make sense of the wide range of resources used in interpersonal exchange. Given some such means of classifying resources, it is possible to ask whether their properties differ, and whether we can find principles determining where each is most likely to be effective. Can the different classes of resource be related to the different conditions under which social exchange takes place? Here the Foas consider two sets of such conditions, one concerning the motivational states of the participants, and the other the appropriateness of the environment. With regard to the first they propose that for each resource class there is an optimal range. When the amount of the resource classes falls below a minimum value it is felt as a need, and when the upper limit is exceeded one is motivated to "get rid of" some of that resource. On merely intuitive grounds it is suggested that the range between upper and lower limits is larger for resources that can be stored outside the body, and that for money the amount that can be stored is infinite (Fig. 3). Certainly not everyone would agree with this scheme, and especially with the view that it is easy to have too much love, but the details are not important for the main thesis.

At first sight the notion of an optional range provides an easy explanation for differences in motivation. If an individual is below the optimal range for a given resource he will have a need to acquire it, and if above he will have a need to give. The latter view is however incompatible with the assumptions in the previous two paragraphs. In the case of particularistic resources, like love, we have seen that giving love to other is associated with giving love to self, and so will not result

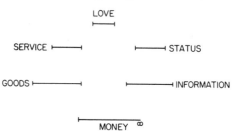

Fig. 3. Foa and Foa's proposed relative widths of the optimal range of various resources (Foa and Foa, 1974).

in depletion. And with non-particularistic resources like money the upper limit is so high that there is seldom or never a surfeit. But this difficulty disappears if giving is a device for getting needed resources —it is nearly always part of an exchange.

Because the resource classes are related, the need states related to them are also likely to be related. For example, a person exposed to loss of love will also feel some need for status. This makes intuitive sense and is supported by test data.

The classification of resource types also provides a classification of types of power—each of the six types of resource can be either given or taken away (see p. 256). And the structure of resource categories provides suggestions about the relations between types of power— money can buy goods or information, possibly status and services, but not love.

We may now consider how the properties of the response classes are related to the motivational conditions under which exchange takes place. We have already seen that giving love to other also involves giving love to self, whereas giving money involves taking money from self. A further proposal is that the degree of ambivalence in a transaction follows the same order: one can love and hate (i.e. give and take away love from a person) simultaneously, but one does not give and take away money at the same time. For these reasons the rules of exchange that apply to money transactions will apply to a lesser degree or not at all to other resource classes: one can simultaneously give love and have more, and one can simultaneously give love and take it away.

Four other properties may be mentioned briefly. First, it is suggested that verbal language is more suitable for transactions at the money end, non-verbal for love. Second, the more particularistic a resource, the more likely that exchange will take place within a resource category: we may exchange money for goods, but usually exchange love only for love. Third, and related to the last, the more particularistic the resource, the narrower the range of other resources with which it can be exchanged. Finally, the more particularistic resources are more likely to require a face-to-face exchange.

Turning now to the manner in which the appropriateness of the environment affects exchange, the Foas suggest the following issues to be important:

(a) *Time.* Money can be exchanged quickly, love takes time. In a busy environment, the more particularistic resources are likely to receive lower priority.

(b) *Delay of Reward.* The rewards of an exchange of love are likely to be reaped only after several encounters, while money can bring immediate reward. Thus in an environment where most encounters are with strangers, the less particularistic resources are more likely to be used.

(c) *Group size.* Small group size favours the more particularistic resource categories.

Given these differences in the manner in which resource classes are related to the conditions under which exchange takes place, it is clear that the laws of exchange for the more particularistic resources need be no less hard-headed and respectable than those for the laws of exchange of money and goods. The Foas describe a number of investigations concerning such questions as not only, "Given a particular resource, what sort of resource does a subject prefer in exchange?"; and "If a particular resource is removed, how would the subject choose to retaliate?"; but also "How does cognitive distance between the resource category of which a subject has been deprived and the resources available for retaliation affect the intensity of his response?"; "Does deprivation affect the probability of occurrence of positive and negative behaviour?" and so on. These studies involve questionnaires or experiments with confederates, with all the dangers attendant thereon. Space does not permit the detailed exposition which would be necessary to enable the reader to evaluate them: the reader is referred to the Foas' book (1974) and to the papers cited there.

The Foas thus support their proposed structure of resource classes with evidence drawn from considerations of development, from the nature and properties of the resources themselves, and from evidence on perceived similarity and perceived equivalence drawn from studies of adults. Their classification seems to make sense of a number of aspects of the ways in which rewards operate, including some admittedly rather gross generalizations about the environmental contexts in which they are efficacious.

It is of course possible to make many comments. Since the scheme is in part intuitive, it is fair to criticize it on the same grounds. Consider first the categories themselves. Might there not be other ways to carve up the resources used in interpersonal exchange in ways that would fit the data even better than that proposed? How far should one generalize about interpersonal relationships from experiments carried out mostly with undergraduates? Do not the Foas come near to reifying each class when they write of "a wide range of actions each conveying the same resource"? Do the Foas stick to their definition of the classes as classes of meaning assigned to actions? For instance, what are the properties of tangible goods given as tokens of love? Is the acquisition of status easily separable from that of other attributes? And could some of the apparent differences between the categories be due to the particular way in which the resources have been categorized, rather than to intrinsic properties of the "meanings assigned to actions". For instance, love is heterogeneous and can be expressed in many ways, whereas money passes in relatively few. Is not that reason enough why love is often exchanged for love, but not money for money?

Again, is not the evidence supporting the developmental sequence a little thin? Is it really the case that love is intermediate between status and services on a dimension of concreteness? Is it really so easy to have too much love (see Fig. 3)? And if love does indeed have a narrow optimal range, and the way to get rid of a surfeit is by taking love away from other (and thus also from self), would not one expect lovers' quarrels to be much more common than they are?

And how much value should one attach to this sort of questionnaire data about perceived similarity, equivalence and boundary permeability? Although the classes of resources are said to be classes of meaning assigned to actions, has not *meaning* somehow been left behind? Perhaps the greatest difficulties arise with the category of information. Information may concern the external world and be valued because it may enable the recipient to acquire more tangible rewards at a later date. Surely such information is more closely related to the response class to which it may later give access, than to its neighbours in the Foas' scheme? Take for instance the issue of reciprocation. If I moved to a new town and asked my neighbour where the post office was, it would not be inappropriate for him to ask me to post his letters as well as my own (services); but if he told me where I could pick blackberries (goods), I might well bring him a box in gratitude.

Another type of information may also concern the external world, but be of importance to the hearer because he sees it as agreeing or disagreeing with opinions he holds himself. This will be relevant in the context of consensual validation, and thus pertinent to the perceived status of the hearer.

Yet another type of information may concern the speaker. Here it may be relevant in relation to consensual validation, or it may be interpreted by the hearer as love, or as directly providing status, or as evidence that the speaker may render him services in the future. Or it may provide the hearer with guidance in a situation that is potentially stressful or in which he is unsure of his abilities (Wheeler, 1974). How the hearer interprets it may depend crucially on the sort of relationship he already has with the speaker. Consider, for instance, how the statement "I am devoted to you" could be interpreted in any of the above ways. The meaning of a piece of information will thus be affected by contextual cues, and may have primary relevance to any of the other resource classes.

This last point applies not only to information. Items in any one of the resource classes may be valued because they give access to others. Their meaning may change with the personality and temporary needs of the recipient, and even with the stage of the relationship.

And finally, what about "understanding" of the type implied by similarity in constructs (see p. 87)? This may not be closely related to love, though it may be conducive to it; and it need not be closely related to information.

What all this amounts to is that the properties of a given reward may depend on the nature of the interaction and relationship in which it is exchanged. That rewards should be classified is essential, but the classification required is one that will interdigitate with a classification of relationships. The Foas do not sufficiently emphasize that the meaning attached to one of their resource category labels will vary with the context. To continue the examples given on p. 242 and in Table 3, what A would expect in return for services would depend on whether those services involved A scratching B's back or changing a wheel on his car. And if it was back-scratching, the expected return would differ if A were scratching his wife's back from if Mata Hari were scratching the back of an important general, while if A was changing a wheel it would depend on whether the car were his neighbour's or a stranger's.

We may pursue this question of the relation between a classification of rewards and a classification of relationships a little further. We have seen that there are differences in what individuals expect from the relationships in which they are involved. In exchange theory terms, the ratio of rewards to costs for a given sort of relationship varies between individuals: some expect more, others less. And what any one individual expects from one relationship is not what he expects from another, even when he can measure both in the same currency. Thus we cannot study how the value of a reward changes with the context in which it is exchanged until we can describe and classify relationships. If exchange theorists are to meet the difficult problems which arise from the varying effectiveness of rewards, both an adequate classification of relationships and an adequate classification of rewards are essential.

It is in fact the case that practically any one of the statements that the Foas used in their questionnaires could take on diverse meanings according to the context of the relationship in which it was given. The words "I love you" could mean something different in parent-child, sibling or peer-peer relationships (i.e. in relationships of different content); they would be almost meaningless in a uniplex relationship; their value changes with the degrees of intimacy, interpersonal congruency and commitment that characterize the relationship. In the latter cases their value might well change in a complex way, perhaps first increasing with increasing intimacy and then decreasing. The value of money or goods would vary also with the content of the relationship, with many of its qualities, with the relative status (financial and otherwise) of the participants (i.e. complementarity), and again with intimacy, interpersonal congruency and commitment.

However that is not all. The interactions and relationships between two individuals cannot be seen as the mere sum of giving and receiving of rewards. Were each participant to be concerned merely with maximizing his own rewards and minimizing his costs, with no thought for his partner, that partner might soon find a better option elsewhere. He must, therefore, consider not only his own probable rewards and costs, but also those of his partner (Thibaut and Kelley, 1959). The issues again depend on the characteristics of the relationship. If the relationship is uniplex and involves reciprocal interactions it may in theory be a relatively straightforward matter, for each partner's gains and costs are measurable in the same currency. If the relationship is uniplex and complementary, the situation is a little more complex because, although gains and losses occur in the same interaction, they differ in kind: what a teacher gains from teaching is not the same as a pupil gains from learning. If the relationship is multiplex, the issue is one of extraordinary complexity, and must involve assessing one's own gains and one's partners losses on the swings against one's own losses and one's partner's gains on a multiplicity of roundabouts. Thus the properties of the relationship will affect the nature and meaning of the exchange that takes place.

What general conclusion can be drawn? On the one hand, many studies based on exchange theories seek to extract principles about relationships without asking whether similar conclusions would have been reached with a different type of relationship or a different type of reward. On the other, on the basis of a battery of questions, the Foas have sought to establish that resources exchanged are more likely to come from resources classes which are neighbours in their scheme (Fig. 2) than from more distant ones, without considering that equivalences may change with the nature of the relationship. What is needed therefore is not only an adequate classification of relationships and an adequate classification of the rewards used in interpersonal exchange, but further research to marry the two.

It thus seems likely that substantial modification to the Foas' present scheme will be required. However this does not greatly diminish their achievement. They have demonstrated, more effectively than any other theorists, that the several rewards used in interpersonal exchange differ in their properties, and that such differences must be taken into account if interpersonal relationships are to be understood. While categorizing rewards does not in itself indicate how they can be measured (see pp. 219–221), it may be a necessary preliminary.

Summary

Exchange theories are based on principles of learning derived from studies of individual animals. The animals used in such studies are usually highly motivated to work for food rewards. The question therefore arises as to whether the rewards used in social exchange have properties similar to that of food for hungry animals. Some evidence on this issue drawn from studies of social approval is discussed.

If rewards vary in their properties, it may be necessary to classify them. Such a classification has been provided by Foa and Foa (1974). They divided rewards into love, status, information, goods, services and money. These categories can be arranged in a circular order, those which are neighbours having more in common than those opposite to each other. Two important dimensions concern how much it matters whom the reward comes from (particularism) and concreteness. Another concerns the consequences of giving; a person who gives money has less, but a person who gives love has more.

Since the meaning of a resource varies with the context, this classification of rewards needs to be related to a classification of relationships.

18

Conflict and Power

Conflict

We have seen that, because the participants in a relationship each strive to maintain a balance between their inputs and their outputs, there will be a tendency towards fairness in their dealings. Whether fairness is ever achieved is another matter: quite apart from the difficulties of measuring rewards and costs on the same scale, the participants may not agree on what sort of justice should prevail. Beyond this, social exchange involves obligations and expectations for the future which can never be specified precisely, so that the balance at any moment cannot be stated (pp. 221 and 229). Just because rewards given may create obligations for the future, each participant in a relationship may strive to build up credit. Thus in addition to the "strain towards reciprocity", there is likely also to be a "strain towards imbalance". In Blau's (1964) view, even in the most intimate relationships tendencies towards balance and imbalance exist side by side. If partner A is better able to provide services for the other B, B must reciprocate if only by acknowledging obligations for the future. Thus balance depends on an imbalance in power in favour of A and an imbalance in obligations by B. The exchange, though asymmetrical, may be considered equitable by A and B. But it may not: if A is too liberal in bestowing favours on B, B may accumulate obligations or lose status to an extent unacceptable to him.

In practice, some degree of conflict is usual. Even in intimate personal relationships, the goals of the participants are unlikely to be wholly compatible in every sphere all the time: there is likely to be some area in which one desires a higher pay off than the other is willing to concede. Interests usually partially overlap and partially conflict, and a *modus vivendi* is worked out between the partners. Commitment to the relationship can play an important role here. But if A sees B to be more committed than he is, he may feel free to try out alternative sources: B's error perhaps lay in revealing his commitment, but had he not done so the relationship itself might have been in jeopardy.

Conflict can be constructive (Deutsch, 1969). If the incompatible goals are trivial, conflict may provide a focus round which a relationship is built. Tennis rivals can become friends if tennis does not matter to them too much. Even if the goals really matter, conflict can be constructive, especially if both partners are committed to the relationship and there is a norm of trust. In a lover's quarrel A may become more convinced of B's commitment, and thus his own trust may be augmented. The process may be mutual. Conflict can pave the way for discussion and understanding.

Indeed some would argue that conflict is almost necessary for real intimacy to be achieved. This is most easily argued in role theory terms. Fit between the role identities (see p. 135) of two individuals is unlikely to be perfect. Increasing intimacy thus requires adjustment of each individual's role identities—the further development of some and the suppression of others. Or, to put it in other terms, the definition of the relationship is bound to need adjustment by both parties.

However, to be constructive, conflict must be concerned with the details of the relationship, not with its central core. Alienation from the focus of a close personal relationship is most likely to stem from dissatisfaction with one's own role identity, or with the role support one is given, or with the demands made on one for role support, any of which may well lead to a decrease in intimacy and a disruption of the relationship (M. McCall, 1970).

Destructive conflict becomes probable if commitment is lacking, if the ability of the partner to reciprocate in the future is doubted and, of course, if important goals conflict. Conflict arising from a real conflict of goals is often contrasted with "autistic" conflict—that is, conflict which has no objective basis in the situation, but stems from the internal states of the participants (Holmes and Miller, 1976). In practice, such a distinction is difficult to maintain. Real conflict may become partially autistic if one or other participant "goes too far" (i.e. disregards the societally imposed standards of behaviour which normally operate to keep conflict in check). Or a dispute involving a genuine conflict of interest may spread to areas of the relationship in which there are no conflicting goals, and the resulting "autistic" elements may then be seen by the participants as real. This is especially likely to occur if the primary issues in the conflict are intangible.

It is of more interest to consider the differing views of the two partners. While the complained-of actor tends to excuse his behaviour in terms of extenuating circumstances, outside influences, or his/her current physiological or psychological state, the complaining partner tends to explain it in terms of the actor's personal characteristics or attitudes. While the latter course can be destructive, and by bringing in general issues facilitate spread of the conflict, it can also serve as a challenge to the actor to prove the attribution wrong by doing better in future (Kelley, 1979).

Perhaps the most potent factor in the escalation of conflict is distrust. Distrust may be, and often is, fostered by misperception of the partner (see p. 120), and results in perceived threat. Threat, distrust and misperception represent three interrelated factors promoting the initiation and escalation of conflict (Holmes and Miller, 1976). Each partner is likely to attribute blame to the other.

A number of techniques have been used in attempts to measure, in the laboratory and consulting room, the amount of conflict present in a relationship. As an example, Epstein and Santa-Barbara (1975) used "Prisoner's Dilemma" and "Chicken" (see p. 216) to study married couples. Each couple was given 300 trials, during which a stable pattern of responding was usually reached: this served to classify the couples as showing stable cooperation ("Doves", criterion 20/25 choices Cooperate–Cooperate; high mutual conflict ("Hawks", 12/25 Defect–Defect); one gaining at the other's expense (Dominant— submissive, 12/25 C–D); or as showing no stable solution (Mugwumps). During the pre-asymptotic period all groups predicted more cooperation than defection, with the doves perceiving more cooperation and actually cooperating more than the other groups (Table 1 (a and b)). In other groups expected reciprocation was not reciprocated. It will be noted that pre-asymptotic predictions were above chance only amongst the doves. However the data also showed that couples who became doves retaliated at their partner's defections during the pre-asymptotic period at a higher rate than did members of the other groups, and the authors suggest that a degree of firmness is necessary for the development of stable cooperative play.

Choices were related to the personalities of the individuals concerned, as measured by a Thematic Apperception Test. Thus subjects high on need for achievement tended to cooperate (predict C and play C), whilst high power-oriented subjects played exploitively (predict C play D). Dove husbands expected their wives to defect quite often even after

TABLE 1a

Proportion of cooperative responses predicted by each outcome group over pre-asymptotic, criterion and post-criterion trials

	Pre-Asymptotic	Criterion	Post-Criterion
Doves	0·718	0·789	0·806
Dom-Sub	0·623	0·697	0·621
Mugwumps	0·650	0·647	0·640
Hawks	0·597	0·652	0·601

TABLE 1b

Proportion of correct predictions by each outcome group over pre-asymptotic, criterion and post-criterion trials (from Epstein and Santa-Barbara, 1975)

	Pre-Asymptotic	Criterion	Post-Criterion
Doves	0·565	0·761	0·736
Dom-Sub	0·428	0·413	0·386
Mugwumps	0·422	0·440	0·424
Hawks	0·429	0·364	0·404

criterion was reached, but dove wives did not show comparable suspicion of their husbands (see also Kelley and Stahelski, 1970, a,b,c).

Other techniques include the transport and train games, where one player may block or facilitate the passage of the other to a goal (e.g. Deutsch and Krauss, 1965). An example is provided by the Ravich interpersonal game/test. Two electric trains, hooked up to a computer, run on a pattern of tracks. They may collide with or avoid each other at gates. Each partner controls one train and a gate, and depending on the time taken, can win imaginary pennies. Ravich and Wyden (1974) claim that, during the course of 30 trials, a pattern emerges in the couple's behaviour. About 25% show a dominant-submissive pattern, 20% a cooperative one, 14% a competitive one and the remainder various combinations of these (Dominant-subordinate competitive, 16%; Dominant-subordinate cooperative, 12%, Competitive cooperative, 5%; etc.). However Liebowitz and Black (1973), on the basis of a factor analysis of data from 75 couples, argued that the game measures two separate aspects of marital decision making—the degree to which one spouse actively impedes the other's activity, and the extent to which conflict is characteristic of the couple as they negotiate. In their view the latter does not relate to the success of the decision once made—or, in general terms, a good healthy fight does no harm, but impeding the partner does.

It is difficult to know how seriously these games should be taken. As laboratory tools, they are useful in revealing the processes involved in conflict resolution and cooperation, and for studying those processes under different conditions. Since the stategy of each player (cooperative *vs* competitive) depends at least in part on that of the other (e.g. Apfelbaum, 1966; Kelley and Stahelski, 1970 a,b,c), it is certainly more an index of the relationship than of the personality of the individual. But as clinical tools for studying the relationship such procedures must surely leave out most of what is important about the subjects' relationship in particular and their lives in general, and thus be of very limited use. And the assumption that the results of such a test will generalize to other aspects of the dyadic relationship in life situations seems extremely dubious.

Power

The goals of the two participants in a relationship may not coincide. It is thus natural to ask whether, and to what extent, the behaviour of one partner is controlled by that of the other—who holds the power? However we shall see that, while the concept of "power" has an obvious value in some contexts, its usefulness is limited.

We may take Thibaut and Kelley's (1959) definition of power as a starting point. "Person A has power over B to the extent that by varying his behaviour he can affect the quality of B's outcomes." With dyads such as teacher/pupil, officer/soldier or doctor/patient it is obvious, at any rate at first sight, where the main power lies. But the ability of A to affect B's outcomes by no means rules out the possibility that B can affect A's.

Power is in fact rarely absolute (see also Chapter 16). In the first place, it is inevitably limited by the capacities of both individuals. Second, it usually involves at most an influence by one partner on the relative probabilities of actions by the other (see p. 215). Third, the exercise of power is usually limited by the controlled party: the worker can strike, or seek employment elsewhere. Even in the parent-child relationship, where the parent seems to hold the power since he controls the tangible resources, the child can in fact control the parent by eliciting care-giving behaviour, or by punishing himself by self-inflicted injury or starvation (see Chapter 19). Fourth, in many relationships one partner has power in some contexts and the other in others, the power distribution being the result of negotiation between them (cf. discussion of complementarity on p. 111). These two latter points indicate that power is a property of the relationship and not of one or other individual.

POWER AND THE RESOURCE EXCHANGED

In terms of exchange theory, the primary determinant of A's power over B will be the resources under A's control that B needs. However this will not be the only issue, for A's power will also be affected by the costs he incurs in transferring resources to B, and by the dependency of B on those resources. Here the issues that arise differ somewhat with the type of resource in question.

Using the Foas' classification of resources (Chapter 17), we consider first the costs for A of transferring resources to B. If A influences B by giving him goods or money, his own stocks will thereby be depleted. If A imparts information to B, B may become better informed and A therefore less able to influence him in the future. But A may also acquire information, in the sense of increased understanding, in the process of teaching. If A gives status to B, he may thereby diminish his own superiority or increase his own inferiority. If A gives services to B, he may or may not limit his capacity to help B in the future. But if A gives love to B, he may thereby augment his own resources. The important point that Foa and Foa (1974) (see p. 243) have made here does not depend on the precise details of their classification of resources (see Chapter 17, Fig. 2): the nature of the change in the donor's resources, consequent upon giving, depends on what has been given.

The point must be taken even further. Another cost of resource exchange concerns the time involved. Performing a service for another involves time that could have been spent in other ways. Actions falling within the Foas' category of love, and to a lesser extent many of those classed as involving status, may be peculiar here also. For whilst the cost in time of giving most resources involves the time involved in the transaction and the time involved in acquiring (or replacing) the resource, the giving of love (or status) may involve commitments of time extending into the future.

So far as dependency of B on A is concerned, this will be determined both by the ability of A to produce rewards and minimize costs for B, and by the availability of other partners who could do likewise. The crucial issue, in Thibaut and Kelley's terms, is the comparison level for alternatives. Whichever of the two partners is closer to his comparison level is likely to be more willing to jettison the relationship. He therefore has the greater power.

However the Foas' dimension of particularism introduces a further consideration. In principle, whilst any type of resource could be available elsewhere, transactions with any particular supplier often tend to increase the probability that future transactions will involve the same individual. This is the case even with non-particularate resources like money—we tend to go to the bank clerk we know. In so far as B has a tendency to return to the same supplier, that supplier's power over B is increased even if alternative sources of reward are available, for by making use of those alternative sources B would be incurring extra costs. This is of course even more the case with particularate resources, such as love—especially when the exchange of love involves commitment. Furthermore sanctions imposed by society, or by individually held beliefs about monogamy, limit some transactions to particular individuals. In such cases the nature of the relationship makes alternative relationships less desirable.

In summary, then, the issues that actually arise over the power in a relationship vary with the resource in question.

TYPES OF POWER

It will already be apparent that the ways in which "power" may operate in a relationship may be diverse, if only because of the varied natures of the resources involved. We may consider a classification of types of influence due to French and Raven (1959), which to some extent cuts across the classification of resources referred to above. Five categories are recognized.

Reward Power

This depends on A's potential for providing rewards to B. Any type of resource may be involved. In general, reward power may influence any aspect of B's behaviour that involves dependence on A, but it is unlikely to be effective for actions that B believes will remain unknown to A.

Coercive Power

This depends on A's capacity for punishing B. Punishment here includes not only physical punishment, but also the removal of resources. One form of coercion whose importance in intimate relationships has been neglected is silence: the power of non-disclosure will be familiar to the parents of teenagers.

As with reward power, any type of resource may be involved. However the exercising of coercive power is apt to be more difficult (and thus more costly) than that of reward power, since B is prone to display actions that he believes will be rewarded but to hide actions that he believes will be punished (Thibaut and Kelley, 1959). Furthermore the consequences of coercive power may be complex. Pain inflicted as punishment, and frustration induced by the non-availability of resources, may have complex consequences, including aggression directed towards the supposed frustrating agent (Ulrich and Symannek, 1969; Dollard, *et al.*, 1939).

In most cases, of course, the effectiveness of a reward or punishment is heavily dependent on the previous experience of the individual concerned. Very often, rewards and punishments are symbolic.

Expert Power

This depends on special knowledge or skill, possessed by A, on which B depends in some way. It is obviously characteristic of relationships such as that between doctor and patient or teacher and pupil. Its effectiveness depends not only on B's dependence on A's knowledge or skill, but also on the esteem in which B holds A relative to other potential sources of expertise. Often expert power involves the dispensation of information, as in the teacher-pupil case. However in this and other cases its effectiveness may depend on further, perhaps more tangible, resources that thereby become available to B. The patient values the doctor not only because he wishes to cease to be ill, but because he values the opportunities that health will bring.

Apart from fatigue, time, and the opportunity to obtain other rewards, the exercise of expert power may involve A in little cost. However it must be remembered that in exercising it A may diminish his ability to influence B in the future: the ill patient is more dependent on his doctor than the healthy one; and the more a teacher teaches his pupil, the less does the pupil need him.

Legitimate Power

This refers to the exercise of power by A over B by virtue of B's acceptance of A's authority, often as a consequence of conventions current in the society. Thus it may be usual to accept the authority of A because of his age, his relationship to B or his status in society. The extreme case is of course acceptance of the power of a supernatural being.

Acceptance of A's status by B may depend on expectations of future rewards or escape from future punishment consequent upon the relationship. Thus in multiplex relationships status may bring legitimate power even to situations in which that status is irrelevant, as when teacher meets pupil out of school. In other cases legitimate power can be ascribed to B's satisfaction consequent upon behaving in a manner congruent with his own values and norms (cf. p. 217). To the extent that A can evoke such norms, he is asserting power over B.

Legitimate power may involve any of the resource classes. The cost to A is usually small.

Referent Power

This is based on the identification of B with A. B is attracted to, admires or envies A, and therefore models himself on A and is influenced by A's behaviour. Referent power may develop out of reward power, perhaps because the exercise of reward makes A more attractive to B. It may also arise from the need for consensual validation: if B sees A as similar to himself, or desires to see himself as similar to A, he may imitate his behaviour and use him as a model with which to interpret his own experiences. It is also possible for A to exert negative referent power over B: if B finds A distasteful, he may attempt to behave in ways different from him.

Referent power usually involves no cost to A. Indeed it may occur in A's absence, and even continue for years after his death. It may operate even in the absence of any awareness by A or B that it is doing so.

French and Raven's classificatory system considerably extends the notion of power, as used in everyday life, to encompass a much wider range of influences exerted by one individual on another. It is possible to look at it in a number of ways. From the point of view of exchange theory, expert power differs from the others in terms of the resource exchanged, legitimate power usually in terms of the sanctions for non-compliance, and referent power in the abstract nature of the rewards that must be postulated to bring it within the confines of exchange theory.

From another point of view, Kelvin (1977) points out that the five forms of power fall into two groups whose psychological characteristics are quite different. Reward and coercive power are rooted in sanctions and lead to *compliance*. Expert and referent power, by contrast, depend on *acceptance*: an expert is not an expert unless he is accepted as such. Legitimate power also involves acceptance by the less powerful of the right of the more powerful to influence him, though indirect sanctions may operate. Homans (1976) had made a similar point in distinguishing between power and authority. In the latter case A has control over B's outcomes, but only because B believes that obedience will bring favourable outcomes from the external social or physical environment.

Operation of the different types of power is however related to the probability of open conflict. The more reward and coercive power the participants in a relationship have over each other, and the smaller the discrepancy between their power over each other, the more likely is "autistic" conflict (see p. 252) to develop. Where there is a large power difference, it seems that guilt on the part of the more powerful tends to reduce "autistic" conflict. Expert and referent power, by contrast, are often associated with mutual respect, and thus the probability of "autistic" conflict is reduced. Legitimate power tends to reduce conflict because of the associated norms specifying the rights and duties of the parties (Holmes and Miller, 1976).

In any case, the exercise of power is usually limited by the emergence of norms. If a powerful partner A threatens to use his power, B may appeal to a norm of fairness. Or B may threaten to leave the relationship, whereupon A may appeal to a norm of loyalty (e.g. Thibaut 1968). Limitations on the use of power are reviewed by Gruder (1970).

ASSESSMENT OF POWER; THE USEFULNESS OF THE CONCEPT IN REAL LIFE

That assessments of the power structure of on-going relationships in terms of responsibility for decision-making can be made in a valid manner is demonstrated, for instance, by the work of Kreitman and his colleagues (cited on p. 106). But it will be noted that their analysis was not only limited to a particular level of analysis ("Who decides that . . .") but also showed that, at that level, power was usually shared (see also Haley, 1963).

A study by Stewart and Rubin (1976) exemplifies the dangers of using the "power" concept at too high a level of analysis. Members of 63 dating couples were assessed on need for power using a Thematic Apperception Test with verbal items. The state of their relationship was also assessed. Two years later the couples were contacted again. Men high in need for power saw their relationships as less satisfactory, and such couples were more likely to have broken up by the two year follow-up. However for women this finding did not hold. The authors advance a number of possible explanations—for instance women may express power in long-term relationships rather than in short-term conquests, or perhaps women can manage conflict within a relationship better than men. Such suggestions seem to boil down to a certain slipperiness in the power concept as used in this way.

A number of other authors have presented evidence that the concept of power has been insufficiently analysed to be much use in practical situations. One basic issue is that the diverse dependent variables used to measure power show little intercorrelation (Sprey, 1972). The further reasons for this are interesting. In a lucid discussion of the use of the power concept with respect to marriage, Rollins and Bahr (1976) point out that a conflict of goals must exist for "power" to be meaningful. These authors distinguish between "power", referring to potential for control; "control attempts", in which it is exercised; and "control", where the attempt is successful. However, beyond that, we have already seen that it is also necessary to discriminate between who makes decisions and who decides who should make decisions. Indeed Safilios-Rothschild (1970) emphasized that "family power structure" is a multidimensional concept, measured through the outcome of decision making, patterns of tension and conflict management, and division of labour (see also Hadley and Jacob, 1976). And Sprey (1972) questioned the usefulness of a definition of power based on decision making on the grounds that decisions need not be based on "power". In the marital situation, Sprey pointed out that decisions are not of an A wins, B loses type, but may have long-term consequences for both A and B. It is therefore expedient to ask not only who decides, but also why A got involved in the decision making process and why B went along with A's view.

Again, Turk (1974) argues that much research on power in interpersonal relationships assumes that the members of a dyad have stable ends which can be arranged in an order of priority. However it is almost impossible to measure people's intentions, especially as they may have both short- and long-term goals which change with time. Turk reviews attempts to measure power in family situations, and points out the difficulty of finding decision making areas that are of equal importance to all family members in all families. He recommends instead that one should proceed on the assumption that group action emerges from the multiplicity of interests and actions of the group members. One can then attempt to account for outcomes not in terms of one individual's power, but as the result of a pattern of interactions (see also Cromwell and Olson, 1975).

It is thus necessary to be clear about where the concept of power is useful and where it is not. We have seen that it is clearly useful in relationships of the A bosses B type, and in relationships in which A controls resources that are crucial for B. However it is rare for power to be absolute, and B usually has alternative sources of supply. Control of B's behaviour by A then occurs only within limits. Use of the power concept must not then imply that power is a property of A. Rather A has power because of the total situation, including the alternatives open to B. Furthermore A may have more power than B in some contexts, while B has more than A in others. The power structure may then depend on complex and continuing negotiation on a number of levels in the different but interrelated areas of the relationship. The concept begins to lose its value.

Some of the problems involved in teasing apart the roles of the partners even in a relatively simple dyadic relationship are considered in the next chapter.

Summary

Some degree of *conflict* occurs in most relationships. It can be constructive. Destructive conflict usually results from threat, distrust and misperception. Conclusions drawn from some laboratory or clinical measurements of conflict are of doubtful generality.

Power is rarely absolute, and must be seen as a property of the relationship rather than of one or other partner. Seen in exchange theory terms, the issues that arise vary with the resource exchanged.

French and Raven's classification of types of power is discussed.

Attempts to assess power in practical situations have been successful only when the dependent variables were adequately defined. In general the concept of power has been inadequately analysed and there are limits to its usefulness.

19

.

Who Determines What?

It may seem obvious enough that, as indicated in previous chapters, most relationships involve mutual influences of each partner on the other. But the history of research on child development indicates that it needs to be emphasized. Until 1968, most students of child development thought that control in the mother-infant relationship rested firmly in the hands of the mother. For pediatricians this view was natural enough: they could tell a mother what to do, but not a baby. But in 1968 R. Q. Bell pointed out that the picture is not so simple as that, and that many aspects of the ongoing interactions are controlled by the infant. The result has been a number of important studies on the "effects of the infant on his caregiver" (Lewis and Rosenblum, 1974). By contrast students of animal behaviour, accustomed to analyse both the stimuli from the parent that elicit filial behaviour from the infant and the stimuli from the infant that elicit parental behaviour, already usually regarded the parent-offspring relationship in terms of mutual influences (Harper, 1970). However they sometimes tended to take the opposite view, assuming that the temporal course of the relationship was largely determined by the physical development of the young—a view which, as we shall see later, is almost equally inaccurate.

But if relationships do depend on mutual influences, how can one tease apart the roles of the two partners? The concepts of rewards, costs and dependencies can take us some way towards understanding and even predicting the course of particular interactions within a relationship, and even help towards predicting the effect of each interaction on subsequent ones. But it must not be forgotten that individuals change as a consequence of their experiences. Each exchange of a resource will result in a change in the interactants, and the assumption of stationarity cannot be made (see Huesmann and Levinger, 1976). If A gives X to B, the whole situation is changed not only because X has changed hands from A to B, but because A's view of B changes (someone who has a potential need for X, or who will no longer need X), B's view of A changes (e.g. to someone who supplies X or who can no longer supply X); A's view of

B's view of B changes (e.g. to someone who acknowledges his need of X); A's view of B's view of A changes (e.g. A knows that B now knows that A can be persuaded to supply X) and so on. Thus any analysis in stimulus-response terms is likely to founder. In addition A may grow or change, in ways that depend wholly, partly or not at all on interactions with B, but which affect his future interactions with B.

One consequence of these considerations is that measures or observations made of the social behaviour of one partner within a relationship cannot be taken as a direct measure of the behavioural propensities of that partner. How much a baby cries depends on how the mother responds to its crying: how quickly the mother goes to it when she hears it crying depends on how much it has cried recently. Therefore measures both of how much a baby cries and of how quickly the mother responds to its cries are characteristics of the relationship rather than of baby or mother as individuals. Systems theory might offer a way to resolve this difficulty, but we are as yet so far from being able even to ennumerate the important variables, let alone to evaluate them and assess their interactions, that it could give only an appearance of precision which would serve too easily as a cloak for ignorance.

In this chapter another approach is considered. It depends on the observation of ongoing relationships, and the use of correlations between measures to tease apart the "direction of effects". That is, given a change in a particular characteristic of the relationship, we are concerned with questions of the type "Is change in this partner or that responsible?" Such an approach demonstrates that, in studying the development of, or changes in, a relationship, it is necessary to frame the questions being asked very precisely. To demonstrate this, we may consider the relatively simple case of mother-infant interaction in rhesus monkeys.

It is first necessary to introduce three measures. One is the amount of time infant and mother spend out of contact. The second is the frequency with which the mother rejects the infant's attempts to gain contact. The third is a measure of the infant's role in the amount of contact observed. If, every time contact between mother and infant is broken, we record whether the make or break was due to mother or infant, we can calculate the percentage of makes due to the infant (% Mk_I) and the percentage of breaks due to the infant (% Bk_I). The difference between these two (% Mk_I–% Bk_I) will give an index of the infant's role, relative to that of the mother, in ventro-ventral contact. If the infant is responsible for a higher proportion of Makes than of

Breaks, and is thus primarily responsible for contact, the index will be positive. In the opposite case, where the mother is primarily responsible for proximity, the index will be negative. The changes in these measures with age are shown in Fig. 1.

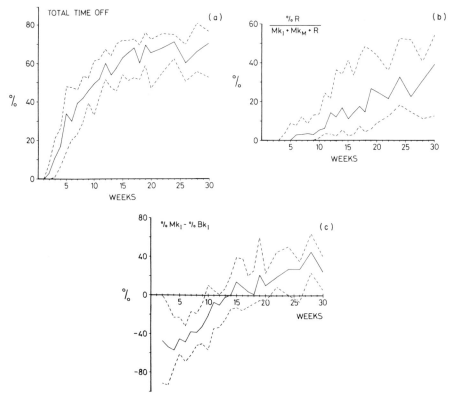

Fig. 1. The course of mother-infant interaction in small captive groups of rhesus monkeys. (a) Total time off mother (number of half minutes infant was off mother as percentage of number watched). (b) Relative frequency of rejections, expressed as the ratio of the number of occasions on which the infant attempted to gain ventro-ventral contact and was rejected by the mother (R) to the number of occasions on which it made contact on the mother's initiative (Mk_M), made contact on its own initiative (Mk_I), or attempted unsuccessfully to gain contact (R). (c) Infants' role in ventro-ventral contact (number of contacts made on infants' initiative, as percentage of number made, minus number of contacts broken by infant, as percentage of number broken ($Mk_I/(Mk_I + Mk_M) - Bk_I/(Bk_I + Bk_M)$).

The argument which follows concerns correlations between the first of these measures and the other two. It would apply to any two measures of a relationship, so long as one could be said to affect the other. It does not depend on the particular properties of those used here to exemplify it. However it may be as well to make a few points concerning the index of the infant's role in contact, since they apply to many comparable measures:

(i) There are practical difficulties in recording who is responsible for a given make or break: the individual who actually breaks contact may be responding to inconspicuous signals from the partner. There are several points here. First, we could treat the index as representing the relative role of the infant as a matter of definition: in that case what we would mean by saying that the infant has the primary role in ventro-ventral contact would be that it was responsible for a higher proportion of Makes than of Breaks. Second, even if some Makes or Breaks are initiated by subtle signals from the partner, use of the index involves only the assumption that responsibility for proximity assessed from the index is adequately correlated with conclusions that would be drawn from a more detailed analysis. Finally, even if Makes and Breaks apparently due to one partner were actually triggered by subtle signals from the other, those signals might themselves be responses to the behaviour of the first individual. Indeed it could be argued that the initiations and terminations of the interactions of higher animals nearly always involve some degree of negotiation. The present argument could be related to any behavioural change considered to be indicative of primary responsibility.

(ii) The value of the index depends to a limited extent on the number of observations. However, given reasonable assumptions about what constitutes a constant relative role, this index varies less than others that have been employed in this context (Hinde and White, 1974).

(iii) The index is concerned only with the relative role of the two partners: there are of course differences between, for instance, mother-infant dyads in which the infant is responsible for all the Makes and half of the Breaks in contact and one in which he is responsible for half the Makes and none of the Breaks, yet both give a similar index. However the argument below would not be affected.

(iv) The index is a summary of events over a period of time: it tells us nothing about any particular sequence.

We may now consider three questions about the mother infant relationship.

(i) Is infant or mother primarily responsible for determining the length of contacts during each period? As indicated above, the difference between the percentage of makes and the percentage of breaks that were due to the infant is a direct index of this. Figure 1 shows that in the early weeks the index was negative—that is, the infants were responsible for a smaller proportion of the makes than they were of breaks, and the mothers were therefore primarily responsible. Later, when the index became positive, the reverse was the case.

(ii) Are the age-changes in the time spent off the mother due more immediately to changes in the mother or to changes in the infant? This can be approached by examining the relation between the changes in the measures. If the time out of contact increased due to a change in the behaviour of the infant, we should expect the index of the infant's role and the frequency of rejections to decrease, but if it increased due to a change in the behaviour of the mother, we should expect both to increase. In general, positive correlations between the two pairs of measures indicate that the mother's role is primary, whilst a negative correlation indicates that the infant's role is primary. Figure 1 shows a positive correlation, and thus it seems that it is changes in the mother that are responsible for the increase in independence of the infant.

However two assumptions must be mentioned. First, a degree of stationarity is implied, i.e. it is assumed that the infant responds similarly to the mother's rejections at successive ages. Second, there is an assumption of limited flexibility in the members of the dyad. For instance, if the infant seeks proximity to the mother more, it is assumed that the mother will reject the infant more, but will nevertheless let him on a little bit more. Each of these assumptions seems reasonable, the former especially over limited age spans. In practice, of course, the argument usually involves many more measures than the two or three discussed here.

The prime importance of changes in the mother is at first sight a surprising finding, since the increase in independence is correlated with, and seems at first sight to be due to, the infant's physical growth and increased tendency to explore his environment and seek for solid food. Nevertheless it is in harmony with the finding that infants reared on inanimate surrogate mothers, and infants reared without mothers but in pairs, maintain a considerable amount of ventral contact to a greater age than do infants reared on natural mothers (Hansen, 1966;

Harlow and Harlow, 1965); the explanation in both cases no doubt lies in the rejecting behaviour of the natural mother.

This emphasis on the importance of changes in the mother's behaviour in promoting the increasing independence of the infant does not imply that the infant could not achieve independence on its own in the end: infants reared on inanimate mother surrogates do in fact leave them more and more as they grow older. Nor does it imply that the changes in the mother arise endogenously: they may be initiated by the infant's increasing demand for milk or its more vigorous locomotor play. But these activities in turn depend on maternal care, which in turn depends on communication with the infant, and so on. Development involves a constant interaction between mother and infant which, to be understood, must be gradually teased apart. This is only a first stage to that end. But the present analysis demonstrates the importance of changes in the mother's behaviour in permitting and promoting the increasing independence of the infant, and shows that it is the changes in her behaviour that immediately regulate the speed with which independence is achieved.

The importance of this conclusion in the present context is this. During the first 12 weeks or so it is the mother who is primarily responsible for ventral-ventral contact ($(\% \ Mk_I - \% \ Bk_I)$ is negative, Fig. 1). Nevertheless, even during this period it is *changes* in the mother that are immediately responsible for the increasing independence of the infant. Thus the questions of who is responsible for the amount of contact at any one age, and that of changes in which partner are primarily responsible for changes in the relationship with age, are separate questions, not to be confused.

(iii) At any one age, are the differences in the amount of time off between mother-infant dyads due primarily to differences between mothers or to differences between infants? Here again examination of correlations between measures can be helpful. If, at any one age, those infants who spent most time off their mothers are the ones who play the least role in contact (that is, for whom $\% \ Mk_I - \% \ Bk_I$ is least) and are rejected the least, the differences in the amount of contact would be primarily due to differences between the infants. If the correlations were significantly positive, the differences in contact time would be due primarily to differences between the mothers. Data are available only for the correlations with the frequency of rejections. The correlations were low, indicating that inter-mother and inter-infant

differences were both important. However they did show interesting and consistent age changes. In the early weeks they were consistently (and in one case significantly) positive, but after week 30 they were consistently (and in some cases significantly) negative. Thus while inter-mother differences are more important than inter-infant differences with young infants, later the reverse is the case. The age at which inter-mother differences become more important than inter-infant differences in determining inter-dyad differences in contact time is two or three months later than that at which infants become primarily responsible for contact.

The need for keeping the questions distinct will be apparent. The three questions posed so far are all of the general type, "Is this partner or that partner responsible?", but the answers are very different. It might have been thought that, as the mother is primarily responsible for contact in the early weeks, the decrease in contact with age would be due to developmental changes in the infant "winning out" over the mother's protectiveness. However such an approach neglects the fact that both mother and infant are changing, and it is important to address the issue of whether it is *changes* in the infant or *changes* in the mother that determine the *changes* in contact with age. In the same way, at any one age both mothers and infants differ between dyads, and we have been concerned with whether inter-mother or inter-infant *differences* are more important in producing the inter-dyad *differences* observed. The answer, as we have seen, depends on the age of the infant.

These arguments can be generalized in terms of the scheme shown in Table 1. The symbols at the left represent four possible types of change in the relationship or four possible differences between relationships. These types of change are respectively the mother seeks contact with the infant more, the mother seeks contact less, the infant seeks contact more, and the infant seeks contact less. They may apply to changes in one dyad, or in the mean for a group of dyads, over time; or to differences between dyads at one age; or to differences between two (groups of) dyads living under different conditions; or to differences between measures before and after treatment, etc. The measures considered so far are shown in columns 1, 2 and 3, but in each case predictions can be extended to include more measures—for instance the time the infant spends off but at a distance from the mother and an index of his responsibility for time in proximity. (It is of course an open issue whether the measures concerned with contact should show simi-

TABLE 1

Predicted direction of changes (or differences) in five measures of the mother-infant relationship, given the four types of change (or difference) shown on the left. (See text.)

	Contact			Proximity	
	(1)	(2)	(3)	(4)	(5)
		Infants	Mother rejects	Proportion of time	Infants
	Time	relative	infant's	off infant	relative
	infant	role in	attempt at	away from	role in
	off mother	contact	contact	mother	proximity
M–I →	−	−	−	−	−
M–I ←	+	+	+	+	+
M–I ←	−	+	+	−	+
M–I →	+	−	−	+	−

lar correlations to measures concerned with proximity: usually they do, but there are cases where they do not (Hinde, 1974).) The symbols indicate the predicted direction of change in the measure indicated at the head of the column, given a change or difference in the relationship(s) of the type shown on the left. It will be apparent that columns 1 and 2, 1 and 3 and 4 and 5 change in the same directions if the change or difference is primarily maternal, and in the opposite direction if due to the infant.

The scheme is equally applicable to many aspects of human relationships. For example, mothers and infants engage in play sequences involving bouts of engagement in mutual gaze and a variety of social actions interspersed with intervals when eye contact is broken (Stern, 1977). The interactions themselves are complex, apparently involving both simple responses to stimuli and pre-programmed sequences on the part of both mother and infant. The questions of whether differences in the frequency or duration of such sequences between mother-infant dyads, or changes over age, are due more to differences between (or changes in) mothers or infants could easily be answered from data on who initiated or terminated them. Or, to take a more mundane and obvious example, similar methods could be applied to how often husband and wife go out together, given information on how often each proposes and/or agrees to a plan. An extension of this method to triadic situations is given in Hinde (1977).

Another type of question that has been asked concerns the influence of measures of the relationship during one time period on a different measure in a later period. Suppose that two variables (X and Y) are measured at two points in time (1 and 2). This will generate six correlations—two synchronous correlations (X_1 vs Y_1 and X_2 vs Y_2) of the type considered in the preceding paragraphs; two auto correlations (X_1 vs X_2 and Y_1 vs Y_2) of the type that might be used to assess consistency over time; and two cross-lagged correlations (X_1 vs Y_2 and Y_1 vs $X\rho$). The difference between the two cross-lagged correlations ($\rho X_1 Y_2 - \rho Y_1 X_2$) is termed the cross-lagged differential. If it is positive, it suggests that X causes Y, but if negative, that Y causes X. Equality of the two cross-lagged correlations would indicate that the relationship between X and Y is due to an unmeasured third variable and not to causation of one by the other. For example Clarke-Stewart (1973), studying mother-infant dyads longitudinally, recorded how often mother and child were in the same room, and how often the child looked at the mother. Figure 2 shows the correlation coefficients bet-

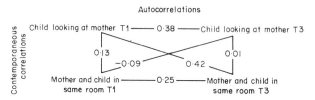

Fig. 2. Correlations between frequency with which child looks at his mother and the amount of time they spend together at two times (1 + 3). (Redrawn from Clarke-Stewart, 1973.)

ween these two measures both within time periods and between two time periods. Clarke-Stewart (1973) noted that how much the child looked at its mother in one time period correlated hardly at all with how often they were together in the same time period, but reasonably closely with how often they were together in the next, and that there was an almost zero correlation between mother and child together in one time period and child-looking in the next. She therefore concluded that an effect of child looking on how much child and mother were together subsequently was more likely than the reverse.

In cross-lagged analyses the synchronous and autocorrelations are used to reject the trivial explanation that a correlation between X_1 and Y_2 is due to correlations between variables within each time period and consistency in one of them between time periods, and to assess whether the basic assumptions of the model are satisfied. For example, the model assumes stationarity—that is, that there is no change in the causal relations between the variables over time. Evidence that this assumption is met is given by similarity in the synchronous correlation coefficients, provided reliability of the variables does not change (Kenny, 1975). Although this technique has been used as much for the study of mother-infant relationships as for adult relationships, the assumption of stationarity makes it more suitable for the latter. With a developing infant, it is by no means always clear that a measure at one age is measuring the same thing as the same measure at a different age. For example, does infant crying at one age mean the same thing as infant crying at another? Some of the precautions that must be observed in using cross-lagged analysis are discussed by Eron *et al.* (1972) and Kenny (1975).

In this chapter it has been assumed that mutuality is inherent in the relationships with which we are concerned: each partner is seen as continuously or intermittently influencing the other. In such a situation a stimulus-response analysis, however sophisticated, is likely to prove inadequate. It seems more likely that understanding will come through a gradual teasing apart of the roles of the two partners in the relationship. The questions posed here of course represent only the first stages in such an enterprise. Further progress depends on answering further questions. For example, if changes in the mother rhesus monkey are more important than changes in the infant in determining changes in mother-infant contact with age, we can then ask "In what ways does the mother's behaviour change with age?" Similarly we can ask "In what ways does the behaviour of mothers whose infants spend little time in contact with them differ from that of mothers whose infants spent much?" These will lead to further questions, to answer which correlations between measures may again be useful.

Summary

Relationships involve mutual influences by each partner on the other. A method for teasing apart the relative roles of the two partners in producing changes in the relationship, or differences between relationships, is discussed.

20

Negative and Positive Feedback

Some interpersonal relationships retain their characteristics over long periods in spite of changes in the participants and in spite of opportunities for, or pressures towards, change from outside. Others, having remained stable for a period, are suddenly disrupted or undergo dramatic metamorphosis. So far most of our discussion has concerned factors shaping the course of relationships in the relatively short term, though in the last chapter we examined a means for assessing the role of changes in the partners in producing more permanent changes in the relationship. Now we must consider further the determinants of stability and/or change.

Stability of a relationship in spite of changes in the participants or external stresses could be due to compensatory interactions within the relationship. In such a case, negative feedback could be said to operate. And where slight change led to gradually accelerating change and metamorphosis or disruption, the sequence could be described in terms of positive feedback.

Whilst we can use the language of control systems in a qualitatively descriptive way here, it requires caution; the veneer of sophistication it provides can easily obscure the complexity of real-life relationships. For one thing, the same course of action can have both positive and negative feedback effects depending on the dependent variable examined—when a parent encourages independence in an adolescent daughter, he/she may be diminishing consistency (positive feedback) but promoting continuity (negative feedback).

Furthermore discussion in terms of feedback can be taken to imply the operation only of relatively simple rewards and costs. In real life the consequences of interactions are evaluated, and whether stability is enhanced or diminished may depend on a fine balance between diverse factors. For example, Bandura (1976), taking a social learning theory approach, has argued that self-regulatory processes operate on the participants in interactions, people responding to their own actions in self-rewarding or self-punishing ways. In his view, the process involves three stages:

(a) An individual observes his own behaviour in terms of certain relevant dimensions.

(b) A judgemental process, which depends on subsidiary processes including comparisons with perceived internal standards, valuation of the activities, and appraisal of the determinants of the process.

(c) Response to the judgemental process, involving positive and negative self-evaluation and/or self-applied consequences. Self-reward and self-punishment will affect subsequent responsiveness.

Thus some individuals, who have adopted codes involving a high valuation of aggressive behaviour, feel better as a result of physical conquests, and become subsequently more likely to indulge in further aggression. But other individuals have personal standards which condemn aggression. For them, aggressive acts are followed by self-condemnation, and anticipated self-condemnation may serve to prevent potential aggression. Such controlling mechanisms can be rendered ineffective in a variety of ways—Bandura discusses, for instance, moral justification, euphemistic labelling, dehumanization of the object, and other processes with a similar end result. It will be apparent that a delicate balance may control whether positive or negative feedback effects occur. In dyadic relationships the issues are even more complex.

However, in spite of this complexity, a distinction between positive and negative feedback provides a framework for discussing the long-term patterning of interactions within a relationship.

Negative feedback

Theorists with widely differing orientations have argued that a stabilizing tendency is intrinsic to many relationships. Amongst exchange theorists, the view that participants in a relationship actively seek a balance between their profits and costs is basic to the theories of Thibaut and Kelley (1959) and Homans (1974). That dyadic relationships and families have powers for self-regulation has been emphasized for many years by clinicians (e.g. Jackson, 1959; Watzlawick et al., 1967; Wertheim, 1975c): negative feedback produces stability within a defined range whilst, in healthy families, permitting limited change in specified directions. Psychiatric illnesses are seen by some as means for maintaining certain aspects of the *status quo*. Whilst processes describable in terms of negative feedback are thus widespread, it is important to remember that either the continuity or the consistency or both of many relationships may also be ensured by external constraints, such as physical propinquity, convenience or social forces. In such cases stabilizing mechanisms internal to the relationship are unnecessary.

The operation of negative feedback can conveniently be illustrated by the effects of a brief separation experience on the mother-infant relationship in rhesus monkeys—a case for which reasonably hard data are available. If a 6–8 month old infant is separated from its mother for 1–2 weeks it shows initially a phase of protest, marked by active searching for the mother and distress calling (the analogue of human crying), and then a phase of despair involving reduced locomotor activity and sitting in a hunched depressed position. Eventually, if the separation is prolonged, some apparent re-adjustment may occur. These phases are comparable to those seen in human infants (Bowlby, 1969). Upon reunion with the mother the infant behaves in a demandingly filial manner. It gives frequent distress calls and may follow its mother around continuously. If the mother responds by picking the infant up and cuddling it, the relationship is likely soon to be re-stabilized. Over a period of a few weeks the infant's demands decrease, and the relationship returns to its original course. This could be described as negative feedback.

However experiments show that recovery can be delayed by certain types of treatment. If the separation is accomplished by removing the infant from the home environment and isolating it in a strange place, it continues to protest for at least several days, and despair sets in only gradually. However if the mother is removed, leaving the infant in the physical environment and with the social companions to which it is accustomed, the phase of acute protest is much more brief and "despair" sets in more rapidly. On reunion, such "depressed" infants appear to be much less effective in gaining their mother's attention than infants still protesting vigorously. The same manipulations affect also the mother's responsiveness. If she has been left in the home pen, she is usually ready to meet her infant's demands when he is restored to her. But if she has been away herself, she must also re-establish her relationships with her other social companions, and is more likely to reject the demands of her infant. Thus the most acute effects are found when the severity of the infant's separation-induced depression reduces its overt demands, and the mother's responsiveness is low. Such a finding could be described in terms of positive feedback, the lack of responsiveness of the mother exacerbating the depression of the infant, and vice versa (Hinde and Spencer-Booth, 1971a; Hinde and McGinnis, 1977). In most cases both positive and negative feedback operate, the outcome depending on the balance.

When negative feedback operates, the nature of the changes necessary for a relationship to accommodate external stresses or changes in the participants will depend on the nature of that relationship. Small changes in the behavioural propensities of one partner require different changes in the other according to whether the relationship is predominantly reciprocal or complementary. Where reciprocal interactions are involved, if one partner changes, the other should change in a similar fashion to preserve stability. Thus with two peers, if one changes in such a way that he tends to play more, the other should change in a similar fashion. By contrast, as we have just seen, the mother-infant relationship is predominantly complementary and, if one partner changes in one direction, stability may be best preserved if the other changes in a complementary fashion. We may note here that special problems are perhaps liable to arise with relationships that are in some contexts reciprocal and in others complementary: changes in either partner must be met by appropriate changes in appropriate areas by the other.

In either reciprocal or complementary interactions there is a third way of coping with change that must be mentioned: if change occurs in one partner, it can be altered or reversed if the other fails to produce a complementary change. Thus if an infant becomes more demanding, the mother might ignore its demands. This would be the equivalent of an extinction procedure, and may be a powerful way to decrease the frequency of an operant response, even in a social situation (e.g. Etzel and Gewirtz, 1967). However extinction may have far-reaching effects on other aspects of the relationship, including the induction of aggressive behaviour. Thus, whilst the infant's demands may disappear if they are ignored, the relationship may also be changed in other, perhaps undesirable, ways. Similar considerations apply to punishment (Feshbach, 1970).

It may seem that two potentially contradictory principles have been introduced here. On the one hand it has been suggested that consistency in the infant-mother relationship may be aided if an increase in the infant's demands is met by the mother. The evidence here is largely observational or correlational; for instance, Ainsworth and Bell (1974) claim that their data indicate that infants whose mothers most frequently ignore their crying in one quarter year are likely to be amongst the most frequent criers during the next quarter year (though see Gewirtz and Boyd, 1977). On the other hand, there is evidence that extinction (e.g. by ignoring) or punishment of a response may decrease its frequency, and may also have ramifying effects through the relationship. It may be suggested that this contradiction is more apparent than real. In the former case we are dealing with changes in the whole relationship whose effects are being assessed by a single symptom, while in the latter we are dealing with the treatment of a symptom which has ramifying effects on the relationship (see e.g. Porter, 1968).

The existence of stabilizing tendencies is of crucial importance for studies of child development. As we learn more about the complexity of human mother-infant interactions, we cannot fail to be amazed by their subtleties. But this does not necessarily mean that their every aspect *matters*. Absence or excessive presence of a so-called "normal" aspect of the relationship may lead to divergence or disruption, or it may be adequately compensated by stabilizing mechanisms (Bell, 1974; Dunn, 1976; Bateson, 1976). We cannot tell, without empirical data, what aspects of a relationship are essential to its nature—and indeed the answer to that question is liable to depend on circumstances. And where stabilizing mechanisms do operate, we must expect them to operate only so long as the divergence lies within certain limits—small divergencies may be unnoticed, and moderate ones adequately compensated, whilst larger ones are disruptive. This point was well illustrated by the experiments on rhesus monkey mother-infant separation: only when both the infant was markedly depressed and the mother was unresponsive were the effects of the separation long term and severe (Hinde and McGinnis, 1977). Furthermore the consequences of a given degree of disruption may depend on the impact of other variables on the system: regulation may occur in some circumstances but not others (e.g. Sameroff and Chandler, 1976; Bateson, 1976).

Stabilizing mechanisms may act to maintain a relationship in the short term, yet permit gradual changes on a longer time scale. This is especially evident in relationships where the behaviour of one participant is directed towards supporting or inducing change in the other. In teacher-pupil and parent-child relationships, teacher and parent strive to maintain the relationship in the short term, but in the long term to produce change which will be incompatible with the initial nature of the relationship. Much unhappiness could perhaps be prevented if it were more clearly recognized that such relationships contain the seeds of their own disruption or transmutation.

Positive feedback

Bateson (1958) pointed out that both reciprocal and complementary interactions may have a built-in tendency to escalate. Thus if boasting by A induces boasting by B, boasting will tend to escalate. If A is assertive, and B replies with submission, this may reinforce A's assertiveness. A may then become more and more assertive and B more and more submissive. The extent to which each partner confirms or disconfirms the other's claims (see pp. 65–7) will determine the degree and duration of feedback.

In practice positive feedback can operate to hinder or help the future course of a relationship. As a short-term example of the former, if one partner in a marriage is unwilling to interact in a particular way, the other may show frustration-induced anger and aggression, and this may enhance the uncooperativeness of the former.

Anger may be invoked also by separation from a parent or loved one. Bowlby (1973) suggests that such anger is usually functional in (a) assisting the separated individual to overcome obstacles to reunion and/or (b) discouraging the loved one from going away again. Negative feedback thus operates. (Of course if the separation is permanent, as in bereavement, the anger is without function, but may nevertheless appear.) However if separation or threats of separation invoke intense, frequent or persistent anger, the affectional bond between the partners may be weakened and alienation occurs. Bowlby suggests that such dysfunctional anger, whose effects can be described in terms of positive feedback, is the more likely to occur because separations, especially when prolonged or repeated, have a double effect. On the one hand anger is aroused, and on the other love is attenuated. Similar considerations can apply to marital infidelity.

An example showing the subtlety of the factors determining the balance between negative and positive feedback is provided by a

sensitive analysis of the "melancholy marriage" by Hinchliffe *et al.*
(1977). On the basis of tape and videotape recordings of patient and
wife interacting, they write:

> In a good relationship the wife would respond to the distress of her
> husband by being reassuring and protective. In many instances this
> would be effective, but when the stress increases or when the wife is
> unable to respond in a manner which meets his needs he may develop
> depressive symptoms. The failure to meet his needs can also be under-
> stood in terms of the shift in roles which occurs . . .; as the wife becomes
> more caring and mother-like the husband becomes child-like and depen-
> dent. The system becomes less stable at this point and psychological
> symptoms emerge which further constrain or regulate the pattern of the
> interaction. The husband becomes ambivalent about his needs, since he
> has on the one hand the security and comfort of the regression and
> dependence, while on the other he experiences the pain and discomfort of
> his impoverished self-image and loss of self-esteem. His behaviour can be
> confusing to his wife as he emits cues suggesting a dependency need and
> at the same time rejects her. As she fails in her efforts to meet his distress
> she becomes anxious, irritable, frustrated and depressed and begins to
> feel alienated. Any motivation for a change in his behaviour would
> depend on his tolerance of the altered equilibrium (p. 140).

Further consideration of positive feedback leading to a gradual
deterioration of a relationship is not possible here, though the issues are
of crucial importance for psychopathology. Turning to cases of positive
feedback acting to facilitate the course of a relationship, one case has
already been mentioned (p. 185). The belief that effort has been put
into a relationship is dissonant with its dissolution, and conducive to
further effort. Commitment to the relationship is consistent with seeing
its good aspects, and with dispensing rewards in the expectation of
future returns.

It seems likely that the development of dyadic relationships often
depends on positive feedback consequent upon the initial dyadic
attraction. Liking may lead to being liked and this to increased liking
(e.g. Newcomb, 1961; Backman and Secord, 1959). This effect of
perceiving that one is liked can operate even when one is initially
prejudiced against one's evaluator (Byrne, 1971).

The means by which liking may lead to liking are certainly diverse.
At a simple level, liking may lead to greater proximity in terms either of
immediate interpersonal distance or of frequency of encounters. Proximity enhances familiarity, which in turn increases liking (p. 194; see
also Homans, 1961). Indeed even the anticipation of future interaction

can, in some circumstances, induce liking (Darley and Berscheid, 1967).

An effect of being liked on liking would be predicted by balance theory. If A likes himself, and A perceives that B likes A, a balanced state in which A likes B will be facilitated. It would also be predicted by reinforcement theory: B's esteem is rewarding to A, and increases A's liking for B. It will be noted that the latter prediction is independent of A's own self-esteem. By contrast, balance theory would predict that, if A does not like himself, perception by A that B likes him would make A less likely to like B in return. As discussed earlier, the evidence here is indecisive, but in harmony with the view that both the reward value of B's esteem and the congruency of B's perceived evaluation of A influence A's feelings about B, the former being the more important (Deutsch and Solomon, 1959). If A does not think highly of himself, B's esteem will induce less liking of B than if A has high self-regard.

A number of other conditions influence the effectiveness of positive evaluations in producing liking. Whether a positive evaluation that is believed to be inaccurate produces liking for the evaluator depends on the precise meaning ascribed to it by the evaluatee (Skolnick, 1971; Tedeschi, 1974; Stroebe, 1977). As discussed earlier, evidence that temporary deprivation of esteem from others will increase its effectiveness is not yet conclusive. However evaluations that change from negative to positive are, in some circumstances at least, more effective than evaluations that are consistently positive (Aronson and Linder, 1965; see p. 76).

The effect of being liked on liking may be further augmented in another way. Equal sharing of scarce resources may induce or augment friendship, and friends are more likely to share equally (Lerner, 1974). Furthermore there is considerable experimental evidence that people tend to help those who help them, harm those who harm them, and confide in those who confide in them (Tedeschi, 1974; Davis and Skinner, 1974; Rubin, 1975). Of course this does not mean that a "reciprocity norm" is ubiquitous: the questions of how far the postulation of such a norm is useful as either a descriptive or an explanatory device, and what its bases may be, are still open (La Gaipa, 1977).

One possibility is that people are guided by social conventions dictating that they should reciprocate benefits received. Should such a convention operate, its force certainly varies with a number of factors such as the needs of the recipient, the resources of the donor and the motives imputed to him. Whether the operation of such a convention can be deduced from more basic postulates, as suggested by equity theorists, is also still an open issue. However it is not clear under what circumstances or in what kinds of relationships it is necessary to invoke a norm of reciprocity as a causative agent at all. If the fact of reciprocity can be explained in terms of intervening variables, such as effects of giving and receiving on liking, there is no need to postulate anything else (Altman and Taylor, 1973).

And there is in fact evidence that, if we like someone we may be willing to do things for them, even without expectation that the favours will be returned. And a person who does favours without expectation of reciprocation tends to be liked. There are thus considerable possibilities for positive feedback. For example, in one study it was found that receiving led to liking, liking led to giving, and giving led to liking (Gross and Latane, 1974). In another, children were more prone to share possessions with children they liked than with children they disliked (Staub and Sherk, 1970). Just how far such studies can be generalized is, as usual, open to question: there are circumstances in which subjects think less highly of donors when there is no requirement to reciprocate than when there is (Gergen et al., 1975). And of course, just how far any act is "genuinely" altruistic is often difficult to assess; it may be that the children in the study cited were more willing to lend their things to those who could be relied on to return them, or who might lend them their things in return. It could even be that they lent because they wanted to be liked by those they liked.

Be that as it may, the very act of behaving generously, or of believing that one has behaved generously, can provide further opportunity for feedback. One likes oneself for having behaved generously, and attributes to oneself liking for the person to whom one has been generous (Blau, 1964). Thus liking induces generosity and generosity induces liking. But generosity induces liking only when it is perceived as generosity. If A confers favours on B that B feels were owed to him, there will be no inducement for B to like A, and if B saw A's favours as constraining his own freedom of action, he might even resent them.

Yet another issue here involves the relation between self-disclosure and liking. Intuitively it seems that we are more likely to reveal ourselves to those we like, and that we like those who are open with us. It has also been suggested that revealing oneself to another person increases liking for that person (Jourard, 1971)—possibly because one likes oneself for being honest. And if B already has some positive feeling for A, A's disclosures may be additionally rewarding because they mark B as worthy to receive information. Also, the act of disclosure may be cathartic for the discloser. The possibilities for positive feedback are clearly considerable.

However the issues are not entirely straightforward. In the first place, reciprocity may be overestimated by the people involved. There is considerable evidence that spouses or roommates believe that what they give and receive is correlated to a greater extent than is actually the case: the degree of reciprocity as measured by a third party may be considerably less than that which the partners believe to be occurring. La Gaipa (1977) thus proposed that there is a 'bias' towards perceiving that social relationships are reciprocal. La Gaipa also found that members of a dyad each *expected* the same degree of reciprocity in intimacy from the other: furthermore this index of the perceived likelihood that the other would reciprocate in intimacy was more predictive of growth in the relationship over time.

Second, although a degree of reciprocity has been found in a number of laboratory experiments, the generality of any "norm of reciprocity" for intimacy must be questioned. Most experimental studies of reciprocity of intimacy have used subjects who were initially strangers to each other, and there is evidence that reciprocity within any one encounter is more usual in encounters between strangers than in those between friends (Thibaut and Kelley, 1959; Altman and Taylor, 1973; Derlega et al., 1976). Furthermore, in a laboratory context special factors may act to enhance reciprocity. Two people confined together quickly reach levels of self disclosure that in ordinary circumstances would be achieved only by very close friends (Altman and Haythorn, 1965). And the subjects in shorter-term laboratory experiments may not be sure how they should behave, and look to each other for cues. Reciprocity is thus enhanced by modelling. In one study (Davis, 1976) it was found that subjects did indeed disclose information about themselves to similar extents, but not as a result of mutual reciprocity. Rather one partner assumed responsibility for prescribing the level of intimacy, and the other then reciprocated.

In longer-term relationships confidence is selective; we are more likely to be intimate with some people than others, in some situations than others, and about some things than others.

Another issue is that, while there is good experimental support for the view that liking leads to disclosure (Worthy et al., 1969), it is less clear that disclosure leads to liking of the discloser by the person with whom the secret is shared. While a positive effect has been found, other studies have found no effect, or a curvilinear relationship with most attraction at moderate levels of disclosure. In the latter case, very intimate disclosure may be interpreted by the recipient as indicative of a personality problem (reviewed Cozby, 1973; La Gaipa, 1977; Ajzen, 1974; Rubin, 1975). Sex differences may be important here however. For at least some subjects in some circumstances revelation of intimate information by women is indicative of better adjustment than is absence of self disclosure, but for men the reverse is the case (Derlega and Chaikin, 1976).

The issue here is similar to that discussed in the context of the effect of similarity on interpersonal attraction. Presumably what matters is not how much is disclosed, but what and when. Ajzen (1977) reports a study in which students were shown a set of statements purporting to come from a fellow student, and asked to evaluate her. The statements varied in the intimacy *vs* superficiality and the desirability *vs* undesirability of the information conveyed. Desirability of the information had a significant effect on liking, but its intimacy did not. However there was an interaction. Attraction was greater when the information concerned undesirable items and was intimate than when it was undesirable and superficial, perhaps because the hypothetical stranger was then viewed as honest: there was virtually no effect of intimacy with desirable information. There is also evidence that a person who reveals intimate information may be regarded as open and trusting and liked on that account, even though the information imparted has undesirable implications.

Again, Altman and Taylor (1973) emphasize that progressive disclosure requires mutual trust and rewarding exchange. They thus picture a sequence of mutual trust, rewarding exchange, projected future trust and anticipated positive outcomes as necessary for the cycle to continue. But self-disclosure by A will not prompt reciprocation by B if B perceives that A's self-disclosure was motivated by self-interest, or that it was the product of an unsound mind. B's interpretation of the meaning of A's behaviour (Nemeth, 1970) or the information contained in the self-disclosure, is crucial. Such facts indicate that attempts to treat mutual self-disclosure in terms of exchange theory, with disclosure as a reward, are likely to need qualifications specifying when it is rewarding and when it is not. Once again, the problem of specifying in advance what is reinforcing necessarily arises.

The preceding discussion of the manner in which liking, rewards, disclosure and/or services may be reciprocated indicates some ways in which positive feedback *could* occur, and provides some (not necessarily incompatible) suggestions as to the mechanisms involved. Comparable data showing an influence of hate on hating could no doubt be obtained. As yet, however, little is known about the circumstances in which feedback does and does not occur. Laboratory experiments, often rather contrived, can provide very interesting data about what can happen, but more natural history-type description is necessary to indicate when it will. We have seen that the meaning attached to a gift, to an evaluative statement or to a confidence may be a crucial determinant of its potency for inducing reciprocation, and this may well depend on the nature of the relationship (e.g. Davis and Martin, 1978). For example, a crucial issue may well be the stage of the relationship; not only may the explanatory value of exchange theory be reduced in relationships of long duration, but the rules of reciprocity may also be quite different. Commitment expressed publicly or privately or implied for instance by the use of plural pronouns, may well be an important intervening variable at some stages in a relationship, but less effective in mediating positive feedback in early stages or in mature relationships.

Finally, in real life many of the processes mentioned above may operate together and mutually sustain each other. This will already have become apparent from the preceding discussion, and may be especially important in the process of "falling in love". Tesser and Paulhus (1976) have suggested that love increases dating frequency and dating frequency increases love by a number of interrelated mechanisms. These include exposure learning, classical conditioning resulting from the good times experienced together, enhanced similarity in attitudes and values as a consequence of shared experiences (but see p. 92), rationalization justifying the time and energy spent in meeting, and private and public commitment. Although some of the assumptions in their empirical work have been questioned (Smith, 1978) their conclusions probably stand (Tesser and Paulhus, 1978).

Summary

Long-term stability in a relationship in spite of changes in the participants or external stresses may be due to compensatory interactions within it. Such a tendency can be described as involving negative feedback. An example, taken from studies of mother-infant interaction in rhesus monkeys, is described. The nature of the compensatory changes required will depend on the nature of the relationship.

Some types of progressive change in a relationship can be seen as the consequence of positive feedback. Positive feedback can operate to hinder or help the course of a relationship. Some examples of disruptive positive feedback are given, and some mechanisms involving positive feedback that may be important in the growth of dyadic relationships are discussed.

IV

Developmental Considerations

21

Developmental Aspects of Relationships between Adults

In Chapters 12–20 we saw that any stability shown by a relationship over time must be dynamic in nature, and discussed some groups of principles likely to aid understanding of the mechanisms involved. In discussing positive feedback, we became concerned with some of the mechanisms by which relationships change. Change is the focus of this last section, where we shall consider some more general issues concerned with the development of relationships. This chapter is concerned with the development of relationships between adults, most of the research discussed being concerned primarily with heterosexual relationships. The next takes up a few special issues concerned with relationships in infancy and childhood.

Stages in a relationship

For some purposes it is useful to contrast the properties of a relationship at different points in time, and in such cases it *can* be useful to describe the changes as involving a succession of stages. A number of attempts to describe stages in the development of adult-adult relationships have been made and it is convenient to review some of them briefly here. However it is important to remember that:

(a) They were intended to be primarily applicable to relationships, usually heterosexual, between late teenagers or between potential marriage partners in the U.S.A. Their generality may therefore be extremely limited. They may have relatively little relevance, for instance, to the strangely close but insulated relationships that can grow up in an air raid shelter or on a long sea voyage, to the spontaneous intimacies shared between strangers in a train, or to many formal relationships such as that between doctor and patient.

(b) There is no suggestion that all stages are to be distinguished by discontinuities. The division of any continuous process into stages is likely to depend on arbitrary criteria, and has the danger of implying the occurrence of sudden changes or the existence of transition periods which have no counterpart in real life (Hinde, 1971). This danger is even greater when the process goes in fits and starts, sometimes progressing forwards and sometimes sliding backwards, as in the growth of a relationship. While some of the forces in a long-term relationship can be seen as facilitating or hindering major changes (e.g. getting married, having a baby) (Ryder *et al.*, 1971; Cowan *et al.*, 1978), for most of the time a relationship proceeds without discontinuities.

(c) The description of each stage in terms of characteristics over a limited time period omits historical aspects which may be important for understanding the dynamics of the relationship (see p. 147).

In spite of these reservations, a brief review of the developmental stages through which various authors suppose a growing relationship to develop will serve to call attention to an important problem.

Thibaut and Kelley (1959) distinguished four stages. First, "Sampling", in which an individual selects those with whom he wishes to interact. Second "Bargaining", in which an acquaintanceship is formed and the individuals assess the probability of future profit. If this seems high, they may enter some form of private or public "Commitment", and this may in turn lead to "Institutionalization" in marriage or some other appropriate form.

Levinger and Snoek (1972) distinguish three "Levels of relatedness" which succeed each other in the development of a relationship. In the first, "Unilateral Awareness", one participant perceives the other as a collection of attributes which are evaluated according to the extent that they confirm his values or are likely to further his goals. This is the level at which many experiments on interpersonal attraction operate, especially those involving questionnaires from a bogus stranger (see p. 83). However at this level there is no relationship in the sense used in this book.

The second level is termed "Surface contact". Here Levinger and Snoek include two rather different situations. One involves transitory meetings in which two individuals interact and reveal limited information about themselves. This is the situation of two people who meet at a party or a dance—another type of situation sometimes artificially contrived in experiments on attraction (e.g. p. 90), but not necessarily involving a relationship in the sense used here. The other situation included in the level of "Surface contact" involves relationships between individuals who meet repeatedly in a particular role context, but exchange little more than a token "hello". For a teacher, Levinger suggests, these might include the bus driver, the building custodian and the colleague in the office down the hall. Transition from "unilateral awareness" to "surface contact" is likely to depend on physical characteristics, including perceived similarity and assumed co-orientation, as well as estimates of probable costs.

At the third level, of "Mutuality", the participants share knowledge, assume responsibility for furthering each other's goals, and share private norms for regulating their association. Two processes are emphasized as necessary to this level—interpersonal discovery and mutual investment in the common bond. Interaction is likely to be extended beyond areas required by the participant's social roles, self-disclosure increases, and each accommodates to the other's needs and values. This third level is further subdivided into three stages from minor interaction to total unity.

Murstein (e.g. 1977), concerned primarily with courtship and marriage in the U.S.A., also recognizes three stages, but only the first shows some correspondence to those postulated by Levinger. In the first or "Stimulus Stage", initial judgements are formed on the basis of perceptions of or information about the other.

The second stage is labelled "Value Comparison": here the primary focus is the gathering of information by verbal interaction with the other. This information concerns background, attitudes, values, interests etc. Discussion proceeds to more intimate items according to the extent to which the couple feel comfortable with each other, the effects of this disclosure on each other, and so on. If it proceeds sufficiently far, consensus on the more important values is reached. During this phase the importance of stimulus variables wane and "role comparisons" begin. In the "Role Stage" the latter predominate. By "role" Murstein refers to one participant's perception of the behaviour that is expected of him by the other or by him of the other. These may be in part moulded by the culture, but stem also from his own attitudes and predilections (see Chapter 13). In this stage "role compatibility" is assessed by comparing expectations with perceptions of the degree to which these expectations are fulfilled over a wide range of behaviour.

Altman and Taylor (1973), while emphasizing that any attempt to break up the "social penetration" process (see pp. 115–6) is bound to be artificial, nevertheless suggest that the postulation of stages may be useful for some purposes. They recognize successive stages of orientation, exploratory affective exchange, full affective exchange and stable exchange, the names being self-explanatory.

It will be apparent that, whilst these authors differ in the number of stages they recognize, they all, to differing degrees, emphasize that the characteristics of the partner or of the relationship that are important for the future of the relationship change as it develops. We shall return to this issue shortly.

Distinguishing degrees of relatedness

Whether or not the stages described by psychologists are useful, in every day life we do apply labels which have implications about how involved the members of a dyad are with each other. We say they are "just friends", "good friends", "lovers" and so on. What is more important, the participants in a relationship may see themselves as having a relationship of one type or another, and how they label it may be important for its future. It is thus of some importance to document what the individuals of a particular culture mean by the labels that they use.

One such attempt, concerned with the distinction between "liking" and "loving" (Rubin, 1974), has been mentioned. Liking appeared to involve primarily perceived attributes of the other participant, while the criteria of loving involved the relationship itself. These criteria were validated for North American students.

Levinger (1974) cites a study of Mark in which an attempt was made to specify the criteria by which members of a particular subculture would recognize relationships of various types. Undergraduates were asked how likely couples, described as "casually acquainted", "good friends not in love", "romantically attached" and "much in love, fully committed", would be to show certain types of behaviour. Not surprisingly, certain types of behaviour (e.g. "smile at each other") were judged as almost equally likely in all degrees of acquaintanceship, whilst others (e.g. "give back rubs", "go camping together" and "refuse to date other persons") were considered to be progressively more likely, the more deeply involved the couple (see also Kurth's (1970) distinction between friendly relations and friendship).

Levinger points out that the information about the relatedness of two individuals that is available to a third depends on the latter's relatedness to them. If he can observe them at his Level 1 (i.e. Unilateral Awareness, see p. 290), only behavioural data are available, but if he can observe them at Level 2 (i.e. Surface Contact) he can also use what they say about themselves, about each other, and about their relationship. Table 1 shows some possible indices of relatedness that he consid-

TABLE 1

Levinger's possible indices of pair relatedness. Modified from Levinger (1974)

| | Data from | |
	One member of pair	Both members
Level 1	Gazing at the other	Mutual gazing
	Approach behaviour	Pair proximity
	Offering (or asking for) space	Shared space
	Reaching toward other	Mutual touch
	Doing something for other	Doing it together
	Helping or asking for help	Mutual helping
	Lending or borrowing	Shared possession
Level 2	Knowledge about other	Shared knowledge
	Liking for other	Reciprocated liking
	Love for other	Reciprocated love
	Commitment to relationship	Mutual commitment
	Pronoun usage	
	Perceptual distortion	
	Memory distortion	
		Agreement on various items
		Past joint activity
		Future joint goals

ers to be potentially useful. Each item may refer either to one member of the pair (left-hand column) or to both (right-hand column). The items available through behavioural observation would all be included in the categories of Content or Quality of interactions in the present scheme, whilst those obtainable at Level 2 include aspects of interpersonal perception and commitment, as well as overall assessments of attraction. On the present view, the extent to which these various dependent variables are correlated with each other, and thus the extent to which it is useful to regard "pair relatedness" as a unitary dimension, are open issues.

Changes in the relative importance of context and attributes

Whether or not it is useful to recognize a series of stages in the development of a relationship, it is clear that the attributes that are most important to the participants change as it progresses.

EXTERNAL FACTORS

The early stages of a relationship are always determined by external factors—the chances of life that bring two individuals into proximity, and/or the discovery of an interest common to individuals who for external reasons are often thrown together. The importance of proximity has already been mentioned, but it must be emphasized that it can lead to aversion between two individuals as well as to attraction.

PHYSICAL ATTRIBUTES

Physical attributes are clearly of primary importance in the very early stages of relationships of many types. They have been shown to be important not only for young adults (e.g. Walster *et al.*, 1966; Byrne *et al.*, 1968; Byrne, 1971), but also for nursery school age children (Dion and Berscheid, 1974) and adolescents (Dion *et al.*, 1972; Cavior and Dockecki, 1973; Cavior *et al.*, 1975). In general the evidence supports the view that physical attractiveness is rather more important for young adult males than females (e.g. Miller and Rivenbark, 1970), and that it becomes progressively less important as a relationship develops (Stroebe *et al.*, 1971). Just what constitutes physical attractiveness is difficult to specify (Berscheid and Walster, 1974b), and certainly differs between cultures. But those judged to possess desirable physical attributes are likely to be regarded as having also many other desirable qualities, not of a physical nature, and to be assessed—more favourably (Byrne *et al.*, 1968; Dion *et al.*, 1972; Seligman *et al.*, 1974; Goldman and Lewis, 1977).

Of course, in any type of relationship, physical characteristics are not assessed merely along a dimension of attractiveness. As we have seen, every individual presents himself in such a way that he conveys an impression as to the sort of person he is—and there may be all degrees of deliberateness in how he does this. Posture, manner, clothes, speech and behaviour may all be involved (Goffman, 1959).

The "stimulus stage" therefore inevitably merges with that of "value comparison", to use Murstein's terms (see p. 291). But what "stimuli" suggest what "values", as well as which values are preferred, is again likely to be a subcultural matter.

ATTITUDES AND NEED COMPLEMENTARITY

Evidence that similarity in attitudes and values may be associated with interpersonal attraction was reviewed in Chapter 7. In experimental situations in which no actual interaction takes place, attitudinal similarity appears to be a powerful determinant of attraction. However once a relationship has been initiated, differences in attitude similarity are less adequate predictors of its future progress. For example Canters (1975) found no differences in attitudinal similarity between couples with different degrees of involvement, and Hill *et al.* (1976) found no differences in initial attitudinal similarity between dating partners still together two years later and those who had broken up.

Evidence that complementarity of needs is associated with interpersonal attraction and friendship was also reviewed in Chapter 7. Neither attitudinal similarity nor need complementarity is ubiquitously important, and the conflicting experimental data can in part by reconciled on the view that what matters to the participants in a relationship varies in part with what sort of relationship it is, and in part with the stage it has reached.

Some studies concerning the former were cited on pp. 103–4. To add one more, Rychlak (1965) assessed the influence of need similarity (need Dominance and need Dominance), need complementarity (need Nurturance and need Succorance) and need incompatibility (need Order and need Change) on interpersonal selection among strangers. He arranged that subjects should solve two problems when in groups of six. The subjects were later asked which other person in their group they would like most and least as an employer, an employee and as a neighbour. The more highly nurturant subjects chose a highly succorant subject as preferred neighbour, but this dimension was irrelevant to the employer or employee relationships. Subjects with a high need for order preferred a boss with a low need for change, but a neighbour with a high need for change. It is interesting that in this study need compatibility *vs* incompatibility provided a basis for some selections, but need similarity did not. Rychlak suggests that people make their initial choices on the basis of compatibility/incompatibility, and only later single out for longer friendships those who have a need pattern similar to their own.

Turning to studies concerned with the influence of the stage in the relationship on what matters to the participants, common observation indicates that needs may change in long-term relationships. For instance, marriage partners may need nurturance and support from each other early on, but this may become less important as they mature and become established. If, in a more traditional marriage, one partner becomes established in the external world while the other plays a child-rearing role of diminishing importance, difficulties may follow. It is perhaps not surprising that marital satisfaction has tended to be greatest early and late in marriage, with a trough in the middle—though this trend accounts for only a small part of the variance (Rollins and Cannon, 1974; see also Spanier *et al.*, 1975).

However there is considerable evidence for changes in what is important at much earlier stages. In a well-known study Kerckhoff and Davis (1962) found similarity in backgrounds and interests to be important early in courtship, then similarity in attitudes or values, and later still need complementarity. Although Levinger *et al.* (1970) failed to replicate this finding, they suggested a number of factors which could account for the differing conclusions of the two studies.

Using a different type of approach, La Gaipa (reviewed 1977) demonstrated directly the changing perceived importance of different aspects of a relationship as it progresses. La Gaipa focussed on four levels of friendship (*Best friends*, *Close friends*, *Good friends* and *Social acquaintances*). He obtained a large number of statements about the characteristics to be expected at each, and used judges to reduce these to 80 items. Students were then asked to rate these for the extent to which they are essential at each level of friendship. Factor analyses of the data for each level of friendship revealed major factors—"self disclosure", "authenticity", "helping behaviour", "acceptance", "positive regard" (enhancing one's feeling of self warmth etc.), "strength of character" (conformity), "similarity", "empathic understanding" and "ritualistic social exchange". These factors were not all present at each level of friendship, indicating that friendship is perceived in different ways as it develops. Subsequent studies provided data on how the importance attached to each factor varied with the level of friendship. Data for six of the factors are shown in Fig. 1. It

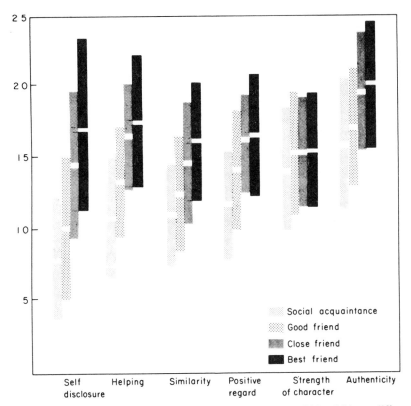

Fig. 1. Variability of importance attached to various factors of friendship at different levels of friendship. (From La Gaipa, 1977.)

would seem, for example, that self-disclosure was not considered very important until the relationship had reached the stage of close friend, but authenticity was important at all levels. In a series of studies La Gaipa has validated scales assessing the several aspects of friendship, and shown that they can be used to predict the growth of friendship (reviewed La Gaipa 1977).

Whilst La Gaipa (1977) used labels from everyday life in this study, it is apparent that many of them were more closely related to the categories of intimacy, interpersonal perception and commitment than to the issues of similarity and complementarity emphasized in so many previous studies. Other workers have likewise emphasized the importance of mutual understanding: relationships in which the partners see themselves the ways their partners see them, define their relationship similarly and are mutually involved, are more likely to progress (Lewis, 1973; Hill *et al.*, 1976).

In an attempt to assess what is necessary for a relationship to progress, Lewis (1973) studied pre-marital dyads by questionnaire methods. Distinguishing the "pair-processes" indicated in Table 2, he

TABLE 2

Successive "pair processes" necessary for the continued development of a relationship (from Lewis, 1973)

(A) The achievement of pairs perceiving similarities in each other's
    (1) Socio-cultural background
    (2) Values
    (3) Interests
    (4) Personality
(B) The achievement of pair rapport, as evidenced in a pair's
    (1) Ease of communication
    (2) Positive evaluations of the other
    (3) Satisfaction with pair relationships
    (4) Validation of self by the other
(C) The achievement of openness between partners through a neutral self-disclosure
(D) The achievement of role-taking accuracy
(E) The achievement of interpersonal role-fit, as evidenced by a pair's
    (1) Observed similarity of personalities
    (2) Role complementarity
    (3) Need complementarity
(F) The achievement of dyadic crystallization, as evidenced by a pair's
    (1) Progressive involvement
    (2) Functioning as a dyad
    (3) Boundary establishment
    (4) Commitment to each other
    (5) Identity as a couple

assessed the present state of each relationship and subsequently its progression to the next. The hypotheses that each stage was necessary before the next could be reached were for the most part confirmed.

PERSONALITY AND PERSONAL CONSTRUCTS

A possible way to integrate some of these research findings has been suggested in a stimulating discussion of the bases of friendship by Duck (1977b). He suggests that attitudinal and personality variables do not differ in kind, but represent stages in a continuum. In the development of close personal relationships, attempts to define and consensually to validate the self are present at all stages. But it is necessary for an individual to validate not only his attitudes and values, but also the constructs he uses to enforce order on the world and to embody predictions of the future (see p. 85). This is especially the case with the most subjective and otherwise untestable constructs—those that are concerned with the personalities of others and that are used to provide explanations of their behaviour. It is here that friendship plays a crucial role. It is not only that the more A's constructs are like B's, the easier will he find it to understand him and to communicate with him, though this will in itself provide a basis for mutual attraction. But beyond that similarity in construct systems provides opportunities for validation at a new and more basic level of personality functioning. And that in turn facilitates extension and elaboration of the construct system. In other words, it provides opportunities for growth. It may be because growth is important that conventional personality tests have proved to be such poor predictors of the development of friendship or love. Most personality tests are constructed to measure stable characteristics. For friendship, flexibility and the ability to modify and extend the construct system may be as or more important than similarity or complementarity in specified areas. There is indeed evidence that, in this context as well as in so many others (Bateson, 1973), a degree of dissimilarity against a background of similarity is attractive.

Duck supposes that comparison and elaboration go on at a number of different levels from early on in a relationship. It is necessary for each participant to build up a picture of the attitudes and personality of the other, to convince himself of the other's value as a person with which to compare himself, and against whom to validate his own views of the world; and also to compare himself against this picture. These different processes may all start from very early in the relationship. However their relative importance changes. For that reason, Duck suggests, the sort of psychological test able to predict the growth of friendship will change as a relationship progresses. Experimental data supported this view (Duck and Craig, 1978). Twenty male and twenty female students, living in the same campus residence, were followed over an eight month period. At one month, 3 months and 8 months after first acquaintance they reported their sociometric choices and completed three personality tests. The tests were (a) The California Psychological Inventory (CPI), a personality test in which subjects are invited to agree or disagree with a set of statements to provide a gross personality profile; (b) The Allport-Vernon Study of Values (AVSV), which provides rather less easily accessible information about value systems; and (c) A Kelly Repertory Grid, which deals with the minutiae of personal experience and ways of thinking (see p. 85). On the last, each subject's constructs were categorized into one of four mutually exclusive and exhaustive categories. Although in other studies similarity on the CPI has been found to be correlated with attraction after acquaintanceships of a few minutes (e.g. Duck, 1977b), here none of the tests was correlated with friendship after one month. The AVSV was correlated with sociometric choice at 3 months, and the rep grid at 8 months. Thus different tests were related to friendship choice after different periods of acquaintanceship. Duck and Craig (1978) argue that this supports the view that different types of personality information will be sought in support of one's own personality at different stages in an acquaintanceship. If this is the case, there may be times when no test (out of a limited number) would be related to friendship choice. This, the authors suggest, is what happened at one month.

These ideas are certainly stimulating, and seem capable of putting new life into an area of research which was in danger of becoming constrained by its own techniques. It remains to be seen how generally important similarity in construct systems will prove to be. Duck's evidence suggests that it becomes progressively more important as friendship progresses, but that does not necessarily mean that it is important in all close relationships. One might guess, for example, that it would be much more important in marriages that Bernard (1964) would describe as "interactional", and of little importance in "parallel" marriages (see p. 113). The nature of the relationship must be taken into account in assessing its dynamics.

The view that friendship permits personal growth raises the question of why it is that some relationships become boring. In most of our everyday business relationships, we value predictability. We tend to go regularly to the same bank cashier although the money he gives us is no better than anyone elses', and even though he is unlikely to remember us, perhaps just because we value his familiarity. That we should prefer predictable over unpredictable interactions is understandable in terms of balance or personal construct theory. It is equally easily interpreted on the view that costs are thereby minimized and gains maximized. But why then do some relationships become boring? Here Duck's ideas, discussed in the preceding paragraphs, link to some speculations by

Kelvin (1977). Kelvin points out that repeated interaction within a relationship leads to adaptation. Each participant habituates to the other's range of behaviour. This may be useful in so far as it is accompanied by enhanced sensitivity to change, but produces a decrease in "arousal" and a progressive deadening of the relationship. Kelvin suggests that there may be an optimal predictability for continued arousal and for the maintenance of a live relationship. But he is quick to emphasize that there is no merit in the retention of a personal mystery. This soon becomes a bore, and is habituated to as such. Rather relationships are likely to remain active in so far as the partners develop jointly as individuals, exploring new areas and furnishing each other with new insights.

SELF-DISCLOSURE

Increasing knowledge of each other's attitudes, values and needs implies increasing intimacy. To Altman and Taylor (1973) progressive self-disclosure is regarded almost as *the* criterion of a progressing relationship, yet they stress that intimacy is likely to be achieved slowly. There are a number of reasons for this. First the outcomes of interactions similar to those already experienced, and the consequences of exchanges involving areas of the personality adjacent to those already penetrated, are more certain than are those of new types of interaction or exploration of new areas of the personality. Second, as a relationship progresses, penetration of the central areas involves not only greater rewards but also greater costs in increasing the individual's vulnerability. Self-disclosure not only enables another individual to understand you better and therefore to protect you, but also puts him in a position to exploit you (Kelvin, 1977). Any advance therefore involves a gamble and progress is likely to be slow. Third, progress towards deeper levels of intimacy depends not only on current rewards and costs of interactions, and expectations of comparable exchanges in the future, but also on forecasting rewards and costs at more intimate levels. Development therefore requires successive forecasts, comparisons of outcomes, and decisions on whether or how to proceed.

In addition, reciprocity of disclosure may be more important in the early stages of a relationship than later. Early on it may be necessary to reciprocate in order to prove trust. Later it may be more appropriate to discuss the issues that a friend reveals than to reciprocate with intimacies of one's own, at any rate at the moment. Possibly this merely means that reciprocity comes to operate over a longer time base. In any case the nature of the relationship, the risks involved in particular types of relationships and many other factors, as well as the stage of the relationship, are likely to affect the degree of self-disclosure.

Finally, Altman and Taylor stress that increasing intimacy does not necessarily mean intimacy about everything. Some areas of the personality may become "sealed off" by mutual agreement, in order to avoid the risks involved in certain types of intimacy or the possibility of disruptive experiences, by cultural convention as to what is appropriate, or in relation to the particular roles the participants see themselves as playing. But the retention of areas of privacy may have a more subtle importance. Schwartz (1968) and Kelvin (1977) stress that areas of privacy are areas in which the individual is not exposed to the power or influence of others. In Kelvin's view, an individual sees himself as the agent of his own actions in so far as he sees his actions as not governed by social constraints. His sense of continuity across roles and across situations provides him with a view of himself as a unique person, and this sense of uniqueness in turn derives from the areas of privacy that he carries with him wherever he goes. Kelvin admits that evidence for such a view is hard to find, but points to the way in which lack of privacy in total institutions, such as armed forces and prisons, leads to loss of the sense of being oneself.

But at the same time, as we have seen, each individual's concept of self can only be validated by others, and this must apply even to those central areas of privacy. Here, Kelvin argues, lies one of the essential tasks of love. The privacy of these central areas becomes a shared privacy, maintaining the continuity of a shared self. On such a view the others with whom an individual forms intimate relationships become a part of his perceived world, and in so far as the construction and validation of his own self depends on them, part of his self. Because they come to define his position in the world, they have power over him. He is vulnerable to their criticisms or rejection, because they undermine the beliefs that he holds about himself. But at the same time it is only to them that he can open up the most intimate areas of himself, only with them that he can validate the most essential aspects of his being (Kelvin, 1977).

The vulnerability and protection that intimacy brings raises the question of the relation between cognitive and physical intimacy. Kelvin, stressing the enormous power of physical intimacy, compares lovers' exploration of each other's body images with the exploration of their self-concepts. Each involves both positive gains on the one hand and increased vulnerability on the other. Although Kelvin does not take it that far, one is led to speculate that, at least for people who have what would now be called conventional norms, the vulnerability consequent upon physical intimacy may be ameliorated by trust, and that trust occurs more readily with cognitive intimacy.

SOCIAL PRESSURES

The studies of the changing importance of different attributes as a relationship develops have been conducted in Western Europe or North America, and have paid little attention to cultural factors. But it is of course the case that the attributes valued will be culturally influenced. Lewis (1975) has emphasized that these cultural forces will be mediated by significant others in the lives of the individuals concerned. He cites data showing that parents may exert a large influence on the companions their children seek, and that friends may facilitate liaisons both in a practical manner and by treating the two individuals as a pair (see also p. 167). It is crucial to remember that the formation of a dyadic relationship takes place within a social group, and is influenced both by cultural norms and by other relationships in which the participants are involved (see Chapter 13).

SOCIAL SKILLS IN DEVELOPING RELATIONSHIPS

At all stages in a relationship, each partner is likely to strive to present himself to his partner as he believes himself to be, or at least as he would like his partner to see him. Each must also convey the nature of the relationship he wants or needs, and each must interpret correctly the reciprocal messages from the partner. It is here that social skills are important, especially perhaps in the early stages of a relationship (e.g. Argyle and Kendon, 1967; Cook, 1977).

As we have seen, progress towards greater involvement in a relationship is seldom smooth. Progress may occur, there may be a pause, perhaps for consolidation, or the relationship may regress. While similarity in attitudes and complementarity in needs may be important, the process of friendship formation is also affected by impressions and judgements made at every stage in its progress. Whilst first impressions may be self-fulfilling, each partner striving to fulfil the expectations created, they may also prove to have raised expectations too high and be self-defeating. And each change in the relationship must involve a change in the definition of the relationship. Since this may involve costs to one or both parties, moves towards a change in the definition of the relationship are likely to be tentative, and to involve a sounding out of one partner by the other before further commitments are made. A sensitive analysis of the processes involved is presented by Kurth (1970).

The way in which A interprets and evaluates B's behaviour also changes as a relationship develops. With someone we know little, we are inclined to equate his behaviour with his personality, believing for instance that he was rude because that was his nature. This is, of course, no more sophisticated than the use of the concept of instinct in an explanatory way—"the canary builds its nest because it has a nest-building instinct". However as we get to know him we better appreciate the diversity of his behaviour, explaining his rudeness as the temporary consequence of his indigestion or preoccupation. As we get to know him even moderately well we acquire an ability to predict his behaviour in a wide variety of circumstances—with a greater or lesser degree of accuracy. We present this to ourselves as a picture of what he is like, but of course in so far as it is based on how he has behaved to us, it can be no more than a picture of his nascent relationship with us. If we see him with others, and hear other's opinions of him, our picture of him gains depth, but it will never be entirely freed from our own biases and our own interpretations of other's biases (see e.g. Eiser, 1978b).

EXCHANGE THEORIES AND DEVELOPING PERSONAL RELATIONSHIPS

Changes in what matters to the participants in a relationship have many implications for exchange theorists. In so far as the changes in a relationship can be identified as consequences of preceding interactions, it should be possible to develop exchange theories to take account of this. A formal approach has been developed by Huesmann and Levinger (1976). Starting from a payoff matrix of the type employed by Thibaut and Kelley (1959) (see p. 217), they assume that higher payoffs are expected as a relationship deepens. They picture this as a sequence of movements from one payoff matrix to another, the extent of the movements depending on the current payoff. In their model, each individual takes into account not only his own rewards, but also the probable responses and rewards of the other. However, the model, though of theoretical interest, is likely to be difficult to apply in any practical way.

But although exchange theorists have discussed close personal relationships in general terms, many (e.g. Blau, 1964), argue that notions of fair exchange become less easy to apply precisely as the participants become more committed, as rewards to the partner become *ipso facto* rewards to self, and as the main point about interactions becomes doing something together (but see Kelley, 1979).

Another issue concerns the changes in the quality of relationships that occur with time. Exciting relationships often come to seem more ordinary, unsatisfactory ones more tolerable. Secord and Backman (1974) have attempted to accommodate such issues by suggesting that in the former case the comparison level rises, so that the amount by which the profit exceeds the comparison level declines, whereas in the latter case it declines. The explanation is, however, *post hoc* and, so far as initially stimulating relationships go, less satisfactory than that in terms of habituation (see p. 300–1).

In so far as the classification of types of power presented by French and Raven (1959) is useful, it is apparent that their incidence will change as a relationship develops. As the relative importance of personal attributes change, reward power will change. But in addition, the exercise of reward power over time may result in the establishment of the conditions for referent power. Conversely, continued use of coercive power by A is likely to diminish B's identification with A and thus reduce his referent power (Secord and Backman, 1974). In the longer term, the exercise of power within a relationship is likely to lead to the establishment of norms, which render the actual use of reward or coercion unnecessary (e.g. Thibaut and Kelley, 1959).

Summary

Some suggested sequences of stages in the development of close personal relationships are described.

As a relationship progresses, there are changes in the relative importance of external factors, physical attributes, attitude similarity, need compatibility, and aspects of mutual understanding and construct similarity. These and other changes pose problems for exchange theories.

The progress of self-disclosure and the importance of social skills are discussed briefly.

22

Aspects of Relationships in Infancy and Childhood

The last two decades have seen considerable advances both in our understanding of parent-child relationships, and of interpersonal relationships in general. Although work in each of these fields is clearly of considerable potential importance to the other, contact between them seems to have been minimal. One possible reason for this is that parent-child relationships are different from the interpersonal relationships of adults. But how different and in what ways? And do the descriptive differences imply also differences in their fundamental dynamics? Perhaps an attempt to answer these questions will facilitate a rapprochement between the two sub-disciplines.

That is the limited aim of this chapter. It is not an attempt to distill an essence from the rapidly growing literature on child development. Rather it contains a brief discussion of some aspects of the relationships of infants and young children, selected to illustrate points arising from the preceding chapters.

The special properties of the parent-child relationship

The parent-child relationship is often regarded as the source of all interpersonal relationships. It may be, but if so, it differs markedly from the relationships to which it gives rise. It is convenient to emphasize this point by considering first certain categories of dimensions that illustrate its unique qualities.

COMPLEMENTARITY, INTERPERSONAL PERCEPTION, INTIMACY AND COMMITMENT

Babies are probably a great deal more clever than they were thought to be twenty or thirty years ago. Yet however clever they are, the difference in cognitive abilities between parent and infant is greater than in all other human relationships. The newborn infant, we believe, has no view of his mother as an individual person in the sense that he does not discriminate her from other persons. It is even often assumed, though with rather less substantial evidence, that he does not discriminate her from himself. Whilst he rapidly comes to respond specifically to some of her stimulus characters, and more slowly to appreciate her as an individual, the sort of view he has of his mother (as revealed by his behaviour) remains different in kind from hers of him for at least months if not years.

This difference in cognitive levels has several immediate consequences. It means that all parent-infant interactions are complementary. It means also that interpersonal perception tends to be unilateral. Dissonance and balance are irrelevant to the young infant: he cannot compare his views with his mother's, or adjust his goals to hers, if he does not recognize her as a distinct individual. Again, intimacy has no meaning for the infant—he has no choice to reveal or conceal, and could not appreciate intimacies received. And when intimacy does come to be meaningful, it remains one-sided. Exogenously the parents are committed biologically and socially, but they also become increasingly committed emotionally (endogenously). Commitment is irrelevant to the new born, but can be said to become meaningful as he comes to distinguish his parents from other individuals, and more so when he starts to show fear of strangers.

These are statements of the obvious, but they serve to emphasize that the parent-child relationship not only differs from any other, but also changes more dramatically than any other. Whilst we may look for rules governing the consistency and continuity of adult-adult relationships, here we shall clearly need rules governing the changing of rules.

COMPLEMENTARITY—THE CONTRASTING CONTRIBUTIONS OF MOTHER AND INFANT

Complementarity in the early mother-infant relationship is of course an inevitable consequence of the differing contributions of the partners. In the first place, babies provide from the start stimuli especially effective in eliciting parental care. These include many of their general anatomical features—their large head, protruding forehead, large eyes low down on the face, protruding cheeks and uncoordinated movements (Ahrens, 1954; Gardner and Wallach, 1965). The newborn also has a repertoire of relatively simple movement patterns, the size of this repertoire increasing over the early weeks. This includes movements of finding the nipple, sucking, movements conducive to mother-infant contact, various signal movements including smiling, crying, etc. (Dunn, 1977). Each is elicited by a range of situations which can be specified with some precision, and each is meaningful to the mother. During the early weeks they are modified by experience in all of their aspects—the situations in which they appear, the readiness with which they are elicited, their form and sequencing. In particular they become more readily elicited by the stimuli that usually elicit them, and less so by others.

While many of these movements serve obvious immediate ends, others appear to be important primarily in eliciting affective responses in the mother. An obvious example is the smile, which usually first appears regularly when the infant is a few weeks old, can then be elicited by a very simple stimulus configuration such as a white oval with two black dots on it, and subsequently comes to be elicited by stimulus situations which the infant can control (Papousek and Bernstein, 1969; Watson, 1972) and by familiar caregivers—especially, of course, the mother (Ahrens, 1954; Spitz, 1965). Closely related to this are the perceptual constraints which make the infant especially likely to focus on his mother's face during early feeding sessions, and later to fixate his mother's eyes (Stern, 1977).

Although virtually all babies possess these stimulus characters and action patterns, individuals differ in their general activity, in the thresholds of the several patterns, and in their modifiability through experience. Such differences may be perceived by adults as involving differences in "cuddliness" or other dimensions relevant to the developing relationship (Schaffer, 1977).

Of course this emphasis on the stimuli that the infant provides does not imply that he is a mere passive partner in the mother-infant relationship. Not only do infants learn rapidly, but they soon show evidence of intentionality and emotional expressivity which is said to be directed especially towards persons rather than objects (Bower, 1974; Trevarthen, 1977, 1978a). Trevarthen regards the combination of subjective intentionality with emotion-laden communicative ability having affective consequences on the perceiver as evidence for "primary intersubjectivity" in 2–3 month old infants. By this he means "the linking of subjects who are active in transmitting their understanding to each other" (1978a). While properly emphasizing the infant's inherent propensity to form a relationship with its mother, and the importance of learning during communicative interaction in the formation of that relationship, "proto-intersubjectivity" would perhaps be more appropriate at this age. The term "intersubjectivity" *sensu stricto* (or "interpretation of viewpoints", Asch, 1952) could then be reserved for the changes that occur later in the first year, and especially when the infant is about 9–10 months old (Trevarthen, 1978b).

Be that as it may, the mother's part in these communicative exchanges is clearly very different. Whilst description in terms of a repertoire of movement patterns takes us quite a long way with the baby, what is important on the maternal side is responsiveness to the stimuli the baby provides. Of course she does provide some stimuli to which the infant is especially responsive—mere contact with her body is soothing. But the central issue is her readiness to respond to, and even to anticipate, the infant's signals. However, she shares with the baby a readiness to interact in ways that are not related to immediate biological ends, to interact for the sake of interacting.

In addressing the baby, the mother uses facial expressions similar to those used with adults, but modified in certain important ways. They are limited in number, but adequate to initiate, maintain, modulate, terminate or avoid social interaction with the baby. Their performance is usually both exaggerated in space and extended in time (Stern, 1977)—differences from adult-adult performance which are similar to the evolutionary changes that have made many animal signal movements more effective for a signal function (Tinbergen, 1952), and presumably facilitating both appropriate responding and social learning by the baby. Her verbal utterances are also simplified, exaggerated in certain ways, slowed, and repetitive (e.g. Snow, 1972; Nelson 1973). She looks at and speaks to the infant in a manner quite different from that in which she looks at adults. Frequently she looks at and talks to the baby simultaneously for many seconds at a time, and mutual gazes may last for half a minute or longer—both very unusual in interactions between adults. These mutual gazes may have a dramatic effect on the mother, making her feel in a relationship with her baby (Stern, 1977).

For such a sequence to continue, the mother must adjust her behaviour according to the ongoing behaviour of the infant, for he lacks the capacity to adjust his to hers. But by about three months the baby has good control of his head and eye movements, so interactions involving mutual gaze become rather more like interactions between equal partners. Episodes of mutual attention become part of longer sequences of engagement and disengagement, of mutual stimulation and withdrawal, in which the infant plays an important part in regulating the mother's behaviour. The mother's responses to the baby's movements are a great source of delight to the baby, and probably make an important contribution to his learning how to control the world (Watson, 1972). However, whilst infants often initiate such episodes, they are also easily over-stimulated and attempt to withdraw. Appropriate sensitivity to the baby's needs to interact or to withdraw from interacting are an important aspect of sensitive mothering—especially as the baby's needs change from day to day (Ainsworth in press; Richards, 1971; Brazelton et al., 1974; Dunn, 1977; Kaye, 1977; Stern, 1977; Schaffer, 1977).

Whilst it has become customary to liken many of the interactions between mothers and babies to "conversations" because of their turn-taking character, it must be remembered that they are due largely to the sensitivity of the mother, who must hold back when the baby is active and fill in when he pauses. It is difficult to say when turn-taking can reasonably be said to be due to mutual adjustment—perhaps by the time give-and-take games develop towards the end of the first year (Bruner, 1977).

But natural responsiveness is neither ubiquitous nor indiscriminate. As mentioned already, babies differ markedly in the stimuli they provide and in their responsiveness to adults, and adults show similar divergence (e.g. Bennett, 1971; Sander, 1969, 1977). And it is probably as well that mothers are not continuously responsive. If a mother were perfectly responsive all the time, the baby would have little opportunity to learn to mesh with her, and an important element in his socialization would be lost.

As a largely stimulus-response account of early mother-infant interaction, this glosses over many important issues, but it suffices to emphasize two points important to the theme of this book. The first concerns the contrast between the mother's and the infant's contribution. The baby's behaviour is at first largely reflexive and controlled by its internal state. Whilst socially elicited aspects rapidly become more and more important, not for some months is it reasonably to think of the baby as using his behaviour in an instrumental way to control the mother so that she will minister to his needs. With the mother, the situation is quite different. While there are aspects of her behaviour that are largely biologically determined, the important issues concern how she sees her role as a mother, how far she feels motivated and competent to fill it, and the manner in which she interprets and responds appropriately to the infant's behaviour.

The second issue is that both partners respond to the other "for the sake of responding", with no other immediate biological consequence (Bowlby, 1969). Whilst both baby and mother appear to engage in bouts of social interaction, and obtain great delight therefrom, the longer term consequences of this behaviour are rather different for the two participants. The baby learns about his mother, about himself, about the world and how to affect it, at the same time as the bond between them is developing. The baby's responsiveness and pleasure in her gives the mother a feeling not only of having a special person but of being something special and having a special relationship. For her, and thus for the baby, it is not just having a relationship that matters, but also what she thinks about it.

THE IMPORTANCE OF THE DIVERSITY OF INTERACTIONS

During the first few weeks after birth, a baby can hardly be aware of the mother as an individual, but rather responds to particular aspects of her in particular contexts—the touch of her skin, smell of her breast, the feel of her nipples, the shape of her face. But just because several of these different sets of stimuli are likely to be present in the course of most types of interaction, each may become associated with responses other than those to which it was first most relevant. It is presumably in this way that the infant comes to respond to the mother not as a heterogeneous collection of stimuli, but as an individual. The complexity of the processes involved and the extent to which they can be described as involving the formation of sensory-motor schemata (Piaget, 1937, 1955) is not the issue here. Under experimental conditions with animals the stimuli relevant to the several responses can be kept separate, so that the young animal comes to have not one all-purpose mother, but several (Hinde, 1974). Furthermore, the young animal may be especially attracted to the mother when she looks a *little* (but not too much) unusual—a fact which presumably helps him to learn more about her and to respond to her as an individual in contexts other than those in which he has previously encountered her (Bateson,

1973; Kagan *et al.*, 1966). It thus seems likely that the diversity of things that mother and infant do together contributes to the infant's growing view of the mother as an individual.

QUALITIES

As in most relationships, mother-infant interactions vary with time and between dyads. Some differences are such that we can ascribe them to idiosyncracies of one or other partner—gentleness, roughness, sensitivity or insensitivity on the part of the mother; malleability, mood, and so on on the part of the baby. But it is usually very difficult to tell whether qualities of the relationship at any one time result from inherent properties of one or other individual, whether they have been affected by previous aspects of the relationship, and whether they will matter in the long run (see Chapter 20).

CATEGORIES OF MOTHER-INFANT RELATIONSHIPS

In studies of parent-infant interaction, categorization of relationships into three groups on the basis of a number of different characteristics has been possible and profitable. The division depends in the first instance on the Ainsworth (e.g. 1979) Strange Situation procedure. In this, infants, usually about one year old, are brought into a laboratory playroom with their mothers. There follows a series of episodes in which the mother leaves and re-enters the room, during which a stranger may or may not be present. On the basis of data on the baby's behaviour in this situation, babies can be categorized into three groups. "Securely-attached" babies (Group B) are characterized by seeking to gain or maintain proximity to or contact with the mother during the reunion episodes, with little or no evidence of attempts to avoid or resist her. Group A babies show little or no proximity seeking in the reunion episodes, but avoid the mother and turn or look away. Group C babies seek proximity and contact with the mother in the reunion episodes, but are at the same time resistant to close contact with her. Although these categories are usually presented as categories of babies, they are perhaps more accurately described as categories of mother-infant relationships, the more so as the same infant may fall into different categories when tested with his or her mother and father (Main and Weston, pers. comm.). Although characterized only briefly here, each depends on a number of dimensions—frequency of crying, proximity seeking, qualities of interactions, and correlations between qualities. Furthermore categorization in the strange situation correlates highly with a number of characteristics in the home situation. For example the securely attached (B) babies cry less at home, show less distress in brief everyday separations there, greet the mothers more frequently on reunion, and are more ready to comply with her wishes than A or C babies. The A babies do not respond positively to being picked up, do not show active contact behaviours with their mothers, and more often show angry behaviour than the others. There are also differences between the mothers—for instance mothers of B babies are more sensitive to signals, acceptant, cooperative and accessible, and A mothers are more rejecting than the others. It is suggested that the A babies have built up a severe approach-avoidance conflict with respect to close bodily contact with their mothers as a consequence of unpleasant experiences in that context (Main, pers. comm.).

In summary, Ainsworth and her colleagues have defined three categories in terms of characteristics of both babies and mothers. For the reasons given above (see also p. 16), these categories can properly be regarded as properties of mother-infant relationships. They are correlated with behaviour outside the situation in which they were initially defined. (It is not of course implied that this is the only way to classify parent-offspring relationships. Factor analytic and circumplex orderings have recently been reviewed by Martin (1975).)

Stability and change

In Chapter 12 a distinction was made between the continuity of a relationship, implying continued interaction between the two participants, and consistency, or constancy in the content of those interactions. In the parent-child relationship, of course, the former is paramount. The content of the interactions inevitably changes as the child gets older. And of course that is not all: both the quality of the interactions and the child's role in initiating and terminating them alter as development proceeds (see e.g. Chapter 19). Thus while we may search for principles relevant to the stability of adult relationships, throughout childhood (and in some adult relationships) the principles are constantly changing. Parental sensitivity must involve sensitivity to these changes as well as to the child's moment-to-moment needs.

Evidence from rhesus monkeys that it is changes in the mother's behaviour, rather than changes in the infant, that determine the rate at which an infant gains independence has already been discussed (see p. 268). This evidence is in harmony with considerations of the adaptive value of continued association to the two parties concerned. From the point of view of natural selection, the benefit to the mother (in terms of the eventual propagation of her genes by herself and by other individuals sharing genes with her) decreases as the infant becomes better able to look after himself, and the costs (in the same terms) increase. The infant will continue to benefit at least to some extent, and the costs will increase more slowly for him than for the mother. There will therefore come a time when it is in the mother's interests to reduce their association and in the infant's to prolong it (Trivers, 1974). Conclusions of this sort apply to a very wide range of species, and it is likely that they apply also to man. Certainly casual observation suggests that most human mothers tend to "push babies on"—to move them from breast to solid food, from cot to bed, or from home to school, before the child could or would make the choice itself.

It may well be important that the mother should over-estimate the child's maturity. Mothers not only facilitate their children's attempts to explore their environment (Ainsworth, 1969; Bowlby, 1969; White and Watts, 1973), and elaborate on those attempts (Schaffer, 1977), but also provide them with opportunities for achievements a little beyond their current accomplishments. It is thus often argued that the mother must constantly over-estimate the child's capacities (e.g. Trevarthen, 1977).

POWER

The difficulties inherent in the use of the concept of power were discussed in Chapter 18, and are nowhere more apparent than in the parent-child relationship. Whilst parents ultimately control virtually all the resources that are essential to the child's development, the course of much moment-to-moment interaction is determined by the child. The rate at which many aspects of the relationship change are immediately determined primarily by changes in the mother, but inter-dyad differences are determined both by differences between parents and by differences between infants (p. 269).

The several forms of power discussed by French and Raven (1959) change in importance at different rates as the child grows older. Throughout development, many episodes of parent-child interaction can profitably be regarded as attempts by the child to redefine the power structure in the relationship. Contrariness in childhood and bloody-mindedness in adolescence, not to mention punishment, coercion and bargaining by parents at all stages, certainly often have a limited redistribution of power as a consequence, though it is not always necessary to impute such a motive to the initiator.

REGULATION

In the short term, the intensity of many sequences of mother-infant interaction remains within certain limits. Games in which the parent stimulates the child, to produce smiles or excited and gleeful laughs, can escalate to a point where further stimulation is aversive to the child. When this happens the baby turns away and shows other signs that, for the moment, he has had enough. The sensitive parent responds appropriately (Stern, 1977; see also Thoman, 1974).

Even when the parent is insensitive, and behaves in such a manner that the whole relationship seems to be endangered, regulation may yet occur. Stern (1977) describes such a case. An over-intensive mother regularly insisted on interaction with her baby long after the baby indicated that it had had enough, forcing the baby to develop and employ a variety of techniques to avoid the excessive input. The baby regularly avoided eye contact with the mother. Just as Stern felt that he must intervene, he noticed a slight improvement. Subsequent analysis of videotaped material showed that this improvement had actually started a fortnight earlier—though the reasons were not apparent. The improvement continued, and although the relationship continued to have difficulties, a happy outcome seemed possible. However that is not always the case: Tinbergen and Tinbergen (1972) have accumulated considerable evidence that some forms of childhood psychopathology may be due to, or exacerbated by, the perpetuation of such approach/avoidance conflicts.

A particular case of regulation after an external stressor, concerning the effect on monkey mother-infant relationships of a brief period of separation, was considered in Chapter 20. In most cases regulation occurred, and although the relationship was disturbed for a few weeks after reunion, it subsequently regained something very close to its original course. Only when a number of factors were present together (e.g. tensionful mother-infant relationship and a particular type of separation experience) were there long-term effects. A similar conclusion seems to emerge from the data on short periods of separation between human children and their families: long-term effects are much more likely to occur or to be severe if the home had been initially tensionful or disadvantaged (Douglas, 1975; Quinton and Rutter, 1976). As another example, the effects of perinatal trauma are usually not detectable in measures of child development amongst children born into families from the more privileged classes, but are in under-privileged homes (Sameroff and Chandler, 1975). It would seem that the mother-child relationship, and perhaps the growing child itself, possess limited powers of regulation such that minor deviations from the course of development leave no permanent trace. Just how effective these powers of regulation are is of course an important issue for child developmentalists (Dunn, 1976).

The role of regulative processes in the longer term epigenetic course of development is central to Sander's (1969, 1977) conception of development. He sees development as involving reciprocal regulation in the system "infant-caregiver" to give patterns of behavioural organization. Adaptation is supposed to occur with regard to a series of "issues", which Sanders describes as "Initial Regulation" (1–3 months), "Reciprocal Exchange" (4–6 months), "Initiative" (7–9 months), "Focalization" (10–13 months) and "Self-assertion" (14–20 months). Wertheim (1975b, c) has amended this system in some respects.

INTERPERSONAL PERCEPTION AND SOCIALIZATION

As the child's cognitive capabilities develop, he comes to apprehend those around him in more and more complex ways. He responds not merely to others' behaviour, but interprets that behaviour as expressing subjective processes in those others. The subjective processes of others become meaningful to him, and he achieves understanding of the physical and social worlds in which others live, and takes over those worlds himself. Through a continuing dialectic he reaches towards his own identity and moves towards something which can perhaps be described as full intersubjectivity with others. The processes involved embrace both cognitive and affective components, and changes both in cognitive and in moral levels (e.g. Piaget, 1937; Kohlberg, 1976).

The extent to which children can enter into the worlds of others has come to be appreciated only recently. As an example, Shatz and Gelman (1973) found that four year olds adjust their language according to the age of the person they are talking to—two year old, peer or adult. Whilst this could be ascribed to simple imitations of the way in which adults address individuals of different ages, it surely indicates the beginning of an appreciation of the way in which others differ, including the sort of language they can understand (see also Snow, 1972; Gelman and Shatz, 1977).

Consistencies in the ways in which parents, siblings and others behave to him, similarities in and differences between the behaviour of others, and comparability between relationships (e.g. his relationship to his parents and his siblings' relationships to them) permit the differentiation of roles—a process which is of course greatly facilitated by the linguistic labels applied to them. The child thus acquires the norms of the relationships, family and social groups in which he is growing up. The processes of socialization depend on and lead to increasingly intricate interpersonal perception in the relationships in which he is involved (Kelley and Thibaut, 1978; Kelley, 1979).

However two ways in which the relationships of childhood differ from later ones must be emphasized here. First, the child enters into them with far fewer preconceptions than will ever be the case again. There is no suggestion here that the child is a *tabula rasa*, but merely an emphasis on the fact that, whilst early relationships may affect the course of later ones, there were no prior relationships which could have played the same role for them.

Second, the relationships of childhood change with more inevitability and rapidity than is the case for most adult relationships. As the child gets older, both its biological needs and the roles appropriate to it change. The child's definition of self both depends on and influences its relationships. As the child comes to see himself differently, in part as a result of the changing perceptions of others, he will continuously require others to confirm his new definitions of self. And the changes in perception required from others, and especially from parents, may require changes in their own definitions of self.

The relationships that are important to the child, and thus probably the relationships that are important for the child, change markedly with age. Whilst most children in most cultures interact more with their natural mothers during the first few days of life, fathers and other adults become increasingly important. From an early age, the relationship with the father differs from that with the mother, even outside the feeding context, and the father has important influences on the course of development (e.g. Lamb, 1976). Similarly interaction with siblings and peers may begin very early, and durable relationships may be formed within the year (e.g. Lewis and Rosenblum, 1975). Inside the family, relationships with mother, father and siblings may affect each other, and be affected by outside influences (e.g. reviewed Hinde, in press b). These relationships will vary with the number of siblings—for instance parental attitudes to the first-born may be very different from those to later children (e.g. Fortes, 1974); and, perhaps for biological reasons (Trivers, 1974), the mother-last-born relationship may have special properties. As times goes on, the relative importance of the various relationships inside and outside the family change, with siblings and peers increasing in importance relative to adults. Furthermore the several relationships within the family must differ in their long-term effects on the child's development: for instance Kohlberg (1976) has stressed the long-term importance of the mother in giving comfort and a sense of security, and of the peers in learning to appreciate the view of others.

While peers outside the family may start to play a significant role from the second year on (Lewis and Rosenblum, 1975; Hartup, 1975), the rate at which relationships outside the family become important varies greatly both between and within cultures. The child's relationships to individuals outside the family may be affected by the attitudes of family members to those individuals, and vice versa. If A loves B and B loves C, then A is likely to love C (e.g. Lewis and Weinraub, 1976). The mechanisms involved are certainly complex (see Chapters 9 and 14). In Western societies extra-familial adults may be important as the adolescent begins to establish himself outside the family (Miller 1970).

Of special interest are changes in what the child sees as important. Not surprisingly, physical attractiveness is important in the initial stages of friendship over a wide age range (Kleck *et al.*, 1974; see also p. 294). But what children expect from their best friends change considerably. Bigelow and La Gaipa (1975) content-analysed children's essays on what they expected in their best friends. The data were coded on 21 "friendship expectation" dimensions. The incidence of three dimensions, *"reciprocity of liking"*, *"ego reinforcement"* and *"sharing friend as giver"* did not change with age. Assessments along sixteen dimensions increased with age. The grade levels at which these were first significantly greater than zero were *help-friend as giver* and *common activities* (2); *propinquity, stimulation value, organized play, demographic similarity* and *evaluation* (3); *acceptance, admiration* and *incremental prior interactions* (4); *loyalty-and-commitment* (5); *genuineness* and *help-friend as receiver* (6); *intimacy potential, common interest* and *similarity in attitudes and values* (11). Assessments along two dimensions, *sharing-friend as receiver* and *general play*, declined with age. The changes appear to represent transitions from egocentric to sociocentric to empathic friendship expectations. However the authors are careful to point out that the data are inherently verbal, and that the changes may partly reflect linguistic development (see also Peevers and Secord, 1973).

THE SOCIAL WORLDS OF CHILDHOOD AND ADULTHOOD

It has long been traditional, especially amongst psychoanalysts, to regard an individual's relationships as in some sense derivative from the mother-child relationship. On this view, though the nature of the child's relationships change dramatically, they do so gradually. Intrafamilial relationships affect extra-familial ones (e.g. Bowlby, 1969), and early relationships affect later ones (Sullivan, 1953; Mannarino, 1976). Such a view emphasizes continuity.

However it is worth while also to consider the marked differences between the social worlds of infant and adult. An extreme position is taken by Harré (1974). He recognizes first an "autonomous social world", based on child-mother attachment, flourishing until the end of the third year, and declining thereafter. But he rejects Bowlby's (1969) view that this social world of early childhood leads to that of adulthood, and that adult attachment behaviour is a continuation of attachment in childhood. Rather Harré suggests that this mode must perish before adulthood is possible. In his view the adult social world is not generated by the emotional side of our nature, but emerges as the product of two processes. One of these, shared with the autonomous social world of childhood, involves an ability for social makebelieve in preparation for social action. The other involves an ability constantly to create and/or maintain social order by ceremonial means (see e.g. Goffman, 1971). In this adult social world, Harré suggests that skills acquired in the early autonomous social world are useless and the expectations are a source of social danger. Between the two lies the "precursor" social world of childhood, with skills and ceremonies essentially similar to those of the adult world, but differing from it in content. This precursor world of childhood has its own ritual, and is complete itself.

It is a pity that, to make his case, Harré is driven to overstate it. Whilst it may be true that "The astonishing thing about the adult social world, *as revealed by ethogenic analysis*, is that it forms and transforms itself with little reference to emotional bonds. . ." (my italics), this is more a comment on the shortcomings of the ethogenic approach than a description of the social world of adults. Certainly the student with whom I spent an hour this morning discussing the relative merits of taking a job in one country and living with her boy friend in another would feel that Harré's account of the adult social world is rather impoverished. Yet his overstatement must not be allowed to distract attention from the differences he emphasizes between adult's and child's social worlds. We have already seen the value of viewing social skills as depending on a complex cognitive structure of the type that he suggests. But it seems unnecessary to suppose a complete break with the autonomous world of childhood, which surely permeates and, some would say, gives substance to the adult social world. Harré's approach here appears to be almost an anti-developmentalist one: the three social worlds, autonomous, precursor and adult, are seen as stopped frames, and not as part of a developmental sequence. A conceptual scheme with more emphasis on continuity is clearly needed.

CULTURAL DIFFERENCES

This brief sketch of developmental issues peripheral to our main theme must not be allowed to distract attention from the extent to which the practices of child-rearing and the processes of socialization vary between cultures. Ariès (1962) has provided a provocative account of how child-rearing practices in France have changed over the centuries; Bronfenbrenner (1970) has contrasted childhood in contemporary U.S.A. and U.S.S.R.; and a number of workers have compared childhood both between industrial and between non-industrial societies (e.g. Benedict, 1935; Whiting and Whiting, 1975; Leiderman *et al.*, 1977).

Summary

The parent-infant relationship, sometimes regarded as the source of all relationships, differs in many ways from virtually all adult-adult relationships. The differences stem, of course, from the great differences in physical abilities, and in the cognitive and moral levels of the participants, and thus involve marked complementarity.

One way of categorizing parent-child relationships, based on Ainsworth's strange situation technique, is mentioned briefly.

As the child grows, the content and power structure of the relationship changes; continuity demands changes by both partners. Regulatory mechanisms, both short and long term, play an important role.

The major changes that occur in the parent/child relationship as the child develops depend on, and demand, great sensitivity on the part of the parent.

The infant may begin to form relationships in addition to those with his parents within the first few months. These relationships multiply and change in nature as he develops. Through his relationships with others the child achieves both understanding of his own identity and socialization.

V

Conclusion

23

Limitations

It is customary, in a concluding chapter, to review the achievements of the preceding pages. Those pages have been concerned primarily with establishing that the development of an integrated science of interpersonal relationships is possible, and with indicating the sort of shape it might have. But at this point it seems to be more appropriate to emphasize limitations than achievements—limitations both in the subject matter covered and in the degree of understanding reached.

It has been argued that a science of interpersonal relationships must rest on a basis of description. But it is not yet possible to specify precisely the dimensions that will be most valuable. In Part II a number of *categories* of dimensions were discussed, but only further research can tell whether they are adequate to contain all potentially useful aspects of relationships and, within them, which dimensions will prove valuable. Even the question of how far global characterizations of relationships, such as "affectionate" or "competitive", will prove useful, is far from closed. Although the dimensions discussed here mostly involve a finer level of analysis, global terms such as "affectionate" are useful in some contexts to summarize more detailed measures or to represent the characterizations of relationships made by the participants themselves or by outsiders.

Indeed, since the properties of relationships depend on characteristics at very varied levels of analysis, and since the participants themselves assess relationships at a number of levels, description must span those levels. In so far as description involves analysis, we must remember that analysis can lead to the neglect of emergent properties, and that the participants themselves respond to their own perceptions of the relationship, which may be in quite holistic terms—i.e. as good or bad, satisfying, etc. rather than in terms of specific dimensions. Much work remains to be done before the relations between these levels can be fully understood.

It is clear that a science of relationships must have contact with the psychology of the individual, and with the social psychology of groups.

In so far as relationships involve individuals acting to further their own ends, principles of individual psychology may aid their explication. But since interactions have properties which are not present in the behaviour of individuals in isolation, and relationships have properties not present in their constituent interactions, the study of relationships must come to terms with phenomena that lie outside the study of individual behaviour. And in so far as the participants see the relationships as an entity, principles derived from the psychology of groups may become applicable. But dyadic relationships lack properties such as deviance and collusion, which can appear only in larger groupings.

Arising from this, the present emphasis on relationships has led to an inadequate emphasis on dialectics of two types. First there is that between the relationship and the individuals that enter it. Whilst it has been emphasized that the properties of a relationship do not depend solely on either participant, they will be influenced by both of them. Although the influence of personality differences on relationships has generally been regarded as outside the scope of the present discussion, they have inevitably entered at a number of points. But the reverse is equally important. Our definitions of self, our view of reality, our attitudes and personality are continuously influenced by our interactions and relationships with others (see p. 119). The reciprocal influences of their relationships on individuals and of individuals on their relationships have usually been by-passed in the preceding chapters.

Focus on the interpersonal relationship has led also to neglect of the dialectic between interpersonal relationships and society. While I have stressed the influence of societal norms on interpersonal relationships, it is of course also the case that the interpersonal relationships existing at any one time affect the norms that shape subsequent relationships. A full science of interpersonal relationships must thus take account not only of the dialectic between personality and relationships, but also of that between relationships and society.

For understanding the dynamics of relationships, we have seen that relevant principles may be found in at least four general areas. In each case, formidable obstacles remain to be overcome.

(i) *Interpersonal perception.* Dissonance and balance theories have been discussed, and attribution theory mentioned. These can be applied both to relatively short-term interactions and to broader aspects of relationships seen as wholes, and have important implications for the dynamics of relationships. However their very fluidity is a danger, and they could easily become unverifiable.

(ii) Learning theories and exchange theories based on them. The learning theories that have so far been most used in the explanation of behaviour are in origin low-level, stimulus-response theories. Although they can be of value for understanding relations between selected variables in laboratory situations, for real-life relationships it is necessary to buttress them well with cognitive concepts. (Strangely, research by psychologists in this area seems to have made little use of cognitive theories directly.) When this is done, some aspects of interpersonal relationships become almost equally well interpreted in either balance or reinforcement terms. For instance the attitude-similarity/attraction relation can be ascribed to consensual validation or to the reinforcing nature of positive beliefs. Other phenomena, traditionally described in balance terms, become perhaps more readily explained in exchange theory terms (e.g. Curry and Emerson, 1970; review by Chadwick-Jones, 1976). But at that point the difficulty of predicting *a priori* what will and will not be reinforcing arises, and the danger of unverifiability arises again. Here the study of relationships must be integrated with that of personality, to their mutual benefit. The importance of the overall properties of the relationship, and of abstract outcomes, including self-fulfilment, have been stressed by workers from several theoretical backgrounds (Chapter 6, pp. 144–145, 191, 217), and Kelley (1979) has provided a means for conceptualizing such issues. In addition, further work on the different properties of resources (Chapter 12), and attempts to couple learning theory to a knowledge of the structure of behaviour (p. 209), are urgently needed.

(iii) Social influences and norms. Many characteristics of relationships can be traced to extra-dyadic influences from other individuals or to the operations of norms. Such norms may be obligatory or have less compelling power, and may be general to the society or more or less specific to the dyad. But explanation of the characteristics of relationships in terms of norms is inevitably incomplete unless consideration is given also both to how norms are acquired by the individual and how they affect him, and to how they develop in the group as a whole. Once again reinforcement concepts in a cognitive framework seem essential, and once again circularity is a clear danger.

(iv) Feedback systems. Finally, to understand either the stability of relationships or their ability to change, not only the consequences of interactions but the consequences of consequences must be understood. Here the concepts of positive and negative feedback seem likely to be useful, but at present they can be applied only in a *post hoc* descriptive way.

Attempts at rigorous theory-building thus seem inappropriate at the moment. Such attempts as have been made previously involve in essence the statement of propositions concerned with individual behaviour, supposedly of a high degree of generality, and attempts to derive statements about social behaviour from them. However it is not even immediately obvious that this is the right way to proceed. It might well be more profitable to start with social behaviour and to regard individual behaviour as a special instance involving a potentially reactive but not interactive environment. Whether it is more useful to regard social behaviour and relationships as involving complexities simply not present in individual behaviour, or individual behaviour as simplified social behaviour, is by no means a foregone conclusion.

Rather than attempt theory-building, I have tried to map the field, using the conceptual and theoretical tools that seemed suitable to the part of the task most immediately in hand. An urgent task is to relate those theories and concepts to each other. To an outsider, one of the characteristics of the studies of interpersonal relationships is the extent to which approaches have multiplied with little effort to interrelate them. However we have seen that relations between exchange and balance theories may well be attainable, and exchange theories suitably buttressed with cognitive concepts may not be too far from symbolic interactionism (Singelman, 1972). Some agreement about the way in which personal relationships develop seems not impossible (Chapter 21).

A necessary step towards integration must involve relating the descriptive and explanatory concepts used in the different approaches. In this book I have been eclectic, using most terms in their everyday sense (Shorter Oxford or Webster's Dictionary), indicating special usages where that seemed necessary. Deliberately avoiding discussion of the question of reductionism, in the belief that too many pates have already been bloodied in that argument to too little avail (see review by Chadwick-Jones, 1976), I have taken the view that successive levels of complexity involve emergent properties, so that full understanding will require study at every level. Whilst a precise glossary of the concepts used, or at least one commanding general agreement, would be either unattainable or tedious, it seems worthwhile, with the aim of facilitating future theory-building, to indicate the varied natures of those concepts. What follows is not intended as an exhaustive list, though I believe that the reader will have no difficulty in assigning the descriptive and explanatory concepts used in earlier chapters to their several categories. Consideration of these categories will also perhaps justify the special emphasis laid on certain concepts in Chapter 2.

(1) Descriptive terms. These can be placed in three categories according to the level of analysis.
    (a) Descriptions of behaviour/action. These may refer to:
        (i) Discrete movement patterns or actions, e.g. eyebrow flash, smile.
        (ii) Categories having common consequences or presumed common causal bases or goals (see below), e.g. signal, dissembling, aggressive behaviour, competitive behaviour.
        (iii) Sequences extended over time, e.g. interaction, episode, relationship.
    (b) Descriptions of properties of interactions.
        (i) Qualities referring to the properties of actions of one or both participants, e.g. tenderness, passion, savageness.
        (ii) Relations between the actions of the two participants, e.g. meshing, disconfirmation, complementarity.
    (c) Descriptions of properties of relationships.
        (i) Assessments of behaviour or propensities of one partner in relation to those of the other which may apply to one or both partners. Their usefulness increases with the number of contexts in which they are relevant, e.g. compatibility; intimacy, interpersonal perception; degree of involvement.
        (ii) Assessments of relationships which depend on the sharing of properties between interactions of different types. Again their usefulness increases with the number of types of interaction involved, e.g. dominance/subordinance, nurturance/succorance, control/permissiveness.
        (iii) Overall qualities which depend on assessments of diverse characteristics, e.g. love, warmth.
These descriptive categories overlap to a considerable extent: for

instance complementarity and compatibility could apply to interactions or relationships, and the distinction between the last two subcategories (c(ii) and c(iii)) has a degree of arbitrariness.

(2) Intervening variables (or hypothetical constructs) commonly used in the analysis of individual behaviour (e.g. motivation, need, learning and reward or reinforcement). These are susceptible to operational definition, at any rate for use within restricted theoretical systems, but may also have, to varying degrees, implications about process. They may refer to phenomena which can be correlated with events at the neural level. Such concepts have not been considered in any detail here, but extensive discussions are available elsewhere (e.g. Kling and Riggs, 1971). It must be noted, however, that in studies of interpersonal relationships they often have considerable cognitive implications.

(3) Pivotal concepts. The concepts of perception, expectancy, goal direction, emotions/feelings, values and norms, together with the view that experience is stored in an orderly fashion as symbols which can be manipulated, seem to be of special importance for a science of interpersonal relationships, and were for that reason discussed in some detail in Chapter 2.

The six named above are all susceptible to operational definition, and are frequently used in studies of individual behaviour. They may also be regarded as having experiential (subjective) correlates, whose possible causal efficiency was discussed on p. 34. Schemata of cognitive representations are compatible with the views of some theorists of non-social behaviour, but would be disowned by others: some such concept seems essential here if it is accepted, for instance, that interactions may be affected by prior rehearsal of events that may never happen.

In the building of a concise theory, the list could perhaps be reduced. For example goal directedness implies a concept of expectancy, while norms are clearly related to values and thus to reward; norms and values could also be related to emotions.

Many of the other concepts used in this book are clearly closely related to these pivotal ones. For example misperception is related to perception; cost, resource, dependency, profit, equality, equity, justice, altruism, social approval and status to value; anxiety, distress, anger, positive and negative affect, cognitive dissonance, cognitive balance and consensual validation to some usages of emotions; and roles, rules and metanorms, in spite of the several ways in which these terms are used, to norms. In some of these cases, however, "schemata of cognitive representations" also seem necessary. Thus justice implies a comparison of values, and dissonance one between attitudes and/or beliefs.

(4) Concepts referring to individual characteristics. These must depend on analysis in terms of one or more of the above pivotal concepts. Thus "attitudes" and "personality", as assessed by any test, must depend on the individual's perceptions, expectancies, values, etc. The same is true of Goffman's concept of the "character" as a person with a distinctive organization of personal characteristics, and his (somewhat idiosyncratic) use of "role" as a plausible line of action truly expressive of the personality of a character.

(5) Higher level explanatory concepts. In a similar manner, higher level explanatory concepts can be described in terms of cognitive schemata and one or more of the pivotal concepts. For example "role identity", as a person's imaginative view of himself as an occupant of a particular social position, will involve perceptions, expectancies, goals, norms, emotions and values. Whilst "role identity" can legitimately be seen as cause and consequence of social behaviour (see p. 135), and may provide a useful shorthand, specification of which aspects are at issue, and when, will be essential for systematic theory-building. Furthermore, it will be necessary to clarify how far, if at all, such a concept is intended to imply emergent properties not present in the norms, values, expectancies etc. it embraces. Similar comments could be made about such concepts as "definition of the situation", "ideal self", "self-evaluation" and so on.

Thus, whilst the study of interpersonal relationships can perhaps be pursued more fruitfully and economically by the introduction of special concepts, it is important, if we are to have an integrated science of interpersonal relationships, that such concepts be tied to a limited number of lower level concepts, themselves susceptible to rigid definition.

Finally, the integration of knowledge about interpersonal relationships is not merely a matter of theorizing. Empirical studies bridging the different approaches to relationships, or linking the study of relationships to other branches of psychology, are urgently needed. Some studies tackling aspects of the dialectic between societal norms and relationships are already available (e.g. Araji, 1977; Tajfel, 1978), and the dialectic between personality and relationships could now be brought under scrutiny. For example simultaneous assessments of the individual characteristics of parents and later of the infant, and of their mutual relationships, over the time of the birth of a first child would provide a fascinating field of study: the work of Cowan *et al.* (1978) suggests a possible direction. Any life event that produces changes in a relationship and in the participants could similarly be taken as a focus. The need for conceptual integration of different approaches to the study of interpersonal relationships is important, but integration at the practical level is equally important.

References

Abelson, R. P. (1959). Modes of resolution of belief dilemmas. *J. Conflict Resolution* **3**, 343–352.

Abrahamsson, B. (1970). Homans on exchange: hedonism revisited. *Amer. J. Sociol.* **76**, 273–285.

Adams, J. S. (1965). Inequity in social exchange. *In* "Advances in Experimental Social Psychology." (Berkowitz, L., Ed.) Vol. 2, 267–299. Academic Press, New York.

Adams, J. S. and Freedman, S. (1976). Equity theory re-visited: comments and annotated bibliography. *In* "Advances in Experimental Social Psychology" (Berkowitz, L. and Walster, E., Eds). Vol. 9, 43–90. Academic Press, New York.

Ahrens, R. (1954). Beitrage zur Entwicklung des Physiognomie und Mimikerkennes. *Z. exp. ang. Psychol.* **2**, 412–454, 599–633.

Ainsworth, M. (1969). Object relations, dependency and attachment: a theoretical review of the infant-mother relationship. *Child Development* **40**, 969–1027.

Ainsworth, M. D. S. (1972). Attachment and dependency: a comparison. *In* "Attachment and Dependence." (Gewirtz, J. L., Ed.) Wiley, Washington, D.C.

Ainsworth, M. D. S. (1979). Attachment as related to mother-infant interaction. *Adv. Study Behav.* **9**, 2–52.

Ainsworth, M. D. S. and Bell, S. M. (1974). Mother-infant interaction and the development of competence. *In* "The Growth of Competence." (Connolly, K. and Bruner, J. S., Eds) Academic Press, London.

Ajzen, I. (1974). Effects of information on interpersonal attraction: similarity vs. affective value. *J. Pers. soc. Psychol.* **29**, 374–380.

Ajzen, I. (1977). Information processing approaches to interpersonal attraction. *In* "Theory and Practice in Interpersonal Attraction." (Duck, S., Ed.) Academic Press, London.

Allport, G. W. (1964). The fruits of eclecticism—bitter or sweet? *Acta Psychol.* **23**, 27–44.

Alperson, B. L. (1975). In search of Buber's ghosts: a calculus for interpersonal phenomenology. *Behav. Sci.* **20**, 179–190.

Altman, I. and Haythorn, W. W. (1965). Interpersonal exchange in isolation. *Sociometry* **28**, 411–426.

Altman, I. and Taylor, D. A. (1973). "Social Penetration." Holt, Rinehart and Winston, New York.

Andrew, R. J. (1974). Arousal and the causation of behaviour. *Behaviour* **51**, 135–165.

Apfelbaum, E. (1966). Etudes experimentales de conflit: les jeux expérimentaux. *L'Année Psychologiques* **66**, 599–621.

Araji, S. K. (1977). Husbands' and wives' attitude-behaviour congruence on family roles. *J. Marriage and the Family* **39**, 309–320.

Argyle, M. (1975). "Bodily Communication." Methuen, London.

Argyle, M. and Dean, J. (1965). Eye-contact, distance, and affiliation. *Sociometry* **28**, 289–304.

Argyle, M. and Kendon, A. (1967). The experimental analysis of social performance.

In "Advances in Experimental Social Psychology." (Berkowitz, L., Ed.) Vol. 3, 55–99. Academic Press, New York.

Ariès, P. (1962). "Centuries of Childhood." Cape, London.

Aronson, E. (1969). The theory of cognitive dissonance: a current perspective. *In* "Advances in Experimental Social Psychology." (Berkowitz, L., Ed.) Vol. 4, 2–35. Academic Press, New York.

Aronson, E. and Linder, D. (1965). Gain and loss of esteem as determinants of interpersonal attractiveness. *J. exp. soc. Psychol.* **1**, 156–172.

Aronson, E. and Worchel, P. (1966). Similarity versus liking as determinants of interpersonal attractiveness. *Psychon. Sci.* **5**, 157–158.

Asch, S. E. (1952). "Social Psychology." Prentice Hall, New York.

Asch, S. E. (1959). A perspective on social psychology. *In* "Psychology: a Study of a Science." (Koch, S., Ed.) Vol. 3. McGraw Hill, New York.

Austin, J. L. (1962). "How to do things with words." Oxford University Press.

Backman, C. W. and Secord, P. F. (1959). The effect of perceived liking on interpersonal attraction. *Human Relations* **12**, 379–384.

Backman, C. W. and Secord, P. F. (1962). Liking, selective interaction, and misperception in congruent interpersonal relations. *Sociometry* **25**, 321–335.

Baerends, G. P. (1976). The functional organization of behaviour. *Anim. Behav.* **24**, 726–738.

Bailey, R. C., Finney, P. and Bailey, K. G. (1974). Level of self-acceptance and perceived intelligence in self and friend. *J. genetic Psychol.* **124**, 61–67.

Bambrough, R. (1960/61). Universals and family resemblances. *Proc. Aristot. Soc.* 1960/61, 207–221.

Bandura, A. (1971). "Social Learning Theory." General Learning Press, Morristown, N.J.

Bandura, A. (1976). Self-reinforcement: theoretical and methodological considerations. *Behaviorism* **4**, 135–155.

Bandura, A. (1977). "Social Learning Theory." Prentice Hall, Englewood Cliffs, N.J.

Bannister, D. and Fransella, F. (1971). "Inquiring Man." Penguin, Harmondsworth.

Barker, R. G. (1963). On the nature of the environment. *J. social Issues* **19** (Kurt Lewin Memorial address), 17–38.

Barker, R. G. (1965). Explorations in ecological psychology. *Amer. Psychol.* **20**, 1–14.

Barker, R. G. (1978). "Habitats, Environments and Human Behavior." Jossey-Bass, San Francisco.

Barry, W. A. (1970). Marriage research and conflict: an integrative review. *Psychol. Bull.* **73**, 41–54.

Barth, F. (1966). Models of social organization. *Roy. Anthrop. Inst. Occ. Papers* No. 23, 1–33.

Bartlett, F. C. (1932). "Remembering." Cambridge University Press.

Barton, M. (1965). "Roles." Tavistock, London.

Bateson, G. (1958). "Naven." Stanford University Press.

Bateson, G., Jackson, D. D., Haley, J. and Weakland, J. (1956). Toward a theory of schizophrenia. *Behav. Sci.* **1**, 251–264.

Bateson, P. P. G. (1964). Effect of similarity between rearing and testing conditions on chicks' following and avoidance responses. *J. comp. physiol. Psychol.* **57**, 100–103.

Bateson, P. P. G. (1968). Ethological methods of observing behavior. *In* "Analysis of Behavioral Change." (Weiskrantz, L., Ed.) Harper and Row, New York.

Bateson, P. P. G. (1971). Imprinting. *In* "Ontogeny of Vertebrate Behavior." (Moltz, H., Ed.) Academic Press, New York.

Bateson, P. P. G. (1973). Preference for familiarity and novelty: a model for the simultaneous development of both. *J. theor. Biol.* **41**, 249–259.

Bateson, P. P. G. (1976). Rules and reciprocity in behavioural development. *In* "Growing Points in Ethology." (Bateson, P. P. G. and Hinde, R. A., Eds) Cambridge University Press.

Bateson, P. P. G. (1978). Sexual imprinting and optimal outbreeding. *Nature* **273**, 659.

Bateson, P. P. G. and Reese, E. P. (1969). The reinforcing properties of conspicuous stimuli in an imprinting situation. *Anim. Behav.* **17**, 692–699.

Beach, F. A. and Jordan, L. (1956). Sexual exhaustion and recovery in the male rat. *Q. J. exp. Psychol.* **8**, 121–133.

Beach, F. A., Westbrook, W. H. and Clemens, L. G. (1966). Comparison of the ejaculatory response in men and animals. *Psychosom. Med.* **28**, 749–763.

Becker, W. C. (1964). Consequences of different kinds of parental discipline. *In* "Review of Child Development Research." (Hoffman, M. L. and Hoffman, L. W., Eds) Vol. 1. Russel Sage Foundation, New York.

Bell, R. Q. (1968). A reinterpretation of the direction of effects in studies of socialization. *Psychol. Rev.* **75**, 81–85.

Bell, R. Q. (1974). Contributions of human infants to caregiving and social interaction. *In* "The Effect of the Infant on its Caregiver." (Lewis, M. and Rosenblum, L. A., Eds) Wiley, New York.

Bell, S. M. and Ainsworth, M. D. S. (1972). Infant crying and maternal responsiveness. *Child. Devel.* **43**, 1171–1190.

Bem, D. J. (1967). Self-perception: an alternative interpretation of cognitive dissonance phenomena. *Psychol. Rev.* **74**, 183–200.

Bem, D. J. (1972). Self-perception theory. *Adv. exp. soc. Psychol.* **6**, 1–62.

Bem, D. J. and Allen, A. (1974). On predicting some of the people some of the time. *Psychol. Rev.* **81**, 506–520.

Bem, D. J. and McConnell, H. K. (1970). Testing the self-perception explanation of dissonance phenomena: on the salience of premanipulation attitudes. *J. Pers. soc. Psychol.* **14**, 23–31.

Benedict, R. (1935). "Patterns of Culture." Houghton Mifflin, Boston.

Bennett, S. L. (1971). Infant-caretaker interactions. *J. Amer. Acad. Child Psychiatry* **10**, 321–335.

Benthall, J. and Polhemus, T. (Eds), (1975). "The Body as a Medium of Expression." Allen Lane, London.

Benton, A. A. (1971). Productivity, distributive justice and bargaining among children. *J. Pers. soc. Psychol.* **18**, 68–78.

Berg, B., Balla, D. and Zigler, E. (1976). Satiation and setting-condition components of social reinforcer effectiveness. *Child Devel.* **47**, 715–721.

Berger, P. L. and Luckman, T. (1966). "The Social Construction of Reality." Doubleday, New York.

Berger, S. and Lambert, W. W. (1968). Stimulus-response theory in contemporary social psychology. *In* "Handbook of Social Psychology." (Lindzey, G. and Aronson, E., Eds) Addison-Wesley, Reading, Mass.

Bergman, I. (1974). "Scenes from a Marriage." Calder and Boyars, London.

Berkowitz, L. (1972). Social norms, feelings and other factors affecting helping and altruism. *Adv. exp. Soc. Psychol.* **6**, 63–108.

Berkowitz, L. and Friedman, P. (1967). Some social class differences in helping behavior. *J. Pers. soc. Psychol.* **5**, 217–225.

Bernal, J. (1972). Crying during the first ten days of life, and maternal responses. *Devel. Med. child Neurol.* **14**, 362–372.

Bernard, J. (1964). The adjustments of married mates. *In* "Handbook of Marriage and the Family." (Christensen, H. T., Ed.) Rand McNally, Chicago.

Berne, E. (1967). "Games People Play." Penguin, Harmondsworth.

Berscheid, E. and Walster, E. H. (1969). "Interpersonal Attraction." Addison-Wesley, Reading, Mass.

Berscheid, E. and Walster, E. (1974a). A little bit about love. *In* "Foundations of Interpersonal Attraction." (Huston, T. L., Ed.) Academic Press, New York.

Berscheid, E. and Walster, E. (1974b). Physical attractiveness. *Adv. exp. soc. Psychol.* **7**, 157–215.

Berscheid, E., Dion, K. K., Walster, E. and Walster, G. W. (1971). Physical attractiveness and dating choice: a test of the matching hypothesis. *J. exp. soc. Psychol.* **7**, 173–189.

Bigelow, B. J. and La Gaipa, J. J. (1975). Children's written descriptions of friendship: a multidimensional analysis. *Devel. Psychol.* **11**, 857–858.

Bindra, D. (1976). "A Theory of Intelligent Behavior." Wiley, New York.

Bindra, D. (1978). How adaptive behavior is produced: a perceptual, –, motivational alternative to response-reinforcement. *Behavioral and Brain Sciences* **1**, 41–91.

Bischof, N. (1975). A systems approach toward the functional connections of attachment and fear. *Child Devel.* **46**, 801–817.

Black, M. (1975). "The Literature of Fidelity." Chatto and Windus, London.

Blau, P. M. (1964). "Exchange and Power in Social Life." Wiley, New York.

Block J. (1977). Advancing the psychology of personality. *In* "Personality at the Crossroads." (Magnusson, D. and Endler, N. S., Eds.) Erlbaum, Hillsdale, N.J.

Bolles, R. C. (1972). Reinforcement, expectancy and learning. *Psychol. Rev.* **79**, 394–409.

Bott, E. (1957; 2nd Edn 1971). "Family and Social Networks." Tavistock, London.

Bower, T. G. R. (1974). "Development in Infancy." Freeman, San Francisco.

Bowers, K. S. (1973). Situationism in psychology: an analysis and a critique. *Psychol. Rev.* **80**, 307–336.

Bowlby, J. (1969). "Attachment and Loss. Vol. 1. Attachment." Hogarth Press, London.

Bowlby, J. (1973). "Attachment and Loss. Vol. 2. Separation." Hogarth Press, London.

Bowlby, J. (1977). The making and breaking of affectional bonds. 1. Aetiology and psychopathology in the light of attachment theory. *Brit. J. Psychiatry* **130**, 201–210.

Brackbill, Y. (1958). Extinction of the smiling response in infants as a function of reinforcement schedule. *Child Devel.* **29**, 115–124.

Brannigan, C. R. and Humphries, D. A. (1972). Human non-verbal behaviour, a means of communication. *In* "Ethological Studies of Child Behaviour." (Blurton Jones, N. G., Ed.) Cambridge University Press.

Brazelton, T. B., Koslowski, B. and Main, M. (1974). The origins of reciprocity: the early mother-infant interaction. *In* "The Effects of the Infant on its Caregiver." (Lewis, M. and Rosemblum, L. A., Eds) Wiley, New York.

Brehm, J. W. (1976). Responses to loss of freedom: a theory of psychological reactance. *In* "Contemporary Topics in Social Psychology." (Thibaut, J. W., Spence, J. T. and Carson, R. C., Eds). General Learning Press, Morristown, N.J.

Broadbent, D. E. (1958). "Perception and Communication." Pergamon, London.

Broadbent, D. E. (1971). "Decisions and Stress." Academic Press, London.

Brock, T. C. and Buss, A. H. (1962). Dissonance, aggression and evaluation of pain. *J. abn. soc. Psychol.* **65**, 197–202.

Brockner, J. and Swap, W. C. (1976). Effects of repeated exposure and attitudinal similarity on self-disclosure and interpersonal attraction. *J. Pers. soc. Psychol.* **33**, 531–540.

Bronfenbrenner, U. (1970). Reaction to social pressure from adults versus peers among Soviet day-school and boarding-school pupils in the perspective of an American sample. *J. Pers. soc. Psych.* **15**, 179–189.

Bronfenbrenner, U. (1977). Toward an experimental ecology of human development. *Amer. Psychol.* **32**, 513–531.

Brossard, L. M. and Décarie, T. G. (1968). Comparative reinforcing effect of eight stimulations on the smiling responses of infants. *J. child Psychol. Psychiatry* **9**, 51–60.

Brown, G. W., Birley, J. L. T. and Wing, J. K. (1972). Influence of family life on the course of schizophrenic disorders: a replication. *Brit. J. Psychiatry* **121**, 241–258.

Brown, G. W., Bhrolchain, M. N. and Harris, T. (1975). Social class and psychiatric disturbance among women in an urban population. *Sociology* **9**, 225–254.

Brown, R. and Gilman, A. (1960). The pronouns of power and solidarity. *In* "Style in Language." (Sebeok, T. A., Ed.) Technology Press, Cambridge, Mass.

Bruner, J. S. (1977). Early social interaction and language acquisition. *In* "Studies in Mother-Infant Interaction." (Schaffer, H. R., Ed.) Academic Press, London.

Bruner, J. S. and Tagiuri, R. (1954). The perception of people. *In* "Handbook of Social Psychology." (Lindzey, G., Ed.) Addison-Wesley, Cambridge, Mass.

Bugental, D. E. and Love, L. R. (1975). Nonassertive expression of parental approval and disapproval and its relationship to child disturbance. *Child Devel.* **46**, 747–752.

Bugental, D. B., Love, L. R., Kaswan, J. W. and April, C. (1971). Verbal-nonverbal conflict in parental messages to normal and disturbed children. *J. abn. Psychol.* **77**, 6–10.

Burgess, E. W. and Locke, H. J. (1960). "The Family from Institution to Companionship." American, New York.

Burgess, R. L. and Akers, R. L. (1966). Are operant principles tautological? *Psychol. Record.* **16**, 305–312.

Burton, L. (1975). "The family Life of Sick Children." Routledge and Kegan Paul, London.

Byrne, D. (1961a). Interpersonal attraction and attitude similarity. *J. abn. soc. Psychol.* **62**, 713–4.

Byrne, D. (1961b). The influence of propinquity and opportunities for interaction on classroom relationships. *Human Relations* **14**, 63–69.

Byrne, D. (1971). "The Attraction Paradigm." Academic Press, New York.

Byrne, D. and Blaylock, B. (1963). Similarity and assumed similarity of attitudes between husbands and wives. *J. abn. soc. Psychol.* **67**, 636–640.

Byrne, D. and Clore, G. L. (1967). Effectance, arousal and attraction. *J. Pers. soc. Psychol.* Monograph 6. (whole No. 638).

Byrne, D. and Griffitt, W. (1966). Similarity versus liking: a clarification. *Psychon. Sci.* **6**, 295–296.

Byrne, D. and Nelson, D. (1965a). Attraction as a linear function of proportion of positive reinforcements. *J. Pers. soc. Psychol.* **1**, 659–663.

Byrne, D. and Nelson, D. (1965b). The effect of topic importance and attitude similarity-dissimilarity on attraction in a multi-stranger design. *Psychon. Sci.* **3**, 449–450.

Byrne, D. and Rhamey, R. (1965). Magnitude of positive and negative reinforcements as a determinant of attraction. *J. Pers. soc. Psychol.* **2**, 884–889.

Byrne, D. and Wong, T. J. (1962). Racial prejudice, interpersonal attraction, and assumed dissimilarity of attitudes. *J. abn. soc. Psychol.* **65**, 246–253.

Byrne, D., Nelson, D. and Reeves, K. (1966). Effects of consensual validation and invalidation on attraction as a function of verifiability. *J. exp. soc. Psychol.* **2**, 98–107.

Byrne, D., London, O. and Reeves, K. (1968). The effects of physical attractiveness, sex and attitude similarity on interpersonal attraction. *J. Personal.* **36**, 259–271.

Byrne, D., Clore, G. L., Griffitt, W., Lamberth, J. and Mitchell, H. E. (1973). When research paradigms converge. *J. Pers. soc. Psychol.* **28**, 313–320.

Byrne, D., Lamberth, J., Mitchell, H. E. and Winslow, L. (1974a). Sex differences in attraction. *J. soc. econ. Studies* **2**, 79–86.

Byrne, D., Rasche, L. and Kelley, K. (1974b). When "I like you" indicates disagreement: an experimental differentiation of information and affect. *J. Res. in Pers.* **8**, 207–217.

Candland, D. K., Fell, J. P., Keen, E., Leshner, A. I., Plutchick, R. and Tarpy, R. M. (1977). "Emotion." Brooks/Cole, Montway.

Cattell, R. B. and Nesselroade, J. R. (1967). Likeness and completeness theories examined by 16 personality factor measures on stably and unstably married couples. *J. Pers. soc. Psychol.* **7**, 351–361.

Caudill, W. and Weinstein, H. (1969). Maternal care and infant behavior in Japan and America. *Psychiatry* **32**, 12–43.

Cavior, N. N. and Dokecki, P. R. (1973). Physical attractiveness, perceived attitude similarity, and academic achievement as contributors to interpersonal attraction among adolescents. *Devel. Psychol.* **9**, 44–54.

Cavior, N., Miller, K. and Cohen, S. H. (1975). Physical attractiveness, attitude similarity, and length of acquaintance as contributors to interpersonal attraction among adolescents. *Soc. Behav. Pers.* **3**, 133–141.

Centers, R. (1975). Attitude similarity-dissimilarity as a correlate of heterosexual attraction and love. *J. Marriage and the Family* **37**, 305–314.

Chadwick, B. A., Albrecht, S. L. and Kunz, P. R. (1976). Marital and family role satisfaction. *J. Marriage and the Family* **38**, 431–440.

Chadwick-Jones, J. K. (1976). "Social Exchange Theory." Academic Press, London.

Chomsky, N. (1959). Review of verbal behavior by B. F. Skinner. *Language* **35**, 26–58.

Cicirelli, V. G. (1975). Effects of mother and older sibling on the problem solving behavior of the younger child. *Devel. Psychol.* **11**, 749–756.

Clarke-Stewart, K. A. (1973). Interactions between mothers and their young children: characteristics and consequences. *Monog. Soc. Res. Child. Devel.* **38**, 153, Nos. 6–7.

Clore, G. L. (1977). Reinforcement and affect in attraction. *In* "Theory and Practice in Interpersonal Attraction." (Duck, S., Ed.) Academic Press, London.

Clore, G. L. and Byrne, D. (1974). A reinforcement-affect model of attraction. *In* "Foundations of Interpersonal attraction." (Huston, T. L., Ed.) Academic Press, New York.

Collins, J., Kreitman, N., Nelson, B. and Troop, J. (1971). Neurosis and marital interaction. III Family Roles and Functions. *Brit. J. Psychiatry* **119**, 233–242.

Connor, J. W. (1974). Acculturation and family continuities in three generations of Japanese Americans. *J. Marriage and the Family* **36**, 159–165.

Cook, M. (1977). The social skill model and interpersonal attraction. *In* "Theory and Practice in Interpersonal Attraction." (Duck, S., Ed.) Academic Press, London.

Cooley, C. H. (1956). "Human Nature and the Social Order." The Free Press, Glencoe, Illinois.

Coombs, R. H. (1966). Value consensus and partner satisfaction among dating couples. *J. Marriage and the Family* **28**, 166–173.

Cowan, C. P., Cowan, P. A., Coie, L. and Coie, J. D. (1978). Becoming a family: The impact of a first child's birth on the couple's relationship. *In* "The First Child and Family Formation." (Miller, W. B. and Newman, L. F., Eds). Caroline Population Center, Chapel Hill.

Cozby, P. C. (1973). Self disclosure: a literature review. *Psychol. Bull.* **79**, 73–91.

Crick, M. (1975). Ethology, language and the study of human action. *J. Anthrop. Soc. Oxford* **6**, 106–118.

Cromwell, R. E. and Olson, D. H. (1975). "Power in Families." Halstead Press, Wiley, New York.

Cromwell, R. E., Olson, D. H. L. and Fournier, D. G. (1976). Tools and techniques for diagnosis and evaluation in marital and family therapy. *Family Process* **15**, 1–49.

Crowne, D. P. and Marlowe, D. (1964). "The Approval Motive." Wiley, New York.

Crystal, D. (1975). Paralinguistics. *In* "The Body as a Medium of Expression." (Benthall, J. and Polhemus, T., Eds). Allen Lane, London.

Curry, T. J. and Emerson, R. M. (1970). Balance theory: a theory of interpersonal attraction? *Sociometry* **33**, 216–238.

Dabbs, J. M. (1971). Physical closeness and negative feelings. *Psychon. Sci.* **23**, 141–143.

Danziger, K. (1976). "Interpersonal Communication." Pergamon, New York.

Darley, J. M. and Berscheid, E. (1967). Increased liking as a result of the anticipation of personal contact. *Human Relations* **20**, 29–39.

Davis, D. and Martin, H. J. (1978). When pleasure begets pleasure: recipient responsiveness as a determinant of physical pleasuring between heterosexual dating couples and strangers. *J. Pers. soc. Psychol.* **36**, 767–777.

Davis, J. (1973). Forms and norms: the economy of social relations. *Man* **8**, 159–176.

Davis, J. D. (1976). Self-disclosure in an acquaintance exercise: responsibility for level of intimacy. *J. Pers. soc. Psychol.* **33**, 787–792.

Davis, J. D. and Skinner, A. E. G. (1974). Reciprocity of self-disclosure in interviews: modeling or social exchange? *J. Pers. soc. Psychol.* **29**, 779–784.

Demarest, W. J. (1977). Incest avoidance among human and non-human primates. *In* "Primate Biosocial Development." (Chevalier-Skolnikoff, S. and Poirier, F. E., Eds). Garland, New York.

Denzin, N. K. (1970). Rules of conduct and the study of deviant behavior: some notes on the social relationship. *In* "Social Relationships." (McCall, G. J. *et al.*, Eds). Aldine, Chicago.

Derlaga, V. J. and Chaikin, A. L. (1976). Norms affecting self-disclosure in men and women. *J. consult. clin. Psychol.* **44**, 376–380.

Derlega, V. J., Wilson, M. and Chaikin, A. L. (1976). Friendship and disclosure reciprocity. *J. Pers. soc. Psychol.* **34**, 578–582.

Deutsch, M. (1969). Conflicts: productive and destructive. *J. soc. Issues* **25**, 7–41.

Deutsch, M. and Krauss, R. M. (1965). Studies of interpersonal bargaining. *J. Conflict Resolution* **6**, 52–76.

Deutsch, M. and Solomon, L. (1959). Reactions to evaluations of others as influenced by self evaluations. *Sociometry* **22**, 93–112.

Dion, K. K. and Berscheid, E. (1974). Physical attractiveness and peer perception among children. *Sociometry* **37**, 1–12.

Dion, K. K. and Dion, K. L. (1975). Self-esteem and romantic love. *J. Pers.* **43**, 39–57.

Dion, K. K., Berscheid, E. and Walster, E. (1972). What is beautiful is good. *J. Pers. soc. Psychol.* **24**, 285–290.

Dollard, J., Doob, L. W., Miller, N. E., Mowrer, O. H. and Sears, R. R. (1939). "Frustration and Aggression." Yale University Press, New Haven.

Douglas, J. W. B. (1975). Early hospital admissions and later disturbances of behaviour and learning. *Develop. Med. Child Neurol.* **17**, 456–480.

Drewery, J. (1969). An interpersonal perception technique. *Brit. J. Med. Psychol.* **42**, 171–181.

Drewery, J. and Rae, J. B. (1969). A group comparison of alcoholic and non-psychiatric marriages using the interpersonal perception technique. *Brit. J. Psychiatry* **115**, 287–300.

Driscoll, R., Davis, K. E. and Lipetz, M. E. (1972). Parental interference and romantic love: The Romeo and Juliet effect. *J. Pers. soc. Psychol.* **24**, 1–10.

Duck, S. W. (1973a). Similarity and perceived similarity of personal constructs as influences on friendship choice. *Brit. J. soc. clin. Psychol.* **12**, 1–6.

Duck, S. W. (1973b). "Personal Relationships and Personal Constructs: A Study of Friendship Formation." Wiley, New York.

Duck, S. (1977a). Tell me where is fancy bred: some thoughts on the study of interpersonal attraction. *In* "Theory and Practice in Interpersonal Attraction." (Duck, S., Ed.) Academic Press, London.

Duck, S. (1977b). Inquiry, hypothesis and the quest for validation: Personal construct systems in the development of acquaintance. *In* "Theory and Practice in Interpersonal Attraction." (Duck, S., Ed.) Academic Press, London.

Duck, S. W. and Craig, G. (1978). Personality similarity and the development of friendship: a longitudinal study. *Brit. J. soc. clin. Psychol.* **17**, 237–242.

Duck, S. W. and Spencer, C. (1972). Personal constructs and friendship formation. *J. Pers. soc. Psychol.* **23**, 40–45.

Duncan-Jones, P. (in press). "The Interview Measurement of Social Interaction." International Sociological Association. World Congress, Uppsala.

Dunn, John (1978). Practicing history and social science on realist assumptions. *In* "Action and Interpretation." (Hookway, C. and Pettit, P., Eds) Cambridge University Press.

Dunn, Judy (1976). How far do early differences in mother-child relations affect later development? *In* "Growing Points in Ethology." (Bateson, P. P. G. and Hinde, R. A., Eds) Cambridge University Press.

Dunn, J. (1977). "Distress and Comfort." Fontana/Open Books, London.

Dunn, J. and Kendrick, C. (in prep. a). The arrival of a sibling: I. Changes in patterns of interaction between mother and first-born child, and the reaction of the first-born.

Dunn, J. and Kendrick, C. (in prep. b). The arrival of sibling: II. Factors associated with the reaction of first-born children.

Dunn, J. and Wooding, C. (1977). Play in the Home and its Implications for Learning. *In* "Biology of Play." (Tizard, B. and Harvey, D., Eds). Heinemann, London.

Dymond, R. (1954). Interpersonal perception and marital happiness. *Canad. J. Psychol.* **8**, 164–171.

Efran, M. G. and Cheyne, J. A. (1974). Affective concomitants of the invasion of shared space: behavioral, physiological, and verbal indicators. *J. Pers. soc. Psychol.* **29**, 219–226.

Eibl-Eibesfeldt, I. (1972). Similarities and differences between cultures in expressive movements. *In* "Nonverbal Communication." (Hinde, R. A., Ed.) Cambridge University Press.

Eiser, J. R. (1978a). Cooperation and competition between individuals. *In* "Introducing Social Psychology." (Tajfel, H. and Fraser, C., Eds) Penguin, Harmondsworth.

Eiser, J. R. (1978b). Interpersonal attributions. *In* "Introducing Social Psychology." (Tajfel, H. and Fraser, C., Eds) Penguin, Harmondsworth.

Ekman, P. and Friesen, W. V. (1969). The repertoire of nonverbal behavior. *Semiotica* **1**, 49–98.

Ekman, P. and Friesen, W. V. (1975). "Unmasking the Face." Prentice Hall, N.J.

Elms, A. C. (1975). The crisis of confidence in social psychology. *Amer. Psychol.* **30**, 967–976.

Epstein, N. B. and Santa-Barbara, J. (1975). Conflict behavior in clinical couples: interpersonal perceptions and stable outcomes. *Family Process* **14**, 51–66.

Eron, L. D., Huesmann, L. R., Lefkowitz, M. M. and Walder, L. O. (1972). Does television violence cause aggression? *Amer. Psychol.* **27**, 253–263.

Etzel, B. C. and Gewirtz, J. L. (1967). Experimental modification of caretaker-maintained high-rate operant crying in a 6- and a 20-week-old infant (Infant tyrranotearus). *J. exp. Child Psychol.* **5**, 303–317.

Fazio, R. H., Zanna, M. P. and Cooper, J. (1977). Dissonance and self-perception: an integrative view of each theory's proper domain of application. *J. exp. soc. Psychol.* **13**, 464–479.

Fentress, J. (1976). Dynamic boundaries of patterned behaviour: interaction and self-organization. *In* "Growing Points in Ethology." (Bateson, P. P. G. and Hinde, R. A., Eds) Cambridge University Press.

Ferreira, A. J. and Winter, W. D. (1968). Decision-making in normal and abnormal two child families. *Family Process* **7**, 17–36.

Ferreira, A. J. and Winter, W. D. (1974). On the nature of marital relationships: measurable differences in spontaneous agreement. *Family Process* **13**, 355–369.

Feshbach, S. (1970). Aggression. *In* "Carmichael's Manual of Child Psychology." (Mussen, P. H., Ed.) Vol. 2. Wiley, New York.

Festinger, L. (1954). A theory of social comparison processes. *Hum. Rels* **7**, 117–140.

Festinger, L. (1957). "A Theory of Cognitive Dissonance." Row, Peterson, Evanston, Illinois.

Firth, R. (1965). "Primitive Polynesian Economy." Routledge and Kegan Paul, London.

Fishbein, M. and Ajzen, I. (1975). "Belief, Attitude, Intention, and Behavior." Addison-Wesley, Reading, Mass.

Fletcher, R. (1966). "The Family and Marriage in Britain." Penguin, Harmondsworth.

Foa, U. G. and Foa, E. B. (1974). "Societal Structures of the Mind." Thomas, Springfield, Illinois.

Fortes, M. (1974). The first born. *J. child Psychol. Psychiatry* **15**, 81–104.

Fransella, F. and Bannister, D. (1977). "A Manual for Repertory Grid Technique." Academic Press, London.

Fraser, C. (1978). Communication in Interactions. *In* "Introducing Social Psychology." (Tajfel, H. and Fraser, C., Eds) Penguin, Harmondsworth.

French, J. R. P. and Raven, B. H. (1959). The basis of social power. *In* "Studies in Social Power." (Cartwright, D., Ed.) University of Michigan Press, Ann Arbor, Michigan.

Freud, S. (1914). "The Psychopathology of Everyday Life." Fisher Unwin, London.

Fromkin, H. L. (1972). Feelings of interpersonal undistinctiveness: an unpleasant affective state. *J. exp. Res. Pers.* **6**, 178–185.

Fromm, E. (1957). "The Art of Loving." George Allen and Unwin, London.

Gardner, B. T. and Wallach, L. (1965). Shapes of figures identified as a baby's head. *Percept. Motor Skills* **20**, 135–142.

Garfinkel, H. (1967). "Studies in Ethnomethodology." Prentice-Hall, New Jersey.

Gath, A. (1973). The school-age siblings of mongol children. *Brit. J. Psychiat.* **123**, 161–167.

Geest, S. van der (1976). Role relationships between husband and wife in rural Ghana. *J. Marriage and the Family* **38**, 572–578.

Gelman, R. and Shatz, M. (1977). Speech adjustments in talk to 2-year-olds. *In* "Interaction, Conversation and the Development of Language." (Lewis, M. and Rosenblum, L. A., Eds) Academic Press, New York.

Gergen, K. J. (1969). "The Psychology of Behavior Exchange." Addison-Wesley, Reading, Mass.

Gergen, K. J., Ellsworth, P., Maslach, C. and Seipel, M. (1975). Obligation, donor resources and reactions to aid in three cultures. *J. Pers. soc. Psychol.* **31**, 390–400.

Gewirtz, J. L. (1961). A learning analysis of the effects of normal stimulation, privation and deprivation on the acquisition of social motivation and attachment. *In* "Determinants of Infant Behaviour." (B. M. Foss, Ed.) Vol. 1. Methuen, London.

Gewirtz, J. L. (1976). The attachment acquisition process as evidenced in the maternal conditioning of cued infant responding (particularly crying). *Human Devel.* **19**, 143–155.

Gewirtz, J. L. and Baer, D. M. (1958). Deprivation and satiation of social reinforcers as drive conditions. *J. abn. soc. Psychol.* **57**, 165–172.

Gewirtz, J. L. and Boyd, E. F. (1977). Does maternal responding imply reduced infant crying? A critique of the 1972 Bell and Ainsworth report. *Child Devel.* **48**, 1200–1207.

Gibson, E. J., Walk, R. D. and Tighe, T. J. (1959). Enhancement and deprivation of visual stimulation during rearing as factors in visual discrimination learning. *J. comp. physiol. Psychol.* **52**, 74–81.

Glass, D. C. (1964). Changes in liking as a means of reducing cognitive discrepancies between self-esteem and aggression. *J. Pers.* **32**, 531–549.

Glenn, N. D. (1975). Psychological well-being in the post-parental stage: some evidence from national surveys. *J. Marriage and the Family* **37**, 105–112.

Goffman, E. (1959). "The presentation of Self in Everyday Life." Doubleday Anchor, New York.

Goffman, E. (1961). "Asylums." Aldine, Chicago.

Goffman, E. (1963). "Behaviour in Public Places." Free Press, New York.

Goffman, E. (1967). "Interaction Ritual." Doubleday Anchor, New York.

Goffman, E. (1971). "Relations in Public: Microstudies of the Social Order." Penguin, Harmondsworth.

Goldman, W. and Lewis, P. (1977). Beautiful is good: evidence that the physically attractive are more socially skillful. *J. exp. soc. Psychol.* **13**, 125–130.

Goody, E. (1972). "Greeting", "begging", and the presentation of respect. *In* "The Interpretation of Ritual." (La Fontaine, J. S., Ed.) Tavistock, London.

Goody, E. (1978). Towards a theory of questions. *In* "Questions and Politeness." (Goody, E., Ed.) Cambridge University Press.

Goody, J. (1959). The mother's brother and the sister's son in West Africa. *J. Roy. Anthrop. Inst.* **89**, 61–88.

Gottman, J., Markman, H. and Notarius, C. (1977). The topography of marital conflict: a sequential analysis of verbal and nonverbal behavior. *J. Marriage and the Family* **39**, 461–478.

Greenspoon, T. (1955). The reinforcing effect of two spoken sounds on the frequency of two responses. *Amer. J. Psychol.* **68**, 409–416.

Griffitt, W. (1974). Attitude similarity and attraction. *In* "Foundations of Interpersonal Attraction." (Huston, T. L., Ed.) Academic Press, New York.

Griffitt, W. and Veitch, R. (1971). Hot and crowded: influences of population density and temperature on interpersonal affective behavior. *J. Pers. soc. Psychol.* **17**, 92–98.

Griffitt, W. and Veitch, R. (1974). Preacquaintance attitude similarity and attraction re-visited: ten days in a fall-out shelter. *Sociometry* **37**, 163–173.

Gross, A. E. and Latané, J. G. (1974). Receiving help, reciprocation and inter-personal attraction. *J. appl. soc. Psychol.* **4**, 210-223.

Gruder, C. L. (1970). Social power in interpersonal negotiation. *In* "The Structure of Conflict." (Swingle, P., Ed.) Academic Press, New York.

Grusec, J. and Mischel, W. (1966). Model's characteristics as determinants of social learning. *J. Pers. soc. Psychol.* **4**, 211–215.

Hadley, T. R. and Jacob, T. (1976). The measurement of family power: a methodological study. *Sociometry* **39**, 384–385.

Haley, J. (1963). "Strategies of Psychotherapy." Grune and Stratton, New York.

Hall, E. T. (1966). "The Hidden Dimension." Doubleday, New York.

Hansen, E. W. (1966). The development of maternal and infant behavior in the rhesus monkey. *Behaviour* **27**, 107–149.

Harcourt, A. H. (1977). Social relationships of wild mountain gorilla. Ph.D. Thesis, Cambridge.

Harlow, H. F. and Harlow, M. K. (1965). The affectional systems. *In* "Behavior of Non-human Primates." (Schrier, A. M., Harlow, H. F. and Stollnitz, F., Eds). Academic Press, New York.

Harlow, H. F. and Zimmerman, R. R. (1959). Affectional responses in the infant monkey. *Science* **130**, 421–432.

Harper, L. V. (1970). Ontogenetic and phylogenetic functions of the parent-offspring relationship in mammals. *Adv. Study Behav.* **3**, 75–119.

Harré, R. (1974). The conditions for a social psychology of childhood. *In* "The Integration of a Child into a Social World." (Richards, M. P. M., Ed.) Cambridge University Press.

Harré, R. (1975). The origins of social competence in a pluralist society. *Oxford Rev. Educ.* **1**, 151–158.

Harré, R. (1977). Friendship as an accomplishment. *In* Duck (1977).

Harré, R. and Secord, P. F. (1972). "The Explanation of Social Behaviour." Oxford University Press.

Harrison, A. A. (1977). Mere exposure. *Adv. exp. soc. Psychol.* **10**, 40–85.

Hartup, W. W. (1975). The origins of friendship. *In* "Friendship and Peer Relations." (Lewis, M. and Rosenblum, L., Eds). Wiley, New York.

Harvey, O. J., Kelly, H. H. and Shapiro, M. M. (1957). Reactions to unfavourable evaluations of the self made by other persons. *J. Pers.* **25**, 393–411.

Hassan, S. A. (1974). Transactional and contextual invalidation between the parents of disturbed families: a comparative study. *Family Process.* **13**, 53–76.

Hayden, B., Nasby, W. and Davids, A. (1977). Interpersonal conceptual structures, predictive accuracy, and social adjustment of emotionally disturbed boys. *J. abn. Psychol.* **86**, 315–320.

Heath, A. (1972). Exchange theory. *Brit. J. political Sci.* **1**, 91–119.

Hebb, D. O. (1949). "The Organization of Behavior." Wiley, New York.

Heider, F. (1958). "The Psychology of Interpersonal Relations." Wiley, New York.

Henderson, S. (1974). Care-eliciting behaviour in man. *J. nerv. ment. Dis.* **159**, 172–181.

Hendrick, C. and Brown, S. (1971). Introversion, extraversion and interpersonal attraction. *J. Pers. soc. Psychol.* **20**, 31–36.

Hewitt, J. and Goldman, M. (1974). Self-esteem, need for approval and reactions to personal evaluations. *J. exp. soc. Psychol.* **10**, 201–210.

Hildum, D. C. and Brown, R. W. (1956). Verbal reinforcer and interviewer bias. *J. abn. soc. Psychol.* **53**, 108–111.

Hilkevitch, R. (1960). Social interactional processes. *Psych. Rep.* **7**, 195–201.

Hill, C. T., Rubin, Z. and Peplau, L. A. (1976). Breakups before marriage: the end of 103 affairs. *J. soc. Issues* **32**, 147–168.

Hinchliffe, M. K., Vaughan, P. W., Hooper, D. and Roberts, F. J. (1977). The melancholy marriage: an enquiry into the interaction of depression. II Expressiveness. *Brit. J. Med. Psychol.* **50**, 125–142.

Hinde, R. A. (1970a). "Animal Behaviour: a Synthesis of Ethology and Comparative Psychology." McGraw Hill, New York.

Hinde, R. A. (1970b). Behavioural habituation. *In* "Short-Term Changes in Neural Activity and Behaviour." (Horn, G. and Hinde, R. A., Eds). Cambridge University Press.

Hinde, R. A. (1971). Some problems in the study of the development of social behaviour. *In* "The Biopsychology of Development." (Tobach, E., Aronson, L. R. and Shaw, E., Eds). Academic Press, New York.

Hinde, R. A. (ed.) (1972a). "Non-verbal Communication." Cambridge University Press.

Hinde, R. A. (1972b). Concepts of emotion. *In* "Physiology, Emotion and Psychosomatic Illness." Ciba Foundation Sym. 8. Elsevier, Amsterdam.

Hinde, R. A. (1974). "Biological Bases of Human Social Behaviour." McGraw Hill, New York.

Hinde, R. A. (1976a). On describing relationships. *J. Child Psychol. Psychiatry* **17**, 1-19.

Hinde, R. A. (1976b). Interactions, relationships and social structure. *Man* **11**, 1–17.

Hinde, R. A. (1977). On assessing the bases of partner preferences. *Behaviour* **62**, 1–9.

Hinde, R. A. (1978a). Dominance and role—two concepts with dual meanings. *J. Social Biol. Struct.* **1**, 27–38.

Hinde, R. A. (1978b). Interpersonal relationships—in quest of a science. *Psychol. Med.* **8**, 373–386.

Hinde, R. A. (1978c). Social development: a biological approach. *In* "Human Growth and Development." (Bruner, J. and Garton, A. Eds). Clarendon Press, Oxford.

Hinde, R. A. (1978d). Field Workers Questionnaire. *Primate Eye* and *Laboratory Primates Newsletter* (in press).

Hinde, R. A. (1978). The nature of social structure. *In* "The Great Apes, Perspectives on Human Evolution Series." (Washburn, S., Ed.). Vol. 5. Benjamin/Cummings Publishing Company, Menlo Park, California.

Hinde, R. A. (in press b). Family influences. *In* "Scientific Foundations of Developmental Psychiatry." (Rutter, M., Ed.) Heinemann, London.

Hinde, R. A. and Herrmann, J. (1977). Frequencies, durations, derived measures and their correlations in studying dyadic and triadic relationships. *In* "Studies in Mother-Infant Interaction." (Schaffer, H. R., Ed.) Academic Press, London.

Hinde, R. A. and McGinnis, L. (1977). Some factors influencing the effects of temporary mother-infant separation—some experiments with rhesus monkeys. *Psychol. Med.* **7**, 197–212.

Hinde, R. A. and Simpson, M. J. A. (1975). Qualities of mother-infant relationships in monkeys. Ciba Foundation Sym. No. 33. Elsevier, Amsterdam.

Hinde, R. A. and Spencer-Booth, Y. (1971a). Effects of brief separation from mother on rhesus monkeys. *Science* **173**, 111–118.

Hinde, R. A. and Spencer-Booth, Y. (1971b). Towards understanding individual differences in rhesus mother-infant interaction. *Anim. Behav.* **19**, 165–173.

Hinde, R. A. and Stevenson, J. G. (1969). Goals and response control. *In* "Development and Evolution of Behaviour." (Aronson, L. R., Tobach, E., Rosenblatt, J. S. and Lehrman, D. S., Eds). Vol. 1. Freeman, San Francisco.

Hinde, R. A. and Stevenson-Hinde, J. (Eds) (1973). "Constraints on Learning: Limitations and Predispositions." Academic Press, London.

Hinde, R. A. and Stevenson-Hinde, J. (1976). Towards understanding relationships. *In* "Growing Points in Ethology." (Bateson, P. P. G. and Hinde, R. A., Eds). Cambridge University Press.

Hinde, R.A. and White, L. (1974). The dynamics of a relationship—rhesus monkey ventro-ventral contact. *J. comp. physiol. Psychol.* **86**, 8–23.

Hoffman, L. R. and Maier, N. R. F. (1966). An experimental re-examination of the similarity-attraction hypothesis. *J. Pers. soc. Psychol.* **3**, 145–152.

Hoffman, M. L. (1975). Developmental synthesis of affect and cognition and its implications for altruistic motivation. *Devel. Psychol.* **11**, 607–622.

Holmes, J. G. and Miller, D. T. (1976). Interpersonal conflict. *In* "Contemporary Topics in Social Psychology." (Thibaut, J. W., Spence, J. T. and Carson, R. C., Eds). General Learning Press, Morristown, N. J.

Homans, G. C. (1951). "The Human Group." Routledge and Kegan Paul, London.

Homans, G. C. (1961). "Social Behaviour: Its Elementary forms." Routledge and Kegan Paul, London.

Homans, G. C. (1970). The relevance of psychology to the explanation of social phenomena. *In* "Explanation in the Behavioural Sciences." (Borger, R. and Cioffi, F., Eds). Cambridge University Press.

Homans, G. C. (1971). Attraction and Power. *In* "Theories of Attraction and Love." (Murstein, B. I., Ed.) Springer, New York.

Homans, G. C. (1974). "Social Behavior: its elementary forms." (Revised edn) Harcourt Brace Yoranovich, New York.

Homans, G. C. (1976). Commentary. *In* "Advances in Experimental Social Psychology." (Berkowitz, L. and Walster, E., Eds.), 231–244. Academic Press, New York.

Huesmann, L. R. and Levinger, G. (1976). Incremental exchange theory: a formal model for progression in dyadic social interaction. *In* "Advances in Experimental Social Psychology." (Berkowitz, L. and Walster, E., Eds). Vol. 9. Academic Press, New York.

Humphrey, M. (1975). The effect of children upon the marriage relationship. *Brit. J. med. Psychol.* **48**, 273–279.

Humphrey, N. K. (1976). The social function of intellect. *In* "Growing Points in Ethology." (Bateson, P. P. G. and Hinde, R. A., Eds.). Cambridge University Press.

Huston, T. L. (1973). Ambiguity of acceptance, social desirability and dating choice. *J. exp. soc. Psychol.* **9**, 32–42.

Huston, T. L. (1974). A perspective on interpersonal attraction. *In* "Foundations of Interpersonal Attraction." (Huston, T. L., Ed.) Academic Press, New York.

Hutter, M. (1974). Significant others and married student role attitudes. *J. Marriage and the Family* **36**, 31–36.

Insko, C. A., Songer, E. and McGarvey, W. (1974). Balance, positivity and agreement in the Jordan paradigm: a defense of balance theory. *J. exp. soc. Psychol.* **10**, 53–83.

Izard, C. E. (1960). Personality similarity and friendship. *J. abn. soc. Psychol.* **61**, 47–51.

Izard, C. E. (1963). Personality similarity and friendship: a follow-up study. *J. abn. soc. Psychol.* **66**, 598–600.

Jackson, D. D. (1957). The question of family homeostasis. *Psychiat. Q. Suppl.* **31**, 79–90.

Jackson, D. D. (1959). Family interaction, family homeostasis and some implications for conjoint family psychotherapy. *In* "Individual and Familial Dynamics." (Masserman, J. H., Ed.) Grune and Stratton, New York.

Jahoda, G. (1954). A note on Ashanti names and their relationship to personality. *Brit. J. Psychol.* **45**, 192–195.

James, H. (1959). Flicker: an unconditioned stimulus for imprinting *Canad. J. Psychol.* **13**, 59–67.

Jaspars, J. M. F. (1978). The nature and measurement of attitudes. *In* "Introducing Social Psychology." (Tajfel, H. and Fraser, C., Eds). Penguin, Harmondsworth.

Jenkins, H. M. (1973). Effects of the stimulus-reinforcer relation in selected and unselected responses. *In* "Constraints on Learning." (Hinde, R. A. and Stevenson-Hinde, J., Eds). Academic Press, London.

Johnson, D. W. and Johnson, S. (1972). The effects of attitude similarity, expectation of goal facilitation and actual goal facilitation on interpersonal attraction. *J. exp. soc. Psychol.* **8**, 197–206.

Jolly, A. (1966). Lemur social behavior and primate intelligence. *Science* **153**, 501–506.

Jourard, S. M. (1971). "Self-disclosure." Wiley, New York.

Jourard, S. M. and Friedman, R. (1970). Experimenter-subject "distance" and self-disclosure. *J. Pers. soc. Psychol.* **15**, 278–282.

Kagan, J., Henker, B. A., Hen-Tov, A., Levine, J. and Lewis, M. (1966). Infants' differential reactions to familiar and distorted faces. *Child Devel.* **37**, 519–532.

Kandel, D. B. (1978). Similarity in real-life adolescent friendship pairs. *J. Pers. soc. Psychol.* **36**, 306–312.

Kaufman, I. C. and Hinde, R. A. (1961). Factors influencing distress calling in chicks. *Anim. Behav.* **9**, 197–204.

Kaye, K. (1977). Towards the origin of dialogue. *In* "Studies in Mother-Infant Interaction." (Schaffer, H. R., Ed.) Academic Press, London.

Kelley, H. H. (1971). "Attribution in Social Interaction." General Learning Press, Morristown, N. J.

Kelley, H. H. (1979). "Personal Relationships." Erlbaum, Hillsdale, N.J.

Kelley, H. H. and Stahelski, A. J. (1970a). Social interaction: basis of cooperators' and competitors' beliefs about others. *J. Pers. soc. Psychol.* **16**, 66–91.

Kelley, H. H. and Stahelski, A. J. (1970b). Errors in perception of intentions in a mixed motive game. *J. exp. soc. Psychol.* **6**, 379–400.

Kelley, H. H. and Stahelski, A. J. (1970c). The inference of intentions from moves in the Prisoner's Dilemma game. *J. exp. soc. Psychol.* **6**, 401–419.

Kelley, H. H. and Thibaut, J. W. (1978). "Interpersonal Relations." Wiley, New York.

Kelly, E. L. (1955). Consistency of the adult personality. *Amer. Psychol.* **10**, 659–681.

Kelly, G. A. (1955). "The Psychology of Personal Constructs." Norton.

Kelly, G. A. (1970). A brief introduction to personal construct theory. *In* "Perspectives in Personal Construct Theory." (Bannister, D., Ed.) Academic Press, London.

Kelvin, P. (1970). "The Bases of Social Behaviour: An Approach in Terms of Order and Value." Holt Rinehart and Winston, London.

Kelvin, P. (1977). Predictability, power and vulnerability in interpersonal attraction. *In* "Theory and Practice in Interpersonal Attraction." (Duck, S., Ed.) Academic Press, London.

Kemper, T. D. and Reichler, M. L. (1976). Marital satisfaction and conjugal power as determinants of intensity and frequency of rewards and punishments administered by parents. *J. genetic. Psychol.* **129**, 221–234.

Kendon, A. (1967). Some functions of gaze direction in social interaction. *Acta Psychologica* **26**, 22–63.

Kendon, A. and Ferber, A. (1973). A description of some human greetings. *In* "Comparative Ecology and Behaviour in Primates." (Michael, R. and Crook, J. H., Eds). Academic Press, London.

Kenny, D. A. (1975). Cross-lagged panel correlation: a test for spuriousness. *Psychol. Bull.* **82**, 887–903.

Kerckhoff, A. C. (1974). The social context of interpersonal attraction. *In* "Foundations of Inter-personal attraction." (Huston, T. L., Ed.) Academic Press, New York.

Kerckhoff, A. C. and Davis, K. E. (1962). Value consensus and need complementarity in mate selection. *Amer. sociol. Rev.* **27**, 295–303.

Kiesler, S. B. and Baral, R. L. (1970). The search for a romantic partner: the effects of self esteem and physical attractiveness on romantic behavior. *In* "Personality and Social Behavior." (Gergen, K. and Marlow, D., Eds). Addison-Wesley, Reading, Mass.

Kirkpatrick, J. (1972). Some unexamined aspects of childhood association and sexual attraction in the Chinese minor marriage. *Amer. Anthrop.* **74**, 783–784.

Kleck, R. E., Richardson, S. A. and Ronald, L. (1974). Physical appearance cues and interpersonal attraction in children. *Child Devel.* **45**, 305–310.

Kling, J. W. (1971). Learning: introductory survey. *In* "Experimental Psychology." (Kling, J. W. and Riggs, L. A., Eds). Holt, Rinehart and Winston, New York.

Kling, J. W. and Riggs, L. A. (Eds) (1971). "Experimental Psychology." Holt, Rinehart and Winston, New York.

Kling, J. W. and Schrier, A. M. (1971). Positive Reinforcement. *In* "Experimental Psychology." (Kling, J. W. and Riggs, L. A., Eds). Holt, Rinehart and Winston, New York.

Kohlberg, L. (1976). Moral stages and moralization: the cognitive-developmental approach. *In* "Moral Development and Behavior." (Lickona, T., Ed.) Holt, Rinehart and Winston, New York.

Kolvin, I., Ounsted, C., Richardson, L. M. and Garside, R. F. (1971). The family and social background in childhood psychoses. *Brit. J. Psychiatry* **118**, 396–402.

Komarovsky, M. (1946). Cultural contradictions and sex roles. *Amer. J. Sociol.* **52**, 186–8.

Konishi, M. and Nottebohm, F. (1969). Experimental studies in the ontogeny of avian vocalizations. *In* "Bird Vocalizations." (Hinde, R. A., Ed.) Cambridge University Press.

Kreitman, N., Collins, J., Nelson, B. and Troop, J. (1970). Neurosis and marital interaction. I Personality and Symptoms. *Brit. J. Psychiat.* **117**, 33–46.

Kreitman, N., Collins, J., Nelson, B. and Troop, J. (1971). Neurosis and marital interaction. IV Manifest psychological interaction. *Brit. J. Psychiat.* **119**, 243–252.

Krout, M. H. (1942). "Introduction to Social Psychology." Harper and Row, New York.

Kubie, L. S. (1956). Psychoanalysis and marriage: practical and theoretical issues. *In* "Neurotic Interaction in Marriage." (Eisenstein, V. W., Ed.) Basic Books, New York.

Kuhn, T. S. (1969). "The Structure of Scientific Revolutions." University of Chicago Press.

Kummer, H. (1975). Rules of dyad and group formation among captive Gelada baboons (Theropithecus gelada). Symposium 5th Congress International Primate Society, Nagoya, 1974, pp. 129–160. Japan Science Press, Tokyo.

Kurth, S. B. (1970). Friendship and friendly relations. In "Social Relationships." (McCall, G. J., McCall, M. M., Denzin, N. K., Suttles, G. D. and Kurth, S. B., Eds). Aldine, Chicago.

La Gaipa, J. J. (1977). Interpersonal attraction and social exchange. In "Theory and Practice in Interpersonal Attraction." (Duck, S., Ed.) Academic Press, London.

Laing, R. D. (1962). "The Self and Others." Quadrangle Press, Chicago.

Laing, R. D. (1969). "The Divided Self." Pantheon Books, New York.

Laing, R. D., Phillipson, H. and Lee, A. R. (1966). "Interpersonal Perception." Tavistock, London.

Lamb, M. E. (Ed.) (1976). "The Role of the Father in Child Development." Wiley, New York.

Landau, R. and Gewirtz, J. L. (1967). Differential satiation for a social reinforcing stimulus as a determinant of its efficacy in conditioning. J. exp. child Psychol. 5, 391–405.

Larsen, K. S. (1971). An investigation of sexual behavior among Norwegian College students: a motivational study. J. Mar. Fam. 33, 219–227.

Lawrence, D. H. (1950). Acquired distinctiveness of cues. II Selective association in a constant stimulus situation. J. exp. Psychol. 40, 175–188.

Layton, B. D. and Insko, C. A. (1974). Anticipated interaction and the similarity-attraction effect. Sociometry 37, 149–162.

Leiderman, P. H., Tulkin, S. R. and Rosenfeld, A. (1977). "Culture and Infancy." Academic Press, New York.

Lennard, H. L. and Bernstein, A. (1960). "The Anatomy of Psychotherapy." Columbia University Press, New York.

Leonard, R. (1975). Self-concept and attraction for similar and dissimilar others. J. Pers. soc. Psychol. 31, 926–929.

Lerner, M. (1974). Social psychology of justice and interpersonal attraction. In "Foundations of Interpersonal Attraction." (Huston, T. L., Ed.) Academic Press, New York.

Lerner, M. J., Miller, D. T. and Holmes, J. G. (1976). Deserving and the emergence of forms of justice. In "Advances in Experimental Social Psychology." (Berkowitz, L. and Walster, E., Eds). Vol. 9, 133–162.

Leventhal, G. S. and Lane, D. (1970). Sex, age and equity behavior. J. Pers. soc. Psychol. 15, 312–316.

Levinger, G. (1964). Note on need complementarity in marriage. Psych. Bull. 61, 153–157.

Levinger, G. (1974). A three-level approach to attraction: toward an understanding of pair relatedness. In "Foundations of Interpersonal Attraction." (Huston, T. L., Ed.) Academic Press, New York.

Levinger, G. and Breedlove, J. (1966). Interpersonal attraction and agreement: a study of marriage partners. J. Pers. soc. Psychol. 3, 367–372.

Levinger, G. and Senn, D. J. (1967). Disclosure of feelings in marriage. Merrill-Palmer Q. Behav. Devel. 13, 237–249.

Levinger, G. and Snoek, J. D. (1972). "Attraction in Relationship: A New Look at Interpersonal Attraction." General Learning Press, New York.

Levinger, G., Senn, D. J. and Jorgensen, B. W. (1970). Progress towards performance in courtship: a test of the Kerckhoff-Davis hypotheses. Sociometry 33, 427–443.

Lewin, K. (1964). "Field Theory and Social Science." Harper and Row, New York.

Lewin, K., Dembo, T., Festinger, L. and Sears, P. (1944). Level of aspiration. *In* "Personality and the Behavior Disorders." (Hunt, J. McV., Ed.) Ronald, New York.

Lewis, M. and Rosenblum, L. A. (Eds) (1974). "The Effect of the Infant on its Caregiver." Wiley, New York.

Lewis, M. and Rosenblum, L. A. (1975). "Friendship and Peer Relations." Wiley, New York.

Lewis, M. and Weinraub, M. (1976). The father's role in the child's social network. *In* "The Role of the Father in Child Development." (Lamb, M., Ed.) Wiley, New York.

Lewis, R. A. (1973). A longitudinal test of a developmental framework for premarital dyadic interaction. *J. Marriage and the Family* **35**, 16–26.

Lewis, R. A. (1975). Social influences on marital choice. *In* "Adolescence and the Life Cycle." (Dragastin, S. E. and Elder, G. H., Eds). Wiley, New York.

Lickona, T. (1974). A cognitive-developmental approach to inter-personal attraction. *In* "Foundations of Interpersonal Attraction." (Huston, T. L., Ed.) Academic Press, New York.

Lickona, T. (ed.) (1976) "Moral Development and Behavior." Holt, Rinehart and Winston, New York.

Liebowitz, B. and Black, M. (1974). The structure of the Ravich Interpersonal Game/Test. *Family Process* **13**, 169–183.

Lindberg, D. G. (1973). Grooming behavior as a regulator of social interactions in rhesus monkeys. *In* "Behavioral Regulators of Behavior in Primates." (Carpenter, C. R., Ed.) Bucknell University Press, Lewisburg.

Linton, R. (1936). "The Study of Man: An Introduction." Appleton-Century-Crofts, New York.

Lock, A. (1976). Acts instead of sentences. *In* "Neurolinguistics, 5: Baby Talk and Infant Speech." (Raffler-Engel, W. von and Lebrum, Y., Eds). Swets and Zeitlinger, Amsterdam.

Lorenz, K. (1943). Die angeborenen Formen möglicher Erfahrung. *Z. Tierpsychol.* **5**, 235–409.

Lorr, M. and McNair, D. M. (1963). An interpersonal behaviour circle. *J. abn. soc. Psychol.* **67**, 68–75.

Lott, A. J. and Lott, B. E. (1965). Group cohesiveness as interpersonal attraction: a review of relationships with antecedent and consequent variables. *Psychol. Bull.* **64**, 259–309.

Lott, A. J. and Lott, B. E. (1972). The power of liking: consequences of interpersonal attitudes derived from a liberalized view of secondary reinforcement. *Adv. exp. soc. Psychol.* **6**, 109–148.

Lott, A. J. and Lott, B. E. (1974). The role of reward in the formation of positive interpersonal attitudes. *In* "Foundations of Interpersonal Attraction." (Huston, T. L., Ed.) Academic Press, New York.

Lott, B. E. and Lott, A. J. (1960). The formation of positive attitudes towards group members. *J. abn. soc. Psychol.* **61**, 297–300.

Lytton, H. and Zwirner, W. (1975). Compliance and its controlling stimuli in a natural setting. *Devel. Psychol.* **11**, 769–779.

McCall, G. J. (1970). The social organization of relationships. *In* "Social Relationships." (McCall, G. J., McCall, M., Denzin, N. K., Suttles, G. D. and Kurth, S. B.) Aldine, Chicago.

McCall, G. J. (1974). A symbolic interactionist approach to attraction. *In* "Foundations of Interpersonal Attraction." (Huston, T. L., Ed.) Academic Press, New York.

McCall, G. J. and Simmons, J. L. (1966). "Identities and Interactions." Free Press, New York.

McCall, M. (1970). Boundary rules in relationships and encounters. *In* "Social Relationships." (McCall, G. J. *et al.*, Eds). Aldine, Chicago.

MacCorquodale, K. and Meehl, P. E. (1954). Edward C. Tolman. *In* "Modern Learning Theory." (Estes, W. K. *et al.*, Eds). Appleton-Century-Crofts, New York.

MacKay, D. M. (1972). Formal analysis of communicative processes. *In* "Nonverbal Communication." (Hinde, R. A., Ed.) Cambridge University Press, Cambridge.

Main, M. and Weston, D. (in prep.). Quality of attachment to mother in infancy differs from that to father.

Mannarino, A. P. (1976). Friendship patterns and altruistic behavior in preadolescent males. *Devel. Psychol.* **12**, 555–556.

Marsella, A. J., Dubanoski, R. A. and Mohs, K. (1974). The effects of father presence and absence upon maternal attitudes. *J. genetic Psychol.* **125**, 257–263.

Martin, B. (1975). Parent-child relations. *In* "Child Development Research, Vol. 4." (Horowitz, F. D., Hetherington, E. M., Scarr-Salapatek, S. and Siegel, G. M., Eds). University of Chicago Press, Chicago.

Marwell, G. and Hage, J. (1969). Personality and social interaction. *In* "Handbook of Social Psychology." (Lindzey, G. and Aronson, E., Eds). Vol. 3. Addison-Wesley, Reading, Mass.

Maslow, A. H. (1954). "Motivation and Personality." Harper, New York.

Masters, W. H. and Johnson, V. E. (1976). Principles of the new sex therapy. *Amer. J. Psychiatry* **133**, 548–554.

Matarazzo, J. D. Wiens, A. N., Saslow, G., Dunham, R. M. and Voas, R. B. (1964). Speech duration of astronaut and ground communicator. *Science* **143**, 148–150.

Matteson, R. (1974). Adolescent self-esteem, family communication, and marital satisfaction. *J. Psychol.* **86**, 35–47.

Mead, G. H. (1934). "Mind, Self and Society." University of Chicago Press, Chicago.

Medawar, P. B. (1967). "The Art of the Soluble." Methuen, London.

Mehrabian, A. (1972). "Non Verbal Communication." Aldine, Atherton, New York.

Mettee, D. R. and Aronson, E. (1974). Affective reactions to appraisal from others. *In* "Foundations of Interpersonal Attraction." (Huston, T. L., Ed.) Academic Press, New York.

Miller, D. (1970). Parental responsibility for adolescent maturity. *In* "The Family and Its Future." (Elliott, K. Ed.) Churchill, London.

Miller, G. A., Galanter, E. and Pribram, K. H. (1960). "Plans and the Structure of Behavior." Holt, New York.

Miller, H. L. and Rivenbark, W. (1970). Sexual differences in physical attractiveness as a determinant of heterosexual liking. *Psychol. Rep.* **27**, 701–702.

Miller, W. B. and Newman, L. F. (Eds) (1978). "The First Child and Family Formation." Carolina Population Center, University of North Carolina, North Carolina.

Mischel, W. (1968). "Personality and Assessment." Wiley, New York.

Mischel, W. (1973). Toward a cognitive social learning reconceptualization of personality. *Psychol. Rev.* **80**, 252–283.

Moore, B. R. (1973). The role of directed Pavlovian reactions in simple instrumental learning in the pigeon. *In* "Constraints on Learning." (Hinde, R. A. and Stevenson-Hinde, J., Eds). Academic Press, London.

Mowrer, O. H. (1960). "Learning Theory and Behavior." Wiley, New York.

Murray, H. A. (1938). "Explorations in Personality." Oxford University Press, New York.

Murstein, B. I. (1961). The complementary need hypothesis in newlyweds and middle-aged married couples. *J. abn. soc. Psychol.* **63**, 194–197.

Murstein, B. I. (1967a). Empirical tests of role, complementary needs, and homogamy theories of marital choice. *J. Marriage and the Family* **29**, 689–696.

Murstein, B. I. (1967b). The relationship of mental health to marital choice and courtship progress. *J. Marriage and the Family* **29**, 447–451.

Murstein, B. I. (1971a). Self-ideal-self discrepancy and the choice of marital partner. *J. cons. clin. Psychol.* **37**, 47–52.

Murstein, B. I. (1971b). Critique of models of dyadic attraction. *In* "Theories of Attraction and Love." (Murstein, B. I., Ed.) Springer, New York.

Murstein, B. I. (1971c). A theory of marital choice and its applicability to marriage adjustment. *In* "Theories of Attraction and Love." (Murstein, B. I., Ed.) Springer, New York.

Murstein, B. I. (1972a). Person perception and courtship progress among premarital couples. *J. Marriage and the Family* **34**, 621–626.

Murstein, B. I. (1972b). Physical attractiveness and marital choice. *J. Pers. soc. Psychol.* **22**, 8–12.

Murstein, B. I. (1977). The stimulus-value-role (SVR) theory of dyadic relationships. *In* "Theory and Practice in Inter-Personal Attraction." (Duck, S., Ed.) Academic Press, London.

Neisser, U. (1976). "Cognition and Reality." Freeman, San Francisco.

Nelson, B., Collins, J., Kreitman, N. and Troop, J. (1970). Neurosis and marital interaction. II. Time sharing and social activity. *Brit. J. Psychiatry* **117**, 47–58.

Nelson, K. (1973). Structure and strategy in learning to talk. *Monog. Soc. Res. Child Devel.* **38** (102, ser no 149).

Nemeth, C. (1970). Effects of free versus constrained behavior on attraction between people. *J. Pers. soc. Psychol.* **15**, 302–311.

Newcomb, T. M. (1952). "Social Psychology." Tavistock, London.

Newcomb, T. M. (1956). The prediction of interpersonal attraction. *Amer. Psychol.* **11**, 575–586.

Newcomb, T. M. (1961). "The Acquaintance Process." Holt, Rinehart and Winston, New York.

Newcomb, T. M. (1971). Dyadic balance as a source of clues about interpersonal attraction. *In* "Theories of Attraction and Love." (Murstein, B. I., ed.) Springer, New York.

Nye, F. I. (1974). Emerging and declining family roles. *J. Marriage and the Family* **36**, 238–245.

Oki, J. and Maeda, Y. (1973). Grooming as a regulator of behavior in Japanese macaques. *In* "Behavioral Regulators of Behavior in Primates." (Carpenter, C. R., Ed.) Bucknell University Press, Lewisburg.

Olson, D. H. (1972). Empirically unbinding the double bind: review of research and conceptual reformulations. *Family Process* **11**, 69–94.

O'Rourke, J. (1963). Field and laboratory: the decision-making behavior of family groups in two experimental conditions. *Sociometry* **26**, 422–435.

Osgood, C. E. (1969). On the whys and wherefores of E, P and A. *J. Pers. soc. Psychol.* **12**, 194–199.

Ovenstone, I. M. K. (1973). The development of neurosis in the wives of neurotic men II: Marital role functions and marital tension. *Brit. J. Psychiatry* **122**, 711–717.

Papousek, H. and Bernstein, P. (1969). The functions of conditioning stimulation in human neonates and infants. *In* "Stimulation in Early Infancy." (Ambrose, A., Ed.) Academic Press, London.

Parke, R. D., Power, T. G. and Gottman, J. (1979). Conceptualizing and quantifying influence patterns in the family triad. *In* "The Study of Social Interaction: Methodological issues." (Lamb, M. E., Suomi, S. J. and Stephenson, G. R., Eds). University of Wisconsin Press, Madison.

Parsons, T. and Bales, R. F. (1955). "Family, Socialization and Interaction Process." Free Press, New York.

Parten, M. B. (1932). Social participation among pre-school children. *J. abn. soc. Psychol.* **27**, 243–269.

Patterson, G. R. (1975). A three-stage functional analysis for children's coercive behaviors. *In* "New Developments in Behavioral Research: Theory, Methods, and Applications. In honor of Sidney W. Bijou." (Etzel, B. C., LeBlanc, J. M. and Baer, D. M., Eds). Erlbaum, Hillsdale, N. J.

Patterson, M. L. (1976). An arousal model of interpersonal intimacy. *Psychol. Rev.* **83**, 235–245.

Pearlin, L. I. (1975). Status inequality and stress in marriage. *Amer. Soc. Rev.* **40**, 344–357.

Peevers, B. H. and Secord, P. F. (1973). Developmental changes in attribution of descriptive concepts to persons. *J. Pers. soc. Psychol.* **27**, 120–128.

Pepitone, A. and Kleiner, R. (1957). The effects of threat and frustration on group cohesiveness. *J. abn. soc. Psychol.* **54**, 192–199.

Peplau, L. A. (1976). Impact of fear of success and sex-role attitudes on women's competitive achievement. *J. Pers. soc. Psychol.* **34**, 561–568.

Pfaffmann, C. (1965). Behavioral sciences. *Amer. Psychol.* **20**, 667–686.

Piaget, J. (1937, 1955). "The Child's Construction of Reality." Routledge and Kegan Paul, London.

Pierce, R. A. (1970). Need similarity and complementarity as determinants of friendship choice. *J. Psychol.* **76**, 231–238.

Polansky, N. A., Weis, E. S. and Blum, A. (1961). Children's verbal accessibility as a function of content and personality. *Amer. J. Orthopsychiatry* **31**, 153–169.

Porter, R. (Ed.) (1968). "The Place of Learning in Psychotherapy." Churchill, London.

Quick, E. and Jacob, T. (1973). Marital disturbance in relation to role theory and relationship theory. *J. abn. Psychol.* **82**, 309–316.

Quinton, D. and Rutter, M. (1976). Early hospital admissions and later disturbances of behaviour: an attempted replication of Douglas's findings. *Devel. Med. Child. Neurol. 18*, 447–459.

Rapoport, A. (1969). Games as tools of psychological research. *In* "Game Theory in the Behavioral Sciences." (Buchler, I. B. and Nutini, H. G., Eds). University of Pittsburgh Press, Pittsburgh.

Raush, H. L., Dittmann, A. T. and Taylor, T. J. (1959). Person, setting and change in social interaction. *Human Relations* **12**, 361–378.

Ravich, R. A. and Wyden, B. (1974). "Predictable Pairing: the Structure of Human Atoms." Peter H. Wyden, New York.

Rheingold, H., Gewirtz, J. L. and Ross, H. W. (1959). Social conditioning of vocalizations in the infant. *J. comp. physiol. Psychol.* **52**, 68–73.

Rich, J. (1975). Effects of children's physical attractiveness on teachers' evaluations. *J. educ. Psychol.* **67**, 599–609.

Richards, M. P. M. (1971). Social interaction in the first weeks of human life. *Psychiatria, Neurologia, Neurochirurgia* **74**, 35–42.

Richman, N. (1974). The effects of housing on pre-school children and their mothers. *Devel. Med. Child Neurol.* **16**, 53–58.

Richman, N. (1977). Behaviour problems in pre-school children: family and social factors. *Brit. J. Psychiatry* **131**, 523–527.

Rollins, B. C. and Bahr, S. J. (1976). A theory of power relationships in marriage. *J. Marriage and the Family* **38**, 619–627.

Rollins, B. C. and Cannon, K. L. (1974). Marital satisfaction over the family life cycle: a re-evaluation. *J. Marriage and the Family* **36**, 271–283.

Roper, R. and Hinde, R. A. (1978). Social behaviour in a play group: consistency and complexity. *Child Devel.* **49**, 570—579.

Roper, R. and Hinde, R. A. (in press). A teacher's questionnaire for individual differences in social behaviour. *J. child Psychol. Psychiat.*

Rosenblatt, P. C. (1974a). Cross-cultural perspective on attraction. *In* "Foundations of Interpersonal Attraction." (Huston, T. L., Ed.) Academic Press, New York.

Rosenblatt, P. C. (1974b). Behavior in public places: comparison of couples accompanied and unaccompanied by children. *J. Marriage and the Family* **36**, 750–755.

Rubin, Z. (1974). "From Liking to Loving: Patterns of Attraction in Dating Relationships." Academic Press, New York.

Rubin. Z. (1975). Disclosing oneself to a stranger: reciprocity and its limits. *J. exp. soc. Psychol.* **11**, 233–260.

Runciman, W. G. (1967). Justice, congruence and Professor Homans. *Arch. Eur. Sociol.* **8**, 115–128.

Rutter, M. and Brown, G. W. (1966). The reliability and validity of measures of family life and relationships in families containing a psychiatric patient. *Social Psychiatry* **1**, 38–53.

Rychlak, J. F. (1965). The similarity, compatibility, or incompatibility of needs in interpersonal selection. *J. Pers. soc. Psychol.* **2**, 334–340.

Ryder, R. G., Kafka, J. S. and Olson, D. H. (1971). Separating and joining influences in early courtship and marriage. *Amer. J. Orthopsychiatry* **41**, 450.

Ryle, A. (1966). A marital patterns test for use in psychiatric research. *Brit. J. Psychiatry* **112**, 285–293.

Ryle, A. and Breen, D. (1972). A comparison of adjusted and maladjusted couples using the double dyad grid. *Brit. J. med. Psychol.* **45**, 375–382.

Ryle, A. and Lipshitz, S. (1975). Recording change in marital therapy with the reconstruction grid. *Brit. J. med. Psychol.* **48**, 39–48.

Ryle, A. and Lipshitz, S. (1976). Repertory grid elucidation of a difficult conjoint therapy. *Brit. J. med. Psychol.* **49**, 281–285.

Ryle, A. and Lunghi, M. (1970). The dyad grid: a modification of repertory grid technique. *Brit. J. Psychiat.* **117**, 323–327.

Safilios-Rothschild, C. (1970). The study of family power structure: a review 1960–1969. *J. Marriage and the Family* **32**, 539–553.

Sager, C. J. (1976). The role of sex therapy in marital therapy. *Amer. J. Psychiatry* **133**, 554–558.

Sameroff, A. J. and Chandler, M. J. (1975). Reproductive risk and the continuum of caretaking casualty. *In* "Review of Child Development Research." (Horowitz, F. D., Hetherington, M., Scarr-Salapatck, S. and Sregel, G., Eds). Vol. 4. University if Chicago Press, Chicago.

Sampson, E. and Insko, C. (1964). Cognitive consistency and performance in the autokinetic situation. *J. abn. soc. Psychol.* **68**, 184–192.

Sander, L. W. (1969). The longitudinal course of early mother-child interaction:

cross-case comparisons in a sample of mother-child pairs. *In* "Determinants of Infant Behaviour." (Foss, B. M., Ed.) Vol. IV. Methuen, London.

Sander, L. W. (1977). The regulation of exchange in the infant-caretaker system and some aspects of the context-content relationship. *In* "Interaction, Conversation, and the Development of Language." (Lewis, M. and Rosenblum, L. A., Eds). Wiley, New York.

Sander, L. W., Stechler, G., Burns, P. and Julia, H. (1970). Early mother-infant interaction and 24 hour patterns of activity and sleep. *J. child Psychiatry* **9**, 103–123.

Sarbin, T. R. and Allen, V. L. (1968). Role Theory. *In* "The Handbook of Social Psychology." (Lindzey, G. and Aronson, E., Eds). Addison-Wesley, Reading, Mass.

Schachter, S. (1964). The interaction of cognitive and physiological determinants of emotional state. *In* "Advances in Experimental Social Psychology." (Berkowitz, L., Ed.) Academic Press, New York.

Schachter, S. and Singer, J. E. (1962). Cognitive, social and physiological determinants of emotional state. *Psychol. Rev.* **69**, 379–399.

Schaffer, H. R. (1977). "Mothering." Fontana/Open Books, London.

Schaffer, H. R. and Emerson, P. E. (1964). The development of social attachments in infancy. *Monogr. Soc. Res. Child Devel.* **29**, 1–77.

de Schazer, S. (1975). Brief therapy: two's company. *Family Process.* **14**, 79–93.

Schellenberg, J. A. and Bee, L. S. (1960). A re-examination of the theory of complementary needs in mate selection. *Marriage and Family Living* **22**, 227–232.

Schiffenbauer, A. and Schiavo, R. S. (1976). Physical distance and attraction: an intensification effect. *J. exp. soc. Psychol.* **12**, 274–282.

Schutz, W. C. (1960). "FIRO: A Three-Dimensional Theory of Interpersonal Behavior." Holt, Rinehart and Winston, New York.

Schwab, J. J., Holzer, C. E., Warheit, G. J. and Schwab, R. J. (1976). Human ecology and depressive Symptomatology. *In* "The Range of Normal in Human Behavior." (Masserman, J. H., Ed.) Grune and Stratton, New York.

Schwartz, B. (1968). The social psychology of privacy. *Amer. J. Sociol.* **73**, 741–752.

Schwartz, S. H. (1977). Normative influences on altruism. *Adv. exp. soc. Psychol.* **10**, 221–279.

Scott, M. B. and Lyman, S. M. (1968). Accounts. *Amer. Sociol. Rev.* **33**, 46–62.

Secord, P. F. and Backman, C. W. (1974). "Social Psychology." McGraw-Hill Kogakusta, Tokyo.

Seeman, M. V. (1976). The psychopathology of everyday names. *Brit. J. med. Psychol.* **49**, 89–95.

Seligman, C. Paschall, N. and Takata, G. (1974). Effects of physical attractiveness on attribution of responsibility. *Canad. J. Behav. Sci.* **6**, 290–296.

Seligman, M. E. P. and Hager, J. L. (1972). "Biological Boundaries of Learning." Appleton-Century-Crofts, New York.

Seyfarth, R. M. (1976). Social relationships among adult female baboons. *Anim. Behav.* **24**, 917–938.

Seyfarth, R. M. (1977). A model of social grooming among adult female monkeys. *J. Theor. Biol.* **65**, 671–698.

Seyfarth, R. M., Cheney, D. L. and Hinde, R. A. (1978). Some principles relating social interactions and social structure among primates. *In* "Recent Advances in Primatology." (Chivers, D. J. and Herbert, J., Eds). Academic Press, London.

Seyfried, B. A. (1977). Complementarity in interpersonal attraction. *In* "Theory and Practice in Interpersonal Attraction." (Duck, S., Ed.) Academic Press, London.

Seyfried, B. A. and Hendrick, C. (1973). Need similarity and complementarity in interpersonal attraction. *Sociometry* **36**, 207–220.

Shatz, M. and Gelman, R. (1973). The development of communication skills: modifications in the speech of young children as a function of the listener. *Monog. Soc. Res. Child Devel.* **38**, No. 5.

Shepher, J. (1971). Mate selection among second generation kibbutz adolescents and adults: incest avoidance and negative imprinting. *Arch. sex. Behav.* **1**, 293–307.

Shils, E. (1951). The study of the primary group. *In* "The Policy Sciences." (Lerner, D. and Lasswell, H., Eds). Stanford University Press, Stanford.

Sigall, H. and Aronson, E. (1967). Opinion change and the gain-loss model of interpersonal attraction. *J. exp. soc. Psychol.* **3**, 178–188.

Simpson, M. J. A. (1973). The social grooming of male chimpanzees. *In* "Comparative Ecology and Behaviour of Primates." (Michael, R. P. and Crook, J. H., Eds). Academic Press, London.

Simpson, M. J. A. and Howe, S. (in press). Interpretation of individual differences in 8-week old rhesus monkey infants. *Behavior.*

Simpson, R. L. (1976). Theories of social exchange. *In* "Contemporary Topics in Social Psychology." (Thibaut, J. W., Spence, J. T. and Carson, R. C., Eds). General Learning Press, Morristown, N. J.

Singelmann, P. (1972). Exchange as symbolic interaction: convergences between two theoretical perspectives. *Amer. Soc. Rev.* **37**, 414–424.

Skinner, B. F. (1953). "Science and Human Behavior." Free Press, New York.

Skolnick, P. (1971). Reactions to personal evaluations: a failure to replicate. *J. Pers. soc. Psychol.* **18**, 62–67.

Slater, E. and Woodside, M. (1951). "Patterns of Marriage." Cassell, London.

Slater, P. (1969). Theory and technique of the repertory grid. *Brit. J. Psychiatry* **115**, 1287–1296.

Smith, E. R. (1978). Specification and estimation of causal models in social psychology: comment on Tesser and Paulhus. *J. Pers. soc. Psychol.* **36**, 34–38.

Snow, C. (1972). Mother's speech to children learning language. *Child Devel.* **43**, 549–564.

Solomon, R. L. and Turner, L. H. (1962). Discriminative classical conditioning in dogs paralyzed by curare can later control discriminative avoidance responses in the normal state. *Psychol. Rev.* **69**, 202–219.

Sommer, R. (1959). Studies in personal space. *Sociometry* **22**, 247–260.

Sommer, R. (1965). Further studies of small group ecology. *Sociometry* **28**, 337–348.

Spanier, G. B., Lewis, R. A. and Cole, C. L. (1975). Marital adjustment over the family life cycle: the issue of curvilinearity. *J. Marriage and the Family* **37**, 263–276.

Spencer-Booth, Y. (1968). The behaviour of twin rhesus monkeys and comparisons with the behaviour of single infants. *Primates* **9**, 75–84.

Spitz, R. (1965). "The First Year of Life." International University Press, New York.

Sprey, J. (1972). Family power structure: a critical comment. *J. Marriage and the Family* **34**, 235–238.

Sroufe, L. A. and Waters, E. (1977). Attachment as an organizational construct. *Child Devel.* **48**, 1184–1199.

Stafford, R., Backman, E. and Dibona, P. (1977). The division of labor among cohabiting and married couples. *J. Marriage and the Family* **39**, 43–57.

Staub, E. (1974). Helping a distressed person: social, personality, and stimulus determinants. *Adv. exp. soc. Psychol.* **7**, 293–341.

Staub, E. and Sherk, L. (1970). Need for approval, children's sharing behavior, and reciprocity in sharing. *Child Devel.* **41**, 243–252.

Stebbins, R. A. (1969). On linking Barth and Homans: a theoretical note. *Man* **4**, 432–437.

Stern, D. (1977). "The First Relationship: Infant and Mother." Fontana/Open Books, London.

Stevenson, H. W. and Odum, R. D. (1962). The effectiveness of social reinforcement following two conditions of social deprivation. *J. abn. soc. Psychol.* **65**, 429–431.

Stewart, A. J. and Rubin, Z. (1976). The power motive in the dating couple. *J. Pers. soc. Psychol.* **34**, 305–9.

Stroebe, W. (1977). Self esteem and interpersonal attraction. *In* "Theory and Practice in Interpersonal Attraction." (Duck, S., Ed.) Academic Press, London.

Stroebe, W., Insko, C. A., Thompson, V. D. and Layton, B. D. (1971). Effects of physical attractiveness, attitude similarity and sex on various aspects of interpersonal attraction. *J. Pers. soc. Psychol.* **18**, 79–81.

Sullivan, H. S. (1938). The data of psychiatry. *Psychiatry* **1**, 121–134.

Sullivan, H. S. (1953). "Conceptions of Modern Psychiatry." Norton, New York.

Sutherland, N. S. (1966). Partial reinforcement and breadth of learning. *Q. J. exp. Psychol.* **18**, 289–301.

Suttles, G. D. (1970). Friendship as a social institution. *In* "Social Relationships." (McCall, G. J. *et al.*, Eds). Aldine, Chicago.

Tajfel, H. (1969). Social and cultural factors in perception. *In* "Handbook of Social Psychology." (Lindzey, G. and Aronson, E., Eds). Vol. 3, 315–394. Addison-Wesley, Reading, Mass.

Tajfel, H. (1972). Experiments in a vacuum. *In* "The Context of Social Psychology." (Israel, J. and Tajfel, H., Eds). Academic Press, London.

Tajfel, H. (Ed.) (1978a). The psychological structure of intergroup relations. *In* "Differentiation between Social Groups." Academic Press, London.

Tajfel, H. (1978b). The social psychology of minorities. Minority Rights Group Report No. 38, 1–20.

Tajfel, H. (in press). Individuals and groups in social psychology. *Brit. J. Soc. Clin. Psychol.*

Taylor, D. A. (1968). Some aspects of the development of interpersonal relationships: social penetration processes. *J. soc. Psychol.* **75**, 79–90.

Taylor, D. A., Altman, I. and Sorrentino, R. (1969). Interpersonal exchange as a function of rewards and costs and situational factors: expectancy confirmation—disconfirmation. *J. exp. soc. Psychol.* **5**, 324–339.

Tedeschi, J. T. (1974). Attributions, liking and power. *In* "Foundations of Interpersonal Attraction." (Huston, T. L., Ed.) Academic Press, New York.

Teevan, J. J. (1972). Reference groups and premarital sexual behaviour. *J. Marriage and the Family* **34**, 283–291.

Tesser, A. (1971). Evaluative and structural similarity of attitudes as determinants of interpersonal attraction. *J. Pers. soc. Psychol.* **18**, 92–96.

Tesser, A. and Paulhus, D. L. (1976). Toward a causal model of love. *J. Pers. soc. Psychol.* **34**, 1095–1105.

Tesser, A. and Paulhus, D. (1978). On models and assumptions: a reply to Smith. *J. Pers. soc. Psychol.* **36**, 40–42.

Tharp, R. G. (1963a). Psychological patterning in marriage. *Psychol. Bull.* **60**, 97–117.

Tharp, R. G. (1963b). Dimensions of marriage roles. *Marriage and Family Living* **25**, 389–404.

Thibaut, J. (1968). The development of contractual norms in bargaining: replication and variation. *J. Conflict Resolution* **12**, 102–112.

Thibaut, J. W. and Kelley, H. H. (1959). "The Social Psychology of Groups." Wiley, New York.

Thoman, E. B. (1974). Some consequences of early infant-mother-infant interaction. *Early Child Devel. and Care* **3**, 249–261.

Thompson, W. R. and Nishimura, R. (1952). Some determinants of friendship. *J. Pers.* **20**, 305–314.

Thorpe, W. H. (1961). "Bird-song." Cambridge University Press.

Thorpe, W. H. (1963). "Learning and Instinct in Animals." (1st edn 1956). Methuen, London.

Tinbergen, E. A. and Tinbergen, N. (1972). Early childhood autism—an ethological approach. *Adv. Ethology* **10**, 1–53.

Tinbergen, N. (1951). "The Study of Instinct." Oxford University Press.

Tinbergen, N. (1952). Derived activities: their causation, biological significance, origin and emancipation during evolution. *Q. Rev. Biol.* **27**, 1–32.

Tinbergen, N. (1968). On War and Peace in Animals and Man. *Science* **160**, 1411–1418.

Toman, W. (1971). The duplication theorem of social relationships as tested in the general population. *Psychol. Rev.* **78**, 380–390.

Touhey, J. C. (1974). Effects of dominance and competence on heterosexual attraction. *Brit. J. soc. clin. Psychol.* **13**, 22–26.

Trevarthen, C. (1977). Descriptive analyses of infant communicative behaviour. *In* "Studies in Mother-Infant Interaction." (Schaffer, H. R., Ed.) Academic Press, London.

Trevarthen, C. (1978a). Communication and cooperation in early infancy. *In* "Before Speech: the Beginnings of Human Communication." (Bullowa, M., Ed.) Cambridge University Press.

Trevarthen, C. and Hubley, P. (1978b). Secondary intersubjectivity. *In* "Action, Gesture and Symbol: The Emergence of Language." (Lock, A., Ed.) Academic Press, London.

Triandis, H. C., Loh, W. D. and Levin, L. A. (1966). Race, status, quality of spoken English, and opinions about civil rights as determinants of interpersonal attitudes. *J. Pers. soc. Psychol.* **3**, 468–472.

Trivers, R. L. (1974). Parent-offspring conflict. *Amer. Zool.* **14**, 249–264.

Turk, J. L. (1974). Power as the achievement of ends: a problematic approach in family and small group research. *Family Process* **13**, 39–52.

Uddenberg, N., Englesson, I. and Nettelbladt, P. (1979). Experience of father and later relations to men. A systematic study of women's relations to their father, their partner and their son. *Acta Psychiat. Scand.* **59**, 87–96.

Ulrich, R. E. and Symannek, B. (1969). Pain as a stimulus for aggression. *In* "Aggressive Behavior." (Garattini, S. and Sigg, E. B., Eds). Excerpta Medica, Amsterdam.

Valins, S. (1966). Cognitive effects of false heart-beat feedback. *J. Pers. soc. Psychol.* **4**, 400–408.

Vaughn, C. E. and Leff, J. P. (1976). The influence of family and social factors on the course of psychiatric illness. A comparison of schizophrenic and depressed neurotic patients. *Brit. J. Psychiatry* **129**, 125–137.

Verplanck, W. S. (1955). The control of the content of conversation: reinforcement of statements of opinion. *J. abn. soc. Psychol.* **51**, 668–676.

Wagner, R. V. (1975). Complementary needs, role expectations, interpersonal attraction and the stability of working relationships. *J. Pers. soc. Psychol.* **32**, 116–124.

Walster, E. (1965). The effect of self-esteem on romantic liking. *J. exp. soc. Psychol.* **1**, 184–197.

Walster, E. and Walster, G. W. (1963). Effect of expecting to be liked on choice of associates. *J. abn. soc. Psychol.* **67**, 402–404.

Walster, E., Aronson, V., Abrahams, D. and Rottmann, L. (1966). Importance of physical attractiveness in dating behavior. *J. Pers. soc. Psychol.* **4**, 508–516.

Walster, E., Berscheid, E. and Walster, G. W. (1976). New directions in equity research. *In* "Advances in Experimental Social Psychology." (Berkowitz, L. and Walster, E., Eds). Vol. 9, 1–42. Academic Press, New York.

Walster, E., Walster, G. W. and Berscheid, E. (1978a). "Equity Theory and Research." Allyn and Bacon, Boston.

Walster, E., Walster, G. W. and Traupmann, J. (1978b). Equity and premarital sex. *J. Pers. soc. Psychol.* **36**, 82–92.

Walters, R. H. and Parke, R. D. (1964). Social motivation, dependency and susceptibility to social influence. *In* "Advances in Experimental Social Psychology." (Berkowitz, L., ed.) Vol. 1, 232–279. Academic Press, New York.

Waters, E. (in press). Traits, Relationships and Behavioral Systems: The Attachment Construct and the Organization of Behavior and Development.

Watson, J. S. (1972). Smiling, cooing and "the game". Merrill-Palmer Q. **18**, 323–339.

Watzlawick, P., Beavin, J. H. and Jackson, D. D. (1967). "Pragmatics of Human Communication." Norton, New York.

Weber, M. (1964). The theory of social and economic organisation. (1st Pub. in German 1922). Oxford University Press.

Weiss, R. S. (1974). The provisions of social relationships. *In* "Doing Unto Others." (Rubin, Z., Ed.) Prentice-Hall, N. J.

Wertheim, E. S. (1975a). Person-environment interaction: the epigenesis of autonomy and competence. II Review of developmental literature (normal development). *Br. J. med. Psychol.* **48**, 95–111.

Wertheim, E. S. (1975b). Person-environment interaction: the epigenesis of autonomy and competence. III Autonomy and para-/pre-linguistic and linguistic action systems: review of developmental literature (normal development). *Br. J. Med. Psychol.* **48**, 237–256.

Wertheim, E. S. (1975c). The science and typology of family systems II. Further theoretical and practical considerations. *Family Process* **14**, 285–309.

Wheeler, L. (1974). Social comparison and selective affiliation. *In* "Foundations of Interpersonal Attraction." (Huston, T. L., Ed.) Academic Press, New York.

White, B. L. and Watts, J. C. (1973). "Experience and Environment." Prentice-Hall, N. J.

Whiting, B. B. and Whiting, J. W. M. (1975). "Children of Six Cultures." Harvard University Press.

Wilson, E. O. (1975). "Sociobiology." Harvard University Press.

Winch, R. F. (1958). "Mate-selection: A Study of Complementary Needs." Harper and Row, New York.

Winch, R. F. (1967). Another look at the theory of complementary needs in mate selection. *J. Marriage and the Family* **29**, 756–762.

Winch, R. F., Ktsanes, T. and Ktsanes, V. (1955). Empirical elaboration of the theory of complementary needs in mate selection. *J. abn. soc. Psychol.* **51**, 509–513.

Wolf, A. P. (1970). Childhood association and sexual attraction: a further test of the Westermarck hypothesis. *Amer. Anthrop.* **72**, 503–515.

Wooton, A. J. (1974). Talk in the homes of young children. *Sociology* **8**, 277–295.

Worthy, M., Gary, A. L. and Kahn, G. M. (1969). Self-disclosure as an exchange process. *J. Pers. soc. Psychol.* **13**, 59–63.

Wright, P. H. (1969). A model and a technique for studies of friendship. *J. exp. soc. Psychol.* **5**, 295–309.

Wyer, R. S. Jr. (1975). Some informational determinants of one's own liking for a person and beliefs that the others will like this person. *J. Pers. soc. Psychol.* **31**, 1041–1053.

Yoshioka, G. A. and Athanasiou, R. (1971). Effect of site plan and social status variables on distance to friends' home. *Amer. Psychol. Assn. Proc.* **6**, 273–274.

Zagonc, E. (1968). Cognitive theories in social psychology. *In* "Handbook of Social Psychology." (Lindzey, G. and Aronson, E., Eds). Addison-Wesley, Reading, Mass.

Zigler, E. (1964). The effect of social reinforcement on normal and socially deprived children. *J. gen. Psychol.* **104**, 235–242.

Subject Index

A

Acceptance, 260
Achievement/vicariousness, 80
Action, social, 17–18
  vs behaviour, 17
Actuality, 148
Affection, see relationships, affectionate; love
Affective/cognitive aspects, (see also cognition, emotion), 15, 22–35
Aggressive behaviour, 200–201, 275
Aims of a science, 4
Alienation, 252, 279
Allport-Vernon study, 300
Altruism, 228–230, 282
Analysis vs synthesis, 4, 43, 209–210
Anger, 213–214, 226–227, 279
Animal studies, relevance, 23, 24, 233–236
Anticipation, 24
Anxiety, 42, 80, 182, 195, 211, 226–227
Assertiveness/compliance, 71–72, 279
Attachment, 35–37, 43, 105, 313–314
Attention-seeking, 28
Attitude, 82, 299, 331
  similarity, 82–100, 110–112, 199, 295–296
Attraction, inter-personal, 76–77, 82–84, 194
  and similarity, 82–83, 88–100
Attribution, 78, 112, 114–145, 216–217, 229, 252, 253, 282, 302
Authoritarianism, 184
Authority, 260

B

Balance, 182–189, 281, 308, 326–327

Bargaining, 290
Behaviour episodes and settings, 160–161
Behaviour
  vs action, 17
  ballistic, 25
  goal-directed, 25–30
  rule-guided, 28–30
Behavioural systems, 36, 209
Breadth in relationships, 54, 116

C

California personality inventory, 88, 299
Change, initiation of, 103
"Character", 190
Chicken, 253
Classical conditioning, 195, 197–201, 206–207, 285
Cognitive level, 146, 153, 307–308, 317–318
Cognitive
  structures, 31–34, 199, 206–210
  theory, 31–35, 198, 203–210, 214, 216–217, 327
Commitment, 131–138, 155–156, 167, 251, 280, 285, 290, 304, 308
  and balance, 134, 185
  for consistency vs continuity, 132–133
  and exchange, 134
  exogenous vs endogenous, 132–133
  processes in, 133–138
Comparison levels, 217–219, 221
Compatibility, 103–106, 110–112, 140, 295–296
Competitive relationships, 160, 325
Complementarity, 78–81, 101–112, 188, 277, 295–296, 307–312
Compliance, see assertiveness, 260

European Monographs in Social Psychology

Series Editor: HENRI TAJFEL

H. TAJFEL
Differentiation between Social Groups: Studies in the Social Psychology of Intergroup
   Relations, 1978

M. BILLIG
Fascists: A Social Psychological View of the National Front, 1978

C. P. WILSON
Jokes   Form, Content, Use and Function, 1979

J. P. FORGAS
Social Episodes: The Study of Interaction Routines, 1979

In preparation

A.-N. PERRET-CLERMONT
Social Interaction and Cognitive Development in Children, 1980